The Phenomenology of Play

Also Available from Bloomsbury

Fashion: Seductive Play, Eugen Fink
Husserl's Phenomenology of Natural Language, Horst Ruthrof
The Phenomenology of Virtual Technology, Daniel O'Shiel

The Phenomenology of Play

Encountering Eugen Fink

Edited by
Steve Stakland

BLOOMSBURY ACADEMIC
LONDON • NEW YORK • OXFORD • NEW DELHI • SYDNEY

BLOOMSBURY ACADEMIC
Bloomsbury Publishing Plc, 50 Bedford Square, London, WC1B 3DP, UK
Bloomsbury Publishing Inc, 1359 Broadway, 12th Floor, New York, NY 10018, USA
Bloomsbury Publishing Ireland, 29 Earlsfort Terrace, Dublin 2, D02 AY28, Ireland

BLOOMSBURY, BLOOMSBURY ACADEMIC and the Diana logo
are trademarks of Bloomsbury Publishing Plc

First published in Great Britain 2024
This paperback edition published 2026

Copyright © Steve Stakland, and Contributors 2024

Steve Stakland has asserted his right under the Copyright,
Designs and Patents Act, 1988, to be identified as Editor of this work.

For legal purposes the Acknowledgments on p. xii constitute an
extension of this copyright page.

Series design by Charlotte Daniels
Cover image: Eugene Fink, 1930 (© Imagno Brandstatter / Getty Images)

All rights reserved. No part of this publication may be: i) reproduced or transmitted in
any form, electronic or mechanical, including photocopying, recording or by means
of any information storage or retrieval system without prior permission in writing from
the publishers; or ii) used or reproduced in any way for the training, development or operation
of artificial intelligence (AI) technologies, including generative AI technologies. The rights
holders expressly reserve this publication from the text and data mining exception as per
Article 4(3) of the Digital Single Market Directive (EU) 2019/790.

Bloomsbury Publishing Inc does not have any control over, or responsibility for,
any third-party websites referred to or in this book. All internet addresses given
in this book were correct at the time of going to press. The author and publisher
regret any inconvenience caused if addresses have changed or sites have
ceased to exist, but can accept no responsibility for any such changes.

A catalogue record for this book is available from the British Library.

Library of Congress Cataloging-in-Publication Data
Names: Stakland, Steve, editor.
Title: The phenomenology of play : encountering Eugen Fink / edited by Steve Stakland.
Description: London ; New York : Bloomsbury Academic, 2024. | Includes bibliographical
references and index. | Summary: "Eugen Fink's deep engagement with the phenomenon
of play saw him transcend his two towering mentors, Edmund Husserl and Martin
Heidegger, to become a crucial figure in early 20th-century phenomenology. The
Phenomenology of Play draws on Fink's concept of play to build a complete picture of
his philosophy from its foundations to its applications, featuring newly translated material
including notes from conversations between Fink and Heidegger, and Fink's own essay
'Mask and Cothurnus' on ancient theatre"–Provided by publisher.
Identifiers: LCCN 2023058197 (print) | LCCN 2023058198 (ebook) | ISBN 9781350424630 (HB) |
ISBN 9781350424678 (PB) | ISBN 9781350424654 (eBook) | ISBN 9781350424647 (ePDF)
Subjects: LCSH: Fink, Eugen. | Play (Philosophy) | Phenomenology. | Ontology.
Classification: LCC B3240.F524 .P44 2024 (print) | LCC B3240.F524 (ebook) |
DDC 160–dc23/eng/20240214
LC record available at https://lccn.loc.gov/2023058197
LC ebook record available at https://lccn.loc.gov/2023058198

ISBN: HB: 978-1-3504-2463-0
PB: 978-1-3504-2467-8
ePDF: 978-1-3504-2464-7
eBook: 978-1-3504-2465-4

Typeset by Deanta Global Publishing Services, Chennai, India

For product safety related questions contact productsafety@bloomsbury.com.

To find out more about our authors and books visit www.bloomsbury.com
and sign up for our newsletters.

To my wife, Jesse, and our children, Calvin, Eve, Wesley, and Zara. Without her encouragement, patience, superb editing, and their persistent playing and questioning (e.g., "Why are you making this book?") this project would never have begun or been completed.

Contents

Preface: The Virtues of Eugen Fink	ix
Acknowledgments	xii
List of Abbreviations	xiii

Part One Background and Foundation　　　　　　　　　　　　1

1 Play in the World as Symbol for Play of the World *Christopher Turner*　　3
2 Fink's Position within the Phenomenological Movement and the Origins of His Cosmology of Play *Giovanni Jan Giubilato*　　12
3 Fink's Phenomenology and Ontology of Play and Its Relation to Hans-Georg Gadamer's Philosophical Hermeneutics *Núria Sara Miras Boronat*　　28
4 Fink and Gadamer: Phenomenology, Hermeneutics, and the Aesthetics of Play *Stefano Marino*　　36
5 Fink and Heidegger on Cosmological and Ontological Play: A Confrontation *Ian Alexander Moore*　　41

Part Two History of Philosophy　　　　　　　　　　　　57

6 The Last Temptation of Metaphysics: Eugen Fink's Nietzsche *Dale Wilkerson*　　59
7 Fink, Schiller, and Echoes of Classical German Philosophy *Susanne Schilz*　　70
8 What Is the Problem that Fink Solved for Derrida and Deleuze in 1967? *Hakhamanesh Zangeneh*　　76
9 Phantasy and Play in Husserl, Fink, and Sartre *Daniel O'Shiel*　　85
10 Fink and Plotinus on Play *Emile Alexandrov*　　92

Part Three Application to Philosophical Issues　　　　　　　　　　　　101

11 Music and Ontological Experience: Fink's Importance for Our Understanding of Music *Goetz Richter*　　103
12 The Relation of Play and Education in Fink: Human Play as an Analogical Path to Understanding Onto-Cosmology *Steve Stakland*　　114
13 "The Desert Grows"? On a remarkable Silence in Fink's *Oasis of Happiness* *Holger Zaborowski*　　121
14 Holy Laughter: A Pentecostal Pneumatology of Play in Fink and Wariboko *Jason W. Alvis*　　127
15 Ontology of Play and the Ambivalence of Resilience *Alice Koubová*　　137

16 From *Animal Rationale* to *Ens Cosmologicum:* Eugen Fink on Animality
    Catherine Homan   147
17 Politics as Social Gameplay? How We Might Reconsider a Phenomenology of Play in Terms of Freedom and Responsibility
    Annette Hilt   155

Part Four Translations and Commentaries   163

18 World, Individuation, and Play: A Critical Introduction to Fink's Conversations with Heidegger *Giovanni Jan Giubilato and Ian Alexander Moore*   165
19 Zwei Gespräche mit Heidegger/Two Conversations with Heidegger *Eugen Fink, Edited and translated by Giovanni Jan Giubilato and Ian Alexander Moore*   173
20 Translator's Introduction to "Mask and Cothurnus" *Christopher Turner*   178
21 Mask and Cothurnus *Eugen Fink, translated by Christopher Turner*   180
22 Notes on a Translation: Eugen Fink's *Nietzsche's Philosophy* *Goetz Richter*   192
23 Review of Eugen Fink, *Fashion: Seductive Play* *Chester Mlcek*   195
24 Annotated Bibliography of All Fink English Translations *Anna Luiza Coli and Chester Mlcek*   199

Notes   205
Bibliography   226
List of Contributors   240
Index   244

Preface

The Virtues of Eugen Fink

Eugen Fink took no notes as he sat in his first class with the great inventor of phenomenology. Husserl thought this did not bode well for his exams, but the master was wrong. Fink, so prodigious was his memory, reproduced the lectures verbatim with commentary. Then he wrote a prize-winning essay on imagination that later became part of his dissertation which was supervised by Husserl and Heidegger, the only time the two were on the same committee for a doctoral student. Husserl was so impressed he had Fink became one of his assistants and later his most relied upon interlocutor and systematizer. He came to say that of all the great phenomenon the greatest was Fink. So dedicated was Fink to Husserl, and prescient his sense of goodness, when the Nazis came to power and Husserl was driven from his university and humiliated, Fink remained at his side through his illnesses, old age, and death. He was instrumental in helping to preserve Husserl's collected works by getting them out of Germany. Instead of hiding his affinity for Husserl, he bravely published his collaborative work. Because of his open support of Husserl the political climate in Nazi German made him an outcast and he could not secure an academic position. Consider his courage. Many of us do not just shy away but flee from the prospect of presenting opposition to prevailing cultural and media narratives that support political agendas because of the harm it will do to our professional lives. We play along to get along. Not Fink. How many of us, like Fink, when given ample opportunity show the courage of Socrates?

In Belgium when the Nazis took over, he and his wife were arrested as anti-Nazis, crammed into cattle cars, and sent to separate concentration camps in France. Though others starved to death, he survived and reunited with his wife but for the rest of his life he suffered from health problems. Back in Germany he refused to do officer training for the Nazis where he would have received a comfortable position given his level of education. Instead, he submitted to being a conscript doing aerial surveillance around Freiburg. After the Second World War, when the occupying French were imprisoning all German soldiers, he remained free because he told them, in perfect French, his entire life story. He finished his credentialling in an homage to Husserl and scraped by as an unsalaried lecturer alongside better supported academics who had been Nazis. He and his small family relied on the support of farmers whom he helped during harvest time and from American supporters. He paid dearly for his courageous loyalty to Husserl, but he had an orthogonal relationship with Heidegger. It is in Fink's dedicated self-sacrifice to Husserl and lifelong relationship with Heidegger that some of his virtues are manifest.

When taking classes with the greatest living philosopher of the time his name was underlined in red. According to Heidegger, he made "this sign" because it meant Fink was "likely to *achieve* something." Besides both being close students of Husserl, Heidegger notes he and Fink shared, "the same teachers of Greek and Latin at the grammar school in Constance." The two became intimately bound. Heidegger noted the uniqueness of their relationship by how Fink even helped move his writing desk. He dramatically reflected Heidegger's attitude to Hannah Arendt when she wished to see him. And in 1966, they conducted a seminar together on Heraclitus. Heidegger was so impressed with Fink, at the celebration of his sixtieth birthday he said, "It is my wish . . . that it be given to you to make a genuine necessity out of virtue." In the end, having outlived his student, Heidegger dedicated one of the first published books of his lectures, *The Fundamental Concepts of Metaphysics* to Fink because of how deeply they impacted him. Heidegger applied a paraphrase of Nietzsche, "One repays a teacher badly if one always remains merely a student." Heidegger saw in Fink someone who could maintain philosophy (i.e., thinking) against the ravages of many modern trends including cybernetics.

Despite all he and his mentor Husserl had suffered due to a cause Heidegger had initially vehemently supported, Fink was able to set aside his differences to work with Heidegger. Somehow, he must have forgiven him. But later he would not take his chair of philosophy even though Heidegger said only Fink could be his successor. Why did Heidegger regard Fink so highly?

For those interested in phenomenology, the history of philosophy, and ways to keep thinking in our time of dehumanizing efficiency and algorithms, we might ask, what was Fink's relationship to the later developments of Husserl's thinking? What influence did Heidegger have on him? Ultimately, we might seek to know exactly what was Fink's philosophical value in his own right, that is, *what did he achieve*? This book indicates some of what his thinking opens for philosophy with an emphasis on his engagement with play. Only Fink works out in careful detail a whole systematic treatment of the topic and relates it to many crucial topics in philosophy, for example, metaphysics, ethics, pedagogy, religion, politics, science, and so on. In doing so he shows Plato's insight that all profound questions are necessarily related to all other questions. He shows that play is fundamental to the functioning of our institutions and societies, traditions and language. Fink agrees with Heraclitus, though he thinks there is much to be worked out, that "The course of the world is a playing child, moving pieces on a board—a king's power belongs to the child." This is not at all a move to trivialize the totality of all relations that which allows all beings to come into appearance. Rather it is a path to engagement with the ever unfolding of the iterative interpretive adventure of self-understanding that is philosophy. His meditation on play is so deep and wide-ranging that it is discovered to be a fundamental phenomenon of human existence and a key concept in understanding cosmology and ontology. Play is a phenomenon as profound as love, work, ruling, and death. Among these five, play is the only one that can mirror all the others, even itself. Fink shows how power is the culmination of the history of metaphysics and play has been covered over by the intellectual tradition initiated by Plato. Play must be excavated and rehabilitated. The need for more academic focus on play is to respond to the cankerous power narrative. Fink's work shows that it is play, not power, that is fundamental. We do not cooperate solely because of power. Human unity is truly built on play.

Here in this book is the first ever English collection of essays that relate Fink's philosophy of play to a wide range of topics and philosophers. You will find detailed essays about how his work is related to but also goes beyond Husserl and Heidegger. Moreover, you will see how he influenced his contemporaries like Gadamer, Derrida, and Deleuze. The scope of contributions goes from detailed historical archival work of never before translated and published materials to lofty speculative interpretations and applications.

To live during turbulent times, to be caught between two philosophical fathers, and to have still raised a family, to have exercised the miracle of forgiveness, to live a life seemingly so burdened by cares, pain, and toil, it is surprising that Fink should become *the* philosopher of play. He reflected Charlie Chaplin's insight, "To truly laugh, you must be able to take your pain, and play with it." His fortitude and ability to create were tempered by trauma. He had reserves of resilience and determination that are evidence of his deep understanding of the world. What he wrote shows his talent, character, and dedication. Besides the relevance of play to religion, culture, politics, education, and the history of philosophy, Fink's phenomenology of play is fun. Engaging in his work is to discover what has been lost in the disenchantment of adult life and return to wonder. It helps us to remember the value of the essence of being human. Fink offers a way to find in our struggles of love and mortality an oasis of happiness. Play cannot be aimed at. To be fully actualized it must be allowed to happen. To do so means to create the conditions for play to happen. At the end of a term, he tells his students, "I would now like to let you go on holiday with the wish that, after your term paper, you may experience something of the happy play of human life on your travels and journeys" (PSW p. 272). Fink had a magnanimity of soul born of the wisdom of deep study and experience.

Acknowledgments

Being and world are *the* gifts. They require the piety of gratitude. The beings which most constitute our world and relate us to Being are other people. I thank some of them here. I am most grateful to Holger Zaborowski for proposing the idea of this book. If it had not been for his prompting to reach out to Ian Moore and Chris Turner, it would never have happened. Ian and Chris were vital in introducing me to an international community of Fink scholars who were interested in contributing to this project. If it had not been for their generous participation and help, I would not have met most of the contributors. I am thankful for all the contributors to this volume and all those who participated in our conference in 2022 where we reviewed and commented on each other's drafts. That experience helped to bring this book into focus and make it a reality. Without the collective work of everyone involved this volume would not exist. Ian also eased the load of preparing for that conference by securing the help of undergraduate Chester Mlcek. Chet worked out many of the details and helped make our conference run smoothly. I am grateful for the three anonymous reviewers who enthusiastically supported the proposal for this book. I am happy for the supportive work that the editorial staff at Bloomsbury has done to bring this book forth. We are also grateful for the permission that has been granted to print here for the first time two new English translations of Fink.

Abbreviations

PSW   *Play as Symbol of the World and Other Writings.* Translated by Ian Alexander Moore and Christopher Turner. Bloomington: Indiana University Press, 2016.

OH   "Oasis of Happiness: Towards an Ontology of Play"

Part One

Background and Foundation

1

Play in the World as Symbol for Play of the World

Christopher Turner

> *In human play there occurs the representation and the symbolic recurrence of a far greater, more encompassing play, whose two-faced character we divine throughout the tragedy and comedy of existence. (Fink 2016b: 160)*

Introduction

In the final chapter of *Play as Symbol of the World* (PSW), Eugen Fink suggestively claims that "the prevailing whole can 'shine back' into an intraworldly being, illuminate features there, and bring aspects to light that are distinctive of the movement of the totality" (Fink 2016b: 211). This happens not only in human play but also in each of the fundamental phenomena of human existence: in work, love, struggle, and death.[1] In what follows, I will limit myself to exploring Fink's account of how human play in the world can become a symbol for the play of the world. To begin, we should ask, with Fink: What features are illuminated by the world's shining back into human play? What aspects characteristic of the world's movement or prevalence are brought to light in human play? And let us not merely begin with Fink's questions here but also with his note of caution immediately afterward: "To answer this in even an initial and preliminary manner remains extraordinarily difficult" (2016b: 211). To meet Fink's challenge, we first need to clarify (1) why play *in* the world, games in the world, are distinct from the play *of* the world; (2) what play *of* the world is; (3) what Fink means by the term "symbol"; and, finally (speculatively) (4) how play *in* the world can become a symbol of the play *of* the world.

Play *in* the World

The serious business of life is a drag. We are dragged forward, impelled toward the future in a restless striving after happiness. The metaphor Fink uses in his programmatic essay "Oasis of Happiness" is worth considering here to frame our understanding of play in the world. The serious business of life and our restless movement from one task to another, attempting to secure a flourishing existence for ourselves, is likened to journey across a desert and our striving is likened to the fate of Tantalus, always extending ourselves out toward a satisfaction that remains just out of reach. As Fink puts it,

> We all strive for *eudaimonia*—but are in no way agreed as to what it is. We are not only affected by the unrest of the striving that carries us along, but also by the unrest of having an "interpretation" of true happiness. It belongs to the profound paradoxes of human existence that, in incessantly chasing after *eudaimonia*, we do not reach it, and that, in the full sense of the term, no one is to be counted happy before death. As long as we breathe we are caught up in a precipitous decline of life. We are enthralled by the urge to complete and fulfill our fragmentary Being. We live in the prospect of the future. We conceive the present as a preparation, as a station along the way, as a way of passage. (2016c: 19)

Fink is implicitly referencing the tenth chapter of the first book of Aristotle's *Nicomachean Ethics* here and giving it a distinctive existential twist. This futural-directedness of human life is anxiety-provoking, hence Solon's dictum to count no one happy before death. However, there is perhaps one way to be counted happy before death and that is, with Seneca and Pierre Hadot, to cease conceiving the current moment as a preparation for anything further and instead to make the present alone our happiness.

This is precisely where play comes in, on Fink's account. If serious life is a drag, and we restlessly roam through a harsh desert mostly chasing mirages, play, in contrast, is refreshing release, "like a plunge back into a morning-fresh primordiality and plastic creativity" (2016c: 14) the present moment as paradise, as oasis. We leave the desert behind. According to Fink, "Play *carries* us *away*. When we play, we are released for a while from the hustle and bustle of life—as though transported to another planet where life seems lighter, more buoyant, easier" (2016c: 20). Play as an embodied human practice lightens our load, so to speak, unburdening us from the anxiety-inducing pursuit of serious goals, and filling us with exhilaration. It is not mere recreation that allows us to return to our journey across the desert of striving, however. Play is not a mirage, and players are not lotus-eaters. As Fink explains in *Grundphänomene des menschlichen Daseins*, "Playing is an activity, a practice of engagement with the imaginary. In human play, our existence to a certain degree mirrors itself in itself, we perform ourselves, what and how we are" (1979: 406).[2] This mirroring does not have to occur merely for the players but can also take place for attentive and participating spectators as well, who identify with the players on the field, stage, or screen. In each instance of play, whether an audience observes and sympathetically identifies with the players or not, a singular and yet collective playworld is generated through the embodied play-activity of the players.

As Fink notes, the goals we pursue and the joys we feel while playing are immanent to play, and so play is separate from the ultimate goal, happiness, that we otherwise pursue (and thus "sacred" in a way). Any kind of play with goals external to it is not really play at all, as anyone with a gym membership can presumably confirm. Play's self-enclosure and circularity, the field of the playworld, so to speak, "lets a possibility of human sojourn within time appear, one that does not have the character of tearing away and driving forward but rather allows one to tarry and is, as it were, a glimmer of eternity" (2016c: 21). This glimmer of eternity is a poetic way of expressing that play in the world as sojourn from life's serious business allows for the play of the world to be reflected back into human play. At one point, Fink even wonders if human beings first imagined the blessed life of the gods from out of our own human experience of play's non-actual liberating lightness (2016b: 144–5). When this "shining back" of world-play into human play occurs, we experience this, in temporal terms, as distention, or what Fink calls "a glimmer of eternity."

Fink's conception of ecstatic, world-open human play resembles Kierkegaardian despair in reverse: in despair, the ability to be is related to being as a fall. Becoming something actual is a descent from infinite possibilities to finite actuality. In ecstatic human play, becoming something non-actual or irreal is an ascent from finite, restricted, progressively more determined, and thus ever more constricted existence to infinite possibilities. What we have here is a kind of Kierkegaardian joy, or the opposite of despair. Finkian play is a remedy for Kierkegaardian despair, since for the one who is in despair, "To be self as he wills to be would be his delight (though in another sense it would be equally in despair), but to be compelled to be self as he does not will to be is his torment, namely, that he cannot get rid of himself" (Kierkegaard 1941: 29–30). Play, on Fink's account, is a way to "get rid of ourselves," to free ourselves from being compelled to be a self we do not will, a way to take delight in being the self as we will (which, if it were a serious life-project "would be equally in despair" but fortunately is not), but only in a playworld set in (and against) the ordinary world of simple actuality.

In a similar Kierkegaardian vein, Fink suggestively notes that "the child *is* potentially ... it is still 'everything' ... it still has a thousand open possibilities ... the whole of life still oscillates in it before all determination" (italics mine, 2016b: 89), whereas an old person is the having-been-closed of a thousand open possibilities and the realization of one or a few, often tinged with regret at what was left undone or the paths that were not taken. As Fink puts it,

> The inexorable contraction of our possibilities, which accompanies our course of life and is the implacable law of serious life, is alleviated in its sadness—by play. For in play we enjoy the possibility of retrieving lost possibilities—indeed, even far beyond this, of attaining the openness of a mode of existence that is not determined and not bound. We are able to cast off the burden of our own life history, can "choose" what we wish to be, can slip into any role of existence. However, we are precisely not able to do this actually and truly, but rather only "in make-believe." We can only escape our actual and decided life in an illusory way. Liberation is a mere dream. (2016b: 89–90)

A turn to Freud, along with Ernst Bloch, on dreams here would be one way to critically assess the idea that the liberation attained in play "is a mere dream," though I leave that to the side here as a suggestion for future research. "Mere dreams," it turns out, often contain far more significance than is initially apparent, and play is a fertile ground for imaginative utopian currents that for various reasons may not immediately find direct political expression.

Play *of* the World

To understand what Fink means by play *of* the world, it first helps to know what Fink means by the term "worldly" (*weltlich*). Thomas Franz has explicated Fink's four senses of the term "worldly," three of which belong to human play and one of which belongs to the play of the world (2011: 261).[3] "Worldly" can denote the being-in-the-world of all finite beings: any being that exists, exists *in* the world. This sense of "worldly" of course does belong to human beings engaged in play, since humans and their playthings exist *in* the world. As we will see, however, the playworld that is always also generated by human players playing with playthings does not simply exist *in* the world like other simply actual beings, nor is it just a mirror-like reproduction of the world itself on a smaller scale. "Worldly" can also denote the way in which the human being relates to and extends itself out toward the world with understanding: in this sense, human beings are worldly while any being that does not or cannot relate to the world with understanding is not worldly, although it too exists *in* the world. A third sense of "worldly" is the one typically contrasted with "heavenly" or "divine": as Franz puts it, here we have "a denigrated mode of the human sojourn in the world" (2011: 261). Finally, we arrive at the fourth sense of "worldly," the one that is *not* supposed to be applicable to human play: the prevalence of the world itself, the world's course, or as Heraclitus put it in a word: *aiōn*, a Greek term that we will here take to be equivalent to *das Walten der Welt selbst* (the prevalence of the world itself). While human play is not worldly in this sense, while it is not the world's prevalence itself, as we will see, the world's prevalence can come to appearance *in* human play.

The play of the world is the world's prevalence, but of course articulating the world's prevalence is by no means an easy thing to do and so let us rely on one of a number of equivalent expressions of the world's prevalence offered by Fink: "the tragicomedy of the ascent and decline of all finite things from the nameless nocturnal womb and tomb of every individuation" (2016b: 116). Right here in Fink's own description of the play of the world, we have an example of play in the world: Fink of course is not seriously suggesting that every finite being actually arises from an actually existing "nameless nocturnal womb," nor is he suggesting that every finite being actually descends into the "tomb of every individuation." Rather, Fink is playfully using metaphorical language to symbolically express what defies any simple propositional definition, namely the world's course thought in its entire trajectory as a cycle of ascent and decline, birth and death. World is here conceived as womb and tomb from which every finite being emerges and into which every finite being declines, the place wherein things arise and decline, the space and time in which finite beings play out their existence before exiting and thereby making room for the next round of the cycle. Anaximander, of course, famously conceived of the *apeiron* as the source and end of all beings and compared it to what might be considered a kind of game, or at least a contest, namely a court proceeding in which one party pays what it owes to another (by ceasing to exist) and the other party receives justice (by receiving its turn to exist).

Another pre-Socratic philosopher, Heraclitus, has left us a fragment that is more central to Fink's conception of world-play than Anaximander's, however. I am referring, of course, to Heraclitus' fragment on the child playing: *aiōn pais esti paizōn, petteuōn; paidos hē basilēiē* (B 52 DK). Let us translate this fragment in Finkean terms: "aeon is a child playing, moving playthings around; a child prevails!" Fink himself translates aeon as *Zeit* but in the sense of an indefinitely long span of time, a kind of temporally tinged equivalent of "world." The world-whole, the entire trajectory of the ascent and decline of beings, is here symbolically expressed as a child moving pieces on a gameboard, with the regal seriousness that it is the human being's task to regain, one might add with Nietzsche. Heraclitus has here attempted to think "*the meaning of being from out of play*," while Plato reverses this and attempts to determine "the meaning of play" from out of being, as Fink puts it near the end of his programmatic essay, "Oasis of Happiness" (2016c: 30). Fink argues that Platonic metaphysics is only established through the suppression of play's true significance, in what Thomas Franz helpfully refers to as a "containment" of play by metaphysics. Plato's understanding of play as a (thrice-removed) distortion of reality distorts the reality of play itself, which more neutrally is just an "illusory variation on serious life" (2016b: 87) that is neither mere false distortion nor divine epiphany.[4]

In a further reflection on Heraclitus' fragment, Fink asks, "Are beings as a whole a taxis, a meaningful structure of universal reason, of the concept conceiving itself, or are they the ultimately inconceivable play 'of the child who moves the pieces on the board back and forth'?" (2016b: 116). The possibility of conceiving the world as play is suppressed so that reason may prevail, but the price of this suppression, I would argue, is a return of the repressed. Plato's philosophy is essentially playful, full of humor and "non-seriousness" on nearly every page, even and especially where the most serious and grim topics are discussed. We now turn to an examination of two fundamental interpretations of play, the metaphysical and the religious, through which Fink arrives at his own approach.

Play as Errancy and Epiphany

Fink begins the final chapter of PSW by providing the third answer to the question concerning the essence of play after already providing two other answers: the metaphysical and the cultic interpretation. The metaphysical answer to the question of play's essence is that play is an "illusory variation on serious life" or distortion of reality. Play is here a non-serious reproduction of something serious, a mirroring that distorts. The ontological status of playworldly appearance at this first level is negative: simply actual things that exist in the world are at one remove from the ideas, are copies of them, while playworldly appearances that are non-actual, that do not really exist on their own but only as images of something else that they are not, are copies of copies. Philosophy views the production of such appearances with suspicion and aims to expose its creators as frauds producing counterfeit images of reality.

However, we should recall that mirrors do not have to accurately reflect anything at all and can instead be a means to playful variation of possibilities not actually present in ordinary reality, such as occurs for instance in a fun house or the infinity-mirror. Anyone who pointed out that such mirrors do not accurately reflect reality would be considered a spoilsport. Instead of viewing a mirror image or copy as "derivative," what if we looked at the mirror image in a different way? Fink provides us with a way out of this myopic view of mirrors:

> So long as we suppose play to be derivative appearance, to be mirroring, and suppose mirroring to be a reproduction of archetypical things in residual silhouettes, we are all held under the spell of the Platonic interpretation. We must free ourselves from this spell. (2016b: 88)

Instead of viewing mirrors as either an accurate reproduction of reality or a pernicious distortion, we should understand mirroring as a manifestation of possibilities, playworldly images and scenes, as fabled "magic mirror" rather than as distorted reproduction of what actually exists.

In the second interpretation of playworldly appearance, that of the cult, it has a positive aspect: the religious interpretation of play is that it manifests a higher reality within appearance through the symbol, through a kind of intensification of reality in appearance, the manifestation of the divine in something mundane. In the use of masks, the performance of rites, the ceremonial procession, and the festival, "Play is considered to be a distinguished association with divine powers, the player as that life-form that comes closest to the heavenly ones" (2016b: 206). The Dionysia comes to mind here, but also mystery cults such as the one at Eleusis. Here, something much more real and powerful than an ordinary thing in the world dissembles and is captured like Proteus in Menelaus' net.

In both fields, metaphysics and cult, play is "interpreted as a relation to beings" (2016b: 206): metaphysically, play is a non-actual mirroring or reproduction of actual beings that are themselves distorted copies of real ideas; in the cult, play is association with and the summoning to presence of divine beings, rapture, and even apotheosis. In contrast, Fink himself interprets play as a relation to world, as an instance of the human being's world-openness.[5] In relating to the world-whole in play by ecstatically standing outside of itself (the literal meaning of ecstasy), the human being as player and the activity of play form a conduit through which the world-whole can reflect itself and through which the world-whole can illuminate innerworldly beings, the player and plaything, for example, charging them with symbolic power, whereby the part expresses the whole through a kind of compression or thickening (the radical sense of *Dichtung*).[6] In my concluding section, we will consider examples drawn from literature that deliberately and playfully illustrate this process itself, the play of the world coming to presence in human play.

Shining-Back and Symbolic Expressions of World in Play

In a revealing passage during his analysis of religious play, Eugen Fink suggestively notes that "the cultic symbol . . . is an early form of the most primordial symbol—it is a symbol of the symbol" (2016b: 146). As we have seen, play of the world comes to symbolic light in play in the world, and one of the most interesting ways in which this happens is when human play symbolizes the symbolic itself, attempting to represent a kind of hyperreality, or exceeding of ordinary reality, opening up within ordinary reality, something that Fink calls our attention to in his analysis of religious play as manifestation of the divine within the mundane. In what follows, I will consider literary examples of "the most primordial symbol."

One common form of human play is the telling of *mythoi*, or stories. Literary and artistic representations of human encounters with a symbolic expression of some infinitely greater whole might help shed light on what it means for the world-whole to shine back into human play and illuminate features of the world-whole's prevalence therein. For instance, in Homer's story of Menelaus and Proteus, we find a hero trying to divine the future by capturing a demigod who shape-shifts at will and can become any living being he likes. To learn what will be, the possibilities that will have been closed off and the restricted actuality that will manifest later on, the hero must "capture" a living being who is somehow all living beings, who does not experience the despair arising from "unlived possibilities." The future, and our present anxiety over it, ceases to perplex us once we can "capture" the infinite possibilities at work in the present moment. Several thousand years later, during the Romantic era, Goethe imagined a plant that was somehow all possible plants, an ideal plant in relation to which all existing plants are "variations on a theme," in his conception of the *Urpflanze*.[7] More recently, one of the twentieth century's most fantastical stories has explicitly thematized the boundless world's symbolic eruption into presence *within* the world.

Jorge Luis Borges, in his short story *The Aleph*, provides several symbolic expressions of a finite individual's encounter with infinite possibilities somehow magically present in one place at one time. This theme starts with the story's epigraph itself, the quotation of Hamlet's famous line: "I could be bounded in a nutshell / And count myself king of infinite space." In addition to citing Shakespeare, however, Borges also mentions several parallels to his Aleph drawn from the history of literature and myth: the seven-fold goblet of Kai Khosru (also known as The Cup of Jamshid), for instance, or a magical "glass" from Lucian's *A True Story*.[8] Lucian's own description of the magical glass cited by Borges is worth recalling:

> I saw also another strange thing in the same court: a mighty great glass lying upon the top of a pit of no great depth, whereinto, if any man descend, he shall hear everything that is spoken upon the earth: if he but look into the glass, he shall see all cities and all nations as well as if he were among them. (I.26)

Once again, we find the description of a thing in the world that somehow is the conduit for, a surface upon which appear if not all things in the world, then an indefinite and mind-boggling number of such things. One's ears can hear "everything" on Earth, and one's eyes can see "everything" there; if one could but touch, smell, and taste in a similar manner, we would have a means by which a finite individual can sensuously interact with a near-infinite number of innerworldly things all in "one place."

In closing, let us briefly consider the way in which Borges describes the indescribable, a point in space that is somehow all other points simultaneously. As with Eugen Fink's conception of world-play shining back into human play, as with the Homeric representation of a being who is somehow all living beings at once, and as with Lucian's tale of a mirror through which one can hear and see everything on earth, we are attempting to describe something that is not actual and present like ordinary things in the world but is nonetheless real in play. Borges prefaces his description of the Aleph as follows:

> Really, what I want to do is impossible, for any listing of an endless series is doomed to be infinitesimal. In that single gigantic instant I saw millions of acts both delightful and awful.... On the back part of the step, toward the right, I saw a small iridescent sphere of almost unbearable brilliance.... Each thing (a mirror's face, let us say) was infinite things, since I distinctly saw it from every angle of the universe. I saw the teeming sea; ... I saw the Aleph from every point and angle, and in the Aleph I saw the earth and in the earth the Aleph and in the Aleph the earth; I saw my own face and my own bowels; I saw your face; and I felt dizzy and wept, for my eyes had seen that secret and conjectured object whose name is common to all men but which no man has looked upon—the unimaginable universe. (1999: 283–4)

Borges has here provided us with a notable attempt at articulating what it means to experience the world-whole's shining-back into a finite being, here imagined in the playful realm of fantastic literature as the emergence of a mysterious *Kugelblitz* or phenomenon of "ball lightning" that is somehow—as symbol—everything that is, was, or will be at the same time and in the same place.[9] Of course, in the story, the Aleph is not a symbol of the whole universe but *is* in fact the whole universe bounded in a nutshell. Borges, however, is only playing. What he describes is *irreal*.

Borges has already told us at the outset of his description of the Aleph that since he cannot possibly describe it in ordinary language, he must, like mystics throughout history, find a symbolic way to put into words the entire universe's coming to appearance in a single place at a single time. In this regard, Borges helpfully reminds us that when we come to the limits of what ordinary language can meaningfully describe, we must revert to symbols and images for exactly the same reason Fink gives, namely that it is only through the symbol that the experience of irreality can be conveyed to others in language; the alternative, direct confrontation and perception of the whole itself, were it even possible, would presumably be as successful as Psyche's efforts to behold Cupid's true form.

According to Plato, a being reflects or participates in its idea to be what it is. Thus, all unfolding of being is the repetition of a finite number of being-types condemned to eternally recurring just as they are. In contrast, "It is different in the dimension of play," according to Fink, since play symbolically manifests "the coincidence of the universal and the particular.... The spectator from the play-community becomes witness to a process that does not occur in everyday life ... what he glimpses in the medium of appearance is not any old random fable that concerns other human beings and basically has nothing to do with him" (1979: 395–6). Instead, what such a spectator catches sight of is "the no-man's land" (*das Menschenlos*), or insight into the truth that each one of us is "in the depths of our essence identical to the strange figures" and have within ourselves every tragic hero "as uncanny, terrifying-terrible possibilities" (1979: 396). We thereby discover something that we are unable to in our own increasingly restricted life trajectory, namely that on a deeper level we *are* a teeming of possibilities, in their being-possible within us, whether or not we actually realize them.

We are simultaneously both world-open ecstatic players and played by the world. World-play may be a game without a player, but for us innerworldly players, world-play symbolically manifests itself when we play with the understanding of ourselves as both player and plaything, both playing and played at the same time. We thereby move from being an innerworldly player to a plaything or avatar for world-play and become the conduit for the one to shine back into the other. The soccer-player kicking a soccer ball on a field and intuitively understanding that ball to stand in for the resistance of beings in general and that field to stand in for the world as stage is already ecstatically world-open in this sense, both player and symbol, whose activity is both human play and symbolization of *das Walten der Welt selbst*.

2

Fink's Position within the Phenomenological Movement and the Origins of His Cosmology of Play

Giovanni Jan Giubilato

Introduction

Spiel ("play") represents one of the main pillars of Eugen Fink's thought.[1] It is a concept that allows one to make contact with all the most significant topics and problems of his prolific thinking: from anthropology to metaphysics, from ontology to cosmology, ethics, pedagogy, and, of course, phenomenology. The question that arises in relation to my interest in the origins of his thought, and in the formation of his early philosophy (found in the close confrontation he has with Husserl and Heidegger), is the following: What about that long and productive period during the years 1927–46, before the centrality of a cosmological concept of "play" became visible in Fink's thought and increasingly reached the public? What about a "pre-history" of the concept of play before Fink's remarks on *Nietzsche's Metaphysics of Play* (Fink 2019a), before his lectures from 1955 about the *Grundphänomene des menschlichen Daseins* (*Fundamental Phenomena of Human Existence*; Fink 1979) and his famous main work *Play as Symbol of the World* (Fink 2016)? What I want to consider here is the progressive emergence of the metaphysics of play, of its wide semantic spectrum, and of its systematic function within Fink's own thinking during the twenty-year period (1926–46) of his early thought, that is, a possible "prehistory of the concept of play." To do this I will mainly take into consideration: (1) the few *Studies in Phenomenology* (Fink 1966) that Fink was able to publish during these early years, including his doctoral thesis on *Presentification and Image*; (2) the "texts and drafts" he wrote with and for Husserl, mainly in view of a revision of his *Cartesian Meditations* and a full elaboration of the German version of the Meditations into a broad *System of Phenomenological Philosophy* (cf. Fink 1988b; 2019b); (3) the *Sixth Cartesian Meditation*; and (4) the large number of private notes and disparate materials from Fink's Archive that have been published, since 2006, in the volumes of the *Phenomenologische Werkstatt* (*Phenomenological Workshop*, Fink 2006, 2008, 2023a, and 2023b).[2] On the basis of these materials, I will delve into the course of Fink's laborious construction of his thinking and point out the gradual rise of his own philosophy, trying to outline the main features of this progressive development. The newly released publication of the third and fourth volumes of the *Phenomenological Workshop* provides considerable information on how Fink continuously renewed and defined his own thinking. Thanks to this variegated collection of materials, I hope to be able to illuminate Fink's position within the phenomenological movement, particularly focusing on Fink's relation to Husserl's transcendental project and Heidegger's fundamental ontology.

Moving beyond Husserl's phenomenology

Fink's concept of play soon became a key catalyst of all the most important paths of his philosophy, gradually emerging from a distinctive radicalization and further thinking of Husserl's phenomenology and transcendental project. Already by the early 1930s, Fink conceived "the phenomenological system" as the "system of life," and "life as concretely playing intentionality" (Fink 2008: 424). In fact, as Ronald Bruzina points out at the end of his seminal introduction to the first two volumes of the *Phänomenologische Werkstatt*, "with Fink at Husserl's side," phenomenological "questioning gained a different force and a persistence that opened up new aspects of a phenomenology that, otherwise, might have tended to stiffen in its habits" (Bruzina 2006: xcvii). The innovative and different character that phenomenology acquired in Husserl's last phase of work was due, to a considerable extent, to the overarching methodological relevance that Fink's "meontic interpretation" gave to the reduction process, and to the daring effort to penetrate into the deepest levels of the ultimate "constitutive dimension" of the "absolute origin." The term "meontic," formed from the junction of two ancient Greek particles (μή and ὄν, "non-" and "being"), was introduced by Fink to designate his own philosophical project, devoted to grasping, understanding, and bringing to conceptual explication the absolute, non-existing origin of every being and of what is originated (meontic, i.e., lying "beyond" being).[3] Linking the absolute origin of what is constituted, the "constitutedness of what is in being" (Fink 2008: 140) and the constitutive process of world's becoming, which is not-in-being but constitutes what being "is," Fink's thinking involved a "movement beyond transcendental genesis, towards the absolute" (Giubilato 2018) that ended up in an innovative, vertical displacement of the horizontal structure of Husserl's phenomenology and led to an independent "program of thought beyond Husserl's approach" (Bruzina 2006: xcvii). Fink's own development of phenomenological thinking occurred "not in orthodox following but in the continuation of the intellectual impulses received from Husserl" (Ossenkop et al. 2015: 27), since it brought Husserl's transcendental phenomenology to "the rocks, [to] the problems that lie at the margins of the regressive analytic, in order from that point to receive the motivating impulse for the constructive project" (Fink 1995: 7). This led to an unprecedented "whole movement out beyond the reductive givenness of transcendental life", and to the examination of the "external horizon of [this] reductive givenness" (Fink 1995: 7). Pushing constitutive phenomenology into the transcendental sphere of being that reaches beyond ego and subjectivity, and beyond the moment of intuitional presence altogether,with his architectonic foundation of a constructive phenomenology (Fink, 1995: 7-11: 54-66) that explores the structural relationship between being and "pre-being",Fink was facing a *Meontics* or a *meontic phenomenology as theory of appearance of the transcendental Absolute*:

> The Absolute is only as its manifestation. It is not first the Absolute and then manifests itself (or constitutes the world), but it is insofar as it manifests itself. "Constitution" therefore means ultimately manifestation or appearance of the Absolute. "Phenomenology" = Appearance theory of the Absolute. (Fink 2008: 302)

The philosophical investigation of the original relationship between the "non-being" (meontic) absolute origin and its constituted manifestation, which is also identified by Fink in the concept of "freedom," leads him to develop a whole *ontogonic metaphysics of the absolute*, which can be evaluated as the core of his original and somewhat heretical evolution of Husserl's phenomenology into new philosophical territory. Since its main aspects have been studied and outlined in detail during the past twenty years (Luft 2002; Van Kerckhoven 2003; Bruzina 2004; Giubilato 2017), I will try to summarize the most crucial aspects on which Fink builds and that differ from Husserl's transcendental project.

The Prominence of the Question about the World

Finks philosophical endeavor engages with defining and questioning about the world, as he considers it the true philosophical question par excellence, to which no single science can address itself. He, therefore, manifests a profound affinity with Heidegger—not only with the analyses he carried out in *Being and Time* about "Being-in-the-World" as "fundamental constitution" of human existence and about the "worldliness of the world", but also with the richness of Heidegger's discussion of the *Fundamental Concepts of Metaphysics: World, Finitude, Solitude* presented in the lectures during winter semester 1929/30.[4] (cf. Heidegger 1995). That the question of the world dwelt since the beginning at the center of Fink's thought is proven not only by the texts he wrote, on behalf of Husserl, for the project of a *comprehensive systematic work* of phenomenology (1930–1931) and for the revision of the German version of the *Cartesian Meditations* (1931–1933) (cf. Fink 1988b), but also by the statement with which he introduced in 1946 his first lecture at the Freiburg University. "In spite of all grandiose extension of the human knowledge in the sciences, these never come to the world. Science focuses in principle on beings, and that means: on intraworldly beings. The intraworldly zone is the field of science. There is no science of the world" (Fink 1985: 96). Moreover, in his famous essay The Phenomenological Philosophy of Edmund Husserl and Contemporary Criticism from 1933, Fink already stated clearly that the fundamental question of phenomenology consisted in "the question about the origin of the world" (Fink 1970: 96). There he addressed world in accordance with the phenomenological method of reduction and with the movement of a world-transcending, in opposition to everything mundane, that is, intraworldly form of knowledge referred to intraworldly beings. In fact, by means of the phenomenological reduction, we "transcend the world as encompassing horizon of every knowledge-problematic" and we are "led back to the world-transcendent origin" (Fink 1970: 99).

Particularly important, as an early hint of Fink's profound radicalization of Husserl's phenomenology, is the conception of an "awareness of the play area" in which the world was to be given *ex negativo*, that is, "in its withdrawal" or as "pure un-holding" (Fink 2008: 319). With this paradox of the "ungivenness" or givenness *in absentia* of the space-giving and time-allowing world, Fink distances himself from Husserl's concept of "horizonal awareness" not only because the phenomenological conception of the world as a continuous horizon expansion seems insufficient to him, but also because the concept of "awareness of the play area" is precisely one of "horizon forming," in which the horizons of every possible human experience are firstly constituted by "ontogonic movement" (Fink 1957: 233). As Fink wrote already in the late 1920s in the preparatory notes for his *Dissertation*: "The Meon carries the world and its transfinite edges" (Fink 2006: 72). With his essay from 1933, designed to "defend" Husserl's phenomenology from the various misunderstandings generated by a traditional and worldly understanding of its goals, Fink also took the opportunity to publicly reveal one of the fundamental theses that also lay at the heart of the VI *Cartesian Meditation*, namely the fundamental ontological thesis that underpins his entire *Meontics*, according to which all being is the result of a process of constitution: "Beings are principally the 'result' of a constitution" (Fink 1970: 91); "The world in its entirety [. . .] can, through the reduction, be known as the result of a transcendental constitution" (Fink 1970: 128).[5] Fink's ongoing recasting of phenomenology thus goes in the direction of a *meontic ontogonic metaphysics*, which results in an increasing tension between phenomenology, ontology, and ontogony.

The "meontic" radicalization of phenomenological reduction

Although reduction was initially introduced within the framework of a phenomenological critique of epistemology, as the elimination of all transcendences and their "being accepted and in force" before the so-called "turn" to transcendental idealism, it has been inseparably connected to transcendental-phenomenological idealism since, at least, Husserl's *Ideas I*. Especially in the 1920s and 1930s, reduction emerges as a *pars pro toto* for phenomenology as a whole, presenting itself as the essential key to every phenomenological understanding. Every kind of phenomenology appears to be, ultimately, the respective unfolding of this basic idea. The reduction can be regarded as the fundamental act of phenomenology, because as such it first gives one the possibility to philosophize: it opens up the space of philosophy in opposition to the closedness of natural and pre-philosophical attitude. Thus, it is not surprising at all that a large part of the metamorphosis of Husserl's phenomenology produced by Fink is essentially based on the concept and on the practice of the "reduction."

Regarding the issue of phenomenological understanding, Fink states that phenomenology can be seen as a mode of thinking that is permeated by two opposing and inherently complementary basic tendencies, with the reduction at their center, as connecting point.

> Phenomenological understanding is pulling back from enworlding, is repetition of the enworlding process. Under these at first obscure titles we indicate the basic

philosophical tendencies: phenomenological reduction as 'pulling back from' and constitutional theory as repetition. (Fink 2006: 246)

This twofold spiral movement, brought forth by the enactment of reduction, is both a "pulling back from" the enworlding that has always already been going on, and from its results (i.e., from constituted worldly entanglement), and an analytical and conceptual repetition of this same constitutive process that finds its teleological endpoint in the meaningful world, in the cosmos that we live in. Fink refers to the first movement of "retrieval" as *"ekbasis"* (ancient Greek for "way out of, going out of" but also "end of a person's life") and to the second movement of "repetition" of the enworlding process as *"katabasis"* (ancient Greek for "way down, descent"). The analytical-conceptual repetition of the constitutive process, which retraces in the reverse direction the emanative-teleological movement of the absolute to the world,[6] gives rise to the phenomenological "theory of constitution." Enabled by reduction, the forgotten "drama of world constitution" unfolds before the eyes of the philosopher, who is purely engaged in "phenomenologically theoretical cognition countering ('retroinquiring')" (Fink 1995: 113) the constitutive process directed toward the world, that is, the progressive manifestation into being of the non-being Absolute. Therefore, as the world is considered to be the *Ausschweifung*, that is, the "manifestation of the Absolute, as the movement of the Absolute" (Fink 2008: 168), philosophical knowledge, which is supposed to think both the world *and* the Absolute, and their constitutive relation, is defined by Fink as the "dialectical unity of finite (ontological) and infinite (ontogonic) knowledge" (Fink, Z-XIX/II/6a; cf. Giubilato 2022a).

Though this (dialectical) "counterplay of world-oriented constitution [on the one hand] and phenomenologically theoretical cognition countering it [on the other]" (Fink 1995: 113) implies a prior elaboration of that from which life is to be pulled back, in order to be able to carry out the reductive and philosophical "pulling back from" experience (Fink 2006: 246). In other words, Fink states the true importance of the prior elaboration of a phenomenological ontology of human Being-in-the-world, exploring the situation in which reduction has to be carried out, and delivering a structural analysis of the human natural attitude and worldly life, which he characterizes essentially as *"Weltbefangenheit,"* that is, as "entanglement" or "captivation in the world." In this regard the conversation that Dorion Cairns recalls he had with Fink on September 23, 1932, when they discussed Fink's draft for the VI *Meditation*, is enlightening.[7] Interestingly, Cairns notes that "Fink has long been working on a Hegel interpretation," confirming what we now clearly see also in the new volumes 3.3 and 3.4 of the *Phänomenologische Werkstatt*, and that according to him "the difficulty with the Hegel interpretation is the erroneous application of mundane concepts and logic to what Hegel says. For example, the identity of *Sein* <being> and *Nichts* <nothing> is not a mundane identity, but the identity of constituted and constituting" (Cairns 1976: 97).[8] Moreover, on the relation between *Weltbefangenheit* and the Absolute we can read:

> The term *"natürliche Einstellung"* <natural attitude> is dangerous, as suggesting a sort of (arbitrary?) "attitude". Fink prefers to say *"Weltbefangenheit"* <entanglement in the world>. The transcendental ego lives then as it were in the

superficies of its life. The transcendental reduction makes the third dimension transparent, enables the ego to see the lower levels of world constitution. [...] He suggested that the *Ur*-ego <primal ego>, in which the enduring ego is constituted, that the *Ur*-now <primal now> is not, perhaps, the Absolute, but the first emanation of the Absolute. (Cairns 1976: 95)

However, Fink's meontic radicalization of phenomenological reduction was not only changing the phenomenological understanding of the concept of "natural attitude"; it implied also a contrast to Husserl's methodological concept of reduction as method of revealing "absolute subjectivity." Fink understood the deeper meaning of "reduction" as an act of liberation of human existence from worldly captivation, which produces within its natural entanglement in the world a new dynamic movement of κάθαρσις (Catharsis) and ὁμοίωσις θεῷ (Homoiôsis Theôi), seizing and elevating it as a whole. It is called by Fink also the fundamental experience of *enthusiasm* (cf. Fink 1947) in accordance with the etymology of the word, which is derived from the verb ἐνθουσιάζω, meaning "to be inspired by a god or be possessed by a god, to be in ecstasy." Consequently, it should always be considered that for Fink the reduction also represents:

1) The seizure, that is, the opening of a *"window" into the Absolute*. From the distance of a freely created opening, the philosopher observes the transcendental happening of the constitutive movement of the world. The transcendental onlooker is an uninvolved *panopticum*, looking through a window opened by reduction at the tremendous spectacle of constitution.
2) The *establishing of a medium*. The act of reduction is an act that holds within itself a *medium* for the appearance of the otherwise hidden transcendental dimension, or the Absolute itself. However, the appearance is worldly; it appears within the world. The (philosophizing) human takes on the function of a "mediator."
3) A multilevel process, which from an initial "bracketing" of the world and its ontological validity leads the philosophizing human through a *process of dehumanization, liberation* from the genetically constituted self-apperceptions and the not genetically constituted structures of finitude: the In-Stances, and finally to an absolute "loosening free" from being, called by Fink *"Absolution"* (Fink 2008: 43, 79, 94, 169; cf. Giubilato 2017: 221–42). Hence for Fink the reduction becomes the "path into the absolute origin—a path that is in each case mine" (Fink 1966: 14–15).

Fink's Critique of Husserl's Subjectivism: The Cosmological Perspective

Fink's conception of a meontic phenomenology as appearance theory of the absolute leads to a deep critique of Husserl's pronounced subjectivism, and to the foundation of the possibility of its overcoming by opening up the potential for a cosmological perspective. Fink's final judgment on Husserl's position was that although his phenomenology established unique and fruitful paths that led to the exposition of the question of the world, it did not succeed in bringing this question in such a way that a final overcoming of the "dogmatism of subjectivity" was already in sight. This criticism is particularly prominent in the *"Elemente einer Husserl-Kritik"* ("Elements for a Husserl-critique"), which will be printed in the second section of the fourth volume of the *Phenomenologische Werkstatt*. The text consists of a collection of fifty-six theses, and dates to the early month of 1940—just after the outbreak of the Second World War. The main goal that Fink pursues in his free and highly argumentative annotations is, as the third thesis indicates, "the resettlement of phenomenological research into philosophy (my claim!)" (Fink, Elemente einer Husserl-Kritik/3). The notes contained in these folders allow us today to list the following four main points of his critical questioning of Husserl's phenomenology, but it should be borne in mind that each of these theses has simultaneously served him as a springboard for the development of his own thinking.

Husserl's phenomenology is "ahistorical." What is missing in it is an effective confrontation with the philosophical tradition and especially with antiquity and with the heritage of speculative idealism. Phenomenology, according to Fink's conclusion,

> is ahistorical, because it considers the new encounter with beings as philosophically decisive; it is ahistorical, insofar as it does not come to a confrontation with the historically-past philosophy, i.e., it does not initially take a position on the problem of speculation [. . .]; furthermore, it is ahistorical, because it does not express its inner historicity (the problem of the transcendentals). (Fink, Z-XXVI/38a)

Thus *Husserl's phenomenology is dogmatic*, insofar as it leads to an "absolutization of the finite subject," or of the knowing "egoity." The "immense analytical work" done by Husserl's phenomenology must not obscure the fact that it is exposed to the danger of ossifying into a *circulus vitiosus*, that is, a philosophy of reflection in which "the human runs back into himself" (Fink, Z-XXVII/57a).

Husserl's phenomenology is anti-metaphysical in its essence. By raising the philosophical claim to a new foundation of knowledge, phenomenology at the same time called to examine everything that is given (as being) to consciousness by returning to its original mode of self-givenness. In doing so, however, it implicitly made the precondition that objective being, the being-for-us of beings, is being par excellence—and correspondingly regarded the primordial event of world-constitution and of appearing exclusively as a form of being-for-us of beings.

Within phenomenology there *is operating an enormous leveling of the concept of "being,"* since in Husserl's phenomenology being would be conceived merely "as validity, namely as representational validity" (Fink, Z-XXVII/3a). This one-sided orientation of the interpretation of "beings" toward the model of the "object" is the unmistakable sign of "immobility of the ontological fundamental concepts," of a "standstill of the concept of being" (Fink, Z-XXVII/6a), which can be sensed within Husserl's phenomenological analysis. It consistently operates with a "model of knowledge" that makes use of the intentional schema "consciousness/consciousness-of" and thus promotes an ontic, that is, worldly biased attitude to knowledge. Consequently, Husserl can even regard "essence" as an "object of a higher order." It is therefore unmistakable, according to Fink, that Husserl operates with "an ontologically mutilated concept of being," namely with a purely "cognitive-relative concept of being" (Fink, Z-XXVII/9b).

To contrast the danger, for phenomenology, to become a merely scientific methodism, and to lose its own philosophical/speculative potential, Fink emphasizes that phenomenology can only permanently maintain its place in the historical development of thought if it understands itself *as philosophy and not as a mere research method*. This implies, however, that it should not evade the fundamental responsibility to carry out the original positing of the basic concepts of all human knowledge. This means that it must set itself anew the task of thinking through "what is a thing, what is a quality, what is the universal, the particular, the one and the many, what is existence, what is essence, what is reality and possibility, what is the whole of all things, what is most being in all being, and what is the essence of truth" (Fink 1976: 128). Following Hegel's thesis that philosophy is, first, the giving of its concepts, Fink counters the phenomenological idol of "absence of presuppositions" with the philosophical task of a primordial positing or archetypal presupposition, and precisely the primordial positing of those "primordially illuminating concepts" which make all human understanding of the world, and even science, possible—and thus represent the *a priori opening of world reality*.

Inclusion of the "question of being" in the "question of the world"

From the previous considerations it is clear that Fink's philosophical endeavor did not put the greatest emphasis on Being (conceived as presencing), which is also called "*Seyn*" by Heidegger, but on the basic event of coming into being (*Seinswerden*), that is, the cosmogonic arising of the world. Thus, it could happen that later, during the lectures of 1949 on "*World and Finitude*," in which Fink made good progress with his own cosmological exposition of the world question, starting from a "metaphysical discussion" (above all with Kant and Heidegger) of the world concept, he formulated his leading idea somewhat strikingly:

> World is the arising of Being. For this primordial event, which only grants the range of play [*Spielraum*] to all things and occurrences, we have no right name and we cannot have one; for all names are at home on the opened field of being, we call the opening itself, the arising: "word." (Fink 1990: 205)

And it was not about a *genitivus subjectivus*, as if the world were the unconcealment of being and being could somehow be the "subject" of this unconcealment activity, but about a *genitivus objectivus*, in the sense that being should be considered exclusively as the result of the ontogonic bringing forth. Being is namely "the gift of the world" (Fink 1985: 109), and this "creative, originating movement of being in the arising of the world must be thought from play" (Fink 1990: 207). In fact, already in a set of notes mainly dedicated to Heidegger's idea of a fundamental ontology relating to the winter semester 1931/2—as he was attending Heidegger's lectures "*On the essence of truth*"—Fink wrote his own position:

> Philosophy cannot be determined primarily as ontology. "Being" only [is] in the horizon of world captivation. "Being" [is] in principle the "result" of a non-being process! "Being": a "moment" of the process: the whereto of the world plunge of the Absolute that is unnihilating itself. "World" as "absolute surface"—philosophizing is asking questions about the origin: existentially the annulment [*Aufhebung*] of existence, catastrophic thinking. (Fink 2008: 108–9)[9]

Alternatively, as Fink put it a little more circumspectly twenty years later: "In the rising of the world, the pure gift of being occurs, which allows everything to occur, brings it into existence, by letting it into space and time and into sight" (Fink 2016d: 206). In the primordial event of the rising of the world,

> in letting go into the clearing of the opened world, every being is given its measure of reality; it comes into being, so to speak, only in such going up into the world. But the world is not a previously produced structure, a container, in which now the things have place and duration and appearance, world is the original producing itself. If we call this giving space and letting time, then these are expressions of embarrassment; but they aim at the movement character, at the "giving". There is not world as there is day and night. But world is that which "gives" everything, of which we then say: "there is." (Fink 2016d: 206–7)

At this point it becomes apparent for the first time in which sense the question of being was included by Fink in the world question. But with this we have already come to the next and last topic, which is the confrontation of the young Fink with Heidegger and especially with his major work *Being and Time*.

"Using a Diamond as a Brick": The Confrontation with Heidegger and *Being and Time*

The study here does not claim to be exhaustive, which moreover would be unfeasible in the space of one single chapter; it aims only to present the fundamental points of the young Fink's critical position toward Heidegger. These will be, at least in part, fundamental themes of the debate between them that came to full fruition in the years following the end of the Second World War. At the beginning of the lecture from the winter semester 1955/6 "*Sein—Wahrheit—Welt. Vorfragen zum Problem des Phänomenbegriffs*," Fink allowed the basic orientation that determined his philosophical conversation with Martin Heidegger to emerge by declaring that "the guiding intention was to illuminate the cosmological horizon of the question of being in an encounter with phenomenological motifs of Husserl's and Heidegger's philosophy" (Fink 2018: 208). The problem of a true philosophical understanding of the "world," which Fink saw in Husserl and Heidegger reduced to the common denominator of some sort of "innerwordly horizon," pushed itself to the fore of his genuinely phenomenological interest. What couldn't come into view under these two perspectives was, according to Fink, the essence of the world as the world *wholeness*, as the world *totality*, in which all being that appears within the innerwordly sphere only then comes to light. His persistent phenomenological questioning was directed precisely to this difference between beings within the world and the whole of the world—called the *cosmological difference*. Neither the world as infinite horizon of consciousness' experience nor the world as "existential," in his view, could explain the "cosmos" as the basic event of the appearing that encompasses and governs all that exists in the inner world. And exactly this question comes to the surface during the discussions with Heidegger in the famous *Heraclitus Seminar*. In this regard, even more valuable and decisive for us today are the numerous notes of the young Fink contained in the four volumes of the "*Werkstatt*" edition. In them, one can follow how his cosmological thinking increasingly gained profile not only by criticizing Husserl's intentional analytics of the given world but also by distancing himself from Heidegger's ontological approach and analysis of Dasein.

In doing so, there is no doubt that both Husserl and Heidegger deeply influenced Fink, whose uniqueness can nevertheless be seen in his tireless effort to integrate both Husserl's constitutive transcendental phenomenology and Heidegger's ontology (as hermeneutics of facticity) into an overarching perspective. This tendency to look for a certain *integration* of Husserl's and Heidegger's positions is clearly perceptible already during the late 1920s–early 1930s, when the "relationship of Husserl and Heidegger" is compared to "the quarrel of two people, each of whom claims to put the cart before the horse: Husserl begins with the analysis of ontic knowledge, Heidegger with ontological knowledge. Husserl is blind for transcendence, Heidegger for constitution" (Fink 2008: 122). To the extent that Heidegger's existential analytic sets itself the goal of an "illumination of Dasein with regard to its a priori structures (such as surrounding world, thrownness, projection)," it would provide nothing else than "an elaboration of the 'starting point of philosophy'," namely the ontological elaboration of the human "natural attitude" (Fink 2006: 44). Based on this surely valid and necessary, but still insufficient philosophical inquiry, Fink's ontogonic metaphysics is supposed to gather the transcendental guidelines for the constitutive problematic. What the hermeneutics of facticity thus lacks, according to Fink, is a true insight into the natural world of life as "that which is constituted in end-constitution" (Fink 1995: 138). By not being able to decipher the "intraworldliness" (the "Being-in within Being" [*In-Sein im Sein*]) as a constituted "final layer," that is, as "transcendental surface" hanging over the absolute origin,[10] Heidegger's fundamental ontology remains (trapped) within the (transcendental) horizon of *Being and Time*. In a pivotal set of notes on a working project entitled *System of Philosophy in Outline* (*System der Philosophie im Grundriß*), which represented a "a first collection and review and reassurance of the current direction of [Fink's] own thinking" (Fink 2008: 252), the point is stated,

> Ontology [is] related to the situation of world-entanglement, to the constitutive end-products, to the "transcendental surface". Phenomenology is not a "theory of

Being", but inquires about Being as a structural moment of the meontic process of the world-plunge of the nothing. (Fink 2008: 313)

In this regard the early Heidegger perspective would remain within "what has been originated," without being able to recognize the "cosmological difference" and to take that decisive (and longed-for) step toward the "overcoming of the horizon as such" and "the return into the source" (Heidegger 1996a: 35). The project of *Being and Time* was thus doomed to remain incomplete, since Heidegger does not come to the realization that "the origin" does not mean "Being" but rather "the relation of the absolute to the ontic" (Fink 2006: 269), which is also called constitution or "ontification" (Fink 2008: 7). In fact, Fink summarized the most decisive insight for the understanding of his cosmological philosophy in the thesis: "Being is result" (Fink 2008: 303). Heidegger's peculiar blindness for the dimension of constitution has the consequence that he has no conceptuality that would allow him to adequately determine *the absolute, me-ontic origin of being and time, that is, of finitude*. In Heidegger's hermeneutics of factual Dasein, Fink criticizes the "suppression" (Fink, Z-XXIX/178a) of ontogonic constitutional research in favor of a blind "philosophical ontology", and the loss of the "problematic of the transcendentals, [. . .] which encourages a leveling of the concept of being" (Fink, Z-XXIX/CCCIV/6b-7a). Thus, we read in the following note, dated from the early 1930s:

> The phenomenological analytics of pure consciousness can be evaluated (in misunderstanding of the transcendental sense of the word "consciousness") as a doctrine of the essence of certain structures of consciousness, thus of certain modalities of Dasein previously analyzed existentially in its totality. But in doing so it [i.e., phenomenological analytics] would be deprived of *its philosophical significance*. It would be like using a diamond as a brick. (Fink 2008: 289)

Theory and Practice

One of the most important critical objections formulated by Fink relates to the claim that, according to Heidegger, "theory" is grounded in the moods of praxis, which constitute primordial access to the world. The derivation of θεωρεῖν from a practice that is to be classified as "original," however, could only be grounded, in Fink's view, on a blatant misunderstanding of what "theory" actually is. In no case does "theory" arise from "a deficiency of having to do with the world and taking care of it" (Heidegger 1996a: 57), for instance from an interruption of the primordial practical-manipulating dealing with the world, in which a pre-conceptual, pre-predicative understanding of being is already at work. If Heidegger's notion of "understanding of Being" already implies the thesis of the (ontological) difference (between Being and beings), together with the conception of a primordial and pre-conceptual "understanding" of being and worldly beings, it also—implicitly— implies a theory about the "posteriority of the concept" (Fink, Z-XXIX/198a). The same was the case with Husserl's intentional intuitionism, and the foundation of knowledge in acts of intuition which are contrasted to conceptual representations.

Fink, for his part, is advocating for an original "conceptual knowledge of being" that, in his view, not only characterizes philosophical knowledge but also lies at the ground of every human relation to his surrounding world. The transcendental priori opening of every world reality takes place, as Fink says, in "primordially illuminating concepts."

Moreover, in Fink's view, Heidegger's interpretation of theoretical cognition as a derived, deficient mode of an original practical dealing with things and of knowing oneself within their "context of relevance" completely disregards the mode of being of "in-itself" of things, beyond their "being-for-me" in the sense of their being available for my handling. It is precisely the underdetermination, at least in *Being and Time*, of the essence of nature that causes Fink uneasiness. Apparently, Heidegger considers the concept of "objective presence" (*Vorhandenheit*) sufficient in order not to lose sight of nature, extending beyond the world-forming sphere of Dasein. But as soon as Dasein's "Being-in-the World" is missing, the world-wideness that is open to him due to his original practical dealing with his surrounding is transformed into a mere undifferentiated materiality:

> The world loses its specific character of aroundness, the surrounding world becomes the natural world. "The world" as a totality of useful things at hand is spatialized to become a connection of extended things which are merely objectively present. The homogeneous space of nature shows itself only when the beings we encounter are discovered in such a way that the worldly character of what is at hand gets specifically deprived of its worldliness. (Heidegger 1996a: 104)[11]

According to Fink, Heidegger's ontological approach supposedly makes "the tacit presupposition that theory deals with *the same being* as the handling, only just in a subsidiary attitude (determined by a privation)" (Fink, Z-MH-I/21a). In the idea that "handling opens up a richer ontological fullness of the existing" and that "theory means an 'impoverishment' of the existing," Fink glimpses an absolutely narrow interpretation of theory which arises from an ontology that is "blind to the depths of being, i.e., the graduality of the ontological power of the existing" (Fink, Z-MH-I/21b).

Concept, Truth, and History of Metaphysics

Fink's critical objections to Heidegger and his reflections on "theory and practice" lead directly to his "concept-theory." This *Begriffslehre* developed by Fink stands under the auspices of a "me-ontic" reading and interpretation of Hegel's *Phenomenology of Spirit*. According to Fink, it is beyond all doubt that it was Hegel who produced "the last great ontological project of the Occident, [. . .] a gigantic work"—but "since then the onto-conceptual thinking stands still" (Fink 1976: 128). While Heidegger in his onto-historical thinking presents Nietzsche as the last metaphysician with whom Western metaphysics has come to an end, in Fink's eyes it is Hegel who in fact represents the end of metaphysical thinking and at the same time its culmination. "With Kierkegaard and especially with Nietzsche," Fink thinks, "a new originality" already announces itself.

They are the "heralds of a new ontological experience, even though they remain quite incapable of expressing their ontological intuition in the concept" (Fink 1976: 128). What is most needed today, however, is a new conceptual thinking that can project and design anew the primordial "fundamental concepts that will henceforth form the framework of the world" (Fink 1976: 134)—a new cosmological thinking in which, step by step, "the draft of the ontological basic ideas" can be elaborated. With this creative projection of primordial concepts Fink associates a conception of "being" and "truth" that shows him once more to disagree with Heidegger.

Certainly, Heidegger's lecture *The Origin of Work of Art*—which Fink attended in early November 1935—made an overwhelming impression on Fink. What Fink retained from Heidegger's remarks as "the essential" presented during the lecture was "the problem of the relation of 'being' and 'truth'" or, as he also says, of "Being-itself and being-for-us" (Fink, Z-MH-I/2b). However, Fink did not intend to try to master this problem by appealing to a "pre-conceptual understanding of being." Rather, he resorted to a "primal illumination of the concept" and to a renewed conceptual articulation of the transcendental relations of *ens, unum, verum, bonum* (cf. Fink 2018: 249 ff.; 259 ff.). Therefore, he opposed the idea of a pre-conceptual, existential (ontological-practical) truth or openness, which had led Heidegger in *Being and Time* to throw into the balance of his analysis of Dasein the key concept of "resoluteness," with his (i.e., Fink's) own idea of the "concept as the locus of truth." This thesis, obviously,needs to be read with great caution, since it has not the same "meaning as the thesis of judgment as the locus of truth, nor is an assertion that yields 'propositional truth' the decisive place. 'Truth' is also not primarily 'correspondence,' but 'the light of the concept' ('clearing'). The most original truth is conceptual" (Fink, Z-XXIX/176a). Once again, it is striking how often Fink brings into play the same terms as those used by Heidegger, but with something fundamentally different in mind. In fact, nor does his conception of the history of metaphysics, which around 1939 he emphatically describes as a "history of ἀλήθεια" (Fink, Z-XXIX/177a) that "moves in jerks," necessarily refer to Heidegger's position. Heidegger and Fink even agree in rejecting the traditional discourse of "eternal truths," which means rejecting every conception of truth that does not consider the fundamental event of ἀληθεύειν. But Heidegger's theory is "wrong in assuming that all ἀληθεύειν is only human, i.e., finite," and thus—this is the crucial point of Fink's critique—"that finite human ἀληθεύειν is incapable of a ὁμοίωσις θεῷ, that is, completely off from the possibility of approaching the Νοῦς" (Fink, Z-XXIX/58a). Heidegger's concept of truth as "(ἀλήθεια) = unconcealment"—of this Fink was convinced quite at an early stage—remained basically "insensitive to the graduality of the Being of beings," since he conceived the "human truth as the clearing of a world night and not as the brightness of twilight compared to the solar brightness of divine truth" (Fink, Z-XXIX/83a).

Ethics of Authenticity

A whole series of notes aim at engaging a deep confrontation with the "ethics of authenticity" that Fink imputes to Heidegger, and in which he detects the expression of a certain "interiorization tendency" of human existence—which he wants to unmask. Thus, for example, it is said that the "fundamental attunements" placed by Heidegger at the center of his "hermeneutics of Dasein"—such as anxiety in *Being and Time* and boredom in the already mentioned lectures on *Fundamental Concepts of Metaphysics: World, Finitude, Solitude*—"bring the human to himself," but not to the "verily and truly being" (Fink, Z-XXVI/95a), the "ὄντως ὄν." Only in the painful privation (*Entbehrung, inopia*) of the Absolute, only in the presentiment of it, in the worldly poverty of being, there can open up—for Fink—the way to a speculative development of a "universal science of the absolute" and to a new ontogonic cosmology, which for the first time set its sights on the question of the world wholeness. In contrast, what in *Being and Time* emerges through the "self-selection" of human fate and the "anticipation of death" is a claim of human existence to "authenticity" conceived, essentially, as an act of "essentialization" and as self-sufficiency of autarchy of the human—without any prospect on a possible being by the "verily and truly Being," the ὄντως ὄν, the Absolute. Heidegger's self-sufficient conception of human existence and of its possible "authenticity" would then bear the mark of an "ethics of resoluteness": "authentic is only the human who relates to his 'true state of being', to his 'being to death'" and who understands "himself undisguised from himself" as "thrown into death"—and "exists in this self-understanding of himself." This kind of "self-knowledge" is "a [mode of] being that means being with oneself, not being alienated," and from which a true "action" can "spring" (Fink, Z-MH-I/7a). In the exceptional state of authentic selfhood, in which the human anticipates his death, takes it upon himself as his own, immediate, unsurpassable possibility, the finite freedom of human existence is realized; it gains original concretion—in contrast to the natural tendency of his life, which leads to "Falling Prey and Thrownness" (cf. *Being and Time*, § 38), to being-thrown into "the unpersonal They" (*das Man*), into being alienated from oneself, into the mediocrity of a common existence. The possibility of an ontological-ethical guidance of finite existence of the human thus lies in the "self-selecting existence" (Fink, Z-XXIX/250a).

Fink wants to distance himself from Heidegger's conception of human existence because in it a certain "anthropocentrism" comes to the surface, since the human seems to revolve only around himself, failing in his essential position as "mediator" and his cosmological function of mediation. Basically, Heidegger's ethics of authentic decision, of utmost determination in the face of death still remains within the intraworldly sphere. Fink believes that Heidegger used an ontic model of existence, that he extracted from the analysis and hermeneutics of the everydayness and averageness of human Dasein, for his ontological interpretation of its fundamental constitution. Moreover, the concept of "authenticity" is still oriented to the concept of "self-understanding" and of "openness to oneself," which Dasein would become inwardly aware of, for instance, in some ontologically "sublime" basic moods. For Heidegger authentic existence would come about only "through the truth about oneself, that is through disclosedness; and authentic existence basically still obeys the classical slogan "γνῶθι σεαυτόν."

Fink considers such a "doctrine of the authenticity" that lies in the "self-grasping of the human about his own existence" to be an "anthropocentrism caught in itself" (Fink, Z-XXIX/58b). Heidegger's ontological determination of human existence as "*care*" (*Sorge*)—according to which "the being about which these beings are concerned in their being is to be their 'there'" (Heidegger 1996a: 125)—paradigmatically illustrates the *circulus vitiosus* in which the modern human has entangled himself. If the world is comprehended and illuminated exclusively from the "self-transcendence" of Dasein, that is, starting from its constant self-selection—what Fink also calls Heidegger's "luminary theory of subjectivity" (Fink, Z-XIX/II/4a)[12]—then the "authenticity" of his world-references depends unilaterally "on the authenticity of the human that is staying in the reference," that is, on his "being-himself in all his references" (Fink, Z-XXIX/96b). Although Heidegger rightly polemicized against reducing the human to (psychological or transcendental) subjectivity and immanence, and therefore asserted the "Being-in-the-World" in general as the fundamental constitution of Dasein, he nevertheless considers the human as inevitably "worldly entangled," that is, "imprisoned" within finitude or the intraworldly sphere. Thus, he conceives the world itself as a merely human world, that is, as a world characterized exclusively by the finite transcendence of a metaphysically isolated Dasein.

Conclusion

In an essential note of the folder Z-MH-I, after Fink has briefly outlined Heidegger's "thesis of an ontological historicity" in his work *The Origin of the Work of Art*, we find a summary of his critical objections toward Heidegger's philosophy, counterposed to his own philosophical standpoint:

> 1) Emotional theory of understanding (practice as "handling"). 2) Underdetermination of the being of nature in *Being and Time*—but as problem-preparing distance!? 3) Dasein "is" the original time! 4) Absence of the cosmological concept of world. 5) Pre-conceptual understanding of being. 6) Heidegger's struggle against the "nous"-nature of being! Against antiquity.
>
> My position: Instead of "care" [*Sorge*]- "play". Instead of "pre-conceptual understanding of being"—the primal illumination of the concept. Instead of "finitude"participation in the being of the gods (in liberation from 'entrapment') (Hegel). The human as "mediator." (Fink, Z-MH-I/3a)

After the attempts presented in this chapter to summarize Fink's position with respect to both Husserl's and Heidegger's philosophies, this list should—so we hope—be more understandable and clearly point to several lines of development in Fink's thought. Hopefully it can also help to begin to shed light on the evolution of Fink's early thought, and the continuities and differences that can be traced in relation to the so called second, "mature" phase of his philosophy of play and his extended confrontation with Heidegger.[13] But maybe the best description of the long, complicated, and intricate relation of Fink's thought toward Heidegger's position since their first encounters during Heidegger's lectures of the late 1920s has been—not surprisingly—produced by Heidegger himself. In a letter dated November 7, 1964, which belongs to the still unpublished correspondence between Fink and Heidegger,[14] he sends heartfelt thanks for receiving the text of the speech given by Fink on the occasion of his seventy-fifth birthday,[15] and then writes:

> I didn't know anything about it until now. After reading it, I lingered in a long meditation that culminated in the thought: "He (Fink) would have been the only possible successor." I am not writing this to remind you of your decision,[16] but to tell you that of the many comments made on my birthday, this one, yours, is the only one that hits the mark. You may measure not only my joy from this original text,[17] but first of all my heartfelt thanks for your word spoken from real proximity. Proximity means at the same time: opposite, and therein lies the independence of your own thinking, which ventures into the corresponding dimensions.

The continuous interplay of "proximity and distance" to both Husserl and Heidegger still represents one of the most fascinating features of Fink's own adventure of thinking. It is, at the same time, an invitation to discover its richness in greater detail.

3

Fink's Phenomenology and Ontology of Play and Its Relation to Hans-Georg Gadamer's Philosophical Hermeneutics

Núria Sara Miras Boronat

The History of Effects and Conceptual History: Philosophical Hermeneutics and Its Relation to Time

Philosophical hermeneutics considered as the systematization and inclusion of several methods of interpretation into a comprehensive theory of interpretation was one of the most fascinating philosophical revolutions of the past century. The debate that originated around Gadamer's work involved the most prominent figures of the neighboring philosophical trends such as Richard J. Bernstein, Richard Rorty (pragmatism), Jürgen Habermas (critical theory), Jacques Derrida (deconstruction), and Hans Robert Jauss (reception aesthetics). Most of the debate focused on questions related to truth, interpretation, and normativity but these did not exhaust the richness of philosophical hermeneutics.

One of the core concepts developed in Gadamer's main work is "*wirkungsgeschichtliches Bewusstsein*," a term that is almost impossible to grasp for those who are not fluent in German. In the English translation, the term used is "the principle of the history of effects."[1] The history of the effects (*Wirkungsgeschichte*) of a concept or an event is a consequential development of historical research and can give crucial information about its actual relevance. In other words, when we focus on a historical event, its contemporary relevance can be measured by assessing its impact on our current culture. The history of effects constitutes a sort of immaterial evidence of the importance of our object of study in which one or more of its fundamental but not always obvious dimensions are disclosed. The history of effects also has a significant resemblance to the concept of "reception" popularized by the Konstanzer Schule.[2]

Gadamer distances himself from reception aesthetics when he criticizes Jauss and his school for the implicit idealization of reception theory.[3] The reception of a classic or of any work of art runs the risk of acquiring the status of canonical interpretation. What characterizes a work of art as a classic, however, is precisely the inexhaustibility of its multiple interpretations. Hence, we could provisionally accept the thesis that a given reception of a classic piece of art is part of its possible effects, but such a reception never coincides with the totality of all of its possible effects.

The history of effects is an intrinsic task of the historian, who must become conscious of the historical relativity of his or her present. Thus, the principle of the history of effects is articulated by Gadamer as the concrete form of historical consciousness (Gadamer 2004: 301).[4] To take responsibility for one own's hermeneutical situation is a precondition of every single interpretation of our shared past. The principle of the history of effects is one of the main axes of Gadamer's theory of the hermeneutic experience, which he defines as the *act of understanding*. The ontological assumption at its heart is that every single interpretation is a possibility offered by the historical tradition itself in its temporal occurrence. Philosophical hermeneutics seeks to elucidate the conditions of the possibility of any interpretation within a historical tradition as the result of its temporality and the coming-into-language of things.[5] In both cases—time and language—Gadamer relies on a phenomenological description of play and games that should help to give shape to the aforementioned theory of the hermeneutic experience. In the cases of both art and language, Gadamer relates himself to the phenomenological approaches to play in the German philosophical tradition, in particular, Eugen Fink. For this reason, the present chapter offers a reconstruction of the history of the effects of Fink's concepts of play,[6] with Fink himself serving as the cornerstone of a given *play narrative*.[7]

Eugen Fink is first mentioned in the *Truth and Method*'s chapter devoted to Gadamer's ontology of the artwork. Gadamer makes use of the concept of play (*Spiel*) as the thread for his ontological explanation of what happens when we interpret a piece of art. Gadamer's starting point is German Romanticism, for which the analogy between aesthetic experience and play has become commonplace. Remember that Kant defined the experience of beauty as the "free play of imagination and understanding" (Gadamer 1999a: 38). With Schiller's *Letters upon the Aesthetic Education of Man* (1794), the play instinct becomes intrinsically human.[8] Gadamer praises German Romanticism for having recovered the "ontological dignity of play."[9] For many centuries, play has been considered the conceptual opposite of seriousness and productivity owing to the impact of industrialism in capitalism (Huizinga 1955; Sutton-Smith 2001). By contrast, Hegel and Nietzsche have both contributed to seeing a specific and inherent seriousness in play, while Gadamer likes to refer to play as "its own, even sacred, seriousness" (Gadamer, 2004: 103). But the main problem of German Romanticism is that its phenomenology of play rests exclusively in its subjective aspect, that is, in the inner experience of those who play. This subjective and individualistic approach neglects what Gadamer considers essential for the phenomena that most resemble play: art and language. These are collective phenomena, not in the strong sense that experiencing them makes them objective and univocal but in the agreeable fact that interpreting artistic or linguistic expressions requires being a part of a historical tradition for which these are meaningful. Thus, to adapt the play concept to the intended ontology of the hermeneutic experience, the first task is to de-subjectivize play and grant the "primacy of play to the players" (Gadamer 2004: 105).

To this end, Gadamer relies primarily on Fink's texts on play and aesthetics, specifically the latter's *Vergegenwärtigung und Bild*[10] and *Spiel als Weltsymbol*

(1960/2010). Play, as art and language, is characterized by *representing* something. This is not merely accidental: their being consists mainly in *being a symbol*. Gadamer's discussion can sometimes appear confusing because it refers to a technical debate over the conceptual distinction between allegory and symbol, which are rhetorical forms. When he stresses the *symbolic* in play, he wants to point out that play and games *represent* life on a small scale because they reproduce life in its manifold possibilities. Play and games (as art and language) are *temporal* and *medial events* (Gadamer 2004: 104–5). To put it in Wittgensteinian terms: play and games (as art and language) share their "practical grammar" with life. Representation, however, is more than mere imitation. Concretely, in a work of art, representation opens up new meanings and possibilities. A genuine representation in art thus implies an *"increase in being"* (Gadamer 2004: 135).

The second feature of play and games is that they are *effortless*. If some effort should be required, it would always be compensated for by the joy of playing, its ease and lightness. Games have rules in a given space that limit the movements of players within it. Still, the players enjoy moving in the play space according to the previously accepted rules. They play by the rules, or they play with the rules, but the rules are not lived as a constriction on their playfulness: they channel it. The explanatory value of *Spiel* as casual movement or dance is that it helps to explain the fact that we are constantly involved in linguistic practices without being constantly aware of the rules.

The third feature of play and games is that they are a *representation of something for others*. They represent a shared cultural meaning; they represent themselves in their growing upon a previously existing but not always articulated *common sense*. According to Gadamer, representation only accomplishes itself insofar as it is directed toward someone. This feature is expanded upon in a number of his later writings[11] with the help of some core anthropological concepts such as ritual and celebration (*Fest*). The analogy with rituals and celebrations enables Gadamer to stress two important features of artworks, games, and languages: they are simultaneously *recurrent* and *unique*. Let us take the example of a celebration like Christmas: some repetitive characteristics occur every year on 25 December, but also, each year, some variations may distinguish the current year from preceding ones.

Phenomenologies of Play: Ways of Dealing with the Elusiveness of Games and Play

The huge success of *Truth and Method* (1960) caught its author unawares. Gadamer never expected to garner so much attention from a book that took him roughly three decades of work. In its wake, he never again entertained the idea of engaging in another major philosophical program. After all, the foundation of philosophical hermeneutics was a lifework. However, he did go back, again and again, to clarify or further develop some of the loose ends in his *magnum opus*. In 1985, Gadamer admits that one of the less consistent points in *Truth and Method* is the connection between the play of language and the play of the arts in the first and third parts of the book (Gadamer 1999b: 5). While the main characteristics of play and games concerning the arts are discussed extensively in the first part, the third part leaves matters only lightly sketched in, giving the impression that Gadamer expects his potential readers to link both definitions of play on their own. Another striking point is that in the preface to the second edition of *Truth and Method*, which was written in 1965, Gadamer insists that his analysis of play and games is meant to be "merely phenomenological" (Gadamer 1999b: 446). Complementary to this remark is perhaps the epilogue to the third edition that appears in 1972, in which Gadamer talks about the ontological problem involved in the play concept (Gadamer 1999b: 456). In 1965, he clarified that his use of the concepts of play and games was meant to overcome the subjectivism of Schiller and the German Romantics. But in so doing and by constructing the analogy between language and play, he never intended to instrumentalize language or to overlap with other technical disciplines that study language.

The argument is complex. Even if Gadamer may have thought that he was making a clearer point, I find his explanation to be quite confusing. Consequently, it might be more interesting for our purposes here to focus on what I take to be the key to Gadamer's problem: the tension between phenomenology and ontology. In light of his works on play and games produced between 1930 and 1960, that is, the period when Gadamer started to write philosophy professionally, the working hypothesis in the present study draws upon Brian Sutton-Smith's (2001) philosophy of play and it is twofold. First, different philosophical traditions and disciplines study games and play with distinctive research interests that determine their specific approach to play. Following Sutton-Smith, we can observe how the literature on play and games started to grow exponentially in the early decades of the twentieth century such that we can speak of a "ludic turn" in Western culture (Sutton-Smith 2001: ix). The diverse approaches to play and games might be so divergent that they are not compatible with a single definition of what play and games are (Salen and Zimmerman 2004). Thus, second, the divergence between approaches to play and games depends to a great degree on the paradigmatic model of play and games in each discipline and tradition. In other words, the ontology of play (i.e., the underlying assumption of what play and games *are*) in any given discipline is strongly dependent on the relevant ontic realm of the discipline (i.e., the play and games that the discipline takes as role models).

When Gadamer says that he has given up offering an ontology of play and that his descriptions must be taken as merely phenomenological, this might be his way of tackling the problem. Using multiple linguistic associations and popular images, he avoids committing to any particular play tradition or discipline: rather, he follows the path of language in pointing out quite common universal traits of games and play to illuminate what arts and languages are, simply by picking up the traits in which the analogy works even when remaining in pure abstraction. Curiously, the preferred play narrative to present a phenomenology of play is also phenomenological.[12] By saying this, I am not completely endorsing Sutton-Smith's rhetorical proposal, which divides the rhetorics of play into seven: progress, fate, power, identity, frivolity, self, and imaginary. Sutton-Smith places the main figures of the phenomenological tradition within the rhetorics of the self (Husserl, Heidegger, and Gadamer). However, Heidegger and Gadamer would refuse to define play solely from the perspective of the players. I find it more promising to use an alternative argument put forward by Sutton-

Smith that often gets overlooked in the literature. We can find three kinds of play definitions in any play narrative or tradition: (1) definitions based upon the players and their play experiences, (2) definitions that underlie the intrinsic functions of play, and (3) definitions that point out the extrinsic functions of play. If we combined the types of rhetoric with the kinds of definitions, we would likely come out with a much more complex but pluralistic account of what play and games are, thereby rendering the complexity of the phenomena.

I aim to treat the phenomenological movement as a philosophical tradition in which more than one definition and rhetoric are present while others are absent. This might be illuminating for the way that the tradition has approached play. For instance, the intrinsic value of play was present for many phenomenologists, which made it impossible for them to understand play as something frivolous or monetizable, traits that belong to other rhetorics of play.

I trace the beginning of the phenomenological tradition of play that influenced philosophical hermeneutics to works by the psychologist and philosopher Karl Groos (1861–1946). Groos studied play among animals (which was quite an innovation in his *Tierpsychologie*)[13] and then made important remarks on the importance of play for children and adults. In his 1922 book *Das Spiel* (Play), Groos emphasized that play presents indisputable life values that he set out under three points of view: *Einübung* (practice), *Ergänzung* (aesthetic surplus), and *Erholung* (relaxation). Groos (1922: 17) sees in play a sort of "segregated context of life experience" (*abgesonderter Erlebniszusammenhang*) that is reminiscent of Fink's "Oasis of Happiness" (1968).

The biologist and psychologist F. J. J. Buytendijk (1887–1974) published an impressive work entitled *Wesen und Sinn des Spiels* (Essence and Sense of Play) in 1933.[14] His research sought to bridge the gap between science and life and he therefore starts from the richness of the semantic field of play (Buytendijk 1933: 39). Buytendijk discusses the main existing literature on the evolutionary aspect of play (which would correspond to Sutton-Smith's rhetoric of animal progress). He relates play to life's instincts, so that play as such is part of an individual's development, mainly in childhood and youth. Other intrinsic features of play and games are added, such as rules and movement. But his phenomenology is not to be reduced to biology: play and games open up the realms of fantasy and imagination. As he puts it beautifully: "Human beings need bread and play. Bread to grow and to exist. Play to experience this existence" (Buytendijk 1933: 79).

Johan Huzinga (1872–1945) is probably the greatest play theorist of the twentieth century. The exuberance of *Homo Ludens* (1938), the fine irony and playful writing style, the sheer amount of historical evidence, and the keen sharpness of Huzinga's analysis find no parallel in the history of phenomenology and play. In keeping with earlier authors, Huzinga followed the linguistic associations of play and games, but he complicated the matter even more by compiling them in a multiplicity of world languages. His second chapter is where the tension between the phenomenological and the ontological is expressed with the greatest vehemence. Still, Huzinga was one of the first to offer an exhaustive definition of play and games resulting from his cultural and phenomenological analysis. Play, he states, "is a voluntary activity or occupation executed within fixed limits of time and place, according to rules freely accepted but absolutely binding, having its aim in itself and accompanied by a feeling of tension, joy, and the consciousness that it is 'different' from 'ordinary life'" (Huizinga 1955: 28). Huizinga's phenomenology converges at the end with philosophical anthropology and an epoch-making diagnosis that we can formulate somewhat differently from him thanks to the productive efficiency of temporal distance. I would suggest the following formulation: when playfulness is forced to draw its wings, the spirit of fascism is near.

Playing Traditions: Gadamer's Appropriation of Fink's Ontology

The ludic tone that surfaces in parts of *Truth and Method* is something that Gadamer fully intended. He inherits a phenomenological tradition that has been formed around concepts and definitions of play, and he knows how to make the most of it. Some of his characteristic features of play are borrowed directly from Groos, Buytendijk, and Huizinga, sometimes because he relates explicitly to them and sometimes because the terms were present in the scholarship of the time. What I argue here is that it is precisely Eugen Fink's multidimensional concept of play that can solve most of the problems in reconciling different play narratives. I find a specific clue in the essay entitled "Zwischen Phänomenologie und Dialektik: Versuch einer Selbstkritik" (Between Phenomenology and Dialectic: An Attempt at Self-criticism, 1985). In the essay, Gadamer accepts that he has had enormous difficulty in integrating different concepts of play, namely *Sprachspiel* (the play of language), *Kunstspiel* (the play of art), and *Weltspiel* (the play of the world). Precisely where the concepts are best interrelated from a phenomenological perspective are in the writings of Eugen Fink, which is the reason why Fink has such a strong presence in *Truth and Method*, even if Gadamer reorganizes Fink's phenomenology of play according to his own theoretical interests.

Fink's most well-known text on play (or most well-known text at all) is his short essay entitled "Oasis of Happiness" (1957). The essay, which bears the subtitle "Thoughts on an Ontology of Play," is a quite complete structural analysis of play and games as phenomena. In it, Fink identifies the following elements: delight, meaning, community, rules, equipment, and play-world. As we can see, some of the elements coincide with the main Gadamerian features of arts and language: meaning, delight, rules, play-world, and community. The range of emotions that a player can experiment with while playing is quite broad. But what must prevail is a *delight* (*Spiellust*), the effortlessness of the movement, and the possibility of moving in an interplay of freedom and opportunities within the play space. For Fink, play is essentially a social phenomenon—solitary play is a subsidiary form of it—that is constituted by rules. Rules, as we have known since Wittgenstein (1999) and Kripke (1982), are learned in society and cannot be learned privately. Beyond the existence of rules as a condition for the possibility of play and games, however, play forms (such as but not limited to rituals and celebrations) institute communal bonds. Play, following

Fink, is the creation of meaning. Such a definition fits perfectly with language, arts, and traditions taken as horizons of self-evolving shared meanings. Fink makes an interesting move here by placing meaning as a structural element of play, which allows him to open up a new dimension: its symbolic, magical aspect, that is, the constitution of a play-world that blurs the lines between reality and fiction (2010: 22). The term that is used in *Spiel als Weltsymbol* is *speculative* as a synonym for *reproducing* or *representing*. The "speculative" is a mirroring of the world performed by something which is structurally equivalent to the world. In this sense, play is a *symbol of the world*. A *symbol* in Fink's sense is not a simple imitation but a revelation of the world's deep structure, which reminds us of the structure of human play and human existence (Fink 2010: 111).

Play is one of the key concepts of Fink's philosophical anthropology set forth in the *Grundphänomene des menschlichen Daseins* (Fundamental Phenomena of Human Existence, 1995). But what does Fink mean by "fundamental"? A fundamental phenomenon occurs in any individual existence by which each existence finds itself referring to objects, nature, and other human existences. Although they are all interrelated, they cannot be reduced to any other. Also, all of them share another important characteristic: they are twofold, sometimes ambiguous and sometimes expressing deep human contradictions. Specifically, these phenomena are death, work, power, love, and play. This is to say, a human being is essentially a worker, a player, a lover, a fighter, and a mortal (Fink 1995: 106). Death belongs to our condition; we are constantly confronted with our finitude; work represents our struggle for survival against nature; power represents the struggle for or against domination; love as *eros* is the way that we as individuals transcend our individuality through the perpetuation of the species. And play stands for our imagined, projected possibilities. It might seem that all these phenomena are equally essential, but an interesting twist arises if we take Fink literally. Play is the *representative* human phenomenon par excellence because it can bring every human situation to life: "We play with the serious, the authentic, the real. We play with work and struggle, love and death. We even play with play" (2010: 101).

In my reading, play is the *Totalphänomen* in Fink's writings. We can close the circle[15] by recalling his earlier texts on Heraclitus and Nietzsche. Cosmic play is a recurrent topic that can be traced back to the famous fragment B52: "*Aion* is a child at play, playing draughts, the kingship is a child's" (Heraclitus 1952: xviii). In *The Birth of Tragedy*, Nietzsche explains the metaphor of time as play, likening it to the world's creative power. For Fink, this is "Nietzsche's metaphysical intuition" (2011: 37) since only play can represent how things are in a world in perpetual change, appearing, disappearing, transforming, or evolving. Fink makes himself an heir of a genealogy of cosmological thought that understands life in the universe as perpetual becoming. Only when we understand the play of the world and the play of being as a kind of artistic freedom, as a work of art that creates and recreates itself, can we be open to the great game that occurs all around us and of which we are a part. This understanding of cosmic play leads us to Nietzsche's formula of the *amor fati*: "The will that does not resign itself to fate, but participates in the cosmic play" (Fink 2003: 172).

Concluding Remarks: Hermeneutical Openness and the Fate of Our Times

In this chapter, I have attempted to trace genealogically a sort of phenomenology of play that puts Fink and Gadamer within a lineage of thinkers that not only dignify play as a concept but end up making play a central element of culture. This coincides partially with Sutton-Smith's rhetorical solution but also partially complements it by refining the original idea, since it demonstrates that some streams of thought might inevitably link different narratives and exclude others. Play as a *Totalphänomen* from a phenomenological perspective excludes seeing play solely as an instrument for the development of physiological capacities or as a commodity that we can monetize. Play is neither frivolous nor secondary. Rather, play is the primary and fundamental access to infinite life possibilities because it builds the link between the material and the ideal.

Fink's reappropriation of the Nietzschean *amor fati* is reminiscent of Gadamer's reappropriation of Schlegel's dictum: "All the sacred games of art are only remote imitations of the infinite play of the world, the eternally self-creating work of art" (Gadamer 2004: 105). Cosmic play perfectly suits the temporal and medial character of the historical tradition within which we are situated but can also move as we walk toward remote horizons of meaning. Historical tradition means that things themselves must come into human language. It makes us feel like part of the eternal conversation of humanity. Gadamer, who so liked to open and close hermeneutical circles, also regarded tradition as the primary subject of the hermeneutic experience: "It expresses itself like a Thou" (Gadamer 2004: 352). The historical tradition is the Great Player. It is no accident that Gadamer chose this poem by Rilke to open his work *Truth and Method*:

> Catch only what you've thrown yourself, all is
> mere skill and little gain;
> but when you're suddenly the catcher of a ball
> thrown by an eternal partner
> with accurate and measured swing
> towards you, to your center, in an arch
> from the great bridgebuilding of God:
> why catching then becomes a power—
> not yours, a world's.

4

Fink and Gadamer

Phenomenology, Hermeneutics, and the Aesthetics of Play

Stefano Marino

In the present contribution I will try to sketch an attempt of critical comparison between Eugen Fink's phenomenological account of play and the role played by the notion of play in the context of Hans-Georg Gadamer's hermeneutical philosophy. Due to the limits, in terms of length and structure, of a single book chapter, and also due to the breadth and complexity of this topic in the philosophies of both these great German thinkers, it is not my aim to ambitiously provide here a systematic or all-encompassing investigation of all the aspects of Fink's and Gadamer's philosophies of play. The present contribution must be rather understood only as a preliminary exploration of a topic that I potentially hope to investigate in a more complete, detailed, and systematic way in some future comparative works on these authors. Throughout the decades Fink developed his phenomenological, ontological, and even cosmological interpretation of the concept of play. I will limit myself to some references to Fink's 1957 essay "Oasis of Happiness: Toward an Ontology of Play" (OH) and to his 1969 book *Fashion: Seductive Play* (FSP).

It is noteworthy that fashion is included by Fink in the complex and multifaceted realm of phenomena that can be explained through the concept of play. In particular, with regard to the question as to whether or not there is an aspect that can be taken as a privileged key to gain an adequate access to fashion, Fink's answer is the aesthetic dimension. Fink emphasizes the irreducibility of fashion's play to other dimensions of human existence, such as economics, ethics, or politics. Fink poignantly defines fashion as "an aesthetic realm 'beyond good and evil,'" and then adds that "This relegation of fashion to aesthetic manifestations, which reach their peak in artworks, should not deceive us into applying categories from theoretical aesthetics to fashion" (Fink 2023: 85).

In some passages of FSP what emerges is the relation between fashion and play—and also seduction. Seduction occupies a strategic position of mediation between the two other concepts in Fink's account of these phenomena. For example, Fink observes that sociability plays a fundamental role in the whole of human existence and that, in turn, "Sociability lives in the element of play. The great forms of sociability, with their 'receptions,' their 'festivals,' always have a more or less masked play-character" (Fink 2023: 97). Fink further observes: "Human play is a basic phenomenon that does not occur alongside and outside of the carrying out of serious existence, but rather, in its sphere, replicates and mirrors all serious undertakings in the mode of *as-if*" (Fink 2023: 93). These passages show the continuity of Fink's observations about play since they are comparable to his earlier work in OH (Fink 2016: 19, 24–6, 28–30).

Fink's philosophical work on the concept of play culminates in PSW. There he emphasizes the need to offer today a rehabilitation of the importance of the "worldliness" of human play, starting from the idea of the ecstatic openness of the human being toward the world and eventually arriving at an outline of a phenomenological cosmology. A philosophy centered on the concept of *kosmos*, on a general view of the human being as the *ens cosmologicum*, and on the basic idea of "cosmological difference" (comparable, although not identical, to Heidegger's "ontological difference"). Especially the concepts of play and world assume a central role in this context, up to the point that play, world, and world-totality can be defined as the key concepts of Fink's entire postwar philosophical work (Bertolini 2012: 128).

In the twentieth century there has been an important series of philosophies of play. Let us simply think about the great relevance that the concept of play has acquired in different thinkers such as Huizinga, Caillois, Adorno, Gadamer, Marcuse, Plessner, Wittgenstein, and others. For example, in the philosophy of language, "language game" has become a key concept since Wittgenstein's *Philosophical Investigations* (1953). In aesthetics the philosophical use of the concept of play has often relied on some insights whose original coinage can be traced back to Kant's notion of the "free play" of the "powers of cognition" (Kant 2000) or to Schiller's original concept of the "play-drive" (Schiller 1993).

Compared to others, Fink's philosophy of play stands out because of its breadth, coherence, rigor, and systematic character. Gadamer is one of Fink's contemporaries who can be compared to him on this topic. He wrote of play often (Gadamer 1976: 130–81) and belongs to the so-called *Phänomenologische Bewegung* (Figal 2007 and Gregorio 2008). Of course, it is important to immediately emphasize the explicit hermeneutical orientation that characterizes Gadamer's approach to phenomenology, due to the long-lasting influence of Heidegger's 1920 lectures and the original ontological and hermeneutical interpretation of phenomenology that Heidegger had developed in his 1927 *Being and Time* (see Heidegger 2010, §§5–8, 13–35).

Even a quick comparison between Fink's and Gadamer's philosophies shows that both conceived of play as a basic human phenomenon, as an "existential characteristic" that deserves to be studied at a serious philosophical level. In the same years in which Fink wrote and published PSW, Gadamer also intensively reflected on the phenomenological and hermeneutical significance of play, most notably in the first part of *Truth and Method* (TM).

TM is structured in three parts, respectively corresponding to different fields and steps of development of Gadamer's ambitious "universal hermeneutics." In general, Gadamer's fundamental philosophical task is "to seek the experience of truth that transcends the domain of scientific method wherever that experience is to be found, and to inquire into its legitimacy" (Gadamer 2004: XXI). In fact, "the problem of hermeneutics"—which, for Gadamer, is basically the problem of understanding and "not merely a concern of science," but rather something that "goes beyond the limits of the concept of method as set by modern science" and that "belongs to human experience of the world in general" (Gadamer 2004: xx). The first part of TM is focused on some fundamental aesthetic problems, understood in light of the basic hermeneutic phenomenon of understanding. This part of Gadamer's *opus magnum* starts from a penetrating critique of the "subjectivization of aesthetics" in the modern age—with a specific critique of the notion of "aesthetic consciousness," as inadequate to fully grasp the breadth of "aesthetic experience"—and arrives to the retrieval of the question of artistic truth and the development of a hermeneutic ontology of the artwork. The main contents of the first part of TM are probably summarized by Gadamer's famous statement "*Aesthetics has to be absorbed into hermeneutics*" (Gadamer 2004: 157).

In the first part of TM, Gadamer offers a hermeneutical conception of play that understands it as the "clue to ontological explanation" leading to the center of Gadamer's philosophical theory of art. Besides this, it is remarkable that in other subsequent Gadamerian essays on aesthetics and poetics from the 1970s and 1980s the concept of *Spiel* keeps playing a particularly important role, although sometimes with a light shift from the strictly ontological orientation that characterized TM to a more anthropological one. This is especially the case of two essays from the mid-1970s, "The Play of Art" and "The Relevance of the Beautiful." In the first, play is understood as "an elementary phenomenon" that "determines man as a natural being," and the human "forms of play" are emphatically defined as the "forms of our freedom" (Gadamer 1986: 123, 130). In the second essay, the concept of play, alongside the concepts of symbol and festival, forms the essay's subtitle and thus immediately shows its centrality in the context of Gadamer's attempt to philosophically grasp the essence of art, beauty, and aesthetic experience. The focus is that play is a fundamental communitarian element, tightly connected to the ritualistic dimension of artistic events, that is, the festival (Gadamer 1986: 39–53).

In TM play is vital in overcoming the narrow and subjectivistic orientation of various modern aesthetic theories that Gadamer critically discusses. In fact, for Gadamer this concept offers the possibility of developing an aesthetic paradigm that is finally capable of connecting the phenomenon of the work of art to the fundamental dimensions of understanding and experience (and not merely *Erlebnis*, understood by Gadamer as a reductive idea of human experience). In order to stress the anti-subjectivistic orientation of his hermeneutical conception of play, Gadamer explicitly claims that, "When we speak of play in reference to the experience of art, this means neither the orientation nor even the state of mind of the creator or of those enjoying the work of art, nor the freedom of a subjectivity engaged in play, but the mode of the being of the work of art itself" (Gadamer 2004: 102).

For Gadamer, the experience of movement represents the basis of the idea of play: "The movement of playing has no goal that brings it to an end; rather, it renews itself in constant repetition. The movement backward and forward is obviously so central to the definition of play that it makes no difference who or what performs this movement" (Gadamer 2004: 104).[1] Just like Fink, Gadamer focuses his attention on the fact that, in play, the player is "played." This is what Gadamer emphatically calls "the *primacy of play over the consciousness of the player*," arguing that "The players are not the subjects of play; instead play merely reaches presentation through the players" (Gadamer 2004: 103, 105), so that the main feature of play is "self-presentation" that includes in itself—and actually overcomes—the supposed primacy of the subject. According to Gadamer,

> Play does not have its being in the player's consciousness or attitude, but on the contrary play draws him into its dominion and fills him with his spirit. The player experiences the game as a reality that surpasses him. This is all more the case where the game is itself "intended" as such a reality—for instance, the play which appears a *presentation for an audience*. (Gadamer 2004: 109)

On this basis, assuming a critical stance toward the basic subject/object dichotomy that has been typical of modern epistemology, Gadamer gradually aims to show that art cannot be reduced to a mere object of a subjective aesthetic consciousness, nor can it be properly understood on the basis of the idea of "aesthetic differentiation" that, for him, has characterized modern aesthetics. In this context, play functions as a sort of emblem of art itself, inasmuch as it allows recognition of our experience with art as "a part of the *event of being that occurs in presentation*, and belongs essentially to play as play" (Gadamer 2004: 115). For Gadamer, "Th[e] change, in which human play comes to its true consummation in being art," can be defined as a "*transformation into structure*," and it is "only through this change does play achieve ideality, so that it can be intended and understood as play" (Gadamer 2004: 110).

It is especially, but not exclusively, in the first part of TM, dedicated to the development of his hermeneutical aesthetics, that Gadamer's account of play emerges. In the conclusion of the third part of TM, dedicated to the development of his hermeneutical conception of language, there is included a significant reference to the concept of play. It is understood as a sort of *trait d'union* between the aesthetic experience of beauty and the linguistic dimension of understanding. "*Language games* exist where we, as learners—and when do we cease to be that?—rise to the understanding of the world. Here it is worth recalling what we said about the nature of play, namely that the player's actions should not be considered subjective actions" (Gadamer 2004: 484).

Both Fink and Gadamer assign a fundamental importance to the role "played" by play in human existence. In contrast to less philosophical accounts of play which often considered it as "mere idle amusement, to be valid only as a restful pause which helps us return all the more energized to what is 'really' important," in OH, Fink develops "a speculative phenomenology of play that begins from the sort of play with which we are all familiar and from there attempts to reflect on play, moving from child's play all the way up to cosmic play, where the world itself is conceived as a '*game without a player*'" (Moore and Turner 2016: 1). Gadamer, for his part, understands, "The playfulness of human games [as] constituted by the imposition of rules and regulations that only count as such within the closed world of play," and, for him, this is exactly the element that is constitutive of the collective world of human practices: "this is indeed so universal a structure of human existence that we might well consider the directedness of play to be characteristically human" (Gadamer 1986: 124).

Fink's ambitious phenomenology of play develops a full-blown and somehow all-encompassing account of this phenomenon not only in existential and ontological terms but eventually also in a cosmological direction and, quite surprisingly, even in relation to a human practice that most philosophers have traditionally considered as "the most superficial of all phenomena" (Svendsen 2006: 7), namely fashion. In contrast, Gadamer's interest in the concept of play is more delimited, not arriving to the metaphysical and cosmological vastness of Fink's treatment. In fact, in the case of Gadamer play appears to be especially important in the context of his hermeneutical aesthetics—outlined in the first part of TM and then in many subsequent essays, later collected in the eighth and ninth volumes of his *Gesammelte Werke*—and then, partially, also in some of his contributions on language. With regard to this, it is noteworthy that, especially in some works connected to Gadamer's "turn" to a conception of hermeneutics *as* practical philosophy from the 1970s onward, what seems to emerge is a sort of transition from the strictly ontological paradigm of *Truth and Method* to a more anthropological one. In fact, in late writings such as his important essay "Towards a Phenomenology of Ritual and Language" (Gadamer 2000), it is possible to speak of a primacy of the anthropological dimension in Gadamerian hermeneutics of language.[2] Remarkably, also in aesthetic essays such as "The Relevance of the Beautiful"—in which, as we have seen, the concept of play is fundamental—Gadamer lets emerge the promising and rich anthropological background of his hermeneutics, explicitly speaking of the need to inquire into "the anthropological foundation upon which the phenomenon of art rests" and the "profound anthropological dimension" of aesthetic experience (Gadamer 1986: 5, 47).

However, despite these significant dissimilarities concerning the different breadth and the dissimilar contexts of application of the concept of play in Fink and Gadamer, it is also remarkable to note some fundamental affinities between them. For example, the fact that the notion of play leads beyond a merely subjectivistic conception of human experience, because during the event of playing, for both Fink and Gadamer, the primary role must be assigned to the play itself and not simply to the subject that is playing. From this point of view, it is surely noteworthy that the essence of play for both thinkers seems to consist in a particular dialectics of activity and passivity, of "playing-with" and at the same time "being-played-by." Noting and emphasizing certain commonalities in Fink's and Gadamer's original treatments of the concept of play—without, for this reason, overlooking the differences between them—can be useful to cast a new light on some aspects of their philosophies. For both authors, play does not appear anymore (as it has often been conceived of) as something merely opposed to the sphere of "real" or "serious" occupations; rather, play is something like a constitutive element or pole in the dialectics that, for Fink and Gadamer, underlies the arrangement and development of the human practices, experiences, and forms of life.

5

Fink and Heidegger on Cosmological and Ontological Play

A Confrontation[1]

Ian Alexander Moore

Although absent from the bibliography and mentioned on only a few consecutive pages of *Play as Symbol of the World* (PSW), Heidegger looms large over Fink's opus magnum of 1960, which was first delivered as a lecture course in the summer semester of 1957. In this context, part of the speech Fink gave for Heidegger's eightieth birthday is important to have in mind: "Following your track, all who think today go their way. Yet never have you been an archway where all paths end, no 'house of truth' behind a firmly bolted bar; *your* thought-track points out into the open, into the prodigious, into the homeland: *world*."[2] Here, I have in mind not so much Heidegger's notion of a long-forgotten ontological difference between being and beings, nor even his conception of "world," which he, like Fink, also believes philosophy has long forgotten or passed over.[3] I mean, above all, Heidegger's own scattered remarks on play, which, judging from Fink's explicit discussion of his erstwhile teacher, one might reasonably think had little to no part in the development of Fink's project. Indeed, after critiquing the largely existential-transcendentalist thrust of *Being and Time*, according to which the world is only the projection of Dasein as *Existenz*, Fink outlines Heidegger's later thought after his so-called *Kehre* or "turn" as follows:

> the understanding of Being is [now, after Heidegger's turn,] not to be interpreted from the human being as a fixed point of reference, but rather above all from the horizon of the openness of the human essence for Being itself. And something like this holds also for the other fundamental existentials: for truth, world, temporalization. Truth, world, and temporalization no longer have their "place," so to speak, in the human being, but rather the human being has his noteworthy and thoughtworthy "place"—which is not determinable in any objective system of positioning—in the disclosure and temporalization of the world. We lack the appropriate concepts for this relation to the world. (P: 70 / EFGA7: 68)

Fink then suggests that play may serve as such a concept for the relation between the human and the world, without, however, commenting on the importance of play for Heidegger both before and after his turn. To be sure, in *Being and Time*, the early Heidegger does not identify play as an "existential," that is, as a structural trait of Dasein as the entity whose being is an issue for it, although Heidegger does characterize the openness of possibilities afforded by Dasein's existential projection as a leeway or play-space (*Spielraum*).[4] Further, in a still-untranslated lecture course from the winter semester of 1928–9 titled *Einleitung in die Philosophie* (*Introduction to Philosophy*), which was Heidegger's first after taking over Husserl's chair in Freiburg and was the first lecture course by Heidegger that Fink attended, Heidegger offers an account of the world as transcendental play, which may accordingly be named not *a* but *the* "existential." This world-forming play (*Spiel*) is the condition for the possibility of any and all games or instances of play (*Spiele*) within the world (GA 27: 312; cf. GA 73: 231). Indeed, it is the condition for the possibility of any and all relations to intraworldly beings, which we are always already "climbing beyond" (*trans-scandere*). In Fink's loose transcript of Heidegger's lecture course, one can read heavily underlined passages such as the following (I have converted Fink's underlining to italics):

> We do not play because there are games; rather, there are games because we play. [. . .] *World is the title for the game* [Spiel] *that the transcendence of Dasein as such plays* [spielt]. *This metaphysical play has its freedom, bindingness, necessity. Being-in-the-world is the original playing of the game that every factical Dasein must join in playing* [einspielen] *in order to be able to play out* [abspielen] *in such a way that things come into play* [wird mitgespielt] *in this or that fashion for factical Dasein for the duration of its existence.* (Surely a play with words, but language plays with us!)[5]

> *The play of transcendence is ecstatic; we have always already playfully swirled around beings* [das Seiende umspielt]. *The genuine seriousness of existence is grounded in the metaphysical play of existence, in the play-space of freedom.*[6]

> We characterize transcendence as play [*Spiel*]. Yet this is not an accidental sort of play. The existence of the human is put at stake in the game of the understanding of being [*ist auf das Spiel des Seinsverständnisses gesetzt*]. [. . .] It will be shown that the problem of being, in union with the problem of world, is the theme of metaphysics.[7]

In fact, there is even a moment in the 1928–9 lecture course in which Heidegger implies a reversal of the priority of the human over being (GA 27: 109 and note 1). In retrospect, this allows for a different, more speculative, but nevertheless grammatically plausible rendering of the second sentence of the first block quotation, in which the transcendence of Dasein can be read as a direct object rather than as a subject: not "*World is the title for the game that the transcendence of Dasein as such plays*" but, rather, "*World is the title for the game that plays the transcendence of Dasein as such.*" On this reading, Dasein in climbing beyond beings does not just open up the leeway of possibilities and meaningful relations that constitute the world—Dasein is itself caught up in the more primordial game of the world.

The later Heidegger, for his part, will affirm this reversal in texts such as "The Thing" and *The Principle of Reason*, where, respectively, the human is conceived of as but one fold in the mirror-play of the fourfold of the world, and where being itself is understood as abyssal play. In this chapter I will examine a couple of Heidegger's later texts to show that, despite Fink's critique and failure of acknowledgment, play is in fact an appropriate way for Heidegger to characterize not only the human's *relation* to the world or to being but also the world or being *itself*. For example, in notes from a conversation they had in 1949, Fink asks, "Play not as constitutive of the being of [human] existence, not as an 'existential,' but rather as the *world-play of being*?" And Heidegger replies, "Yes, here alone is where it belongs. You see entirely correctly."[8]

However, my goal here is not just to rectify the historical record or to trace influences (in which case it would be necessary to devote more time to Fink's engagement with Heidegger's thought in the late 1920s and early 1930s,[9] as well as to discuss Heraclitus, Hegel, and Nietzsche, all of whom are more prominently named as precursors in PSW than is Heidegger; the same can be said for these figures in Fink's 1957 booklet *Oasis of Happiness: Thoughts toward an Ontology of Play*). I also want to bring Fink's and Heidegger's writings on the play of being/the world into dialogue. Indeed, whether and to what extent there is a difference between being and the world or between ontology and cosmology, whether and to what extent there is, in short, a difference between Heidegger and Fink on this topic of all topics, will need to be addressed. I will do so in the final section, focusing on the sub-topics of correlationism, finitude, and individuation. But before staging this confrontation (*Auseinandersetzung*) between Fink and Heidegger, it will be necessary to set apart from one another (*aus-einander-setzen*) their respective thoughts on play and on the ultimate issue or matter of philosophy. I will accordingly begin with Fink's philosophical cosmology in PSW and then elucidate a couple of the later Heidegger's most important comments on the play of the world and the play of being.

Fink on the Play of the World

Fink's philosophical interest is less eidetic or phenomenological than cosmological and it lies less in the topic of play for its own sake than in its ability to symbolize the world. But we must be careful about the term "cosmology" (as we must about the term "phenomenology," on which more below). Regarding the second combining form of "cosmology," that is, *-logy*: as what first opens up the possibility of *logos* in its manifold sense, the world, as Fink understands it, cannot be approached "logically." (Whence, I note in passing, Fink's beginning with lightening in his interpretation of Heraclitus and not, as is common, with the *logos* fragment;[10] whence also, as we will see, Fink's interest in play.) Regarding the first combining form, that is, *cosmo-*: the world, in its deepest sense, is not some domain that could be marked off and studied by a discipline. It does not show up as do entities that are subject to description, as do species and genera that are subject to classification, as do domains of being that are subject to regional ontologies, or even as does the beingness of beings (*on hē on*) that is subject to first philosophy. Little wonder, then, that Fink does not present the cosmological aspect of his 1960 opus under the heading of "phenomenology" (something Heidegger was also hesitant to do for ontology already at the end of the 1920s, even if the term would later return under the heading of a "phenomenology of the inapparent"). Indeed, the noun "phenomenology" appears only once in PSW—and in scare quotes at that—to clarify that Fink is not ultimately offering a phenomenology of play.[11]

In the chief sense in which Fink is interested in the term, the "world" is not the sum total of beings within it, let alone a gigantic container. It is not located *in* space or time but rather is *das Raumgebende und Zeitlassende*, that which first "gives space and grants time" (P: 140 / EFGA7: 143). Fink chooses his words carefully here. He does not just make a non-subjective transcendental argument, according to which the condition must differ from the conditioned. He clues the reader in to how this condition is to be understood. If space is properly speaking a gift, then, following a well-known argument by Derrida (himself drawing on Heidegger), that which gives space must not expect anything in return; the giving of space, in other words, escapes the economy of exchange. As "aneconomic" (Derrida), the world is also *ateleological* or "without why" (Meister Eckhart).[12] It is, in Fink's language, literally "groundless," which Fink explains toward the end of PSW:

> The world is *groundless*—but in a quite unique sense. Its groundlessness encompasses the pervasive groundedness of all innerworldly processes and events. *In* the world many acts of striving have immanent goals; [...] but does the world, too, as a whole, have an end, a goal, a *telos*, toward which it moves? [...] The world in itself is aimless, and it also has no value in itself and remains outside every moralistic assessment, is "beyond good and evil." Without ground and without aim, without sense and without goal, without value and without plan—but it holds within it all the grounds for thoroughly grounded intraworldly beings. It encompasses with its universal aimlessness the paths upon which aims and goals are striven after. (P: 212 / EFGA7: 220)

Further, the groundlessness of the world conflicts as much with effective causality as it does with final causality. The world, in Fink's view, is not an *archē* that can be arrived at by connecting causal motion within the world. To this extent, it can be called *an-archic*, although Fink, like Heidegger, avoids this term, presumably because of its political connotations. In any event, Fink is pointing in this direction with his choice of the verb *lassen* to characterize the world's opening up of time. (Christopher Turner and I often render *lassen* as "to grant" in our translation of PSW, although more literally it means "to let.") Heidegger also uses the verb *lassen*, often in conjunction with the language of giving or eventuating, to describe an enabling that is conceptually prior to the distinction between activity and passivity and hence subjectivity and objectivity. The world's granting or letting of time is, one could say, middle voiced.[13]

But what does all of this have to do with play? Play is crucial for Fink for four main reasons: (1) its ultimate aimlessness (or autotelic nature), (2) the distinction it opens up and preserves between actuality and a peculiar kind of appearance, (3) its ability to symbolize the world, and (4) its priority among what Fink calls the "basic phenomena of our existence" (P: 143 / EFGA7: 147).

(1) Play, like the world itself, is ultimately aimless, even if there are immanent goals such as scoring points or winning in the case of some games (see P: 20 / EFGA7: 18). While play is often conceived of as restorative of one's ability to work or as a means to non-play-like ends such as knowledge acquisition or physical fitness, Fink contends that it would be a mistake to think of play solely or even principally in instrumental terms, which fail to capture its essence. (Fink's analysis is thus not altogether "aphenomenological," even if the world—his primary concern—is not literally a phenomenon.) Expressed positively, we might say that play is ultimately "autotelic": complete in any of its moments (rather than only when it achieves its end). The proper answer to the question, "Why do you play?," can only take the form of a tautology: "I play because I play."

(2) In "Oasis of Happiness," Fink succinctly describes several features of play, which can be organized as follows. Play is:

 i. uniquely pleasing (neither simply sensuous nor intellectual);
 ii. meaningful for those involved (whether as participants or spectators);
 iii. communal (in the minimal sense of being open to others, which holds even for solitary play);
 iv. binding yet revocable;
 v. and pervaded by a threefold doubling, which can be seen:

   a. in the *equipment of play* between the thing as object (a stick, a rubber sphere) and the thing as toy or plaything (a doll, a basketball);
   b. in the *participants* between their status as human beings (the child, Michael Jordan) and their status as players (the doll's parent, shooting guard);
   c. and—I might add, although Fink does not use this language explicitly— more broadly within the *domain* circumscribed by the game or instance of play between entities in their significance for the mundane (a grove, a large building) and those same entities in their significance for what Fink calls the "playworld" that encompasses all of the aforementioned features of play (the "house," the basketball game taking place in the arena).

This final feature (v) is most relevant for Fink's cosmological concerns, since it enables us to conceive of something other than entities and their ontological characteristics, something with a different sort of temporality and spatiality, something that is not real in the way entities are but is not mere semblance either. "We play [*spielen*] in the so-called actual world," Fink writes, "but we thereby attain [*erspielen*, i.e., bring about through our play] a realm, an enigmatic field, that is not nothing and yet is nothing actual" (P: 25 / EFGA7: 23; see also 205/213). Indeed, play becomes for Fink the way to attain not just *a* playworld, but the playing world *itself*.[14]

(3) In the third chapter of PSW, Fink turns to cult practices to appreciate the all-encompassing character that play can have. However, for Fink, cult play is still insufficient insofar as it conceives of the relation between the participants in ontic

or entitative terms (such as the relation between humans and gods/God), hence in an *innerworldly* fashion. Is there, however, some way in which play within the world can refer to the play of the world, without the latter's being viewed as the playing of some *thing* or some *one*? This is precisely what Fink tries to show with his theory of symbols. If play is to provide access to the world itself, it cannot do so in the manner of *mimesis*, for the world is not an entity that can be copied or marked off from other entities and pointed out. Rather, human play opens up the non-actuality (which is not to say complete nothingness) of the playworld and, beyond this, the non-actuality of the world itself. Or better: the world offers proof (*Rückschein*) of itself by shining back (*zurückscheinen*) into the instance of play. Human play becomes a "symbol" of the world to the extent that it is a fragment "thrown together" (*sym-ballein*) with the world as its counterpart. In the strange appearing (*Scheinen*) of the playworld, coming-to-appearance as such (*Erscheinung*) becomes manifest as the result (*er-*) of the world's own *Scheinen* (P: 207–208 / EFGA7: 215–16). *Erscheinung* should thus be taken here less as intransitive luminosity than as a transitive *making-to-appear*. Play, in other words, bears witness to the world as the dark *source* of phenomenality, as that which makes anything and anyone appear at all, including ourselves. In play, we are not only taken outside ourselves (outside our goals, our reasoning, our cares) but able to learn about our—indeed about everything's—cosmic source.[15] As Fink writes near the end of PSW:

> What we ordinarily already call the world is the world-dimension of presence, the dimension of coming to appearance wherein things are really separated from each other, but also still integrated in spatial and temporal vicinity and connected to each other by strict rules. But the world is also the nameless realm of absence, from which things come forth into appearance and into which they again vanish [...]. In the problem of individuation [*Individuation ... Vereinzelung*], the coming to appearance of beings is plumbed, thought back into absent depths, which the terrestrial day on the surface for the most part conceals from us. All beings are cosmic playthings but all players, too, are themselves only played. (P: 215 / EFGA7: 223; see also 71/69, 213/221)

(4) Lastly, play is significant because of its primacy for the human being. To be sure, in "Oasis of Happiness," Fink quotes Schiller's claim in *On the Aesthetic Education of Man* that "man only fully is when he plays," but then Fink adds: "it also remains valid that he only fully is when he works, struggles, holds out against death, or loves" (P: 18 / EFGA7: 16; see also 21/19, 204/212). Other passages call into question Fink's emendation, however, suggesting instead that play does not merely point to the fundamental care of existence by temporarily interrupting it (P: 202 / EFGA7: 209), but may as such take precedence over the other basic phenomena of human existence. This would be the case not just insofar as play is the only basic phenomenon that can encompass all of the others (P: 21 / EFGA7: 19) but also to the extent that we are called upon to live in accordance with the way the world itself ultimately is, namely, as playful instead of as laboring, fighting for existence, loving, or engaging in practices related to

death. The alternative would be an ontological—or rather cosmological—pluralism, according to which each of the basic phenomena would reflect either different *aspects* of the one world or different, irreducible *worlds* (cf. P: 211 / EFGA7: 219). That Fink takes play as cosmologically primary (as something like an Aristotelian focal sense of being) is, however, supported by the conclusions of "Oasis of Happiness" and PSW. In the former, Fink writes:

> If the essence of the world is thought as play, it thus follows for the human being that he is the only being in the vast universe who is able to *correspond* to the prevailing whole. Only in the correspondence to what is beyond the human [*Entsprechung zum Übermenschlichen*] may the human being then attain to his native essence. (P: 31 / EFGA7: 29)

In other words, we "become who we are" only when we live in accord with the world, that is, when we live *playfully*. Fink's biblical allusion at the end of "Oasis of Happiness" indicates that the stakes couldn't be higher, even if there is no hope for an afterlife in Fink's this-worldly philosophy: "When thinkers and poets point in such a humanly profound way to the immense significance of play, we should also be mindful of the saying: we cannot enter into the kingdom of heaven if we do not become as children" (P: 31 / EFGA7: 29; cf. Matt. 18:3). Otherwise, we are faced with despair: not exactly the despair of reason (*logos*), let alone that of the inferno, but rather the despair of ever becoming like the world itself (*homolegein*).

The conclusion of PSW is comparably remarkable, if more tentative, in its apotheosis—or better, *apocosmosis*—of play:

> To make the play of the world the theme of speculative thinking is a task that still remains to be accomplished, which perhaps can only be fully ventured when the metaphysical tradition, which conceals play and is hostile to it, has been worked off. Is it not then also a part of this affair that the human being transforms himself—that he no longer seeks his measure above the stars and mistakes himself in the radiance of the gods? Yet it would be questionable [*eine bedenkliche Wendung*, "an alarming/dubious turn"] to say that the human being must henceforth "correspond," not to the intraworldly gods, but to the prevailing, playing world and find his future measure in it. We conclude our course of thought with a still completely unresolved problem. The human being—as a player—exists open to the world most of all precisely when he dismisses all measures and holds himself out into that which is limitless. (P: 215 / EFGA7: 223; trans. mod.)

Additionally, in a folder containing material on Heidegger and other topics in Fink's literary remains, there is a note (presumably from around 1953) in which Fink separates play from the other basic phenomena of human existence:[16]

At the top of the page, Fink experiments with linking the basic human phenomena of dominance/ruling, work/labor, love, and death with Nietzsche's key concepts of the will to power and the eternal return. A horizontal line divides the page in two, suggesting that the bottom portion presents an alternative to the top and thus an alternative to Nietzsche insofar as he is considered to be the "last metaphysician" or a mere inversion of Plato, as Heidegger maintained in his later critique of the nineteenth-century German thinker. In his 1960 book *Nietzsche's Philosophy,* Fink follows Heidegger's critique closely but nevertheless sees Nietzsche as able to escape the confines of "metaphysics" thanks to his "cosmological philosophy of 'play,'" which makes Nietzsche "the albatross [*Sturmvogel*] of a new experience of being."[17] Interestingly, in the lower half of the note, Fink considers not one but two alternatives to the limitations of Nietzschean "metaphysics" or, put more positively, two ways of advancing Nietzsche's own non-metaphysical (albeit conceptually undeveloped)[18] philosophy of play: Fink's own, in which the play of *aiōn* ("the course of the world")[19] is able to hold together unconcealment and concealment, presence and absence (as is, presumably, the human being who, in play, conforms to the play of the world); and the play of Heidegger's fourfold, which is characterized by "mirror-play." Before comparing the different directions in which Fink and Heidegger advance, more needs to be said about Heidegger's later philosophy of play.

Heidegger on the Play of the World and the Play of Being

Mirror-play is the first moment in the later Heidegger's appreciation of play on which I will be focusing. Heidegger develops it in "The Thing," which he first published in 1951 but had already presented in part in 1949 and 1950.[20] Heidegger sent a signed offprint to Fink in December 1951.[21] The text contains Heidegger's famous characterization of the "thinging of the thing" as a gathering of the "fourfold" of sky, earth, divinities, and mortals (or of what Heidegger also calls "the world").[22] When we consider a jug, for example, as a "thing that things," we are not considering it merely as equipment (as something "ready-to-hand" in the language of *Being and Time*, in this case as a vessel for the storage of liquid), let alone as an object for investigation (as something "present-at-hand," in this case as made of a certain material, as having a certain mass, etc.). Rather, we are considering it as the site in which manifestation (sky) and concealment (earth), sanctity (divinities) and finitude (mortals) are mutually implicated, that is, folded in on one another. Heidegger describes this inter-relationality—which is neither the artificial separation of a whole nor the aggregation of independent units—with the language of a "mirror-play" or *Spiegel-Spiel*, which is itself a play on words in German:

> Earth and sky, divinities and mortals—being at one with one another of their own accord—belong together by way of the simpleness of the united fourfold. Each of the four mirrors in its own way the presence of the others. Each therewith reflects itself in its own way into its own, within the simpleness of the four. This mirroring does not portray a likeness. The mirroring, lightening each of the four, appropriates their own presenting into simple belonging to one another. Mirroring in this appropriating-lightening way, each of the four plays to each of the others [*spielt sich jedes der Vier jedem der übrigen zu*]. The appropriative mirroring sets each of the four free into its own, but it binds these free ones into the simplicity of their essential being toward one another. The mirroring that binds into freedom is the play that betroths each of the four to each through the enfolding clasp of their mutual appropriation.[23]

Notice also that Heidegger tries to reconcile freedom and necessity in this mirror-play, or rather to find in this play a domain—or what Heidegger elsewhere calls a play-space—that lies before the emergence of freedom and necessity as dichotomous. Further, as Fink will, Heidegger goes on to challenge the ability of causal language—whether teleological or mechanistic—to capture this play, which is why he prefers to use the tautological or cognate nominative construction, "the world worlds."[24] Heidegger develops this point about causality in the second important set of comments on play in his corpus that I would like to address.

These comments can be found in the lecture course *The Principle of Reason*, which Heidegger delivered in the winter semester of 1955–6 and first published in 1957. Fink attended some, if not all, of the course and corresponded with Heidegger about it during the semester. In this lecture course, Heidegger offers an extended commentary on the principle of sufficient reason as articulated by Leibniz: *nihil est sine ratione*. Taking inspiration from Eckhart and from the baroque poet Angelus Silesius, who sings in one of his most famous couplets of the rose that blooms "without why,"[25] Heidegger playfully shifts the way in which Leibniz's principle is to be heard—or rather, he lets being or language put into play a different way of hearing it. Instead of hearing *nihil* as a pronoun (*there is not anything that is without reason*), Heidegger suggests that we should instead hear it as a noun, as no-thingness or as being itself (*being as no particular thing does not have a ground*). In short, Heidegger moves, in yet another wordplay, from the *principle of* (*Satz vom*) reason or ground to a *leap away from* (another meaning of *Satz vom*) reason or ground.

Heidegger also uses the language of play to understand the groundless no-thingness of being. As he did in late 1920s, Heidegger speaks of a play-space (or rather a time-play-space, *Zeit-Spiel-Raum*) for the appearance of beings; only, it is now being itself rather than the human qua being-in-the-world that opens up this time-play-space,[26] and being brings the human into it. The human is thus, as Fink would put it shortly after Heidegger's course, more fundamentally played than a player (P: 215/EFGA7: 223). Drawing on another couplet by Silesius, Heidegger speaks of Mozart as "The Lute Playing of God."[27] Earlier in the course, he entertains, again as Fink would shortly thereafter, the idea that humans might live most authentically when they are like the rose, "without why."[28] Once again like Fink, Heidegger does not pursue it, although the conclusion of the course corroborates the idea:

> The "because" [*Das "weil"*] sinks away in play. Play is without "why."[29] It plays while [*dieweil*] it plays. [. . .] Being, as what grounds, has no ground, plays as the abyss [*Ab-Grund*, "away from the ground"] of that play that playfully passes us [*uns . . . zuspielt*] being and ground as a fateful sending. The question remains as to whether and how we, listening to the movements [*Sätze*] of this play, play along and join in the play.[30]

Fink and Heidegger: A Confrontation

The parallels between Fink's and Heidegger's later work on play should, by now, be evident. Heidegger no doubt influenced the man whom Husserl called "the greatest phenomenon in phenomenology" and whom Heidegger himself would, in the late

1960s, declare to be the most talented philosopher among Fink's contemporaries (which is saying a lot given the number of prominent former students of Heidegger from the same generation).[31]

But Fink does not follow Heidegger to the letter. Not only does Fink seem to have been the first to center the philosophy of play on a non-existential (and hence non-subjective or non-transcendentalist) conception of the world. Fink also made this conception of play central to his lifework (something that can hardly be said of Heidegger, even if play is operative throughout his corpus, and even if he is occasionally willing to go so far as to characterize being, the world, and the event of appropriation as play[32]). Already in 1936, for example, decades before the composition of PSW, Fink predicated that "the *metaphysics of play*" (here "metaphysics" is used positively) would be crucial for his future life as a philosopher and wrote that "[t]he essence of life = play."[33] In December 1945, requesting permission to habilitate at the University of Freiburg (and hence finally to qualify to give lecture courses at the institution), Fink made this telling remark, which could apply as much to Heidegger as it does to Husserl:

> Although I would consider it a necessity imposed in the interest of intellectual history to resume a tradition [i.e., phenomenology] that was interrupted only owing to external forces, [i.e., the Nazis], and to lay out Husserl's philosophy precisely in its yet unrecognized essence, still I would never do this in the manner of adepts. For wherever philosophy is experienced as destiny Hegel's word holds: "Regarding the inner essence of philosophy there are neither predecessors nor followers."[34]

For his habilitation thesis, Fink submitted the *Sixth Cartesian Meditation*, which he had composed in close collaboration with Husserl in the 1930s. It is an excellent example of how Fink took up and advanced Husserl's philosophy.[35] But for his trial lecture, Fink chose a topic that would foreshadow both his later philosophical preoccupations and his critical dialogue with the other great Freiburg philosopher about the ontological or cosmological significance of play and about Nietzsche's contributions to understanding it. The title of the lecture, which would launch Fink's teaching career at the university, was "Nietzsche's Metaphysics of Play."[36]

Furthermore, Fink also takes speculative leaps with the ontological or cosmological characteristics of play that Heidegger was, with few exceptions, unwilling or at least reluctant to make. In this final section, I will discuss three of these leaps and measure them against Heidegger's efforts. Before doing so, however, a couple of clarifications are in order.

First clarification: it is insufficient to critique Heidegger simply as an ontological thinker, as one may be inclined to do when distinguishing his philosophy from Fink's speculative cosmology. Heidegger himself, already in his winter semester 1929–30 lecture course *The Fundamental Concepts of Metaphysics* (whose published version Heidegger dedicated to Fink), problematizes the term "ontology," as Fink was well aware.[37] Heidegger even calls into question the radicality of the term "being" in his *Bremen Lectures*, that is, precisely where he first discusses the fourfold publicly and attempts to think the relation between thing and "world," to which he considers being to be subordinate.[38] Admittedly, later in the lectures, *Seyn* or "beyng" will return,³⁹ but now it is written with a "y" to mark its difference from the "being" (*Sein*) of "beings" (*Seiendes*) or from their "beingness" (*Seiendheit*). Heidegger's thinking, in other words, cannot readily be classified under the heading "ontology," as he too is trying not merely to think the ontological difference but to discover its *source*. We should also remember that Fink is not always terminologically consistent about the difference between ontology and cosmology. The subtitle of "Oasis of Happiness," after all, is "Thoughts toward an *Ontology* of Play."

Second clarification: Despite the fabled precedence of the *Seinsfrage* or "question of being" in Heidegger's oeuvre, William McNeill is right to note that "the phenomenon of world [. . .] is, one might argue, the singular focus (not to say obsession) of Heidegger's work from 1927 through 1930 and beyond."⁴⁰ Hence Heidegger cannot be said to suffer from *Weltvergessenheit* or "forgetfulness" about the question of "world" in any straightforward sense, as Fink was also well aware.⁴¹ The differences between Fink and Heidegger are more subtle. The most important of these differences can, in my view, be grouped under the headings of (1) "correlationism," (2) "finitude," and (3) "individuation."

1. Correlationism. The first difference I want to highlight concerns the role of the human in Fink's and Heidegger's philosophies. Earlier I noted that, for both Fink and the later Heidegger, the human is fundamentally less a player than someone played by the world/being. The meaning of "played" is not the same for both philosophers, however. Although, for Fink, the human is privileged over other animals in its relation to the world, Fink places little emphasis in PSW on the world's *need* of the human. Fink was accordingly perplexed when he read, in "The Thing," that Heidegger had situated mortals and gods on the same level as sky and earth in the constitution of "world."⁴² For Fink, the cosmos can well be without the human, whereas being itself (or beyng), as Heidegger typically understands it, cannot. Take the following passage from Heidegger's *The Principle of Reason*:

> As the ones standing in the clearing and lighting of being we are the ones bestowed, the ones ushered into the time play-space [*die in den Zeit-Spiel-Raum Eingeräumten*]. This means we are the ones engaged in and for this play-space [*die in diesem Spielraum und für ihn Gebrauchten*], engaged in building on and giving shape to the clearing and lighting of being—in the broadest and multiple sense, in preserving it.⁴³

The root verb of the word translated as "engaged" in this passage, namely, *brauchen*, is one of the most important for the late Heidegger and has the dual sense of "needing" and "using." We are used by being, but we are also needed by it to be the site in which things show up as meaningful. Indeed, late in life, Heidegger declared that "the basic thought of my thinking is precisely that being or the openness of being *braucht* (needs/uses) the human and that, inversely, the human is only human insofar as he stands in the openness of being" (GA 16: 704). To this extent, Heidegger remains more of a correlationist or phenomenologist than Fink.

Still, there are rare moments in which Heidegger, too, suggests the priority of *brauchen* qua "use" over *brauchen* qua "need," where the human would no longer seem to play any role in the unfolding of being. One of the most well-known passages on this priority can be found in Heidegger's essay "The Anaximander Fragment" (first published in 1950), where Heidegger translates one of the fundamental Greek words for being, *to chreiōn*, as *brauchen* and provides the following explanation of how the latter should be understood:

> to use [*brauchen*] is to brook [*bruchen*, in the archaic sense of "having the enjoyment of"], in Latin *frui*, in German *fruchten, Frucht*. We translate this freely as "*genießen*" ["to enjoy"], but *nießen* originally means to be pleased with something and so to have it in use [*im Brauch haben*]. Only in its derived senses does "enjoy" mean simply to consume or gobble up. We encounter what we have called the basic meaning of "use" [*brauchen*] in the sense of *frui*, in Augustine's words, *Quid enim est aliud quod dicimus frui, nisi praesto habere, quod diligis?* ["For what else do we mean when we say *frui* if not to have at hand something that is especially prized?"] *Frui* involves *praesto habere* [literally "having (something) stand there in front of (one)"]. *Praesto, praesitum* is in Greek ὑποκείμενον, that which already lies before us in unconcealment, *ousia*, that which lingers awhile in presence. "To use" accordingly suggests: to let something present come to presence as such [*etwas Anwesendes als Anwesendes anwesen lassen*]; *frui*, to brook, to use, usage [*Brauch*], means: to hand something over to its own essence and to keep it in hand, preserving it as something present.

Heidegger clarifies that this sense of *brauchen*, as a "using" that lets things emerge into presence and guards them as present, is not merely a human activity but, more deeply, an interpretation of "the oldest name in which thinking brings the being of beings to language."[44] Being "uses" and "enjoys" before the human does. Such passages, which tend to appear in Heidegger's interpretations of the pre-Socratics, bring Heidegger closer to the cosmological thinking of Fink.

2. *Finitude*. A second, related difference between Fink and Heidegger concerns the finitude not of the human entity (on which they both agree) but of the fundamental source. Fink maintains that the world, in its independence from the human, is also *infinite* (P: 210–11/EFGA7: 218–19). Already in the early 1930s, Fink was meditating on the absolute as an infinite origin that gives rise to finitude through a process of ontogenesis or "ontification." "Finitude" is, in other words, "a constitutive *result*," not a basic state.[45] In contrast, Heidegger considers not just the human but primordial being (or beyng) itself to be finite. Indeed, according to Fink, this is what distinguishes Heidegger's philosophy from that of all of his predecessors. As Fink remarked in a 1964 radio lecture:

> The thought of finitude seems to be, in our view, the most radical and revolutionary fundamental thought of Heidegger's philosophy—the thought with which Heidegger opposes the entire tradition. [. . .] Not only the human being, who has an understanding of being, not only the *vessel* [Gefäss] that "grasps" ["*fasst*"] being, is finite; *being itself*, the immense, world-penetrating being, the origin itself of all that is, oscillates in time, happens as an "event." Heidegger's late philosophy

revolves around this utmost thought—which is perhaps the most audacious thing that has yet been thought in humanity.[46]

This seems to have been the lecture that prompted Heidegger's comment, in a letter to Fink from a couple of months later, that Fink "would have surely been my only possible successor" (i.e., to the chair of philosophy that Fink had turned down).[47] One year later, Heidegger related that he was planning to address Fink's comment about the finitude of being in a text he was preparing for Fink's sixtieth birthday.[48] Unfortunately, this topic is not broached in the extant version of the text that Heidegger delivered at the celebration.[49]

Heidegger may, however, have been thinking about earlier passages in his corpus, where, to be sure, he does not declare being to be *infinite* (which, to my knowledge, he never does explicitly, even if it is in some sense "everlasting"), but where he nevertheless entertains being's *independence* from the human, thus bringing him closer to Fink.[50] For example, in a 1944 lecture course on Heraclitus, Heidegger begins by recapitulating the point mentioned above about being's need: "Because being is *Logos*, it needs [*braucht*] *legein* [speaking]," which refers to what is essentially "'human' about the human." Yet he clarifies that:

> being requires the latter [namely, human *legein*] for the preservation of its independence [*Das Sein bedarf dessen, zugunsten der Wahrung seiner Unabhängigkeit*]. Here we are thinking within that realm (i.e., the realm of the truth of beyng [*Wahrheit des Seyns*]) where all relations are completely different from those in the region of beings.[51]

3. *Individuation*. The final difference between Fink and Heidegger that should be discussed concerns the problem of individuation. What accounts for the singularity of entities? How does something become "this" and not "that"? For Fink, entities genetically emerge as singulars from the play of the world, into which they again pass away.[52] For Heidegger, in contrast, the question is not, "how are entities *in themselves* individuated?" but rather, "why do they show up as mattering *for me*?" This does not amount to constructivism, since Heidegger grants that entities in their plurality exist independently of the human (even if the *being* of those entities and their total context must *in part* be tied back to the human). When Heidegger does speak of individuation, as, for example, in *Being and Time*, it is rather a matter of Dasein confronting itself by gathering itself together from its dispersion in everyday practices and norms. Heidegger could accordingly tell Fink, in 1953, that "there is no problem of individuation for him."[53]

All three of these differences center on the extent to which philosophy can access the "in-itself," whether this be the in-itself of world (for Fink) or the in-itself of being and the in-itself of beings (for Heidegger).[54] In this chapter, I have shown that to greater and lesser extents, both philosophers use play to characterize the ultimate level of reality, which is neither entitative (a being) nor simply ontological (the being of beings), and both stress its groundlessness, aimlessness, and non-mechanistic/non-teleological causality as a form of "letting." However, whereas Fink believes that philosophy or whatever replaces it at the end of metaphysics (e.g., speculative cosmology) can make the move to the in-itself, Heidegger's ambitions are more modest. In 1974, one year before his death and two years before Heidegger's, Fink sent Heidegger his essay "Weltbezug und Seinsverständnis" ("World-Relation and Understanding of Being"). This prompted the following reply from Heidegger:

> The cosmological direction of your inquiry points to the fullness of the "labyrinthian" world-essence [*Weltwesens*], while my thinking tries to keep on the narrow ridge of the question concerning the peculiarity of being as presencing [*Eigentümlichkeit des Seins als Anwesen*], with the risk that the provenance of being as the nihilating nothing [*das nichtende Nichts*] would withhold itself from thinking and that this withholding [*Vorenthalt*] would announce itself in a beckoning way as the region of the sojourn [*Aufenthalt*] of Dasein.[55]

Fink is no epigone but a thinker deserving of further engagement, not only in his confrontation with Heidegger on the topics of play correlationism, finitude, individuation, and the in-itself, which I have only begun to work out here, but also in his own right. This is, after all, how Heidegger himself saw his erstwhile pupil. As Heidegger said in his aforementioned speech for Fink's sixtieth birthday: "for now I am referring to Eugen Fink the 'student,' and note that from then to the present day he has shown the truth of a well-known saying of Nietzsche's. It runs: 'One repays a teacher badly if one always remains merely a student.'"[56]

Part Two

History of Philosophy

6

The Last Temptation of Metaphysics
Eugen Fink's Nietzsche

Dale Wilkerson

From Nietzsche we find a characterization fitting of Eugen Fink, "To you, bold searchers and tempters and whoever put to terrible seas with cunning sails."[1] Among what is most memorable about the career of Eugen Fink, along with his apprenticeship and collaboration in phenomenology with Edmund Husserl,[2] his complicated personal and professional relationship with Martin Heidegger,[3] and the development and promulgation of his signature contribution to Western thinking as the philosopher of play (and its influence, which is discussed in the present volume), Fink's rather idiosyncratic interpretation of Friedrich Nietzsche remains a hallmark of his professional life. Despite its reputation of good will and sympathy for the subject, however, Fink's Nietzsche interpretation is marked with extreme, even esoteric, ambivalence. According to Fink, this ambivalence is unavoidable, given the main features of Nietzsche's thought: "The great and decisive difficulty of Nietzsche's model of the world is that it pulls the ground out from under its own feet. It shatters this ground and leaves it in ruins; it destroys the path of understanding that this model wants to establish" (1988b: 214). Fink makes the case that Nietzsche's work is nearly lost in self-contradiction, as the iconoclast succumbs to the temptation to re-loom the metaphysical veil his thought seeks to unravel. However, Fink himself also seems conflicted: Should he ultimately write off Nietzsche's thought, as Heidegger had done, as the interesting yet conclusive end of 2500 years of philosophical malpractice? Or, should he conclude that something essentially redemptive is embedded there, something that affirms Nietzsche's intuitions about Western theory, as such, and saves the thought from Nietzsche's flawed methodologies? The problem, for Fink, is found in the subject himself: "Nietzsche is two-headed: he is a philosopher and a sophist" (2003: 35). Fink seems tempted to reach both conclusions and often finds himself playing the middle against these two conflicting possibilities. So, the question I would like to raise here concerns just who is being tempted by bad intentions? Is it Nietzsche? Fink? Or, perhaps both? For this purpose, in the following sections I will examine the thought-path developing through Nietzsche's texts and its relevance to modern notions of human self-alienation and transcendence, his interest in traditional "philosophical" issues such as being, becoming, and values, and Fink's suggestion that maybe, just maybe, Nietzsche can be redeemed as a player in Fink's philosophical game. I will begin by noting Fink's ambivalence toward Nietzsche's methodologies.

Fink's Ambivalence toward Nietzsche's Methodologies

Fink often condemns Nietzsche's methodologies for lacking philosophical depth. They are merely "anthropological" in the way that the ancient sophists related the knowledge of all things back to the human being. Even more radically, Nietzsche's skepticism often throws the human being, as a concept, into doubt. The most important of Nietzsche's methodologies, and the most problematic, involve his considerations and strategic use of language. For him, language does not reveal the royal road to absolute truth, as is often claimed. Language develops modestly out of human needs, which further drive the formation of concepts, truth claims, and the complex value systems that support them. In this way, the "highest concepts"—that is, truth and lies, good and bad, right and wrong, and so forth—are manufactured in order to promote human preservation and enhancement. Moreover, because high moral concepts are crucial for flourishing and maintaining social order, human beings seek to maximize their power. Toward this end, the user of language "forgets" that the highest concepts originate in human need and creativity, and thus we give them the sheen of absoluteness (OTL 1/KSA 1.875–886). Societies that do this successfully seem to flourish, and those that don't fail (GS 110/KSA 3.469–471). Nietzsche's methodological understanding of truth-claims is so skeptical, however, that even the natural sciences are said to rely on a "metaphysical faith" based upon active forgetting (GS 344/KSA 3.574–77). Despite our effectively forgetting these origins, then, "truth" remains nothing but "a mobile army of metaphors," a "counterfeit" emblem of what it seems to be but essentially is not, and a mere trace of the human being's capacity to create a world for ourselves in the service of our needs (OTL 1/KSA 1.880–1).

For Fink, all of this reeks of radical scientistic skepticism, profane decadence, and muddled confusion, unworthy of Nietzsche's most elevated aspirations. Part of Nietzsche's methodological problem is that he rarely "considers metaphysical concepts historically" and conflates logical concepts with lifeless abstraction. If concepts are no more than metaphors and metaphors are empty husks, he seems to deprive himself of the means "to conceptualize his thinking adequately" (2003: 14).[4] This leads to all sorts of confusion about even practical matters. The high concept of evil, for example, as it is deployed to order systems of slave morality, "is not despised as what is insignificant, but [merely] feared and hated as dangerous" without knowing why. Something similar could be said about the high concept of good in noble value systems. Indeed, even though after *Zarathustra* "all philosophical questions" become for Nietzsche "questions of value . . . [t]he being of value itself no longer becomes problematic" for him (2003: 114). We are simply the absent-minded creators of values, in this view, creating haphazardly and hoping for the best. Yet, even this creator of values, as a creating-subject who is claimed to have manufactured a world of truths, would seem to be no more than just another metaphorical concept and therefore an empty fiction. This "makes it easy for [Nietzsche's] opponents to point out the circularity of his argument" (1988b: 213).

Another methodological problem, perhaps even more pernicious than the ones described above, lies in Nietzsche's move away from the tragic worldview of the ancient artist and toward sophistic "anthropology," heightened by his interest and acumen in deciphering psychological motivations. For Fink, this move is regrettable, because it leads not only to confusion but also to disenchantment: "[a]s long as Nietzsche's concept of science remains guided by positivism [as it is, for example, in *Human, All-Too-Human*], it comes to enormous disillusionment."[5] Nietzsche's thought frequently affects a kind of scientific "mask," a "scientific perspective," the "disguise of cold-blooded science" that "sees [only] the biological foundation of all 'ideals.'" The result is "human profanation" where "man is mutilated" (2003: 46). Attempting to mitigate disenchantment, while still guided by anthropological-biologistic presumptions, he resorts to developing concepts related to "organic life," presuming them to lend support to his grandest cosmological claims. Fink, however, cites several methodological problems with this strategy. It implicitly presumes "that the world as a whole" is alive, then it extends the concept of the living "beyond the phenomenon of life" when analyzing the coincidental phenomenon of motion, and most problematically for Fink, it does away with "the difference between the human organism and that of plants and animals, which is evident in the phenomena." This means that "the moment of freedom that characterizes human being is not expressly separated from plant and animal being" (1988b: 215). Thus, the problem of disenchantment remains.

Moreover, even as a modern scientific endeavor, per se, Nietzsche's methods are sloppy. According to Fink, Nietzsche

> pays no attention to replicability, proof, or the preservation of the "things themselves," and . . . shies away from the toil of verification and declares the method of verification itself to be a leading problem. He announces but he does not reveal the way that leads him to his wisdom. (1988b: 215)

Thus, Fink discovers a host of problems with Nietzsche's anthropological methodologies. The ambivalence he feels for Nietzsche's language and concepts, however, lies in the fact that play is itself metaphorical in ways that a Nietzschean worldview would frame it. In Fink's notes from 1954's "The Philosophical-Pedagogical Problem of Play," kept in preparation for articulating a philosophy of play, he writes in the "Seventh Session," entry number 4, that play is a metaphor uniquely well-situated for "symbolic representation of the world (i.e., for a model of philosophical conceptualization)." He then points to Western philosophy's "[f]irst case of the metaphor of cosmic play" in Heraclitus' *Pais Paizon*, the "playing-child" of Diels' fragment 52, which Fink then cites (in Attic Greek): "Eternity is a child at play, moving pieces in a game; kingship belongs to a child" (2016a: 262).[6]

He frequently draws the relation of Heraclitus to Nietzsche through the metaphor of this "playing child." Typically, the relation is drawn explicitly. For example, in *Nietzsche's Philosophy*, he references 1873's *Philosophy in the Tragic Age of the Greeks*, writing that even in Nietzsche's early writings, he finds "the mysterious dimension of play . . . [Nietzsche's] Heracliteanism with Zeus, the playing cosmic child, the *Pais Paizon*" (2003: 171).[7] This is the general conclusion Fink is tempted to draw concerning Nietzsche, the *philosopher*: "Nietzsche's interpretation of Heraclitus thus focuses on the fragment 52 (Diels) . . . . Heraclitus' concept of play becomes Nietzsche's deepest intuition for the grandly symbolic and metaphorical nature of the cosmos" (2003: 32). Moreover, in the 1954 notebook "Seventh Session," entry number 4, he follows the reference to Heraclitus' "first case of the metaphor of cosmic play" with the conclusion: "[a]t the end of Western metaphysics: play as formula for the world in Nietzsche. Innocence, beyond good and evil, productivity, etc." (2016a: 262).

"Play" is said to be a particularly effective conceptual metaphor—for Fink, for Heraclitus, even for Nietzsche. In the trenchant entry from 1954, Fink highlights the historical metaphoricity of play, its suitability for ontological conceptualization—due, in part, to its "element of representation," in part to Heraclitus' "first case" usage of it in Western antiquity, and in part to Nietzsche's use of it "at the end of Western metaphysics." The entry also establishes the historical, metaphorical, and ontological associations of Heraclitus and Nietzsche. Yet, as the next entry (Seventh Session, number 5) makes clear, the basic "features of the phenomenon of play" must be "bracketed out." That is, "symbolic representation . . . must subsequently be factored out of the whole understood as play," even though this representation makes the concept particularly "excellent" as a metaphor, and it serves as "the basis [for which] play is taken to be [a] likeness of the whole" (2016a: 262). Moreover, as the following entry (Seventh Session, number 6) suggests, if the basic feature concretizing play and making it excellent for symbolic articulation of the cosmos must be factored out, then this procedure raises questions concerning "in what way . . . the cosmos [is] understood . . . in the metaphor," if at all (2016a: 262). Or, even, could it be adequately understood with metaphor? Fink will propose that the eponymous character of Nietzsche's novel *Thus Spoke Zarathustra* achieves something like transcendence at the end of Part III through the experience of "play." Yet, Fink has concerns about the way this character is drawn: "it still surprises everyone who seeks to follow the path of Nietzsche's thought that the figure of Zarathustra and the image of the *Übermensch* is remarkably pale." Despite Nietzsche's rationale for drawing Zarathustra in this way, "the figure of Zarathustra remains one-dimensional, the ventriloquist's dummy of the philosopher" (1988b: 208).

Thus, even though the phenomenon of play is "excellent for the symbolic representation of the world" and is a "model for philosophical conceptualization," it nevertheless remains a metaphor and subject to the Nietzschean critique of language and truth-claims. Its usefulness is therefore misleading and Fink recognizes this as a problem not only in the Nietzschean framework but also in his own. Although Zarathustra is the player of the play of a transcendent life, the playing-child in Nietzsche's novel, play is no more than an ontological metaphor threatened by Nietzsche's extreme anthropological epistemology at "the end of Western metaphysics." In this respect the metaphor is like the self that remains alienated because it cannot ground itself adequately for philosophical contemplation,

Nietzsche's Thought-Path and Relevance to Transcendence

Not only is Nietzsche's methodological understanding of language and concepts confused, it is also at times profane. In this, however, he was not alone. One of the overriding questions guiding Fink's study of Nietzsche and other nineteenth-century philosophers is how to deal with the profane in late-modern philosophy, particularly after the death of God.[8] In a real way, the problem of the profane concerned for him issues related to human alienation, freedom, beauty, and the ethical life. But it begins with the question of transcendence. To wit: what does transcendence mean without religion? Beginning with Hegel, according to Fink, and continuing through Feuerbach, Marx, and Nietzsche, modern thinkers leave "the structure of 'transcendence' to the divine" and "philosophy becomes a decided and resolute anthropology" (2016b: 181–2). The question does not concern only whether transcendence is possible or desirable or even worthy of philosophical reflection. Those are secondary issues. For Fink, it surely does not imply a longing for the days when theology lorded over philosophy by providing a clear and decisive image of the Supreme Being. In Chapter Three of PSW, Fink takes up the issue of the cult, the sacred, and the profane in his "explication of human play as an ecstatic relation to the play of the world." For him, "the human being and the world can be reached by philosophical thinking: the gods cannot" (2016: 139). For this reason, philosophy should not be concerned with theological issues. Conversely,

> Only the truth of the understanding of Being and to the human world-relation belongs to philosophy. The truth of religion [in so far as it is metaphysical by nature] certainly does not relate to the truth of philosophy as the "representation" to the "concept". . . . Each attempt to dissolve religion into philosophy leads to a theologization of philosophy. (2016b: 140)

In the context of these insights, Fink interprets Nietzsche's "lament" over "the god of play . . . with the formula [(EH IV.9/KSA 6.374)] '*Dionysus versus the Crucified*'" (2016b: 140). Thus, as this citation from Chapter Three's "The Interpretation of Play in Myth" shows, Fink does not philosophize about the days when God's servants waited at heaven's gate to pass judgment on our souls as they move on from this life to the next. To be sure, the Christian worldview offered an uncomplicated image of transcendence, making it easy to understand. Thus, real transcendence is what happens when we die and our souls leave our bodies to join the Maker in a better place. Not only is transcendence possible, in this image, but it is real. It is really real, the highest, most noble, most beautiful, most free, most fulfilled, most ethical reality thinkable for humans. We don't even need to think it: *es gibt*. It's a given. It just is. It is the promise of the real to human beings—God's promise. A life seeking transcendence in this worldview will surely be spent in preparation for that moment. But not only this, whether such a life is seeking transcendence or preparing for it, human life in this image is a living-towards-transcendence.

What does all of this mean in late modern times? What is to become of human fulfillment, freedom, beauty, and the like? Is there no more promise of transcendence?

Nothing to seek or prepare for? Is there no ethical life? Is transcendence possible through the movement from oneself to another human being? Or, from oneself to an earthly ideal, such as duty to humanity, to reason, to the greatest good, or to the state? Is only an "anthropological" transcendence possible, which is to ask again: "is there no real transcendence at all?" What does transcendence mean after the death of God?

For Fink, Nietzsche at his best thought in preparation for transcendence. This is evident for him in Nietzsche's early writings, especially on Greek tragedy and art: "Nietzsche's first period . . . is essentially determined by Nietzsche's view of the problems of Greek culture and philosophy" (2003: 30). In this phase "Nietzsche foresaw" a profound shift in Western thinking's "ontological understanding" of being, as represented by the struggle of the sophists and Socrates—the anthropologists and the metaphysician—both of whom rejected the ancient Greeks of the tragic age. In this initial phase, he intuited (albeit only in psychological terms) that "In the disputes between the sophists and Socrates Western thinking was turning towards anthropology and metaphysics and that this constitutes an event, which indeed can hardly be overestimated" (2003: 21). This is why Nietzsche called Socrates the "vortex and turning-point of so-called world history," because the latter had renovated Western moral and political thought and ethical life from the ground up (BT 15/KSA 1.100). While Socrates and his epigone generally emerged victorious from the struggle with the sophists, and henceforth ushered Western culture into 2000 years of metaphysics, the anthropologists remained in the shadows, waiting for a chance to reemerge and take their place under the main lights on the stage of Western thought.

Beginning with *Human, All-Too Human* and "to a certain extent" continuing through *Daybreak* and *Gay Science* Nietzsche's thought-path is engaged in the problems and methodologies of the Enlightenment, which Fink characterizes as a "radical turn" away from the focus of the first phase, in which "Nietzsche appears to deny everything he has asserted so far" (2003: 34). Questions of transcendence become "moral problems" of value-positing, an "anthropomorphic cosmology [that Fink assesses to be] extremely problematic as a philosophical assertion" (1988b: 213–14). After succumbing in these texts to the temptations of the anthropological and manifestly profane stage of thought, Nietzsche finds his way back to thinking originary transcendence in *Zarathustra*, whose eponymous character emerges as a surrogate for the author. This non-metaphysical form of transcendence can be seen most prominently in Nietzsche's endorsement of the essential fragments of Heraclitus. For Fink, we see Nietzsche's answer to the questions of transcendence after the death of God in the novel itself, especially after the groundwork for transcendence is laid in Parts I and II, which is articulated specifically in Part I's "Zarathustra's Speeches." This part opens with the chapter, "On the Three Metamorphoses of the Spirit," where it is explained that the spiritual inheritor and defender of values is represented by a "camel," before the spirit transforms into the "no-saying" lion, which then gives way to the spirit as a "playing child" who blesses and affirms all of existence with unadulterated innocence (Z I.1/KSA 4.29–31). Ultimately, for Fink, Parts I and II prepare for the crossing-over that happens with Zarathustra in the later chapters of Part III. The texts produced by Nietzsche after *Zarathustra*, *Beyond Good and Evil*, *On the Genealogy of*

Morals, and so forth are generally polemical in nature and return him to the "denying and rejecting half of [his] task." For this reason, Fink considers *Zarathustra,* especially the end of Part III, to be the pinnacle of Nietzsche's transcendent "yes-saying." Before looking at the moments of Zarathustra's transcendence, we should track a bit more closely the theoretical development of Zarathustra's "father" in Nietzsche's flirtations with anthropology and metaphysics.[9]

The Temptations of Anthropology and Metaphysics: On Being, Non-Being, Becoming, and Value-Positing

Like Heidegger, Fink views Nietzsche's thoughts on metaphysics and ontology, as well as their cosmological implications for values, to be the most important.[10] Fink's question, what is transcendence and how is it possible, is answered in both Nietzsche's anthropology and cosmology. Anthropologically, the human being's transcendence of the alienated self is said to occur in value-positing. "The thesis with which Nietzsche launches his attack [on inherited values] in order to break through man's self-alienation is that the superhuman and transcendent is, in fact, only man's externalization and self-forgetting" (1988b: 209). For Nietzsche, the myth of metaphysical truths is unraveling, epistemically and otherwise, but mostly under the weight of its own defenestrating history, the decay of which should be encouraged to make room for the creation of new and more suitable values. "Granting that I am a decadent, I am the opposite as well" (EH I.2/KSA 6.266). At times, he calls the self-implosion of the highest values "nihilism" (WP 2/KSA 12.350). At other times, he calls the historical activation and marshalling of this disempowering power, "through the struggle against this error" (BGE P/KSA 5.12), the overcoming of metaphysics (HH I.20/KSA 2.41). For Nietzsche, the struggle to overcome metaphysics demands the polemical outing and condemnation of most philosophers not only for having followed "the Eleatics" of the ancient world down the path of bloodless concept creation (PTG 9/KSA 1.836 and TI III.1-5/KSA 6.74–78), but also for having incited a war of convictions based upon the highest concepts. This polemical obligation is necessary because the struggle for such convictions has produced only bloody and violent consequences. "It is not conflict of opinions that has made history so violent, but . . . conflict of convictions" (HH I.630/KSA 2.356–7). Thus, part of Nietzsche's methodology is to reveal the path of bloodless concept formation leading to the bloody founding of convictions. The highest concept for the Eleatic philosophers is "being," which Nietzsche claims is *presumed* to transcend the living world as an objective truth and the highest reality. For Nietzsche, however, this so-called highest concept is merely an illusion, an "empty fiction," created for the purpose of grounding the so-called truths of moral improvement in an "anti-natural" cloud of abstractions (TI III-VII/KSA 6.74–102). Moreover, while moral concepts were *originally* created (in the days of Anaximander, who judged all existence to be an injustice for which the living is doomed to perish) in order to redeem humanity for the crime of simply existing (PTG 4/KSA 1.817–822), from the days of Socrates and Plato onward they have also proven to be useful for establishing, dominating, and exploiting the social order, and for that reason they have been promoted in order to grant advantages to priests, kings, philosophers, and whoever else might have the power to convince the majority of human beings of the superiority of their so-called divine and objective insights. For Nietzsche, the history of metaphysical truth since Plato is an "ancient error" and hostile to life. It continues "to run its ancient course" (D 168/KSA 3.151), moreover, while humanity has and continues to suffer grievously for it.

With respect to being, according to Nietzsche, Heraclitus should be recognized as superior to most philosophers in the Western tradition for standing apart from the Eleatics (TI III.2/KSA 6.75), and as with this reading of Heraclitus, Nietzsche proposes to accept or "impose upon becoming" the true nature of reality. Thus, for Fink, Nietzsche's "second attack" on inherited values for the purpose of transcending self-alienation is to label

> As a fiction the system of categories with which we determine substance, causality, the structure of things, the process of movement, and all forms of thought and objects. It is "being," according to Nietzsche, that is the delusion that conquers and enthralls the human imagination. It establishes a false network of concepts in which men commonly catch themselves and halts, binds and lays to rest the supposedly actual . . . . The truly actual, Nietzsche postulates, is becoming, not being. Being is the lie of reason, the deception of concepts that conceals the surging play of becoming. (1988b: 211)

Marking reality in this way is possible because creativity remains for good and ill purposes the human being's essential nature. Being is the illusory creation of the ancient metaphysicians, from Socrates and Plato onward. However, if becoming is the really real nature of reality, and creativity the true nature of human beings, then human reality is nothing but a force with destructive and creative potential. Notably, according to Fink, Nietzsche does not adequately theorize destruction. He simply "asserts that the increase in power of the quanta of the will and the destruction of the unity of life are equally primordial: to build and to destroy, to join and to set asunder are mutually necessary ways in which the cosmic will to power rules" (1988b: 217).

Nevertheless, the highest values are to be recognized as mere artifacts of human creativity, and they are "posited" (or established) with the intent to impose order upon existence for the purpose of creating ever new values understood to be suitable from this or that perspective. Thus, "value-positing" *as such* becomes through Nietzsche's analysis the newly ordained "highest value."[11] He names the impetus for value-positing the most radical "will to power": "To impose upon becoming the character of being— that is the supreme will to power" (WP 617/KSA 12.312). Moreover, if anything could make becoming more radical than this, then it would be if will to power's outcomes and logic were noticed to be merely "interpretive" (and for this reason self-undermining). Whenever this happens, "so much the better" (BGE 22/KSA 5.37).

This is where Nietzsche's view of the world becomes dangerously problematic for Fink and Heidegger, for whom Nietzsche has both answered the riddle of the essence of metaphysics and crossed the Rubicon for seeming to rationalize metaphysics in willing for willing's sake (in the "will to will"). For this reason, Heidegger calls Nietzsche "the last metaphysician," the one who fulfills metaphysic's promissory and nihilistic logic at this critical juncture in Western history. For his part, Fink is tempted to follow Heidegger's damning interpretation of Nietzsche as the one who best represents Western civilization's final implosion.

Yet, the key point for both Heidegger and Fink is that the destructive history of metaphysics from Plato to Nietzsche unfolds along the greater (i.e., longer and more fundamental) path of the history of being. Thus, while Nietzsche was correct to attack metaphysics for its perverse epistemic and ethical failures, and while Fink certainly appreciates Nietzsche's attempts to transcend the alienated self, Nietzsche's methods for doing so were ham-fisted in so far as they obliterated the issue of being, the promise of which is itself necessary for grounding humanity's saving grace. To put all of this in another way, metaphysical values have always occluded questions of being—of the being of their being—in such a way that the issue of fundamental ontology gets lost in the history of metaphysics. Nietzsche could not discern the difference between metaphysics and ontology and therefore his attack on the former implied for him a charge against the latter. For Fink, this lack of fundamental discernment unmoored Nietzsche and set his intuitions adrift. Henceforth, Nietzsche gleefully sailed into the dark and self-contradictory seas of radical, anthropological cosmology, where celebrating his conceptual incoherencies and confusion was the best he could think to do. "Nietzsche's anthropology is cosmomorphic, and his cosmology is anthropomorphic. . . . Man dissolves in universal becoming" (1988b: 213).

The Cosmological Temptation of Play: Fink, Nietzsche, and Dionysus

Not only was Nietzsche's attack on Western metaphysical inheritances anthropological, in Fink's view, it was also cosmological in a way that for him was "non-metaphysical" in the ways of traditional metaphysics. Fink attempts to play the middle with and against these possibilities. This section will close the present chapter with Fink's claim in 1960's *Nietzsche's Philosophy* that the pinnacle of Nietzsche's thought was achieved in the novel *Thus Spoke Zarathustra*. By focusing on his account of the novel's development and mobilization of "*Spiel*," and on the concept of play in Nietzsche's philosophy as such, Fink's claim also reminds of his encounter with Heidegger. As early as 1946, Fink was asserting Nietzsche's philosophical superiority over Heidegger's turn to poetic thinking in readings of Hölderlin, which Fink judged to be "romantic anti-intellectualism" and philosophically insufficient for opening "any path that points to the future." Nietzsche, on the other hand, offers a way forward:

> My thesis is this: that play is the *central metaphysical concept in Nietzsche* and also in modern philosophy in so far as modern philosophy conceives being as *creative*. [Play is the] unitary phenomenon of the *double visage—Apollo and Dionysus* . . . the essence of play has to be grasped at its most profound level.[12]

Years later, this same idea finds its way into Fink's summary statement in *Nietzsche's Philosophy* (2003: 32). Clearly, Fink saw something in Nietzsche's work that outshined Heidegger's thinking, even while Heidegger was preparing his notes from the 1936–40 Nietzsche lectures for wide-spread publication (Fink did not attend those lectures in person). If Fink's claim in 1946 that Nietzsche's "metaphysical" grounding of play clearly marked it as superior to "anti-intellectual romanticism," by 1960 he was praising Nietzschean play for its "non-metaphysical" features. As if this apparent change in semantics were not confusing enough, Heidegger's allegation that Nietzsche is the "last metaphysician" cast a shadow over Fink's approach to his 1960 study. The relationship with respect to their readings of Nietzsche was complex.

For Fink, even though Nietzsche's questions concerning the overcoming of metaphysics remain essentially within the realm of metaphysics, and for that reason "Nietzsche remains within the ontological dimensions of nothing, becoming, appearance, and thinking like the metaphysical tradition he opposes" (2003: 169). In contrast, Heidegger's reading is reductive. As Fink contends,

> Heidegger's Nietzsche interpretation is essentially based on Heidegger's summary and insight into the history of being and in particular on his interpretation of the metaphysics of modernity. Nevertheless, the question remains open whether Nietzsche does not already leave the metaphysical dimensions of any problems essentially and intentionally behind in his conception of the cosmos. There is a non-metaphysical originality in his cosmological philosophy of "play." (2003: 171)

One could hardly improve upon this claim as a summary statement on Fink's reading of Nietzsche vis-à-vis its standing under the cloud of Heidegger's visage.

Conclusion

As we have seen, Fink's consideration of the "question" concerning whether Nietzsche overcomes metaphysical problems is nuanced at best and fraught with temptations of all sorts. Although Nietzsche "struggles against Western metaphysics... not everyone is free who ridicules his chains" (2003: 165). Still, however, Fink is tempted to read Nietzsche as the one who best attempts the great "event" that Fink claims characterizes any "deviation from the path of metaphysics" (2003: 165). Here, he references Nietzsche's *Ecce Homo*, a text in which Nietzsche "finds the language for the consciousness of his fate." We have also seen that Fink often finds Nietzsche's analysis and use of language to be extremely problematic. What, then, might it mean for Nietzsche to find the language suitable for the way of transcendence that Fink perceives his own thought to be? The reference to *Ecce Homo* is no coincidence. In 1957's "Oasis of Happiness," he tells us explicitly what this means:

> The relation of the human being to the enigmatic appearance of the play-world...
> is *ambiguous*. Play is a phenomenon for which the appropriate categories do not

easily and unambiguously present themselves . . . [However,] great philosophy has always recognized the eminent essentiality of play, which the common understanding does not recognize, because play means to it only something that is idle, something neither serious, nor genuine. . . . [Yet,] Nietzsche puts it in *Ecce Homo* as follows: "I do know any other way of handling great tasks than as *play*." (2016c: 26)

Fink was evidently quite taken by this claim from *Ecce Homo* (EH II.10/KSA 6.297), as he repeats it at the close of *Nietzsche's Philosophy*, where it is further claimed that Dionysus is Nietzsche's name for "the fathomless all-power of play," and through which "transcendence" relieves other Nietzschean concepts—even will to power—of their "characteristics of reifying being for a conscious subject" (2003: 172). More importantly, Fink's critical reading of Nietzsche discloses what is for him "the cosmic concept of play as an extra-metaphysical question" *as such*.

Thus, Fink's discovery of this "cosmic concept" through close examination of Nietzsche's work in *Zarathustra* would likely reward further investigation. Yet, as Fink did in PSW, we should let Nietzsche's so-called son, "the dithyrambic thinker 'Zarathustra' have [today's] last word" (2016b: 215):

If ever I spread tranquil skies over myself and soared on my own wings into my own skies; if I swam playfully in the deep light-distances, and the bird-wisdom of my freedom came—but bird-wisdom speaks thus: "Behold, there is no above, no below! Throw yourself around, out, back, you are the light! Sing! Speak no more!" ("The Seven Seals," Z III.16.7/KSA 4.291)

Fink, Schiller, and Echoes of Classical German Philosophy

Susanne Schilz

Introduction

This chapter will explore the relations between Fink and Friedrich Schiller, and more generally the period of Kantian and post-Kantian philosophy referred to as German Idealism. The goal here is not to enter into technical detail but to simply present an overview of the ways in which these authors have a continued relevance for Fink, how some of their basic ideas echo in Fink's writings, and thereby perhaps suggest further avenues of study and overlooked possibilities for contextualizing Fink's thought.

Eugen Fink's *Spiel als Weltsymbol/Play as Symbol of the World*[1] contains a number of references to the work of the German poet and philosopher Friedrich Schiller. This may seem at first to be a minor or marginal source for Fink. All the citations point to the same phrase by Schiller, found in his *Über die ästhetische Erziehung des Menschen in einer Reihe von Briefen/Letters on the Aesthetic Education of Man*.[2] In this text, Schiller is fundamentally developing an aesthetics of beauty. Readers unfamiliar with Schiller's *Letters* may not be aware that in fact, the concept of play takes a central role in Schiller's work. Because of Fink's sensitivity to engagement with play in the history of philosophy, Schiller is an obvious source. When we examine that repeatedly cited phrase from Schiller more closely, we also find that it contains an expression that, while easily overlooked, constitutes an important theme of research in the history of philosophy. This gives us an additional, well-established philosophical context to which Fink can be seen to be contributing in his book. Furthermore, exploring the relationship between Fink and Schiller will show that instructive parallels can be made between these authors on the themes of appearance (*Erscheinung*), dialectic, interaction/nexus (*Wechselwirkung*) mirroring (*Spiegelung*), and wholeness (*Ganzheit*). The difference between them is that between anthropocentrism and cosmocentrism. As we work through these themes we will also touch upon the works of the other major Classical German philosophers of Schiller's era: Kant, Hegel, and Fichte. While more can be said on the level of pedagogical or anthropological topics (Schiller is a famous philosopher of *Bildung* and Fink taught for many years at a pedagogical institute, *Institut für Erziehungswissenschaften*), we will not enter into that set of topics here. Instead, this chapter will be oriented to Schiller's and Fink's fundamental commonalities in ontology and epistemology.

Wholeness and Unity

The only phrase Fink cites from Schiller is, "the human being only plays when he is in the fullest sense of the word a human being, and he is only fully a human being when he plays" ("der Mensch spielt nur, wo er in voller Bedeutung des Worts Mensch ist, und er ist nur da ganz Mensch, wo er spielt").[3] The key component of this phrase, that is so easily overlooked, is the expression "fully a human being" (*ganze Mensch*). The wholeness of the human being is a significant topic of debate in Classical German philosophy. It refers to how Kant was interpreted in the period. In a letter to Schiller reporting conversations with Fichte on Schiller's philosophy, Wilhelm von Humboldt writes: "The only thing which is still missing is the unity. This unity can be found in your sentiment, but not yet in your system." According to that report, Fichte went on to suggest that Schiller's achieving of systemic unity would have elevated him above all other thinkers of the period and would have inaugurated a new epoch in thought.[4]

The post-Kantian heritage is broad and multifaceted. But I would suggest that a thinking of living unity, *lebendige Einheit*, is a common theoretical aim or goal, despite that variety and plurality of the tradition. The quest for this missing unity pervades philosophy and literature in the nineteenth century after Kant.[5] Both Schiller and Fink are part of this project or can be said to think in this direction. For Schiller this is obvious. For Fink this is less obvious. In fact, while it is common to identify this motif in Classical German philosophy, I would like to suggest that the Phenomenological movement also inherits this reaction to Kant. In particular, the Kantian duality of sensibility and reason, *Sinnlichkeit und Vernunft,* creates a desideratum of thinking an anthropological wholeness. This anthropological wholeness is what Schiller is referring to in the passage quoted by Fink.

Schiller's starting point is not far from Kant's. Based on an exchange with Fichte, Schiller thinks the human being first as composed of—not faculties or *Vermögen*, as had Kant—but opposed drives (*Triebe*).[6] Thus, his starting point is a dualistic conception of the human being in terms of a Material-drive and a Form-drive (*Stofftrieb, Formtrieb*). These drives are parts of the human being and do not exist in isolation.[7] They exist instead in a joint state connected by a third instance. This third instance that mediates the other two is the play-drive (*Spieltrieb*).[8] The phenomenon of play, through the realization of the play-drive (*Spieltrieb*), in the achievement of beauty, is thought to overcome the separation of the Material-drive and the Form-drive.[9] This is why Schiller claims that play makes the human being whole. So, play is responsible for the fullness of the human being, play makes the human being whole and thus makes the human being what it actually is. This wholeness is the overcoming of a Kantian anthropological dualism. Of course, the notion of play, in Schiller, is taken over from Kant's third *Critique*. Kant invokes the notion in describing the relations among the faculties of the soul. Commentators generally take Schiller's elevation of play to the level of a drive to be a sign of his more anthropological and less transcendental orientation.[10] While the fullness and the wholeness, *Ganzheit*, of the human being is achieved in play, the two drives are not exactly dissolved in unification. The living human being is importantly not dualistic because of a failure or incapacity; duality is a condition *sui generis*. Instead, for Schiller, form and matter enter a *Wechselwirkung*, an exchange or a nexus of reciprocal action. We will return to this topic further below. The nexus or *Wechselwirkung* of form and matter described by Schiller in the ideal human being is not, or is only approximatively attainable.

As for the step to unity and to unification, the step where Fink can be connected to the post-Kantian heritage, here is a passage from the closing pages of PSW:

> and the playworld of the play of the world is not an "appearance" [*Schein*], but rather the *coming to appearance* [*die Erscheinung*]. Coming to appearance is the universal emergence of all beings, things, and events into a common presence [*Anwesen*] that integrates everything individuated—in our midst. (215)

Fink's language is a little dense here, but he is connecting the world of play with *Erscheinung* as opposed to *Schein*. Then the former concept is understood as the *universelle Aufgang*, the universal opening, universal emerging, which is, in turn, equated with an *alles Vereinzelte zusammenschliessendes Anwesen*, a presencing which unifies every individuality. So that play, by way of *Erscheinung*, leads to a unification of all individual things. And this unification is *bei uns*, in our midst, at our place. So, the world and us, both, are in unity in play. The unification achieved by Fink is going to be on the level of the human being and the world.

That same idea of a unity in and through play is expressed in the following: "Human play is an especially distinctive way in which existence relates with understanding to the whole of that which is, and in which it lets the whole resonate through it. In human play, the whole of the world is reflected back into itself" (PSW 206). While we will return further below to the language of reflection, what is important at this point is the repeated reference to a whole, *Ganze*. It is in play that we achieve an understanding of the whole, that is, a unification of all beings, "all that is." It is in Play that the whole, the unified totality, becomes phenomenon, as it were.

I will only emphasize one point here: how a thinking of unity and wholeness leads to a thinking of appearance. For Schiller, this wholeness is to be found in the human being where a *Wechselwirkung* unites opposites. For Fink, appearance opens up to the concept of mirroring *Spiegeln*, which describes a wholeness in the relation between the human being and the cosmos. As Fink says: "In human play the whole of the world is reflected back into itself, letting features of in-finity emerge and shimmer in and on something innerworldly and finite" (PSW 206).

Phenomenality and Dialectic

Fink's philosophy of Play is characterized by a triple interwovenness of the concepts of wholeness, negativity, and appearance/appearing. Appearance or *Erscheinung*, and the associated words *Erscheinen, Schein*, are an important component of Fink's thought. It was through his analysis of the dimension of appearance and appearing that Fink achieved that level of unity or reconciliation pointed out earlier. According to Fink's editors, however, the notion of *Erscheinung* in Fink is "withdrawn from the visibility of everything phenomenal, from everything that appears within the world" (PSW 312–13). But this may be an interpretation of 'phenomenon' that is unnecessarily narrow. Certainly, as far as the phenomenological movement is concerned, it has always been characterized by an interest in "not just the things themselves, but more fundamentally towards the dimension of appearance."[11] The appearing that Fink refers to is perhaps not a phenomenon at the level of a mere perceptually defined phenomenality but rather to be understood in a Heideggerian ontological sense of phenomenality. The familiar Heideggerian insistence on the ontological withdrawal and refusal in *Entzug* and *Enteignis* in phenomena seems to be active in Fink's thinking through a dimension of negativity. As Fink writes, "But the world is also the nameless realm of absence, from which things come forth into appearance [*ins Erscheinen einrücken*] and into which they again vanish [*verschwinden*]. . . . The play of the world, if it is to have a sense that can be thought at all, must be conceived as the relation of the world-night to the world-day" (PSW 215). But this manner of thinking appearance is also reminiscent of Hegel, who writes in the *Phenomenology* : "Appearance is emergence and passing away that itself does not emerge or pass away but is in itself."[12] Emphasizing the duality at the beginning of that quote, we are able to appreciate how Fink, too, thinks appearance as structured by duality, in his case, cast as day and night of the world.

Of course, a thinking of appearance based on negativity is something that Fink inherits also from Hegel's *Logic*. In the doctrine of Essence, Hegel thinks appearance and negation explicitly together: "Appearance is the existing mediated by its negation."[13] A distinction here, with respect to Heidegger, lies perhaps in the Hegelian connection of appearance with negativity rooted in the appearance of the entity, the extant, or existant, *das Existierende*. But that was also the context in which Fink, in the above passage, referred to "coming to appearance." The issue for Fink was the coming to appearance of things, in individuation.

The question of phenomenality runs through the entirety of Fink's thinking. PSW dedicates a vast portion to critical engagement with Plato. The criticism is methodological. Plato is accused of a circularity:

Plato takes up particular phenomena from the realm of sensible things—phenomena that prove to be derivative in themselves and furthermore are determined by a moment of reproduction [*Abbildung*]. Such phenomena are, as it were, existing "non-actualities." Plato operates with the phenomena of the "shadow," the "reproduction," [*Abbild*], and "mirroring" [*Spiegelung*]. Shadows, reproductions, and mirror images occur as specific appearances [*Erscheinungen*] within the total realm of sensible things." (PSW 93–4)

This is the familiar vocabulary of imitation, *mimesis*. The derivative is described in terms *copy*, *shadow*, and *mirror-image*. To complete the criticism Fink argues, "Plato thus draws the models for the ontological devaluation of the sensuous sphere from precisely the sphere he wishes to devalue" (PSW 94). This is perhaps not yet significant. But Fink doesn't conclude from this criticism that the concept of mirroring, or

Spiegelung, for example, must be abandoned. In fact, he holds on to the concept and even builds it into his theory of play. He appropriates some of the Platonic vocabulary of the derivative. It is important to note which terms are chosen.

As he develops his analysis of play further, he writes: "The mirror-image [*Spiegelbild*] copies. But insofar as it copies and is dependent on the original, it opens in the first place a region of a strange 'appearance:' [*Schein*] we see into, so to speak, an irreal realm" (PSW 97). Thus, this structure of mirroring is not so much criticized by Fink as it is rehabilitated, or reappropriated. He doesn't dwell on shadow and copy, but he appropriates *Schein* and *Spiegel*, appearance and mirroring, in order to describe the irreality of play, the domain of non-actuality. As Fink says, the question of mirroring is not just any question, an arbitrary point. The importance of mirroring to Fink's understanding of play is made clear in the following statement: "In order to understand *play* we must be acquainted with the *world*, and in order to understand the *world as play* we must achieve a still much *deeper insight into the world*" (P 77). In this quote, we see Fink going from play to world, then from world to play, and then back to world. The movement is perhaps an enactment of the motion of mirroring, the reflecting back and forth. In the following, Fink employs the idea more conceptually and declaratively: "In human play the whole of the world is reflected back into itself, letting features of infinity emerge and shimmer in and on something innerworldly and finite" (PSW 206). The reflecting-back of the world and the shimmering in and on something are both strongly reminiscent of the mirror reflection. This means the mirroring decried by Plato is necessary, in some way, for the achievement of the unity that is achieved in play. This also contrasts strongly with the view of the editors, referenced earlier, according to which phenomenality qua visibility is sidelined by Fink. In fact, Fink's descriptions here rely heavily on the metaphorical language of light, mirror, and luminous reflection.

This is the same thought that in the earlier text, *Oasis of Happiness*, was put as follows: "it depends decisively on whether in fact the whole of Being, in repeat, mirrors itself, from out of itself, in a single being" (P 30). In this quote, Fink in fact reuses the word "mirroring." Now, this thought of mirroring can be found later in the book, as Fink is building his remarks on the Play of the World: "The worldly prevailing of the omni-potent happens without ground and without goal, aimlessly and senselessly, without value and without plan. These are the basic features of the world that shine back [*zurückscheinen*] into human play" (PSW 213). In this passage, the specific term employed is, again, shining back, *zurückscheinen*. The relationship between the human and the world is taken in a structure of *zurückscheinen*, a shining back, and this asserts the movement of mirroring, *Spiegeln*. This mirroring, appropriated of course from Plato, is thus an integral moment of Finkian play.

For Schiller, the corresponding notion to the movement of mirroring is to be found in the notion of reciprocal action, interaction, or nexus of the drives, *Wechselwirkung*. The same dialectical movement that is expressed by Fink in Platonic terms is present here, expressed as follows:

> Both principles are, therefore, at once, subordinated to each other and coordinated with each other, that is to say, they stand in reciprocal relation to one another: without form, no matter and without matter, no form. (Schiller, Letter 13)

The nexus of drives produces that same motion, now between form and matter. Each is subordinated to the other, while each is also coordinated with the other in a dynamical process.[14] Thus we are led from one pole of the opposition to the other, and then back again. This motion of reciprocal action is the engine, so to speak of beauty itself: "We have seen how beauty results from the reciprocal action of two opposed drives and from the uniting of two opposed principles. The highest ideal of beauty is therefore to be sought in the most perfect possible union and *equilibrium* of reality and form" (Schiller, Letter 16). Schiller, in conformity with other Classical German thinkers, emphasizes ideas of harmony and, here, equilibrium, significant for us is the prior term, "most perfect, or most complete, union." The reciprocal action constitutes the union, the unity, or the wholeness. For Schiller and Fink, in *Wechselwirkung* and *Spiegeln*, we find two analogous ways of thinking a unity, of overcoming an initial duality and achieving a unity.

Conclusion

The constellation of themes that have been presented in this chapter will hopefully open doors for further, more narrow, investigations into Fink and Classical German philosophy. While for Schiller play is key to the absolute or complete comprehension of the human being, for Fink, play elucidates the place or position of the human being in the world (PSW 198). Although Fink does not list Schiller as a major source, their commonalities are indeed instructive, for example, in the connection between play and "appearance" (*Schein* and related terms). For Fink, appearance is an important descriptive aspect of Play, but also a key concept for the relation between the human being and the world. While for Schiller "appearance" is anthropocentric (in continuity with Kant's language from the third *Critique*), for Fink it is perhaps cosmocentric. Fink's notion of appearing is also reminiscent of a Hegelian construction involving negativity. In both Schiller and Fink, play also appears to function as a terminological alternative to "dialectic," whereby the notion of play adds a more concretely dynamic implication. In his correspondence with Fichte, Schiller emphasizes a notion of *Wechselwirkung*, or nexus of interaction, which in the *Letters on Aesthetic Education* is crucial for the emergence of the concept of play. Play thus brings together opposites in a dynamical interrelation. This, I have argued, can be fruitfully brought to bear on Fink's language concerning the mirroring play of world. For both Schiller and Fink, finally, though not touched upon in this chapter, it should be intuitive, the notion of limit becomes important here. Schiller insists on the concept of a limit and Fink moving to dissolve it to free play from a metaphysical burden.

8

What Is the Problem that Fink Solved for Derrida and Deleuze in 1967?

Hakhamanesh Zangeneh

Not long ago, it was still possible for a reviewer of a work on Fink and Husserl to end his essay with the following words: "But there is a nagging doubt in mind: in what sense is Fink himself an eminent figure? . . . Who outside of phenomenology has ever heard of him?" (Moran 2007). In this chapter, I will show that two of the most important European philosophers after Heidegger had heard of him, and indeed, that their work was importantly indebted to Fink. I am referring to Jacques Derrida and Gilles Deleuze.[1] I will be focusing on Derrida's *De la Grammatologie* (1967) and Deleuze's *Logique du Sens* (1967b). Given the length limitations here, I will be content to motivate and make plausible that connection, perhaps elucidate it to some extent, while putting off for later the more exhaustive investigation. One might surmise that the previously mentioned reviewer's doubts were rooted in the late translation of Fink's postwar writings into English. It may also be rooted in the de facto division of labor in Anglophone work on European philosophy between Teutonic-centric and Gallo-centric scholars. Whatever the reason might be, the recent translation of Fink's *Spiel als Weltsymbol* (PSW) by Turner and Moore is a good occasion to revisit the question of Fink's intellectual posterity.

Terms, Texts, Method

But first: Play or Game? Both. In German, as in French there is a unified phenomenon: *Spiel*, or *jeu*. English speakers consider this an ambiguity, an obstacle to translation: play *or* game. But perhaps this distinction is already a way of breaking up what the continental thinker approaches as a unitary phenomenon. After all, the ambiguity is not just in French and German: Italian has only *gioco*, Spanish only *juego*, other languages converge in this usage, and English is really the outlier. In this chapter, I am going to heuristically think play and game together and not separately. I do not have a robust argument for this at the outset, but I want to declare it as an operative assumption—it will become useful below.

As to texts, I am focusing on a ten-year stretch of European philosophy, from 1957 to 1967. A glance at the chronology of Fink's publications in original and in French translation makes his importance to this period of the history of philosophy unmistakable. His work on play immediately preceded—maybe even opened—France's golden age of philosophy. (Neither Husserl nor Heidegger, I would note, ever benefited from such rapid translation and reception in French.) Furthermore, the major intellectual stations on Fink's path toward play—Nietzsche and Heraclitus especially—reappear in French works thematizing play during the same period. Kostas Axelos[2] is clearly situated here as a transitional figure between Fink on the one hand, and Derrida and Deleuze on the other. From 1961 to 1964, Axelos published what he called a "tryptic," moving from Marx/Heidegger, to Heraclitus, to what he calls planetary thinking.[3] In addition to his own publications, Axelos was the editor of the book series "Arguments," which published Fink in French, and in 1966 he was guest editor of a journal issue on nihilism, featuring essays on play and reviews of Fink.[4] Apart from Marx, replacing the cosmic with the planetary, Axelos" itinerary maps well onto that of Fink. On the heels of Axelos' book, in 1967, both Derrida and Deleuze published major works with both explicit and implicit, hidden, references to Fink, Axelos, and *jeu*, play/game.

My fundamental orientation here is historical, and a minimal methodological declaration is in order. My *terminus ad quem* is 1967 because of the importance of what was published in French that year. My other end point, my *ab quo*, is 1957, the German publication of *Oasis*. As a result, I will be considering only what was available from Fink before 1967 (so I am ignoring some posthumous Fink publications as well as Axelos' later *Le Jeu du monde*). I am looking at a movement from German to French over a ten-year period, trying to discern what French poststructuralism historically

Table 1 Chronology of Publications

Year	Fink - German	Fink - French	Axelos	Derrida	Deleuze
1957	Oasis				
1960	PSW Nietzsche	Oasis			
1961			Marx Penseur d.l. Technique		
1962			Héraclite et la Philo		
1964/5		PSW Nietzsche	Vers la Pensée Planétaire		
1966			Ein. i.e. k. Denken		
1967				De la Grammatologie	Logique du sens
1969			Le Jeu du Monde		

owes to Fink (this has been completely ignored in the literature[5]). I am not pursuing an atemporal comparison and contrast of doctrines and themes. Incidentally, a conventional comparison and contrast would have a lot to work with—the amount of overlap between these authors is immense and would require a book-length study. So instead, I am going to try to read Deleuze and Derrida as grappling with problems or questions they both try to answer specifically through Fink (and Axelos). Hence my title: what is the problem that Fink solved for Deleuze and for Derrida?

Deleuze, *The Logic of Sense*

In the tenth series of *Logique du sens*, "*du jeu idéal*," "Of the Ideal Game"[6] (Deleuze 1967: 74–82), Deleuze begins by describing a theory of the *normal* games that we play. An attentive reader can already guess where this analysis is going: this normal play will contrast with something else later. We are thus expecting from the outset some sort of dualism of play/game, vaguely recalling a Finkian/Axelosian distinction of the type "play of" versus "play in" the world. At the outset, Deleuze finds a set of principles which he claims are definitive for phenomena of normal play/games. I don't want to elaborate on these in detail, but will point to a few features that resonate with ideas from Fink. Normal games, according to Deleuze, are partial—they only occupy a part of our time. We play, and while we play we are *at play*, but sure enough, we eventually exit the game—we stop playing. This is the kind of play, I would suggest, that is the subject of philosophical anthropology—it is one of the activities of the human. Just as we expect normal play to contrast with some other play, we might thus expect that other play to open a dimension different from the anthropological one.

A second feature of the partial or normal games, one that is essential to Deleuze's interest, is that these have a limited relationship to contingency (Deleuze 1967: 75). Normal play limits and bounds chance, *le hasard*, with mechanical causality. There is a reference here to Stephane Mallarmé's famous poem (which Deleuze interweaves into his Nietzsche book) "A Throw of the Dice." The opening line/page of the poem declares that *Un coup de dés, jamais, n'abolira le hasard*, "a throw of the dice will never abolish chance." Even when, as one might say in English, "the die has been cast," the poet affirms that chance has not vanished. This affirmation of chance, of contingency, surprise, event, is a model for Deleuze's thought. When, in contrast to normal play, one imagines a "pure play," one affirms all of chance, *affirme tout le hasard*, one affirms chance completely. Mallarmé's example of playing dice exemplifies a game where mechanical causality (the throw) and contingency (the outcome) are in contact, but the latter, contingency, is not (or so the claim) eliminated by the former, causality. This motif works as a directive for Deleuze. Thus, what he strives for is some conception of play/game where contingency is no longer bounded, no longer limited, but is rather absolute.

So, the description of the normal games that humans play serves as a reference point or as a foil against which another form of play/game is arrived at. This other play/game is not going to be partial, it is not going to be one of many, and it is not a phenomenon of philosophical anthropology. But also, this other play/game will be chiefly distinguished by its total and unconditioned embrace of contingency. Deleuze calls this *le jeu idéal*, the ideal play/game. It is crucial to note that this ideal or absolute play/game is not a phenomenon that is encountered in human experience. "The ideal game of which we speak can be realized neither by a human being nor by a god" (Deleuze 1967: 76). We do not play this way. In fact, the absolute game notably becomes one *without* players. A surprising development—but of course there are similar passages in Fink's PSW about the play of the world, to which we will return later. In a Heideggerrian ductus we might say that *das Spiel spielt, der Mensch spielt nicht*. This of course sounds quite strange, but only until we recall Heidegger's overarching desire to describe such phenomena as world, space, or language (and he has such Cratylean tautologies for all the preceding: *Welt weltet, Raum räumt, Sprache spricht*) without an anchoring in the agency of a human subject. That is, without an anchoring, and without a subject. So, moving from normal to ideal play moves us out of a framework wherein play would have a ground, an *arche*, outside of itself, as well as displacing the subject as underlying *hypokeimenon*.

Another feature of normal play according to Deleuze is its "mixed" nature (Deleuze 1967: 75). Here he is referring to ways in which normal play/games are dependent on, or at least allegorical for, something heterogeneous. Our normal play/games derive values from morality, from economy, and so on. Absolute play/game, by contrast, is autonomous or perhaps best referred to as auto-telic, it is its own *telos*, it refers to nothing outside of itself. Ideal play is not instantiating some other thing, it is not suggestive of something exterior to it. When play is elevated to this absolute state, without players, without external criteria/goals it is not an object of experience. We might say that it moves from being an object of philosophical anthropology to an organizing principle of ontology. In the case of Deleuze this happens to be univocal ontology. With this connection to ontology I am drawing closer to what I think is the question, the question that Deleuze answers through Fink. At first blush, Deleuze's remarks on ontology seem quite conventional; they are a simplification of a scheme proposed by Etienne Gilson in his massive study of Duns Scotus (Gilson 2019). As Deleuze has it, there are three possible positions in ontology: analogy, plurivocity, and univocity. But *unlike the pre-Heideggerian* discussion of ontology, Deleuze articulates univocal ontology in a formulation highly reminiscent of or at least compatible with Heidegger's articulation of ontico-ontological difference. According to Deleuze: "The univocity of being means that being is Voice, that it is said, and that it is said in one and the same 'sense' of all that of which it is said. That of which it is said is not at all the same. But it [being] is the same for everything of which it is said" (Deleuze 1967: 210). The clarity with which this statement distinguishes being and that of which it is said (beings, the many entities) contrasts sharply with Gilson's classical discussion where being, essence, and entity are used interchangeably.[7]

Now, if we glance at an earlier Deleuze essay carrying references to Axelos, we find this orientation confirmed. What Deleuze explicitly praises in Axelos is the latter's orientation toward an ontology *beyond metaphysics*—in the *Heideggerian* sense of metaphysics. In fact, he endorses Axelos' attempt at moving more forcefully beyond metaphysics than the German phenomenologists.[8] The notions which allow Axelos to do this, to replace the "metaphysical," according to Deleuze, are play and errance (Deleuze 2002: 109). So when play is associated with contingency, indeterminacy, the abyssal, and the an-archic (read *Abgrund*)—and all of these are descriptions of play for Axelos[9] when play is associated with these notions it exceeds metaphysics in the Heideggerian sense. So, play seems to organize an ontology beyond metaphysics.

Finally, this fundamentally critical orientation toward metaphysics is confirmed by Deleuze's elaborations on the temporality of play/game. Here Deleuze's source is iconoclastic but curiously complementary to my reading. Deleuze draws on ancient Stoicism in order to align play/game with the time of Aion as opposed to Chronos (of course, the reference to Aion recalls the famous Heraclitus fragment which employs that term in connection with play, but Deleuze embraces the Stoic and not the pre-Socratic Aion). This has some baroque details in the domain of divisibility and infinity, all rooted in the details of Stoic physics, which I will not pursue. But, there is one feature of the Stoic notion of Aion that is crucial. Drawing on the work of French historians of Stoicisim,[10] Deleuze suggests that the Aion eschews the present. While the time of Chronos is a time of an ever growing present, Aion is a time of infinite past and infinite future with no presence (Deleuze 1967: 69). I would suggest that Deleuze's aligning of ideal play/game with the time without presence could be viewed as his manner of carrying out a deconstruction of the metaphysical present.

Fink's perhaps most compact declarations concerning metaphysics occur actually not in PSW but at the end of his Nietzsche book (Fink 2003).[11] After reviewing Heidegger's Nietzsche interpretation, Fink attempts to highlight that notion in Nietzsche's writing that might allow him to escape Heidegger's determination of metaphysics based on the history of being. That notion turns out to be play, *Spiel*: "There is a non-metaphysical originality in [Nietzsche's] cosmological philosophy of 'play'" (Fink 2003: 171). Also: "Where Nietzsche conceives being and becoming as play he no longer remains within the boundaries of metaphysics" (Fink 2003: 172). In an important passage bringing together the notions of play, contingency and the cosmos, Fink writes: "where the ascent and decline of the finite, temporal forms is experienced as a dance and a round, as the **dice game of divine chance**, . . . man can experience himself in his **play**ful productivity . . . as embedded in the great **play** of the birth and the death of all things and as immersed in the tragedy and comedy of universal being. **The cosmos plays**" (my emphasis, Fink 2003: 171-2). Notably, the passage ends on a declarative statement of the impersonal, a-subjective nature of what Deleuze had called ideal play/game. Recall that a subjective rooting of normal play contrasted with the impersonal nature of ideal play, the one without players; Fink describes this by displacing the agency of the human subject by way of the cosmic: "The cosmos plays." And of course, Fink identifies play with contingency by referencing the dice game and chance. All these conceptual moves appeared in our reading of Deleuze as well.

So in 1960, Eugen Fink is articulating a critical perspective on metaphysics, based, to be sure, on Heidegger's interpretation of the history of being, and he, Fink, is gesturing to an opening in Nietzsche that leads beyond metaphysics. It seems clear to me that some of the crucial features of what has been understood as French poststructuralism and postmodernism was first explicitly articulated, and I say explicitly articulated not implicitly suggested, first by Eugen Fink. This is not immediately legible when one reads Fink and stays there. It becomes obvious when one moves along this sweep from German to French texts from 1957 to 1967. When one reads Deleuze after Fink.

Of course, none of this is meant to suggest that there is one self-same identical problem that traverses Heidegger, Fink, Axelos,, and Deleuze. There is rather something like a structure which undergoes slight modification from one thinker to the next, whereby the transition and modifications are discrete and observable, rational and motivated. Out of the many factors intervening between Heidegger and Fink, I would point to one that was significant for the latter's posterity. It is well-known that among the German phenomenologists, Eugen Fink was the figure who was most sympathetic to Hegel. While it would be hard to discern in Fink's works relevant to play any specific trace of speculative negativity, of determinate negation, it is nonetheless manifest that Fink was a writer who thought by way of contradictions, oppositions, even dualities. This latent, quasi-dialectical, determination of play was also inherited by Axelos and then also by Deleuze.

If that is a factor intervening between Heidegger and Fink, another readily legible one is between Fink and Axelos. Earlier, I had characterized play as an organizing *principle* for an ontology beyond metaphysics. On the notion of a "principle," one can discern a distance especially as we move from Fink to Axelos. The historical complex concerning play has some differentiation here. As Axelos writes, "Play is not definitive, it is not the last word . . . it remains unthought—perhaps unthinkable—unknown, unfeasible" ([1964] 2019). Rather than characterize it as a principle, in fact, Axelos ends by describing play as a question.

Derrida, *Of Grammatology*

The first step toward determining Derrida's relation to Fink is already much harder because his use of play, *jeu*, is not confined to one location in the text, it is not a *thematic* concept, but it is rather employed throughout as an *operative* concept. The most prominent usage of play under Derrida's plume is likely the expression "play of difference," *jeu de la différance*. But we can also find references to play, preliminarily and in isolation as it were, together with citational reference to Fink and Axelos. In order to establish the relation to our constellation of authors I will start with a well-known passage in *Of Grammatology*, from the part on structuralist linguistics, where we encounter a reference to play:

> It is necessary here to think that writing is play in language. This *play*, thought as absence of the transcendental signified, is not a play *in the world*, as the philosophical tradition has always defined it, in order to *contain* it. . . . It is thus *the play of the world* that must be thought *first:* before attempting to understand all the forms of play in the world. (Derrida 1967:73)

As is clear from the invocation of play in a dual reference to both play *in* and play *of* the world, Derrida has here made a Finkian/Axelosian distinction his own, embraced it and operated with it. (This passage is also the reason why I am focusing on *Of Grammatology* and not on the paper from 1966: "Structure, Sign and Play in the Discourse of the Human Sciences.") Despite the abundant literature on Derrida and phenomenology, to my knowledge, no English reader has studied this connection between Fink and Derrida specifically on the dual notion of play. Now admittedly, this duality, while blatant in the French original, is obscured in the published English translation: Spivak renders one *jeu* as play and the other as game. Thus, her translation asserts that "the game of the world" must be thought before "play in world." This problem will recur in the translation. Out of the four authors referenced in the note to this page by Derrida, Fink and Axelos are the only two for whom there is a duality of play *in* and play *of*—no such distinction occurs in Heidegger (despite the references to two specific texts) nor to my knowledge in Nietzsche (for whom no specific text is adduced). If the connection to Fink and Axelos has been established, we can now turn to a closer determination of the value of play in Derrida's text.

The two ideas contained in the above passage are the relationship to writing and the notion of the absence of the transcendental signified. We will revisit writing further below but as for the point about the transcendental signified, another phrase on this page is key: "One might call *play* the absence of the transcendental signified . . . as the shaking of onto-theology and of the metaphysics of presence" (Derrida 1967: 73). We see already the problem or the question facing Derrida to which Fink is to provide the answer or the response. It is through Finkian play that Derrida "shakes" and deconstructs onto-theology and the metaphysics of presence. Why this operation is identified with the absence of the transcendental signified will be explained with another passage below. In the second part of the book, on Rousseau, Derrida writes the following, and it is the second clause of the sentence which is of interest:

> There are many games/instances of play (*jeux*) within the public festival but no play (*jeu*) at all, if one understands by that singular the substitution of contents, the exchange of presences and absences, chance and absolute risk. (Derrida 1967: 433)

I give the French parenthetically to make the connection between the plural and singular recognizable (*jeux* and *jeu*). Again, translating into English forces us to distinguish and to lose the clarity: in Spivak's rendering we have again: many *games* . . . but no *play* . . . But Derrida is not asserting a difference between games and play here. He is distinguishing the plural and the singular of the *same* thing,[12] play, *jeu*. Play in the singular, play as such, is distinguished from the many types and instances of games that can be played e.g. during a festival, a celebration. Play as such is separated from the multiple, different, delimited games that we can occupy ourselves with (and whose study would again constitute a philosophical anthropology). This seems an echo of the distinction between the singular play *of* the world versus the plural play *in* the world.

Now, in that same passage, play as such is characterized by three features: (1) substitution of contents, (2) exchange of presence and absence, and (3) chance and absolute risk. I would say that (1) and (2) are economic features and that (3) is the notion of contingency. If Derrida had characterized play only in economic terms, then his notion would have been a limited one, indeed it would have been the notion of limited play. The addition of contingency, heightened to the "absolute" state, is key here.

The notion of play operating here is one of absolutely contingent economy, absolutely contingent exchange and substitution. What this suggests is that the exchange and the substitution are not perfect, are not closed, as it were. There is loss, surplus, friction, and the whole is aleatory and not rational. I would say that play here is strictly speaking an-economical, the lexical allusion is retained just to be negated conceptually.

It is along these lines that one should think the determination I skipped in the first passage above. In that first quote we saw Derrida associate play with writing as "absence of the transcendental signified." I want to comment briefly on the two components of this connection. How should we understand this idea of play as absence? Play is *not* an arriving at a terminal absence, but rather an infinite referral, an infinite chain of presences which do not terminate the reference but only move it along. The context here is that of the relation of signification, and Derrida wants to suggest that whatever is signified is in turn, itself, a signifying, such that the relation of signification becomes endless, infinite. So play is aleatory and infinite, and I would suggest that because of the latter feature, it must be thought at the level not of human experience. This is not one particular form of play among many that we can undertake, engage in, or more generally experience. The infinite and contingent play, that is not human, is the play of the world.

But what does it mean to assert or posit play as *writing* at the level of the play of the world? Isn't writing considered as play, then, at most, one of the instances of play, one specific form, one activity of the human? Isn't writing just one of many, delimited, bounded activities? After all, we are not always writing—we are not solely writing. Here it is important to recall some of the basic aspects of Derrida's engagement with structuralist linguistics on the issue of writing. Very briefly put, Derrida operates with two notions of writing, one of which is empirical and the other is not. The empirical notion of writing is the writing we are all familiar with and that has also been thematized explicitly since at least *Phaedrus*. The non-empirical is a generalized ontological concept, related to but not limited nor identical to empirical, familiar instances of writing. The ontological concept of writing shares abstract properties with empirical writing, and is therefore named after the latter, but it applies to more phenomena, or underwrites more phenomena than just actual empirical writing. It is this ontological notion of writing that Derrida identifies with play.

So the play of the world is singular, contingent, infinite, and thus not of the order of human experience. At the same time, this play of the world *precedes* human play. This play *precedes* the human, intraworldly, play in the order of thought. This is a transformation of the Finkian perspective; a subtle displacement had already occurred in the first cited passage above. From Fink to Derrida, the two levels of play have changed relationship. Here we encounter a noteworthy development from Fink to Derrida. In PSW, Fink articulates the relationship between play *in* and play *of* in terms of his notion of symbol. While the nature of my examination does not allow me to enter into any one determination in great depth, I would suggest that symbolization is not grounding. In other words, for Fink the two levels of play do not display a relationship of foundation. As we move from Fink to Derrida, the response transforms the question and a more conventional vision of foundation reasserts itself. For Derrida there is hierarchy between the two levels of play—the singular, the absolute, the *haplon*, *must* be thought before and must be thought as the foundation of the determined, conditioned instances.

This "preceding," this priority, when taken in conjunction with the abstract concept of writing, and the reference to a shaking of onto-theology and of the metaphysics of presence, suggests an ontological status for Derridean play.

Now, to be sure, there are passages in Derrida that would seem to contradict my insistence on ontology and on the ontological. A third passage referencing play, from the same work, will allow me to clarify this to some extent. Here, the question is the determination of the human, the *anthropos*:

> But what is the proper of man? On the one hand, it is that whose possibility must be thought before man, and outside of him. . . . It is precisely the play of presence and absence, the opening of this play that no metaphysical or ontological concept can comprehend. Therefore the *proper* of man is not the property of man, it is the dislocation of the proper in general. (Derrida 1967: 347)

There are two basic moves in this passage. First, we find that play is again to be thought *before*, and even *outside* the human. The notion of play has priority and exteriority to the notion of the human. Play is not derived from the human but makes the human possible. This allows us once again to leave the axis of philosophical anthropology. For my construal, this precedence and exteriority suffice to attribute to play an ontological vocation. The priority and exteriority put the investigation on the ontological axis. However, the second point is that we must reform our notion of the ontological. Derrida contends that no metaphysical or ontological concept can grasp play. The reason for this has already emerged earlier: play is absolutely contingent and infinite. If this is the case, then it defies rationality (*qua* contingent) and defies closure (*qua* infinite). And if this is the case, then it defies grasp by metaphysical or ontological concepts *in the strict sense of the tradition of metaphysics and ontology*. So, if the notion of play allows Derrida to access an ontological level of claims, then this ontology displays aspects that have traditionally been excluded from it.

So what is the question that Fink answers for Derrida in 1967? What is the problem Fink solves? As was the case for Deleuze, for Derrida the question is how to articulate an ontology beyond metaphysics, not anchored in the agency of the human subject. This is what Fink's philosophy of play made possible, for both *Logic of Sense* and *Of Grammatology*. And from there, the rest is history.

9

Phantasy and Play in Husserl, Fink, and Sartre

Daniel O'Shiel

Introduction

It is a rather strong platitude to say play is a vital part of human reality, but it is! In fact, play seems to take us way beyond the human and into our evolutionary roots too. Indeed, with play comes pattern recognition, mimicking, rule following, trial and error, learning more generally—all absolutely essential traits in our evolutionary and personal histories.

Play has not been given enough attention in philosophy. This has been changing but there is a lot of catch-up to do. One exception is Eugen Fink, for whom it was one of his main philosophical and phenomenological interests, and upon which he wrote more than perhaps any other subject and more than any other philosopher. This is now available to us in English thanks to Moore and Turner's excellent translation (Fink [2010] 2016). The aim of this brief chapter is to situate Fink generally, as well as certain strands of his investigations into play, into the phenomenological movement, and show he is a key link between Husserl's quite novel essential connection of play to imagination and thinking more generally, and then Sartre's existentialization and ontologization of the concepts a couple of decades later. It is thus a focus on play more on the mental side of the category, which is just as well as the domain is far too large and diverse for any comprehensive chapter—as this edition itself demonstrates.

In all of this, the inherently playful nature of phantasy—which we will see is "imagination in a narrow sense," dealing with irrealities (and idealities for Husserl)—will come to the fore. Phantasy as "playful" may seem obvious and trivial, but when it is situated in the wider phenomenological and existential contexts here, we will see it is rather bemusing how it could have gone relatively unstudied for so long, cropping up in parts of our human realities and irrealities that one might not have even anticipated.

With this overarching trajectory in mind, there are three main steps to this piece. I will open with Husserl and his phenomenology of phantasy, and specifically how play might fit in there—not least in his notion of "eidetic variation." Second, after mentioning Fink's highly detailed analyses on his many explicit pages on the subject, I will focus on showing how play also essentially appears in his lesser-known work on perception and imagination ([1930] 1966), whereby he extends a Husserlian notion with relation to phantasy. The third main section will include Sartre's observations on play and link them to his theory of the imaginary, and ultimately show how he ontologizes the issue and thereby makes it existential, and even normative, as well. In this manner this phenomenological conception of phantasy will be essentially playful, and because of its centrality in our lives, it extends to many facets and elements of human (ir)reality too. With these points in mind, I will conclude with a discussion as to the interrelation and precedence between play and phantasy, particularly from a phenomenological and developmental standpoint, in order to show how play might actually precede phantasy, or at least be co-original and co-constituting.

Husserl

Husserl is quite well-known for many things, and in phenomenology circles he is still considered the unsurpassable "Master" by many. His writings were copious, although his lifetime publications rather sparse. The Husserl Archives in Leuven, Belgium, as well as elsewhere, are still working tirelessly on publishing his remaining works.

One thing Husserl is quite well-known for is "eidetic variation" and the ensuing "reduction." The former is the capacity our minds have to play with all kinds of objects (examples: table, unicorn, circle) in order to get to their "essence," or "*eidos*" following the ancient Greeks and particularly Plato's Theory of Forms or Ideas. Phantasy, or our capacity to imagine—and more specifically our capacity to posit irrealities—is used for this. Here one can take any "object" (mental object in this case—for example, a table, a unicorn, a circle) and play around with it, take things away, add things on, and see if it still remains the same thing. If you take something away and it stops being that thing (the legs of a table, the horn of the unicorn, the curvatureof the circle), then you have an essential property of that object. Essences are conditions sine qua non of the objects they inhere in, and the playful phantasy of eidetic variation is how we get there.

For Husserl, and especially the earlier Husserl (e.g., HUA IX), phenomenology was all about essences, capturing them and describing them, and showing how they all interrelate and interconnect. The capacity for this Husserl precisely called "phantasy," which has an inherently and essential playful element in that it necessarily involves the capacity to manipulate and change objects with one's mind. There is a great freedom to this, and yet it is also anchored in hard Husserlian phenomenological method and rules, as it is all held together by the truth and logic of the Ideas and phenomenological laws as well.

Elements of all of this are not particularly new or novel. I have just mentioned Plato, and empiricists like Hume ([1739] 2000) already well noted the amazingly adaptable and plastic capacity of the imagination and its ideas. However, Husserl elsewhere went on (HUA XXIII) to systematize and categorize this type of imagination quite painstakingly in contrast to many others—most notably memory, visualization, foresight, and empathy, which all fall under the category of "presentification" (*Vergegenwärtigung*), or imagination in the broad sense for him. Add to this "image-consciousness" (*Bildbewusstsein*), and you have the full collection of imagination capacities in Husserl. Whereas the four aforementioned forms of presentification (memory, visualization, foresight, and empathy) involve real, probable, or possible elements of the past, present, future, and other minds respectively, and whereas "image-consciousness" necessarily has a physical component such as a photograph, painting, or in today's day and age a digital screen (see also Richir 2011), phantasy with a "ph-" (or "fantasy" we might say in English here) is the quintessentially playful type of imagination in Husserl, with playfulness, frivolity, and yes even freedom of creation being among its delineating (and thereby essential) characteristics.

I have written about these issues at quite some length elsewhere (O'Shiel 2022: 15–22); suffice it here to repeat that "phantasy" with a "ph-" is a technical term of delineation for a narrow conception of imagination which necessarily has to do with irrealities and idealities, that is, things that do not exist in perception and reality. A table may well exist in reality, but my image of it is an irreality. Unicorns have never (yet) been perceived by anyone, and might never be. And we might all be aware there is no such thing as a "perfect circle" in perception, which is why these mental objects are often given the name of ideality—they only exist through our ideal conceptions, toward which phantasy is a crucial bridge.

Phantasy as play thus has a serious and significant role in Husserl's own phenomenological method, for eidetic variation would not be possible without it. One could even say that the playful fiber to phantasy is essential to eidetic variation. What is more, on top of phantasy being delineated through its realm of irrealities and idealities, the playful tenor to it is also a demarcating and highly significant characteristic, for without it our whole world of fiction, art, and creation would be scarcely possible either. It is thus a massive realm of human thought, experience, and activity, and it is something Fink builds upon in his own studies on the matter.

Fink

Historically Eugen Fink has been largely known to have been a devoted understudy to Husserl, both during the latter's life and after, with Landgrebe, Husserl's wife Malvine, and a young Master's student from Leuven called Mercier; they were responsible for rescuing Husserl's corpus from the Nazis and were instrumental in deciphering Husserl's texts (few could read Husserl's personalized Gabelsburger shorthand), getting them to storage and publication, and passing on knowledge which is still a process continuing today.

In recent years, however, Fink is coming to be known as quite a formidable philosopher and phenomenologist in his own right. Nowhere is this more evident than among his writings on play which, as already mentioned, has been an understudied philosophical topic, and one Husserl did not engage with to the level or complexity Fink did. For what Husserl has said on play itself, there is a general consensus in this edition that his idea was always thought of in more instrumental terms, with play always having a goal. Fink's idea, to the contrary, includes more of a liberation and could even be seen as subversive at times, whereby play can often precisely be when control, and thereby any real goals or aims, is also completely relinquished. What is more, toward later writings play becomes more cosmological for Fink, and thereby comes away from perception and even phenomenology, and thus beyond the latter somewhat (see Moore in this volume).

I will focus here on the earlier Finkian breeds of play specifically in reference to what has already been outlined with regard to Husserl, namely play's inherent relation to certain capacities to imagine, and ultimately the two as quite elemental conditions of possibility for each other.

First of all, to set the scene and at least begin with *Play as Symbol of the World and Other Writings* (Fink 2016), play (*der Spiel*) is often indeed seen as integral to many facets of our existence and experience, from basic ontology, metaphysics, and philosophy to the realms of fiction, myth, and culture. Holding a lot of this together is, though, a familiar Husserlian trope that brings it right back into the realm of phantasy and actually couples the latter with play quite strongly. Fink highlights (id.: 88–89) play's quite obvious "inactuality," "non-seriousness," and "acting as if." These are all essential characteristics of phantasy too and are described as such in a lesser-known work by Fink in the English-speaking world. In section 20 of "Presentification and Image" [1930] (1966), Fink provides a succinct but detailed account of his own Husserlian conception of phantasy. What is more, he goes further in making distinctions between "localized phantasies" which transform and "transfictionalize" elements of the real world—perhaps a child's game with a stick ("Bang! Bang!") a good example—and those "purer phantasies" where the physical world is left largely behind. With purer phantasy comes purer possibility and, in a way, pure play too, a bit like we have already seen with Husserl. However, with Fink there is also an emphasis not just on our thoughts and images of tables, triangles, unicorns, and the like but actually on the whole perceptible and perceivable world too. This inherent capacity to "irrealize" reality, as we will see with Sartre, is already present in Fink's idea of localized phantasy therefore—it allows for activities and phenomena like perceptual play one has in sport for instance, but also our long-standing human culture of seeing whole worlds, images, and symbols in the natural world and its things, as well as creating plethoras of cultural artifacts for similar and other purposes. Indeed, this capacity for treating as-if and not the precise same (identity) allows the image to be born in the first place, because both Husserl and Fink recognized that images necessarily have to have a similarity (*Gleichnis*) to something while at the same time not being absolutely identical to that thing (it would simply be it), nor too different (it would no longer be recognized).

It is only a step from there to see how this type of phantasy, along with purer elevations, then allows for our playful creativity itself, which must be a main mental and phenomenological wellspring for that most human of endeavors, artifice, and industry, from works of art to technological innovations. In this manner, play and phantasy go hand in hand for opening up a gap and slither of possibility, irreality, and creation into many things, and thereby allow us to transcend, control, and manipulate immediate perceptual realities in myriads of ways, from playing games, to artistic creation, to industry and artifice, and then up to more wholly mental forms of image contemplation and reflection, of which Husserl's eidetic variation is already a pinnacle and signature type. This massive human realm moreover ranges from perceptive and affective materiality, all the way up to the more vaporized and abstruse; in essence it is the realm of creation and captivation, and again can be playful in the extreme.

With these considerations in mind, I do not think it is too helpful to read Fink's text as marking a strict line between localized and "pure" phantasies, for indeed every phantasy would pick up elements we have experienced in one way or another, not least in perception (e.g., horse + horn = unicorn). No, it is rather the insight that phantasy is our inherent and absolutely crucial capacity to irrealize and transform, and were it not for this capacity play perhaps would not even surface beyond a rather unreflective instinct. Indeed, the as-if and "pretend" nature of play, even though it can still be serious and significant (e.g. professional sport), are absolutely essential elements for it, just like all kinds of Finkian phantasy, from localized and concrete to the more ethereal. What is more, it seems phantasy, and our ability to irrealize, turns out to be a transcendental condition for play in all its forms; a stick would remain only a stick without it, but with phantasy and its playful fibers, it can be a gun, a wand, a spear, and so on—the options are quite endless!

A question remains here: whether there is an original instinct or drive for play that might open up the realm of irreality and phantasy in general, and thus it is perhaps play that is the transcendental condition for phantasy, or at least it is co-constituting and co-original. I will address this in the final remarks; for now we need to complete the phenomenological picture of the key relation between the two, something which Sartre does quite adeptly.

Sartre

Sartre takes this topic of irrealization and the captivation of phantasy and play even further, with a dedicated 1940 work on *The Imaginary* ([1940] 2004), and then an ontologization and existentialization of the topics in *Being and Nothingness* ([1943] 2005) three years later. In fact, the more I read Fink, the more I am convinced Sartre must have come across some of his writings, or at least heard of some of his ideas, when in Berlin in the mid-1930s. Whether this was the case or not, Fink's work on presentification and image can nonetheless be seen as a key conceptual lynchpin and bridge between Husserl and Sartre.

Sartre was also at this time steeped in the phenomenological tradition and brimming with concepts from Husserl and Heidegger. Indeed, with regard to perception, Sartre remains Husserlian in *L'imaginaire*, but he also pushes the logic of the imaginary to its limits. Here, the imaginary is different to Husserl and Fink because he does not use the German umbrella term "presentification" (*Vergegenwärtigung*), so activities like memory or empathy are not included, and there is a focus on more standard and commonsense cases of "imagining," plus physical images. When it comes to "phantasy" (*Phantasie*) though, another German term Sartre does not use, generally Sartre's understanding maps quite well onto Husserl and Fink's understanding, and ultimately all three can be defined as our capacity to irrealize reality. This is indeed already Sartrean language, and what is more, in his conclusion to the work, he discusses the metaphysics, and in fact states that reality is only ever cognized as real because it is always already set in contradistinction to our phantasies and their irrealitites. This ultimately means we are essentially dual beings, and it is in our nature to be able to experience objects in both a real and irreal manner, often the same or similar objects. In a nutshell, then, in the actual world I perceive whole hosts of objects—"things"—which do not depend on my conscious being; our creations of phantasy, however—imaginary objects—do absolutely. A chair in the room has no need of me in order to keep on existing; the pink throne-chair in my mind (or a more drab real-life copy) right now is nothing without my consciousness positing and experiencing it. Perception and imagination, perception and image, are thus two absolutely fundamental and interrelated modes of human consciousness, necessarily constituting both real and irreal domains in intriguing and complex dynamics that are both opposed and interrelated.

Imaginary objects can replicate real ones (e.g., a chair), or they can be quite fantastical (e.g., a centaur). With this in mind, it should be obvious that the playful nature is again carried over in its fibers. Already in *The Imaginary*, Sartre goes so far as to say that many people even prefer (largely) imaginary lives. The life of mental pathology (e.g., a psychosis) would be one more negative example, but the life of an artist would usually be a more positive one, although the two instances are of course not mutually exclusive. What is more, in today's digital age, this even extends to the physical imaginary, namely our digital screens (O'Shiel 2022), as many already seem to prefer to exist mainly online and through virtual wavelengths (in games, on social media) than in their everyday and confined here and now. In all of this, infinite combinations of real and irreal still always persist, at least for now.

In a last main step, the playful nature of the imaginary is extended and sedimented into our existential and ontological makeup in Sartre's main "phenomenological ontology" three years later, *Being and Nothingness* (1943). Indeed, Sartre is a philosopher of dynamic poles, and one main pole referenced throughout this large work is the "spirit of seriousness" set in opposition to the "spirit of play." The former is more on the side of brute being-in-itself, the laws of physics and matter, and the facts and events which stem therefrom. The main human field of investigation here is now known as science, and to do this properly, one needs to largely strip away any creative or fanciful ideas and stick to observations, facts, hypotheses, tests, and verifications. On the other side is the spirit of play, which is, quite logically, the inverse, and is the realm of creation and freedom—of doing what one likes, sometimes in a structured and rather serious manner (e.g., professional sport or child's play), and oftentimes much more frivolous and even reckless or subversive. The imaginary in its playful guise comes to the fore here. In the spirit of seriousness the imaginary and even play can be significant factors (think of scientific modelling or thinking through a problem with images); but it is on the side of play where the imaginary is unleashed without restriction and really lends itself to our innate Sartrean freedom, which is also something that was presaged in Fink's extended concept of phantasy as libertarian as well.

In these dynamics, Sartre's concept of bad faith claims that dwelling overly in either extreme—in either facts or freedom, seriousness or play—can lead to issues, like the obsessed scientist who cannot even laugh or the entranced artist who cannot even deal with any practicalities of their daily life. These might be caricatures but they do exist; and whichever mixture one lives at any moment, one sees here how play and the imaginary pervade our whole lives, from thinking through serious problems on the one side to pure creations and enjoyments on the other. Play and the imaginary in Sartre, just like play and phantasy in Husserl and Fink, are thus bound together, with the latter even a precondition for the former. And in Sartre, it's not just in a phenomenological manner but is ultimately extended into our existential and ontological fibers—and thereby originate there too.

Final Remarks

I have suggested more than once that our capacity for phantasy or the imaginary is a necessary precondition for our capacity for play. What, perhaps, if it were the reverse? It does seem that play needs an ability to cognize something as-if, not really, and thereby a more general gap between what actually is and what can or might not necessarily be. This is precisely what the imaginary provides at its core and roots. There is, however, a case to suggest that maybe play instigates this in the first place. Looking to human animals, and more generally to many and especially social mammals, play seems to be an absolutely essential and original instinct, namely something which we cannot not do (see: O'Shiel 2013). In the natural world young play has crucial developmental and survival reasons; one establishes comrades and hierarchy, one trains for inevitable conflicts, and one also just gets to have some fun. Indeed, in the human variation it seems little different, with a young human child as predisposed to play as a young lion cub, wolf, monkey, or other creature.

There is thus undoubtedly an original drive to play in us. However, one could say almost the same with imagination and phantasy too. Indeed, it seems in their development children actually have to learn reality as they grow up and bump into things, both metaphorically and literally. Freud uses the term "reality principle" in a different context ([1920] 2003); here I think it works quite well in contradistinction to phantasy and the imaginary too. In this manner, the imaginary would be as primordial as play, and could even be more explicitly dominant in a good portion of the early lives of human children than even perception, as they do more often than not seem to be in their "own little worlds."

Developmentally then, human play and phantasy ultimately seem as fundamentally co-constituting of each other. Indeed, in any usual chick-and-egg scenario the safest bet is usually a bit of both. This would even reinforce the idea of a quite essential link between the two, as has been presented here, because they grow up together and are thus co-original, and this is precisely why they are so developmentally and phenomenologically intertwined and interdependent. In this manner, if one looks to the prism of phantasy first, one would see play as an offshoot; and if one looks to the prism of play one might then see phantasy as an important but secondary component. In ultimate reality though, along with perception and reality, phantasy and irreality are just as significant and primordial, and play grows up in, amongst and around these dynamics and modes of human consciousness as well.

10

Fink and Plotinus on Play

Emile Alexandrov

Introduction

Play as a subject matter of philosophical inquiry was already present in the German tradition before Fink, perhaps most notably in Kant and Schiller. Fink, however, made play central to his philosophical project; play is the problem of thinking. This came with a particular reading of the history of philosophy common in German philosophy. This reading considers the philosophy of Plato and Aristotle as shifting away from the free-play of thinking seen in Heraclitus and the pre-Socratics more generally. This chapter rethinks this reading to show that Fink's play converges with Platonist thought at salient points. This is especially prominent in Plotinus. On a fundamental level, play thinking is built into Plotinian cosmology in a way that resembles Fink's world-play. However, in postulating anagogic thinking of beauty or contemplating "beyond play," Platonist thought diverges from Fink, who saw that any hierarchical thinking of beauty impedes play based on self-imposed restrictions. I show Plotinus' play thinking is a product of his cosmological binding of contemplation and flux; that is, play itself symbolizes the path to hierarchical thinking of beauty. Despite this difference, I argue Fink and Plotinus are consistent.

Play as the Philosophical Problem

In PSW Fink questioned whether play is a topic worthy of philosophical investigation. In posing this question, Fink distinguished between thinking and play as two modes of life. The challenge here is to find compatibility between the former as the "business of abstract thinking and its gloomy seriousness," and the latter as that which "delights in the senses and without qualms mixes the actual and the fantastical." This is a problematic association since play is free from careful examination and forethought (Fink 2016: 35). In other words, Fink sought to interrogate the fundamentally unquestionable or potentially pre-questionable mode of life. Play represents the pre-conceptual grasp of the world before it emerges as a world. We have play only when we find ourselves in the world before conceptualization and amid the most rudimentary forms of understanding. Understanding play, nevertheless, remains the chief task of thinking (Fink 2016: 36). The challenge is, therefore, the philosophical comprehension of one's world-embeddedness before systematic thinking. This is even more warranted since philosophy has hitherto been under the guiding influence of Plato, Aristotle, and the Stoics, who founded various philosophical disciplines that obscure this immanent stance (Fink 2016: 37).

As such, philosophy has restricted the innermost recesses of Being, adding further difficulty to understanding play. Before this philosophical "awakening," however, a mythical-religious disposition accepted "without question the hierarchy of the mythical interpretation of the world" (Fink 2016: 37). This play-predisposition exhibited the human being's dependence on world; the limitations, possibilities, and commonalities among beings.[1] Following the later development philosophy, human beings no longer accept these worldly factors of play as most worthy of reverence. Ultimately for Fink, the historical trajectory of philosophical thinking hitherto covers over the constitution of the world and play.[2]

Despite metaphysics appearing to eliminate all hierarchical differentiation of beings, metaphysics still determines the Being of beings according to their "proper degrees" (Fink 2016: 38). In determining metaphysics as an unprecedented historical event, Fink echoes a Heideggerian reading of history.[3] Like Heidegger, Fink associated Plato with the historical shift from play to theological-hierarchical philosophy since the imposition of a philosophy of the Good impedes play-thinking. Platonic philosophy thereon enabled one standardized mode of questioning to predominate (Fink 2016: 61). So the rise of Platonism coincides with the institution of divine absolute truth into philosophy for the first time in history. Truth and world are suffused together, and the absolute truth of the divine thus far constricts play.

For Fink, the human being is guided by the theology of metaphysics that disguises world-play and has become the "world-problem" (Fink 2016: 64–5). Plato's battle with the poets is symptomatic of world-problem, which resulted in the historical denigration of poetry into derivative appearance; "we are all held under the spell of the Platonic interpretation. We must free ourselves from this spell" (Fink 2016: 88).[4] Platonist metaphysics rigidified a particular world that manufactures afterimages based on the absoluteness of the idea. All metaphorical characterizations of Platonism remain bound to the world of shadows that Plato constructed (Fink 2016: 94).

Fink did see that there was more to Plato's writings than just an artful style. Plato essentially appropriated the manic inspiration of the poets into philosophy to demonstrate the "true mania." In other words, for Plato, philosophy is what poetry claimed to be (Fink 2016: 98). Fink's position can be supported by Plato's praise of the inspired Bacchants who practiced "philosophy in the right way [πεφιλοσοφηκότες ὀρθῶς]" (Phaedo, 69d). In Fink's understanding, Plato affirmed poetry's enrapture with beauty, albeit under the aegis of philosophy. However, the danger is that poetry for Plato does not understand itself as a "prefiguration of philosophy and as able to be superseded by it" (Fink 2016: 98–9). Thus, Plato's philosophy represents a passionate struggle against play in the "wisdom of the mysteries and tragedy, against the poets" (Fink 2016: 98). The unbridled freedom of play is hereby closed off by Plato's metaphysical certainty that "is essentially good, without weaknesses and wretched human features, is unchangeable, constant, continuously identical in his very self." Hence, the idea is "the true god" for Plato (Fink 2016: 99). So in our historical advancement of Platonism, we remain bound to the mirror-image of Plato's shadows (Fink 2016: 104).

Plato's philosophy represents the inaugural event of metaphysics, introducing a dimension of non-actuality (Fink 2016: 93). Despite being influenced by Heraclitus and Parmenides, Plato blended Being and nothing since he could not stick with the Eleatic separating of Being and nothing. Plato could not withstand the obscurity of "the nothing," so freedom to think-play is impeded. Plato's blend instead discloses the perpetual transitionary nature of beings to be participatory in the higher and stronger Being of the ideas. Plato implanted the dichotomous worldview into the history of philosophy that secured a world and restricted play in a move toward a playless world.

Returning to Play

The rise of metaphysics is thus correlated with the neglect of the awe and mystery of world. For Fink, play represents the return to the mystery and back "to the gleam of the beautiful over all wordly things" (Fink 2016: 36). However, philosophy must first seek to understand the "indwelling" of our world (Fink 2016: 36). Play must be investigated despite philosophical speculation's opposition. This involves understanding play not as a firm concept or idea, not even as a problem in its character. Play cannot be an individual philosophical discipline as commonly understood (Fink 2016: 52). Thinking-play represents something more primordial; it is a grasping of the human being's "world-position" under the guidance of a "specific understanding of play" (Fink 2016: 54). To think-play, one *must play*, so understanding play is incumbent upon being immersed in a particular play.

Being guided by play also means that one cannot remain bound to one particular understanding; play-thinking remains ever-changing, for there is a transient nature to play-thinking the world. The starting point is always a "zero-point"; every encounter with beings is subject to change, which perpetually impacts the starting point. In this sense, play-thinking represents the continual perspectival shift where space itself becomes "homogeneous." Thus, one's contemplative starting point within play will determine the worldly relations to beings (Fink 2016: 55). Hence, Fink considered play-thinking to be liberated thinking although it is also pre-philosophical, for the starting point is determined by that which captures one's attention—be it "power, beauty, or the like" (Fink 2016: 55). Once this has been ascertained, one can then play-think (Fink 2016: 55). As such, the preceding activity of building a hierarchy of beings concurrently with a "pre-projected measure" only to each time reset and begin anew can be achieved.

This demonstrates Fink's understanding of the obscurity behind Heraclitus' writings; "the connection with play was the essential thought, under whose guidance and escort we sought to set our own stammering reflections in motion" (Fink 2016: 57).[5] Fink saw Heraclitus as the figure who preceded the theological orientation of metaphysics that later inhibited play (Alvis 2019: 97). Fink also agrees with Heidegger here that theology has no place within philosophy. That theology was nonetheless a part of philosophy from Aristotle to Hegel shows the "entire metaphysical tradition was determined by the suppression of the world-problem" (Fink 2016: 145).

Since Heraclitus precedes this theological imposition, the entire history of Western philosophy can "be written as a commentary on this thirty-second fragment of Heraclitus" (Fink 2016: 57–8).[6] Heraclitus showed that all succeeding philosophies were guided by a theological disposition irrespective of how radical they may appear. The world is always prefixed and bound by its theological constitution, whereas in Heraclitus, the gods are also subjected to play, and Fink also identifies this condition of the gods in Plato's *Laws*; the gods are intrinsic to the human-world-relation. Heraclitus represents the pre-metaphysical age that showed us that philosophy could never fully comprehend play.

Philosophy must instead recognize its guidance by play and always account for an irretrievable reserve in every apprehension of Being. Every contemplative scenario should begin anew since one's comportment to the world is always subject to change; play is an "essential element of man's ontological makeup, a basic existential phenomenon" (Fink 1968: 19). Despite this, play cannot be investigated from other existential phenomena, nor can we contrast play with other phenomena, for play is "existence centred in itself" (Fink 1968: 20). Play always confronts Being in its inextricability to the world-totality; each "game is an attempt at existence" (Fink 1968: 23, 43). Play-thinking decenters the subject and allows limitless creativity and freedom (Fink 1968: 24–5). This unrestrained freedom can also risk the "dark Dionysian moment of panic self-abandon," and so there comes a price with abandoning the contemplative refuge. This risk is mandatory nonetheless and was taken by all the great philosophers from Hegel to Nietzsche. So to play-think is to liberate thinking, overcome the history of metaphysics, and delve into the play-world, a "realm whose reality is open to question" (Fink 1968: 25). In so doing, Platonic ontology that has determined Western philosophy to operate within the "concept of the copy as a shadow and a reflection to interpret the structure of the world" can be overcome (Fink 1968: 27–8).

Platonism and Play

The view that Platonism represents a monumental shift in the history of philosophy is standard within the German philosophical tradition and can perhaps be seen culminating in Nietzsche and Heidegger (Most 2002: 91–7).[7] Despite not unfolding a pre-metaphysical ontology of play, for Fink, Heraclitus was the pre-metaphysical thinker par excellence (Fink 2016: 93). This is evident in Heraclitus' writings, which are fundamentally distinct from the writings of Plato. While Plato was restricted by his commitment to the ἰδέα, Heraclitus remained uncommitted to any divine principle or otherwise. This allowed Heraclitus to employ his "cosmic metaphor of unbelievable boldness" (Fink 2016: 93). This all changes in Plato, and we see the beginnings of the process of grounding of metaphysics, which led to the closure of the problem of world. Plato effectively inaugurated the God of metaphysics that disguises the world (Fink 2016: 64, 93). Fink saw this historical trajectory reaching Kant, who suppressed the play of consciousness and object (Heidegger and Fink 1979: 126).[8]

Fink's play, however, coincides with Plotinus' cosmology in a manner that warrants a rethinking of his Platonism. As Huizinga reminds us, the "comparison of life to a stage" is little more than an echo of Neoplatonism (Huizinga 1980: 5).[9] In *On Providence*, Plotinus described this stage as child play irrespective of an individual's world position (Ennead 3, (47): §3.2.15: [47–62]). Plotinus' description of the "outer shadow of a human being that wails" corresponds to Fink's "innerworldly process" of the human being that "never fully penetrates the Being of beings" (Fink 2016: 201–2). Plotinus' play represents the embodied soul's inherence to the world of multiplicity. Embodiment is the "outer shadow" of the soul that subsists within an infinitely fragmented world that cannot be comprehended in its totality. Excluding the soul, Fink likewise affirmed the limitations of one's particular world-comportment: that the whole cannot be known from the perspective of one's innerworldliness. Hence Fink considered it necessary to always allow for the perpetual renewal of play in the human being's comportment to Being (Fink 2016: 202). In other words, for both Plotinus and Fink, total comprehension of Being is not possible for the previous, at least initially. Whereas Fink remained bound by the perpetual renewal of play, Plotinus understood this as symbolizing the potentiality for higher levels of contemplation.

In Plotinus' view, regardless of theological or philosophical commitments, we remain "playthings [Σπουδάζεται]." Regarding the idea of plaything, Plotinus described Socrates joining "the game" as the Platonic play of the "outer Socrates." For Plotinus, Plato orchestrated Socrates' play through various roles, be it as a defendant at the Athenian court, a guest at Agathon's dinner party, a prisoner in an Athenian cell, and so on.[10] The dialogues are intended to reflect the flux of Plato's cosmological worldview. As such, they are subject to change depending on Plato's setting, a feature that other Neoplatonists, such as Proclus, expanded upon at length (Republic Commentary V1: [6].1–5). This shows that there can be no escaping play for Plato regardless of metaphysical presupposition, whether theological or otherwise.

In Plotinus the embodied soul is subject to the play of the cosmos since the cosmos is intrinsically playful, a Heraclitean insight that Plotinus uniformly adopts (Ennead 4, (6): §4.8.1: [11–17]).[11] Plotinus recognized that Plato's dialogues were fancifully constructed with this in mind: the dialectical process must adapt to the flux of the sensible world while accommodating the purity of the intellect (Ennead 3, (47): §1.3.5: [3–7]). This corresponds to Plato's Heracliteanism, which Aristotle claimed Plato adopted from an early age—that the world is in an ever-present state of flux (Metaphysics, [6].987a29-987b1). As scholars have pointed out, "flow and flux are in play in necessity" and form the backdrop of Plato's cosmological outlook (Mason 2016 127–9). Plotinus saw that both Plato and Aristotle had accepted this Heraclitean view (Ennead 2, (40): §2.1.2: [1–18]). This relates to Socrates' claim that Heraclitus had invoked insights from the days of Cronus and Rhea (Cratylus, 402a-d). This is likely why Plotinus asserted that Plato relied on views more ancient than his own (Ennead 5 (10), §5.1.8: [10–14]).

The Plotinian Cosmology of Play

In *On the Cosmos*, Plotinus repeatedly asserted that the cosmos is in a perpetual state of change (Ennead 2, (40): §2.1.1: [25–30], [5–10], §2.1.3: [1–5], §2.1.6: [1–7]). While this appears consistent with Fink's Heraclitean influence, there are important distinctions. For Plotinus, flux is the "contributing factor to the immortality of the cosmos" (Ennead 2, (40): §2.1.3: [1–5]). In being bound to the cosmos, then, the human being is naturally in play; "a body is always fleeing and in flux [ὑπεκφεύγοντος καὶ ῥέοντος]" (Ennead 2, (40): §2.1.1: [9–10]). Additionally, contemplation is central to the *Enneads* since Plotinus saw the cosmos as being inherently contemplative: "That everything, then, comes from contemplation and is contemplation [θεωρίας καὶ θεωρία]" (Ennead 3 (30): §3.8.7: [1–4]). Thus, flux and contemplation are inextricably bound to one another in such a way that thinking must always accommodate the flux of the cosmos. Whereas Fink sought to cement play as a genuine philosophical problem, it is already Plotinus's unavoidable ground of contemplation. Hence "tears and lamentation" should not be taken as evils, for such events are demonstrative of flux. Considering that contemplation is naturally coextensive with flux, evils and goods only appear as such depending on the human being's world comportment.

Again, Plotinus understood play qua flux as the fundamental ground of thinking, and one always begins by play-thinking on the way to understanding (νόησις). Understanding, however, represents Plotinus' principal divergence from Fink since it symbolizes thinking "beyond the game."[12] This anagogic (ἀναγώγια) feature of contemplation is central to the Platonist cosmic order and built into the framework of the *Enneads*. Fink, in contrast, saw that all ontological hierarchies represent a particular fixed position that exclusively determines the intraworldly relation between beings (Fink 2016: 56). As covered earlier, for Fink, all hierarchies, such as power and beauty, are always interpreted from within a particular relation to Being. The problem for Fink is that instead of being prioritized and understood as the central determinator of a way of thinking, the postulation of anagogic thinking makes play subjacent. While Plotinus and Fink are consistent regarding the starting point of thinking, the Plotinian philosopher holds the capability to think beyond flux. Philosophers are an intrinsic part of Plotinus' cosmological order. This is likened to a theatrical production, where Plotinus noted that the inferior characters also contribute to the "completeness" of the play itself, for contemplation is stratified in nature (Ennead 3, (47): §3.2.11: [5–15]).

The philosopher's pre-eminence is in recognizing beauty as symbolic of the hierarchical nature of contemplation. The philosopher undertakes the anagogic path of contemplation through beauty which is the divine that extends before all things (Ennead 3, (47): §3.2.13: [13–25]). In pursuing beauty, the philosopher is engaged in anagogic thinking that moves to overcome play. The philosopher here contemplates beauty without being swayed by nature's empirical manifestations (Vassilopoulou 2021: 121). Pace Fink, this higher thinking cannot be determined by constancy in time or rationality, fixed position, or metaphysics: "The ordering of the universe comes about through Intellect in such a way that it is done without calculative reasoning [ἄνευ λογισμοῦ]" (Ennead 3, (47), §3.2.14: [1–7]). That understanding stands at the apex of the cosmic order and is beyond calculation is consistent throughout the *Enneads*, for example, "meta-calculative [ἐπιλογισμός]" (Ennead 1 (20), §1.3.6: [8–15]) or rather "prior to calculative reasoning [πρὸ λογισμοῦ]" (Ennead 5 (31), §5.8.6: [16–20]). Moreover, in the Platonist tradition, beauty holds the unique power to reveal the potentiality for nonconceptual thinking amid the cosmological flux, and it is here that Plotinus thought dialectics was critical.

For Plotinus, dialectics adapts to the flux of the cosmos by grappling with what is good and not good, between beings, non-beings, and that which is different from beings (Ennead 1 (20), §1.3.4: [1–9]). It is the philosopher who can utilize this capacity to journey upward toward Beauty itself (Ennead 1 (20), §1.3.3: [1–5]). Plotinus is heretofore making the case that beauty as intrinsic to the natural order of the cosmos must be dialectically apprehended. The philosopher who is "winged" by nature recognizes beauty inherent to the cosmos and, after having been made a "complete dialectician," is transported in "the upward direction" (Ennead 1 (20), §1.3.3: [1–10]). To be sure, Fink recognized this Platonist imperative, although he saw a "seductive daemonic power" to beauty that can oppose thinking and lead it astray. The additional problem with Plato's beauty is that it is ultimately pulled by education παιδεία toward the "true Being of the idea" (Fink 2016: 115–16).

While education is indeed stated as the goal of understanding at the start of book VII in the *Republic* (514a), in the preceding book VI, understanding (νόησις) is also described as unhypothetical ἀρχὴν ἀνυπόθετον; it concludes "without making use of anything visible at all [αἰσθητῷ παντάπασιν οὐδενὶ προσχρώμενος]" (511b-c). This unhypothetical principle is Plato's inconceivable beauty; it "provides both knowledge and truth and is superior to them in beauty [ὑπὲρ ταῦτα κάλλει ἐστίν]," for it is beyond being ἐπέκεινα τῆς οὐσίας (Republic, 509a-b). Scholars have shown this to be the Parmenidean influence on Plato's robust "anti-empiricist epistemology," which he projected in the context of the revelation of Being (Palmer 2002: 17–20).[13] Commensurate with Plato, Plotinus described beauty as not desirable by shape or figure; rather, it is immeasurably "beautiful in a different way, and is beauty beyond beauty [κάλλος ὑπὲρ κάλλος]." There is no "idea" presented; instead, the "productive power of everything, then, is the flower of beauty, a beauty that produces beauty" (Ennead 6 (38), §6.7.32: [25–32]).

It is worth noting that beauty playing an integral role in play was already a part of the German philosophical heritage that Fink had inherited, especially in Schiller and Kant. In his *Ästhetische Briefe*, Schiller saw beauty as not extended over the whole realm of living things nor confined to this realm. Similarly, in Kant's understanding, beauty is presented in a "free harmony" which is nonconceptually appreciated while also being a symbol of morality (Kant 2008: 225–8) (Rogerson 2008: 67). While agreeing with Kant regarding beauty and its relation to morality, Schiller saw more to beauty than pleasure and morality. For Schiller, there is an objective principle in beauty that he, in contrast to Kant, had assigned to practical reason.[14] This beauty requires a reciprocal action—the play impulse between form and matter (Schiller 1954: 70). Hence why beauty, as the intermediary between form and matter, is always in play: "Man shall only play with Beauty, and he shall play only with Beauty" (Schiller 1954: 73–82). Schiller and Huizinga appear more amicable to the Platonist conception of beauty than Fink.[15]

This marks the principal distinction between Plotinus and Fink's rejection of any thinking beyond the world of play. For Fink, all pre-philosophical relations to beauty depict the intraworldly character of a particular world position (Fink 2016: 56). For Plotinus, in contrast, one's marveling at beauty symbolizes the dialectical path to higher contemplation beyond play (Ennead 5, §5.8.8: [8–20]). However, this cannot be understood by those who fail to recognize the intelligible beauty (Ennead 5, §5.8.8: [15–25]). In other words, one must commit to the intelligible beauty in dialectics. In so doing, one can play-think beyond concepts to avoid being lost amid the great theatrical play of the cosmos like those who "do the kind of things they play at in war dances, they prove that every human concern is childlike" (Ennead 3 (47), §3.2.15: [33–35]). Dialectic adapts to the cosmological flux; it "contemplates reality as a whole, every single real being in its interconnection with everything else" (Vassilopoulou 2021: 127). The drawing power of beauty allows the dialectician like Socrates of the dialogues to think-play reciprocally with the flux of the cosmos.

Conclusion

Fink's philosophy of play appears somewhat distinct from contemporary philosophies based on concepts, perhaps even incongruent since at least the Enlightenment age of systems. Thus, Fink's play discloses an insightful problem: whether philosophy can be something other than a serious task of abstract thinking. Fink returned to the pre-Socratics, especially Heraclitus, whom he drew upon to affirm this possibility since play was lost after the inauguration of metaphysics by Plato and Aristotle. As I have shown, the idea of Plato's movement away from play must be reconsidered. Prominent figures of the twentieth century, such as Gadamer, Huizinga, and Derrida, have already shown the play inherent in Plato's writings. However, this chapter showed that this association harks back to Plotinus, who further advanced the play of Plato's dialectics. While Plotinus' play thinking was oriented toward overcoming thinking, it is nonetheless grounded in the inextricability of flux and contemplation. Hence, play-thinking is an inescapable cosmological precondition for Plotinus regardless of theological or philosophical commitments. Despite Plotinus' anagogic imperative, Plotinus and Fink are commensurate on this point. Ultimately, Fink's play draws us toward this comparative study, for it is after understanding his problem of play that we become compelled to turn to the play in Plato and Plotinus.

Part Three

Application to Philosophical Issues

11

Music and Ontological Experience

Fink's Importance for Our Understanding of Music

Goetz Richter

Music is unique in our life and seemingly omnipresent in our culture. For most of us, hardly a day passes without some musical experience—be it as minimal as the fleeting encounter with a song while we wait for the traffic lights to change. The mere realization of listening, of hearing something that seems other than information or a signal requiring our response to action, grants us the opportunity for wonder. Naturally, we can decide to ignore this opportunity and continue to rush on, or we can invite music into our lives. Doing so, we may keep a superficial distance, hearing music merely as delightful decoration. Alternatively, we can become intrigued and involved, perplexed whether music expresses being and intrigued how it discloses identity. We can become enchanted or intoxicated by music finding escape or refuge, using it as a therapy for our traumas and suffering. The diverse possibilities of music and the balance of our relationship to it depends on our intentionality. We must direct our attention actively to differentiate and listen.

We live with and through music in seemingly infinite ways. We move to music with orgiastic abandon or listen to it in silent contemplation. We play and dance as embodied expression of our being. We reach for music at the crucial moments of our life. We sing songs to our lovers and lullabies to our babies. We make music with minded bodies and we experience and play it in our embodied minds. We celebrate marriages, births, and initiations with music. We hearken to music at funerals, silent with anxiety about death, grieving loss and seeking solace in the realization of our ultimate, abysmal loneliness. Music is our most immediate *meditatio mortis*—the contemplation of our peculiar being which, in its finitude, reaches for the infinite. The temporal form of music shadows the ephemeral fleetingness of life. Perhaps, though, our transitory lives reflect a being bound by temporality for which music is the most truthful expression? While we contest the question whether only humans make music, we certainly feel that humans must do so.

Our capacity for "musicking" is a "principal marker of modern humanity" (Tomlinson 2015: 23). Cultural and technological developments have made it possible that all types of historically distinct and diverse kinds of music are available to us.

We hear and learn about the music of the Kaluli people (Kaden 1993: 19), who identify music with weeping birds that yearn to bring together worlds of existence and worlds beyond. The polyphonic masses of the Gothic masters still sound to us in the cathedrals of the twelfth century, as do Wagner's operas in Bayreuth. We listen with renewed perplexity to Beethoven's late string quartets in concert halls, are struck by the visceral frustration of rap music echoing through derelict housing estates or immerse ourselves in mystical abandon to sound art in a transformed water tower in the Australian outback. We can learn the *sitar*, the *erhu*, or the French Horn. We join the local choir or become mesmerized, perhaps annoyed, by the looped playing of *Sakura Sakura* in the local Japanese restaurant. Our involvement with music seems boundless, always available and essentially inevitable. Music seems to say something about us, our being and our world.

Given the infinite variety of musical experience and vast diversity of possible involvement, a desire to understand music appears a forbiddingly complex task. Which of the many *musics* are we going to privilege? What stance and approach to listening are we going to single out? To be sure, we can approach music in the manner of a musicologist or cultural historian. We would then reduce the complexity in line with the requirements of such disciplines, developing either a historical understanding of derivations and influences, interconnections and affinities or a learned understanding of form, notation, practice, and reception. Any such disciplinary ordering, however, would already need to commit to accepted theoretical pathways. It would reach for obvious and accepted methods of explanation and could hardly contemplate an intuition that perhaps the weeping songs of the Kaluli shares much with the *Adagio* of *Schubert's String Quintet in C major*.

Even a philosophical path of questioning that leaves behind disciplinary determinations and asks more fundamentally what music is, however, harbors dangers. Much of the philosophical discussion about music proceeds in accordance with cultural practice and thus remains trapped in metaphysical concepts. The philosophical consideration of music occurs in the subject matter of aesthetics. Making music the topic of aesthetics, however, may no longer allow us to reflect the *topos* or realm in which music, or the musical experience, occurs. A consideration of music as an "art" that properly belongs to the subject matter of aesthetics has already narrowed the view. Music is no longer a phenomenon—it already has been reified. Its "works" and "pieces" are coming into view and are considered through their creation, their structure or their reception. However, the phenomenon of music precedes any artform. The art of music presupposes the realization that sound can become music in the first instance. This realization requires a reopening of ourselves to the question of music in its most fundamental encounter, a clarification of the phenomenon in its phenomenality.

Music and musical experience only occur where tones are heard by those with ears to hear. Mere sequences of sound are not yet music. Music unfolds through playing, singing, and listening—intentional activities which, in their constitution, seem beyond our analytical reach. These abilities are constituted by a need and an ability to play, sing and listen that is integral to the human being. The listening which enables us to attend to music as music seems itself intimately connected to our own playing and singing. Music is performative in an essential way. It reflects the most intimate connection of our phenomenal immersion and human agency in the world. It reflects possibilities of our subjective consciousness and grants opportunities for objectifying reflection. It requires temporal forming and spatial sounding. It exposes human being as a being in a spatio-temporal world and it brings the ultimate reality of such a world into view. Music, in its most fundamental constitutions, discloses characteristics of human being as a being with world and as a being that challenges and even creates world.

Eugen Fink's Importance for Philosophy and Music

At this point, such observations require corroboration. They are vaguely speculative, yet they sketch a constellation of questions. What is music other than a cultural, historical, or anthropological phenomenon? What does the playing, singing, and listening to music say about the human being? What does music have to say to philosophy in its seemingly endless perplexity about the human being that finds itself and its world? These questions provoke curiosity. They may challenge us to voice objection. However, even if they do so, any answer will need to respect the fundamental disclosure that is already articulated in them. Reflection and analysis in themselves cannot answer the unease, the perplexity, and the wonder raised by our experience of music. Clever theoretical progress must ultimately respond adequately and sound out the experience of being, the ontological experience, that seeks to find its voice in us.

In the following I intend to open up these questions and in particular the question of music as ontological experience with reference to the philosophy of Eugen Fink. This is initially obvious, as the concept of "ontological experience" appears uniquely in Fink's discussions of Hegel and Nietzsche, yet, without any obvious reference to music. Furthermore, Fink has made no direct contributions to aesthetics[1] and has nothing to say about music directly. In that respect he resembles many philosophers, but most obviously Heidegger. Is the summon of Fink for this question a diversion or stunt?

The answer depends on how we view philosophy itself and how seriously we might take an intuition that music discloses being and world. Does a philosopher need to say anything about a topic to be relevant to a question? Clearly not, as the setting of a topic may narrow the possibilities of answers to the question. Requiring philosophers to contribute to topics and solve problems through expertise forgets that philosophy may be no subject matter in the first instance. Neither Fink nor Heidegger would in any case wish to be recruited to showcase the business of philosophy.

While there is irony in such assertions, the importance of Fink for the question of music is not determined by his ability to solve problems or answer questions in relation to music. What matters is how the thinking of this (or any other) philosopher discloses phenomena and uncovers a path of questioning! Opening up the phenomena of world and play will test our intuition of music as manifestation of ontological experience. The absence of a theoretical discussion about music seems an advantage here as we are not burdened by operational assumptions. This absence can assist us paradoxically in understanding music and musical experience more directly and fundamentally.[2]

The Conception and Articulation of Ontological Experience

Eugen Fink, student and collaborator of Edmund Husserl and Martin Heidegger, develops his thinking through critical response to Husserl's phenomenology and Heidegger's transformation of phenomenology through the question of Being. His own distinct philosophical voice also emerges through interpretations of Kant, Hegel, and Nietzsche. In this constellation of thinkers, Fink's own philosophical autonomy is not often easy to see, as he moves within the orbit of his teachers. It is at points of conceptual uniqueness, however, that we see Fink's individuality emerge. Fink seems particularly insistent about the philosophical importance of three phenomena: ontological experience, world, and play. All three phenomena are linked and seem centrally important to music.

The concept of ontological experience emerges in the context of a reflection on philosophy itself in general and in response to Hegel in particular. Philosophy is for Fink radically autonomous thinking.

> Without the effort of autonomous (*eigenen*) philosophising there is no path into philosophy. Philosophy is first and foremost thinking (*philosophieren*); not resulting knowledge, but a spiritual movement (*geistige Bewegung*). Every philosophical question leads to philosophy in its entirety, which has no subjects or disciplines, because it is itself no subject matter or discipline. (Fink 1985: 29)[3]

Important philosophers (like Hegel or Nietzsche) seek to articulate ontological thoughts (*Seinsgedanken*) (Fink 1977: 110). Hegel and Nietzsche are accordingly not merely metaphysicians or theoretical philosophers but give voice to a renewed ontological experience.

What is meant by ontological experience?

Fink's early discussions of Hegel introduce the concept of ontological experience as the "fundamental relation (*Grundbezug*) of Being and the human being, which enables and sustains all ontology" (Fink 1977: 80). In Hegel's case, the conception of Being as life, spirit and history achieves a "liquidation of determinations" (Fink 1977: 89) and opens our consciousness toward its own encounter with Being. Ontological experience thus brings to attention the fundamental ways in which being and truth disclose and manifest themselves. Ordinary knowledge "forgets Being and sticks in blind forgetfulness to the things (*das Seiende*)" (Fink 1977: 103). While we hear echoes of Heidegger's ontological difference here, the crucial point is how philosophy deals with—and responds to—such a realization and circumstance. Locating the source of thinking within experience challenges a movement toward traditional metaphysics and epistemology which operates in a ready way with a dualistic ontology of subject and object and objectifies thoughts and ideas. Traditional metaphysics traps itself in these dualities, including the—for Fink—central duality between human subject and world which also determines the more obvious duality of object and world. In the metaphysical context, world is taken to be a horizon and container of objects (*Dinge, Gegenstände*). The human subject is one of such objects distinct in its agency, intentional consciousness, and ability of reflection, however, nevertheless thing-like in a world. Turning away from ontological experience to metaphysical reflection and analysis leads to an operation with objects in a theoretically implied world. Against this, the awareness and attention to ontological experience, a direct experience of Being and its disclosure, enables philosophy to become attentive to its foundation. It renews its attention to the embeddedness of the subject in the world and the concurrent embeddedness of the world in the subject and returns to the origin or "home" of its dynamic thinking.

Ontological experience originates from "attunement" (*Stimmung*), which constitutes the foundation of philosophical thinking. We tend to obliterate it by reaching for ready metaphysical categories. However,

> philosophy is enabled through attunement (*Stimmung*); attunement is nearness of world. World is as the ultimately inconceivable (*Unausdenkliche*) home of thinking; the impulse to thinking is the distinction between world and thing. All things are "individuated" (*selbständig*) and yet they belong to world. (Fink 1977: 83/4)

The challenge for our thinking is to suspend a desire for categorization of ontological experience and allow it instead to find a voice in the thinker. Purely interpretatively, Fink's conception of ontological experience follows Hegel's identification of experience (*Erfahrung*) in the introduction to the *Phenomenology of Spirit* as a starting point for philosophy. It shares Hegelian characteristics by giving rise to speculation. For Hegel, the term "experience" refers to the "dialectic movement, which consciousness exercises in itself in relation to its knowledge and its object of knowledge (*Gegenstand*) in so far as this leads to the creation of the new, true object" (Hegel 1970: 78). The "dialectic movement" of consciousness realizes the nature of the object (*An-sich*) and its givenness or appearance to consciousness (*Für-sich*). This movement does not occur on the level of a mere reflection or abstraction. It constitutes itself as speculation[4]—the object of consciousness is no longer simply determined by analytic attention but by an attention to formations of consciousness (*Gestalten des Bewusstseins*). Transposing the Hegelian concept of experience, Fink seeks demarcations for his concept of ontological experience:

> The title ontological experience must in no way be measured in accordance with familiar or given forms of experience. Ontological experience is not a passive response (*hinnehmendes Verhalten*) analogical to the way in which we otherwise experience a being, a fact, an event, an occurrence . . . ontological experience is neither theoretical nor pre-theoretic experience. (Fink 1977: 72/3)

In addition, ontological experience constitutes itself in a turn away from the inevitable preoccupation with the reifying dimension of being, toward an attention to being itself. Ontological experience (*Seinserfahrung*) forms a "massive contrast" to the experience of beings as things (Fink 1977: 150).

Heidegger's ontological difference (between Being and ontic beings) does not remain the principal focus of Fink's conception of ontological experience. Rather, the focus on Being is replaced by a focus on world. As stated above, thinking emerges from the distinction between world and thing. World itself, however, remains elusive. It is reflected in its ontological constitution as play. This becomes important for Fink as play becomes the conceptual vessel to articulate ontological experience.

Fink develops his approach to the concept of world through the ontological difference between the world as the realm of beings (*Dingwelt*) and World itself which cannot be conceived as a thing and which evades our reifying conceptual grasp. Conceptually, Fink's approach to the question of world emerges through his discussion of Kant, "the metaphysical thinker who poses with the greatest determination the question of the World" (Fink 1990: 98). Kant's realization that the world as a totality can be thought but not imagined (Fink 1990: 39) imposes a particular relation of the human being to world. World is nothing that could become present for our intuition (*Anschauung*). Its formal determinations, space, and time are forms of intuition and this transformation of the concept of subjectivity implies that the human subject itself becomes the "opening of a world field"—the "ego opens up a realm, a field, a horizon. This sphere belongs to the essence of the subject" (Fink 1990: 73).

It is not the theoretical conception of world that is important here but its embeddedness in human being and its connection with experience. World is no object of our reflection or analysis—in fact world is no-thing. It determines our existence and it announces itself as the distinctive possibility of our subjectivity. Further determination of world seems only possible within metaphorical expression. Fink uses the image of flame and light to characterize a new conception of a worlded subjectivity as "the illuminating transcendence of all things" (Fink 1990: 74).[5] How this manifests itself in relation to music and philosophy becomes clearer in Fink's discussion of Nietzsche.

Nietzsche's Ontological Experience and the Importance of Music

Fink's reading of Nietzsche exposes layers which transform his philosophical response to the concept of ontological experience. Initially, Fink approaches Nietzsche's concept of the tragic as an attempt to articulate a fundamental ontological experience. "The tragic is Nietzsche's first fundamental formula for his ontological vision (*Seinserfahrung*)" (Fink 2003: 10). However, almost immediately the Nietzschean conception of art and tragedy transform into an experience of world, into a cosmological conception. The tragic not only is an ontological vision but becomes a cosmic essence.

> Nietzsche has a vision of the cosmos as tragic play. In his tragic vision of this cosmic essence, he refers to the tragic artwork as just that "key" that unlocks and opens up its true understanding. The aesthetic theory of the classical tragedy discloses in this way the essence of being in its entirety. (Fink 2003: 13)

The essence of this transformation is captured in Fink's insistence that we unravel the question of being by focusing on ontological experience provisionally through tragic play. The cosmos, world itself, however, ultimately becomes the focus of Nietzsche's thinking in Fink's reading, and Fink follows through on this path with the Nietzschean (and Heraclitean) conception of world as play.

Unreachable through conceptualization or analysis, the appropriate response to such ontological experience and world is the philosophical "attempt" (*Entwurf*). It is clear now that philosophy can merely attempt to search; however, ultimately such an attempt is set to fail and we will need to commence anew. In that prospect of failure, the temptation is high that we sidestep the experience and hand ourselves over to the conceptual safety of metaphysics. Metaphysics arrests the movement of the concept and we realize that the ontological experience cannot find its voice simply in its ready concepts. This is no indication that we must reject metaphysics as such. It just suggests that we must not allow metaphysics to obscure the dynamic of thinking and the significance of the questions that are embedded in ontological experience.

Fink resists evasive moves into metaphysics that leave the ontological experience behind and ignore its presence—this does not constitute a rejection or overcoming of metaphysics per se. He recognizes in Nietzsche a kindred philosophical spirit in this element of philosophy, that is, the ever-recurring need for renewal of our philosophical attempt as a result of the challenge to give voice to ontological experience. This makes Fink a unique and important interpreter of Nietzsche. It also shows that retreating "endlessly to starting points" (Moran 2007: 30) is in Fink's case no failure but a reflection of the nature of his thinking. Philosophy for Fink has a strongly performative, repetitive dimension reflecting the play-structure of world. The renewed questioning of concepts is not unique to Fink in any case: Nietzsche's philosophy with the hammer or Socrates' aporetic dialogues similarly realize the nature of a philosophizing that commences always anew. Returning endlessly to starting points is no incontinence on Fink's part but rather the reflection of an authentic, single-minded philosophical vision of ontological experience and the manifestation of a renewing search for possibilities of its articulation.

The experience of Being is transformed by Fink through a cosmological focus, into the leading idea of world. World emerges more clearly in Fink's interpretation of Nietzsche. In Nietzsche itself the idea of world already undergoes a transformation. The Dionysian is Nietzsche's most stable and intriguing metaphor for ontological experience. The starting point of its articulation, the tragic pathos of the artist's metaphysics, remains rooted in subjectivity and Schopenhauerian metaphysics with its duality of appearance and thing-in-itself. The voices of Nietzsche's early conceptions of ontological experience make way for *Zarathustra* and its climactic realization of the eternal return of the same. This forms the heart of Nietzsche's philosophy in Fink's reading. Here, Nietzsche shows himself

> as the explorer of a thought which attempts to grasp the world beyond all things... he attempts to reflect beyond things and beyond inner-worldly being... Cosmic harmony and the cosmic stance of human existence become the scale which measures everything now. Human greatness depends on its measure of openness

to the world. The life most exposed to the world has the highest rank." (Fink 2003: 81)

Whether Nietzsche is successful in this exploration is not relevant here. Fink indeed seems to raise questions given Nietzsche's unreflected stance toward temporality in the eternal return. However, the transformation of perspective which moves world and its play into view matter in themselves. This view requires a distinct method of approach. Nietzsche's path reaches its climax and terminates at the end of the third book of *Zarathustra* (also cited by Fink at the end of PSW): "bird wisdom speaks thus: 'Behold there is no above, no below! Throw yourself around, out, back, you who are light! Sing! Speak no more!" (2016b: 215).

While it is not surprising that Nietzsche would privilege music and singing to articulate what propositional language cannot achieve, Fink's reference to Zarathustra's "Seven Seals" at the conclusion of his book on play suggests distinct termination of reflective or analytic consciousness when it comes to the ontological conception of play. Fink shares Nietzsche's "bird-wisdom of his freedom" as the last word on the "unsayable" ontological experience of world in play.

The Importance of World and Play for Music

The focus on play as a way through which we encounter and understand world emerges through Fink's reading of Nietzsche. Originally, Fink's thinking of world proceeds from philosophical constellations defined by Husserl and Heidegger. These constellations move, as in particular Heidegger's challenge to Husserl in *Being and Time* and Husserl's response to this challenge in *The Crisis of the European Sciences* only define starting points—an initial clashing of swords.[6] Fink is conscious of limitations in Husserl's phenomenology notwithstanding his consistent loyalty to his teacher. In particular, while Husserl's focus on intentionality brings into view the manifold ways of our directedness and involvement in the world, the phenomenon of world itself is always occluded in an essentially "subjective" approach. Despite Husserl's radicalization of view on intentionality in the fundamental reflections of a phenomenological reduction, the "objective tendencies of life" and "our abandonment to the things" lead only indirectly to the phenomenon of world. World is not explicitly thematized by Husserl (Fink 1985: 33), but primarily determined as empty horizon.

> World is the paradoxical intentional phenomenon of an empty horizon of experience which leaps ahead and circumscribes it. World as such does not exist for Husserl as little as it does for Kant. If Kant says, it is mere "idea", Husserls says: it is a mere "horizon". World is re-interpreted as an a-thematic, intentional form of experience; it is taken to be an always anticipated realm, which circumscribes the field of experience in an "empty" way. (Fink 1990: 149)

This stance toward world seems, to Fink, evasive—a "peculiar horizon which rejects its fulfilment" (Fink 1990: 149). Husserl does not achieve a compelling thematization of the phenomenon of world, something that Heidegger's identification of *Dasein* seems more ready to face. For Heidegger the human being (*Dasein*) is essentially a being-in-the-world. He seeks to understand this through an existential analytic of *Dasein* in *Being and Time* (Heidegger 1986). However, while we find a "cosmological difference" in Heidegger (a distinction between being-in-the-world and World itself), Heidegger's approach to world remains also trapped in a "subjective" perspective[7] notwithstanding that Heidegger seeks to understand subjectivity in an entirely different way than the metaphysical tradition (Fink 1990: 154). Heidegger's existential analytic looks at the world-hood of the world, distinguishing it from a Cartesian conception of world as *res extensa* before returning to a perspective of *Dasein* as a being in a world. This is for Fink a return to "subjectivity" with Husserlian slant. To be fair, Heidegger himself realises the limitations of *Being and Time* and the existential analytic of *Dasein* and seeks to progress the question of Being further with a conception of truth as *Aletheia* articulated in the essay on art (Heidegger 1980) and in his Hoelderlin and Nietzsche interpretations, before finally turning toward clearing (*Lichtung*), and being-itself in the late *Contributions to Philosophy*.

For Fink, Heidegger's "turn" (*Kehre*) also progresses the conception of world as a characteristic of *Dasein*. In Heidegger, we see a "particular *movement* in the thinking of world from an existential—towards a cosmic concept of world." This movement is initially merely an announcement—Heidegger is "on the way" (*unterwegs*) and this dynamic allows Fink a "leap into the historical presence of the problem of world" (Fink 1990: 150). Our conception of world occurs in "speculative anticipation" which yields further analytical determinations. The determination of human being as being-in-the-world brings forth the realization that world is an ontological modality of human being once this determination is confronted with the question of being. World shows itself in—and through the human existence in particular in our feeling (*Befindlichkeit*) or attunement (*Stimmung*) and in our conscious realization (*Verstehen*).

> The human being is in its world in such a way that it feels such and such. Feeling (*das Befinden*) does not refer to an objective situation, but to a way, how we are feeling, how we are attuned . . . attunement is, however, not an experience inside, in our psychological inner world, it is rather a way in which we are "overall" (*im Ganzen*) and how the entirety of being affects us. In attunement the world as a whole become disclosed. (Fink 1990: 160)

The concepts of feeling (*Befindlichkeit*) and attunement suggest an ecstatic possibility of the human being. We are not just a monadic, isolated consciousness but reach out toward world. The ecstatic possibility of the human being becomes central in Fink's concept of play. That is why play reflects the ontological manifestation of world. The relationship between world and human being cannot be comprehensively conceptualized within philosophy, for its dynamic and paradoxical nature demands constant adjustments in response to the flux of becoming and its continuous mediation of tensions and dissonances. There is nothing we can really say about world except to say that the human being is "open to the world" (Fink 2016: 213). World itself is indeterminate. It "is aimless, and it also has no value in itself and remains outside every moralistic assessment, is beyond 'good and evil'. Without ground and without aim, without sense and without goal, without value and without plan" (Fink 2016: 212).

Music, World as Play and Silence

Fink's thematization of the concept of world suggests reference points through which we might conceive music as a disclosure of world and of the human being's *worldedness*. As a temporal form, music is constituted in its identity through play. While we speak about making music, this "making" does not create any object—it is no *poiesis*. Even in realms where we speak predominantly about "works" of music and establish analytic discourses that refer to music as a canon of artistic objects, the actual works themselves are brought to life in performance and play. The objectification of music is even here never complete and remains open in the face of the essential requirement that music must be played. Our expectation of musical practices is that they conform to determinations of play in the way Fink outlines: "In play the human being 'transcends' himself, surmounts the determinations with which he has surrounded himself and within which he has 'actualized' himself" (Fink 2016: 206).

Musical play achieves an "ecstase of existence towards the world" and affirms realms of freedom in which existence and its actions become possible (Fink 2016: 213). These play characteristics are required by our experience of music as music, which we expect to reflect in spontaneity, authenticity, and immediacy. Play in music is not only restricted to the active play of performance. It also includes the listener, who plays[8] by virtue of the presence of play.

The essential constitution of music as play, however, is merely one factor that makes world strongly significant for music. The presence of world and our existence as beings in a world manifests itself for both Heidegger and Fink in attunement (*Stimmung*) and feeling (*Befindlichkeit*). The concept of *Stimmung* is essentially a musical phenomenon— it is already present in the concept of Greek *harmonia*. *Stimmung* is disclosed most authentically, directly and clearly through music. Its musical manifestations provide us with metaphorical possibilities to extend the concept of *Stimmung* into other contexts of sense, experience, and intellectual life. This makes the case for music as central to world and worldedness rather straightforward.

The second concept (*Befindlichkeit*) that is relevant has a more complex possibility of meanings. We have translated *Befindlichkeit* as feeling; however, this captures only part of the depth of the concept. *Befindlichkeit* rather refers to the way we find ourselves, a specific form of consciousness of self, that discloses our existential situation or condition. It refers potentially to "how we are" in the broadest and most fundamental sense psychologically, spiritually and physically, including, how we are disposed toward ourselves, others, and the world. This disposal and stance toward the world (and its consciousness) opens up world in the first instance for us. We assign music a central role in both reflecting and determining our *Befindlichkeit*. Music is a way to disclose, but also to determine our *Befindlichkeit*. This would amount to a disclosure but also determination of world. Music is a way in which we open ourselves toward the world and allow world to be. Such an opening is not simply receptive or cognizant of world, as if world was already present as the "other" or horizon. Opening ourselves to world constitutes and determines world in the first instance. That explains why music can be experienced as profound. It also explains how we can make music together with others. Our collective playing extends our consciousness beyond our immediate horizon and lived realm determined by our immersion in the things. Music transforms and blends our horizons.[9] One of Fink's achievements is the recognition that such an extension occurs in silence—world is ultimately nothing (*me on*) and music extends its reach into an infinite realm. In this way, music reflects our fundamental being and our mysterious ontological intuition as we reach into such silence to anticipate our being through playing and listening.

The Relation of Play and Education in Fink

Human Play as an Analogical Path to Understanding Onto-Cosmology

Steve Stakland

Introduction

Fink was a philosopher of education. When he became a full professor in 1948 it was as the combined chair of *both* philosophy and pedagogy. His thinking about pedagogy was diverse. Besides publishing prolifically on the topic of childhood, he was always "available for students and to promoting their interests." To continue the possibilities of andragogy, he was instrumental in establishing the Freiburg community college in 1946. Fink was also director of the Freiburg *Studium Generale* from 1954 to 1971, a school dedicated to education and teacher training. "He also played a decisive role in the formulation and implementation of pedagogic reform in Germany, and organized conferences on the themes of pedagogy" (translators introduction to PSW). Here I seek to show a way to combine Fink's philosophy of play with his concern for education.

In the years leading up to the publication of PSW, Fink was preoccupied with questions related to education. Throughout his collected works, there are lectures and notes related to education, though most have not been translated from German. For example, in 1965 he gives attention in his lectures to an American philosopher "*Die pragmatische Erziehungsphilosophie John Deweys*" (John Dewey's Pragmatic Philosophy of Education). He also lectured about Rousseau and Locke, Pestalozzi and Schleiermacher as educational thinkers (see volume twenty of Fink's collected works). The English translation of PSW includes Fink's 1954 lecture notes for the ten sessions seminar titled "The Philosophical-Pedagogical Problem of Play" (PPPP). These notes are outlines not only for his 1957 essay "Oasis of Happiness: Thoughts toward an Ontology of Play" (OH) but also PSW. He cites the same poems, quotes the same philosophers, and poses many of the same questions in these lecture notes as are included in these two major publications on play.

In PSW, educational concerns rarely become explicit, but it does shine through in a few crucial places. For example, "The metaphysical interpretation of play ever orbits around this referential character, play's exceeding of itself, the moment of a strange transcendence, but it interprets this transcendence in terms of a *paideia* that is thought philosophically, as the drawing and e-ducating pull toward the true Being of the idea" (115). The hyphenating of 'e-ducating' carries through into the English translation, the emphasis Fink wished to place on the leading aspect of education. It is derived from *ducere* "to lead," and in Fink's German text it is "*Er-ziehung*," showing the purpose of learning is "to draw out." He finds a place for play in the proper form of education. Play can help us to learn what cannot be learned in any other way. The philosophical advantage of becoming more or being what we are is the sense of education as *Bildung* (upbringing or formation). Such a possibility is rooted in aspects of our nature that make play and the ability to be led out of ourselves possible. The best way to describe the educational value of play is to regard what is learned in play as an analogy.

Fink's thinking on play is inextricably united with his lifelong concern for education. To accommodate the constraints of this chapter and draw attention to what is available in English, I will focus on Fink's thinking about play in PSW as it relates to his 1954 seminar (PPPP). His work in that seminar shows that Fink's engagement with play was initiated by educational concerns. It certainly became more than this, as ontology and cosmology but it began due to his concerns with pedagogy. Although the significance of play for understanding Fink's cosmology and ontology is emphasized in chapters five and ten, I want to make the educational connection explicit (see chapter sixteen as well).

Play and Education

There are many possible ways of relating play to education. In Fink's 1954 lecture notes and throughout PSW and OH, Fink reviews many connections. Here are some: (1) a relation of mimesis, (2) a relation characterized by *poiesis*, (3) a relation that is ontologically and cosmologically instructive, and (4) a relation that is a union of *poiesis* and mimesis. The first possible relation, one of mimesis, is the use or emphasis of play in education as a way of conserving skills by copying. "Some kinds of playing operate as an imitation of a simultaneous serious activity; for example, children can imitate the simultaneous life processes of adults" (109). The mimetic aspect of play, where the student copies in play what they will later do as adults, is the kind of relation that John Dewey emphasizes as well (see *Democracy and Education* ch. 15 "Play and Work in the Curriculum"). However, Fink is quick to note that play is not merely "slavish imitation" (Ibid.).

The second possible relation, *poiesis*, bringing-forth, appears in Fink's writings, especially when he quotes Nietzsche and Schiller. Here the importance of play in education is due to its creative or at least productive importance. Fink quotes Schiller's aesthetic writings, where he says, "man only fully is when he plays" (OH in PSW 18). It is in the play of artistic creation that humans learn to be most fully what they are. Making art is understood as a form of play. By engaging in this sort of play, people learn to appreciate beauty and thus approach what is most unique about being human. Fink quotes Nietzsche, "In this world only play, play as artists and children engage in it, exhibits coming-to-be and passing away, structuring and destroying, without any moral additive, in forever equal innocence"—"The world is the play of Zeus . . ." (from *Philosophy in the Tragic Age of the Greeks* in OH in PSW 30) and "I do not know any other way of handling great tasks than as play" (from *Ecce Homo* in PPPP in PSW 259). Nietzsche, like Schiller, has a similar sense of play as *poiesis*, but his emphasis extends beyond aesthetic creation and appreciation; for example, he is sensitive to the cosmological dimension. Fink's appeal to these two philosophers shows his awareness of the educational relation of production, making and creating to play. Indeed, he often uses the philosophical anthropological formulation *homo faber* in PSW (e.g., 62, 68, 153). In PPPP Fink explicitly takes Nietzsche to be referring to the aspect of "productivity" in his thoughts about play (in PSW 262). Play in education is thus often used to help students become creative.

The third relation is a summary position based on all that Fink has to say about play in PSW. The quote from Nietzsche about the play of Zeus supports Fink's cosmological insights and clearly relates to Heraclitus. The cosmological significance of play is also important to Plotinus's thinking about play. To be both ontologically and cosmologically *instructive*, play must be related to Being and the world. Moreover, this relation of play and education brings together the mimetic aspect as well: "Play and mimesis: not mimesis of a 'thing,' but rather of 'all of existence'!" (PPPP in PSW 262). A certain kind of play is a pantomime of all reality. This introduces the important distinction between human play and cosmic play. This third relation of play and education shows that by thinking about play we *learn* something vital not only about Being but also the world, that is, the sum of all possible relations.

The fourth relation is based on Fink's reading of Heraclitus's 52 fragment. "The course of the world is a child playing, who moves the pieces on the board here and there, is a child's kingdom" (PSW 51). Besides Plato, Heraclitus is the second most referred to philosopher in PSW. His perspective dominates Fink's philosophy of play. Fink uses Heraclitus' insight to show that play is both productive (i.e., creative *poiesis*) and imitative, that is, mimesis. The child's play brings forth a world. However, it is also imitative of some deeper inchoate level of existence, a baseline beyond the endless pattern of the whole of existence. Fink's term 'meontic' is meant to capture what it is that can be imitated in this cosmic sense (see chapter two and eighteen). Heraclitus establishes the philosophical precedence for regarding play as essential. He is the source of the world theater cosmological interpretation of play. Plato's mimetic characterization of play used in his critique of the poets in the *Republic* is opposed to the Heraclitean. However, Fink notes in PSW that in Plato's last work, the *Laws* his understanding of play is a reformulation of what Heraclitus thought, that is, humans are the playthings of the gods (100). Thus, the gods play, and so our play is a version or shadow of how divinities exist. Heraclitus's insight supports Fink's ontological and cosmological thinking. From the perspective of the union of mimesis and *poiesis*, play in the context of education can be used as a way for the student to both imitate and productively create. That is, in their learning they can emulate the forms of art, language, and work while also making new inventions and additions.

Of these four relations, the third is the most important for understanding Fink's philosophy of play. Although he considers play from many different perspectives (e.g., cultural, pedagogical, cultic, etc.), his culminating analysis is ontological and cosmological. His philosophy of play is therefore, onto-cosmological. In PPPP he calls play "a cosmological key concept" (in PSW 264). He emphasizes that our cosmic connection comes through play, "Because he is "worldly"; the human being is a player" (PSW 213). Moreover, the goal of Fink's work is pedagogical. On the last page of PSW the book is characterized as a "conceptual exercise" (215). So, what do we *learn* by thinking with Fink about play? For one thing we are shown the error of the metaphysical tradition since Plato (see chapter six). The keen Fink translator and interpreter Catherine Homan says, "Play is ultimately a mode of understanding" (2013: 289). In play our understanding of ontology is corrected, because, as Fink says, play is a symbol of the world; the world, like play, is not a being. Therefore, ontology cannot be characterized as a hierarchy of beings since not everything is a being. When we play, we learn about the world, a thing that is a non-being in the sense that it is not itself an entity within the world. Thus, human play is educative because it teaches us something through analogy about cosmological and ontological, that from Fink's perspective, nothing else can. This education occurs implicitly as we engage in play or explicitly as we phenomenologize with Fink about play. Such education is potentially analogically valuable for understanding the world and Being because it teaches us the cosmological difference. This difference "characterizes the way in which the human being, while inner-worldly, thinks and expresses this totality symbolically" (Homan 2013: 288). Awareness of this difference comes through human play because it is an analogy of cosmic play.

Education: (Re)Formative versus Nutritive

In PPPP, Fink focuses, at least initially, on the play of the child. The child's perspective is always in general understood from an adult's viewpoint, so it is hard to know it in a pure sense. The play of children introduces the contrast with adult play. "Among children play is 'central,' among adults a 'marginal phenomenon' as a rule" (in PSW 258). Ultimately Fink unites both in what he calls human play, which he then contrasts with cosmic play. Cosmic play will loom large throughout PSW. However, like the lecture notes for PPPP, human play serves as the onramp in PSW to Fink's onto-cosmological insights. In all these writings there is the "transition from the simple taking up of the phenomenon of play to its conceptual grasp" (259). The pedagogical perspective on play is part of the conceptual grasp.[1] Having played as children, adults have learned about the world. This analogical learning, at once both cosmological and ontological, is not necessarily an explicit education. The comprehension of the world and being that comes from play only becomes explicit in a philosophy of play.

In PPPP, Fink argues that in education there are "Two opposed fundamental tendencies: formation and nurturing" (in PSW 264). The former is what he regards as "prescriptive" and is the "traditional aspect" known in German Idealism as *Bildung*. Fink also calls this "reformative" education the "authoritative" kind that is "responsible to society, to culture, to the state" (268). Furthermore, it is the "prescriptive" mode (Ibid.). Formative education makes learning into something that has the potential for failing. It doesn't always succeed, and it is risky. It characterizes a kind of intrusive education where if nothing is done the outcome cannot be actualized. "How are play and the playful manifestly regarded in 'reformative education'? Precisely as means. Learning by playing! Guided striving. 'Prescribed kinds of play': with insight into the situation of the respective stages of life according to developmental psychology. Kinds of play and toys suitable for children" (264). Formative, active or intrusive education roughly characterizes the first ever philosophy of education given by Plato.

The second perspective, the nutritive or natural attitude in education, is the "progressive aspect" of education in the sense of "letting-grow" (264). Nutritive education is responsible "to the child as a future free human being" (268). And "the nurturing" is indirect (266) and it is meant to "follow-along" (268), that is, to simply let the learner be what they are. Thus, whatever is allowed to happen in its purity is the purpose of education. Letting be faces no sense of danger or risk of failure other than if outside shaping forces are allowed to be exposed to the pupil. Fink argues that play is related to this fundamental tendency, "As expression of the substantial core of the young human being, as inner anticipation of his future, as his self-portrayal, as document of unconscious depts, etc." (Ibid.). In this form of education all must be done to not interfere with the student. In relation to play, Fink says, "such educators do not play along. They observe, furtively watching over child's play" (Ibid.). Nutritive educating understands play as a "Principle of self-activity" (Ibid.). Moreover, later PPPP he says, "The adult educators must accommodate themselves to child's play" (266). Despite the prized place of natural play in this form of education, the teachers hold back and do all they can not to engage with students so as not to interfere and potentially corrupt the purity of the young students' natural unfolding. The second great philosopher of education, Rousseau, is representative of this nutritive tendency.

At its most basic level, Platonic education was something done to the student. To be educated a person needed to encounter or at least approximate The Good. This notion assumes that human being, despite innate abilities, is also inherently lacking and in need of completion. The most obvious need of the individual, as demonstrated by Plato, is the truth. And to arrive at the truth a certain kind of teaching method or dialectic is necessary. The dialectic was based on a progressive hierarchy of virtues, in pursuit of The Good, that is, full education. The Platonic view of human being, or at least a powerful interpretation of what Plato might have thought, establishes a dualism between the immutable intellectual world of ideas or forms and the ever-changing perceptual world. Students are engulfed in the later and must be brought more fully into the former through rigorous study, particularly of abstract subjects like mathematics. The fully educated individual, following this dominant interpretation of Plato, is someone who almost completely disparage the material world and even their bodily existence and its perceptual orientation toward impermanent physical reality.

In contrast to Plato's view of physical entanglements through our bodies and our basic lack, Rousseau develops a profoundly different perspective. In his book *Emile* or *Treatise on Education*, he describes the ideal education, the kind that would overcome the degradation of society. Based on his description he prescribes a purely natural education. In contrast to the Platonic view, nothing should be done to the student. Instead, the student's learning should be negative in the sense that everything from society and culture is kept away from the student. The teacher's job is not to share and expose the student to experiences or projects of intersubjective interest but iinstead to shield and harbor the student in an environment where they are exposed strictly to a state of nature. The ideally educated individual can make the necessary cultural reforms simply because they have grown up unperturbed by the errors of the historical intersubjective tradition.

These are both merely rough characterizations of Plato and Rousseau. Some of the differences between the two are developmental. Plato's dialectical method seems to be meant for adults. Rousseau is focused on the initial education of children. However, developmentalism aside, it is similar thumbnail sketches that have had the deepest impact on educational theory and practice. For example, the Romanticism of Rousseau leads to the extreme views of human malleability found in ever-new iterations of progressive education. Indeed, it is the ideas of Rousseau that are the antecedent to the American philosopher of education John Dewey's deeply social and pragmatic ideas for formal schooling. The influence of Plato continues in the extreme emphasis on STEM fields as well as forwarding modernistic subject-object dualism.

Fink dissolves the deadlock between these two views of education by uniting them. For him these "two 'extremes' are not accidental positions. Rather, they are polar "'primal forms' that belong together" (PPPP in PSW 266). Education must therefore be a compromise or mix of the two extremes. The authoritative "paternal" formative education and the passive accepting nutritive "'maternal' element in the educational relationship" must be wed, to educate appropriately (Ibid.). From the dominate progressive modes of education today there is resistance to interfering in the play of children. And the intensity of formative education wants to excise time that is wasted in unrestricted free play, for example, recess. However, Fink explains why *both* rules and freedom are needed:

> One might believe that the charm of wholly free play in unrestricted improvisation is greatest ... that is not the case ... Precisely the child places the greatest value on the observation of and compliance with the rules of the game. The rules of the game are not the cancellation of creative imagination, but rather what is striven for in creative imagination. Setting and observing the rules is a coming-into-constitution. The human being is originally not composed, but strives towards "form," "constitution." (Ibid. 266–7)

Because of our long neoteny, excess drive, and having language and culture, we have a sense that what we are is open and incomplete. As Fink says, "Because the human being is the world-open living being, he is also the rational, the speaking, the erotic, the skilled and political living being who understands Being" (PSW 135). Striving for form in this openness is at once to have a sense of self-creation *and* to know that we are becoming what we are meant to be. The duality of inventing ourselves according to a pattern that we ourselves did not invent is what it means to become fully educated, that is, an individual who has also been socialized but understands their socialization for what it is.[2] Education is an inculcation into live traditions of sociality as the student learns to be with others in the present and engages with the past through explicit study, repetition of institutional patterns, and group norms.

Conclusion

For both formative and nutritive education to be important components of education, the use of play cannot be only the pure improvisational and revealing type without any rules or just the directed kind that follows rules (PPPP in PSW 264). For example, though a student in a theatrical play must conform to many things like the script, the director's vision and the other actors he or she is still able to interpret the role. Indeed, the creative aspect is highly valued. This kind of play, at once conforming to rules and open to improvisation, is what leads to the analogical onto-cosmological education. Play that is both rule oriented and free educates in an original way. We are able to learn that the world is both open to chance and creative invention as well as ordered and full of rules. Despite its constancy it is a world of miracles.

From Fink's philosophy of education and play we can find insights for the practical task of educating and thus fully living. Education should have games and playtime structured by rules but also allow for creative invention and the possibility of failure, that is, the breakdown of play. This is because "Every kind of play is an attempt at life, is an attempt at a mastering of life, and, in the plaything, has hold of resistant beings in general" (Ibid., 267). The possibility of meaning is born from the pushback of entities, that is, objects and particularly other people. Ultimately, the ongoing process of our education is like our quest for *Eudaimonia*, it only ends with death. "We *are* not, we incessantly *become*—and perhaps never arrive at a conclusive form, and until death we are a project for ourselves" (PSW 175). The project of our becoming is brought about by free choice. And in all our choosing we "ultimately chooses only [ourselves]" (Ibid. 207). The tautological form of our coming to be indicates that it is not the specific outcome which is vital but rather exercising our ability to choose. This sense of *Bildung*, where we are formed into what we already are, is different than a natural sense of being left alone, like a feral child. To fully become what we are means coming to understand the full scope of human history, language and culture etc. An understanding which in the time allotted to mortals can only begin.

Freedom is the source of education (Ibid.). Education is the habits that form us into what we are, based on our decisions. Formal education whether early or late provides a space for the formation of habits. If left to nature what we copy (*mimesis*) to form our habits will develop according to a less socialized or integrated mode and be less capable of creativity (*poiesis*). If we are actively exposed and formed for a fuller understanding of ourselves, we have the tautological *Bildung* that is at once both more indicative of a pattern and capable of invention.

When Fink considers the relation of play and education, he emphasizes human play not cosmic play. However, his consideration of human play leads him to cosmic play, the play of the world, because the former is an analogy of the latter. Human play can lead to an understanding of the world as cosmic play, that is, onto-cosmology (PSW 210).

"The Desert Grows"? On a remarkable Silence in Fink's *Oasis of Happiness*

Holger Zaborowski

"Oasis" in Eugen Fink's *Oasis of Happiness*: The Meaning of a Metaphor

Oasis of Happiness. Thoughts toward an Ontology of Play (OH) is one of the best-known texts by the German philosopher and educator Eugen Fink.[1] This does not come as a surprise for play is a phenomenon that is of significance not only in academic disciplines. It is also a phenomenon that is of interest in non-academic circles. It has, as Fink emphasizes at the outset, a "great significance [. . .] within the structure of human existence" (14). If, as Friedrich Schiller pointed out (and as Fink cites him), "man only fully is when he plays" (18), play belongs to the phenomena with which anyone should deal who has an anthropological interest in the human being or who raises the question about oneself—about one's own life and its meaning.

If Fink characterizes play as an "oasis of happiness" or if he compares it to such an oasis, he has found a persuasive image for what play is. He explains this characterization as follows: "In relation to the course of life and to its restless dynamic, to its obscure questionworthiness and its forward-rushing orientation toward the future, playing has the character of a pacified 'present' and self-contained sense" (20). However, the word "oasis" appears—apart from the title—only twice in OH, first, immediately following the sentence that has just been cited: "it resembles an 'oasis' of happiness arrived at in the desert of the striving for happiness and Tantalus-like seeking that is otherwise our condition" (20). In the following, Fink explains further what is meant by this kind of "oasis" and uses the word for the second time:

> For the adult, on the other hand, play is a strange oasis, a dreamy resting point for restless wandering and continual flight. Play gives us the present. Not, to be sure, that present where we, having become still in the depths of our essence, hear the eternal breath of the world and behold the pure forms in the stream of transience. Play is activity and creativity—and yet it is near to eternal and tranquil things. Play

"interrupts" the continuity and context of our course of life that is determined by an ultimate purpose. It withdraws in a peculiar manner from the other ways of directing one's life; it is at a distance from them. (21)

For Fink, play is a relational phenomenon. But it cannot be understood "within the popular antitheses of 'work and play', of 'play and seriousness of life', and so forth" (17). A deeper interpretation is necessary to understand play in its distance to the non-playing ordinary life. The everyday life, Fink holds, is characterized by continuous movement and orientation toward purposes. He does not describe it neutrally but critically: the "dynamic" is "restless"; the "questionworthiness" is "obscure"; the "orientation toward the future" is "forward-rushing"; life is a "restless wandering"; the human being is on a "continual flight"; all other activities are "determined by an ultimate purpose"—that is, they do not find their purposes in themselves, but in some other purpose (cf. 21). Insofar as playing opens up an opposite pole to life in its everydayness—rest rather than restlessness, dream rather than reality, presence rather than absent-mindedness, end in itself rather than instrumental orientation toward ultimate purposes—Fink discovers a distance between play and all other basic phenomena of human existence. This is why the metaphor "oasis" seems appropriate. For an oasis, too, is being understood in relation to what it is not, that is, to the desert, and, as a space of rest, of recreation and refreshment, of encounter and fertility, it stands in distance to its surroundings. And as in human life, the everyday is dominant and play the exception, so is, in relation to the desert, the oasis the smaller space; it is the exception to the rule, the interruption of the continuity, a space of life in an otherwise hostile environment.

It is surprising that Fink does not further explain this powerful metaphor in this text more explicitly. He leaves it to his readers to interpret this metaphor in its depth, in its appropriateness, and in the complexity of its allusions. That the word "oasis" does not appear often in a text that stands under the title *Oasis of Happiness* seems to suggest that Fink has a problem with this metaphor. This is supported by the fact that Fink once uses "oasis" in inverted commas and that, in the second instance, he speaks of a "strange oasis." This interpretation is confirmed by a brief look at other texts by Fink.

In his major work PSW, the word "oasis" does not appear at all. In the lecture course "The Philosophical-Pedagogical Problem of Play" (1954), Fink interprets play only a few times and, in addition, only shortly with respect to an oasis in this lecture course. He does not delve into this metaphor any deeper. There is, therefore, a tension between the title *Oasis of Happiness* and the actual significance of the word "oasis" for Fink's text. Such a tension could be due to coincidence. Maybe it is because the title of the essay was chosen relatively late or just before the text was printed—or to the fact that for Fink, the characterization of play as "oasis" was so self-evident that he thought it was not in need of any further explanation or clarification. But it could also be the case that this "silence" about the "oasis" is philosophically significant. Before I can explain this any further, I will draw attention to two important clusters of associations of the metaphor "oasis."

Clusters of Associations of the "Oasis": A Double Experience of Desert and of Oasis

Oases can be understood, with Foucault, as heterotopias. In the history of ideas, there are many references to oases and deserts as metaphors for human life. One important example is provided by Friedrich Nietzsche, whose philosophy and particularly whose diagnosis of modernity have been important for Eugen Fink (26, 30). In a famous word in his *Zarathustra*, Nietzsche (or better the wanderer or the shadow of Zarathustra) declared: "*The desert grows: woe to him who harbors deserts!*"[2] This exclamation introduced and concluded a poem which is written from the perspective or position of an oasis. This position makes it possible to see, and to reflect on, the growth of the desert: "it just now yawned wide open Its lovely mouth."[3]

Nietzsche is, first of all, a thinker of the desert as a heterotopia. For "[i]n the desert the truthful have always dwelled, the free spirits, as the rulers of the desert; but in the cities dwell the well-fed, famous wise men—the draft animals."[4] For him, it is crucial for free spirits to leave the oases, "for where there are oases, there are idols as well."[5] So he argues as follows: "Truthful—thus I call the one who goes into godless deserts and has broken his revering heart."[6] However, the oasis, too, seems to be a heterotopia for him which—as place *in* the desert, far away from the cities and of European civilization and culture—makes it possible to discover that the desert grows and allows necessary rest from the desert life. In a note that he wrote after the publication of *Zarathustra*, he points out that free spirits, too, are in need of oases: "for we, too, need sometimes oases, oases of humans, in which one forgets, one trusts, falls asleep, dreams again, loves again, becomes human again."[7]

Martin Heidegger hast interpreted Nietzsche's word "The desert grows" in his lecture course "What calls forth thinking?" from Winter Semester 1951/2—a few years before OH was published—as follows:

> Into those words, Nietzsche put all he knew. They are the title of a poem Nietzsche wrote when he was "most distant from cloudy, damp, melancholy Old Europe." Complete, the words run: "The wasteland grows: woe to him who hides wastelands within!" Woe to whom? Was Nietzsche thinking of himself? What if he had known that it was his own thought which would first have to bring about a devastation in whose midst, in another day and from other sources, oases would rise here and there and springs well up?[8]

From far, far away from Europe, Nietzsche, as thinker of the transition, makes the diagnoses of an increasing devastation that is itself devastating. In nihilism, as discovered and proclaimed by Nietzsche, Western metaphysics comes according to Heidegger to a conclusion. For Heidegger, however, a different kind of thinking, the thinking of a new beginning, could lead to oases within the desert of nihilism. These oases, to be sure, are different oases than the ones Nietzsche experienced or was looking for. Even though Fink was close to both Nietzsche and Heidegger, he fails to explore these clusters of associations in his considerations about play although he described his own time in rather critical terms, too (cf. /9).

The metaphor "oasis" opens a second association space which Fink only implicitly addresses: that one of the biblical world. For this world was characterized by desert and, indeed, oasis experiences—unlike the world of ancient Greek mythology, religion, and philosophy that is so important for Fink. "Oasis" goes admittedly back to the Greek word *oasis*, but this is the Greek form of word that was originally Egyptian and that referred to fertile areas within deserts. In the texts of both testaments, oases—and, as in Fink's text, the interplay between deserts and oasis—play a central role. First of all, the desert is taken to be a place of the encounter with God. God appears to Moses in the desert (cf. Exodus 3; cf. also Acts 7.30). Jesus spends forty days in the desert (cf. Matthew 4, Mark 1, Luke 4). However, the desert is also the area of hunger (cf. Exod. 16.3), generally of danger (cf. Deut. 1:19; 2 Cor. 11:26), and of punishment: The people of Israel have to spend forty years in the desert as punishment (cf. Num. 14.33 f.). An image for salvation is that the desert becomes fertile (and will cheer): "The wilderness and the dry land shall be glad; the desert shall rejoice and blossom like the crocus; it shall blossom abundantly and rejoice with joy and singing" (Isa. 35:1-2). And God's shows his goodness in turning the desert into an oasis: "He turned the desert into pools of water and the parched ground into flowing springs" (Ps. 107:35). With the metaphor of the oasis (as polar opposite to the desert) one finds oneself in a complex net of biblical allusions.

In OH, there are indeed occasionally references to biblical texts. But they remain implicit.[9] Fink, for example, raises with respect to the great significance of work and seriousness in the present time the question: "Do we need a little of the divine sense of lightness and the joyous levity of play," in order to again come close to the 'birds of the sky' and the 'lilies of the field'? (17; cf. Mt. 6.26; Mt. 6:28, and also Lk. 12:24 ff.). The biblical story of the tower of Babel could resonate in Fink's reference to the "utter confusion of language" (20/16). And Fink finishes OH with another biblical reference: "we should also be mindful of the saying: we cannot enter into the kingdom of heaven if we do not become as children" (31/30; cf. Mt. 18,3). Fink, however, does not at all draw attention to the dimensions of meaning that are opened up by the biblical metaphor "oasis" even though this would have been obvious.

Fink speaks of religion explicitly in OH. He raises the question "whether the human being as a player stays within the human realm or at the same time necessarily comports himself to a realm beyond the human one [Übermenschlichen] as well" [38/24]). However, Judaism and Christianity and their reservoirs of metaphors do not play a role. Whenever Fink refers to religion, he mentions historically early forms of religion as they relate to play. The cultic sense of religion that he explores no longer has the same significance in the twentieth century. He refers to a rather abstract kind of religion when he, for example, writes *der Gott*, which should appear in English as "the God" (20). At the end of the second part of OH, Fink addresses the "binding" and "community-founding" power of play and illustrates this with respect of the "early human community of play." It "embraces all these stated forms and shapes of being together and brings the whole of existence to complete presence. It consolidates the circle of the phenomena of life as the play-community of the festival" (38/25). This, Fink argues, shows itself at the "archaic festival". This

> is more than the merry-making of a people; it is the elevated actuality—the actuality that has been elevated to the magical dimension—of human life in all its relations. It is cultic dramatic play or spectacle [Schauspiel], where the human being feels the nearness of the gods, the heroes and the dead, and knows himself as having been placed into the presence of all the blessing and frightening powers of the world-totality.

On the basis of this observation, Fink arrives at the following conclusion, "Primeval play also has a deep connection with religion. The community of the festival envelops the spectators, the initiates and epopts of a cultic play, where the deeds and sufferings of gods and humans appear on the stage, whose boards in fact signify the world" (27).

Fink focuses, therefore, on religious tradition for which desert and oasis do not play a role. Even though they play a central role in the biblical tradition and his own cultural horizon, there is no explicit reference in OH to biblical experiences of desert and oasis. This is also surprising because Fink speaks explicitly about the "polysemy" (22) of play and because twentieth century Christian theology has also "discovered" the phenomenon of play.[10]

Fink's Silence: Reasons and Consequences

It is, therefore, possible to observe a double silence: as much as Fink has been influenced by Nietzsche and Heidegger, and would seem therefore to be primed to explore the metaphors of oasis and desert, he doesn't. And as much as he has been at least culturally influenced by the biblical metaphors, he does not draw attention to the biblical dimensions of oasis and desert.

The reason for the latter silence lies in a methodological limitation. Like Heidegger, Fink draws a sharp line between philosophical knowledge and religious faith. This also explains why he only occasionally or, as he admits himself, only superficially deals with the topic of religious cult:

> If we now leave cult-play aside, we must remain conscious of the fact that a great problem is left behind whose surface has hardly been scratched. . . . The cult is not only a problem of play—it is above all a theological problem. The genuine theological question is not a concern for us; it transcends the framework of a philosophizing self-understanding of the finite human being. (PSW 178)[11]

However, the implicit references to biblical texts show that a reference to the biblical experiences of desert and oasis would not have contradicted his phenomenological approach. There was no need for Fink to read them as religious testimonies; he could have interpreted them as cultural points of reference. Because of the difference between philosophy and theology, he omitted this. This may, indeed, be regrettable, but can well be understood.

Philosophically more noteworthy and questionable is Fink's silence about the cluster of associations opened by Nietzsche and Heidegger. This shows, first of all, a specific perspective on the side of Fink in his thinking about play. His lies in "determining *the sense of Being from out of play*" (30). This is to say that he has an interest in play as an "existentiell, fundamental phenomenon" (18), but always with respect to a "speculative concept of play" (30), that combines in itself anthropological, cosmological, and ontological dimensions. This interest is closely related to Fink's interpretation of nihilism as a chance, "As long as one characterizes nihilism only from the perspective of the phenomenon of religion, thus describing and deploring it as the growing wasteland of modern godlessness, the opportunity concealed in it is not caught sight of" (PSW 186). Whereas for Nietzsche and Heidegger, nihilism is a radical phenomenon and the "growing wasteland" or "desert" does not only concern religion but philosophy too. Fink domesticates the nihilistic experience of both thinkers. This is why he does not need to look for oases in the wasteland of nihilism that help him to understand the wasteland or that make a different kind of thinking—that is, a different beginning of or for thinking—possible. He can find in nihilism itself the possibility of a new "openness to the world." Does not, however, this domestication misapprehend the full consequences of the death of God, as diagnosed by Nietzsche and as examined by Heidegger, that also concerns the basic difference between being and appearing and thus a difference that is of crucial significance for Fink's ontology of play?

Fink interprets the "playworld" as "appearance" (28): "Playing is finite creativity within the magical dimension of appearance" (29). For exactly this reason, play can be understood as "symbolic activity of bringing the sense of the world and life to presence" and as "speculative world formula" (30). There is, therefore, no play without the difference between being and appearance. The imaginary of play needs the relation to what it is an image of. Fink's ontology, therefore, makes strong metaphysical presuppositions. Nietzsche, however, would question these presuppositions.[12] For Nietzsche, with the growing wasteland or desert—against the background of the death of God—the difference between being and appearing collapses, too. Everything is now appearance—and therefore dream, dance, and play. Given this, play is no longer an oasis in distance from the wasteland, but an oasis that has itself become a wasteland or a wasteland that is now an oasis. Who could still differentiate between oasis and desert? But it is to be asked if nihilism can really be understood as a chance in light of this finding? Would this not be to disregard its abysmal character? Is Heidegger's approach to Nietzsche and to nihilism not more radical—and more appropriate to the phenomenon of devastation? Is not, against this background, a deeper confrontation with Nietzsche's experience of desert and oasis and with Heidegger's interpretation of it a challenge for Fink's speculative ontology of play? And cannot these questions—after Fink's domesticating "ordering" of the devastation—shed light on the fact that Fink seems to have had issues with the metaphor of an "oasis"?

14

Holy Laughter

A Pentecostal Pneumatology of Play in Fink and Wariboko

Jason W. Alvis

By the mid-1990s, the "Holy Laughter" movement had become quite popular in a number of Pentecostal Christian churches. Also known as "The Toronto Blessing," and via leaders such as Kenneth Hagan, parishioners would remain in church services for hours exhibiting uncontrollable laughter, drunken-like behavior, wild dancing, and speaking in tongues. For many on the outside of Christianity, this movement was laughable. Yet from within Christianity, fiery critiques arose, especially from those who could not imagine how such practices were compatible with a truly pietistic, orderly, and holy pneumatology. And irrespective of religious background, holy laughter at first appears to be a contradiction of terms: the idea of a laughter that is "holy" is directly opposed to everything we have been taught about the serious and respectful posture we should take when we approach that which we deem sacred. Whether one is within or without Christianity, it does us some good to consider what kind of metaphysic is at work within such Pentecostal movements, and the degree to which these movements actually abandon not only past presumptions of the faith but also particularly modern epistemologies of "certainty" and foundationalist ontotheologies.[1] Nietzsche quipped:

> Who Among you can at the same time laugh and be exalted? He who climbeth on the highest mountains, laugheth at all tragic plays and tragic realities . . . I should only believe in a God that would know how to dance. And when I saw my devil, I found him serious, thorough, profound, solemn: he was the spirit of gravity—through him all things fall. Not by wrath, but by laughter, do we slay. Come, let us slay the spirit of gravity! I learned to walk; since then have I let myself run. I learned to fly; since then I do not need pushing in order to move from a spot. Now am I light, now do I fly; now do I see myself under myself. Now there danceth a God in me.[2]

This perspective may have more in common with Pentecostal Christianity than we might at first presume.

Readers of Eugen Fink will recognize the Nietzschean influence upon Fink's work, given its certain emphasis upon dance and the dynamic, the Dionysian and the dramatic. It was precisely this influence that helped Fink develop his praise of play. Although Fink of course had no known associations with Pentecostalism, he did make original observations about Christianity and religion that are strikingly similar to that movement, thus making a juxtaposition between Fink and Pentecostalism worth the effort. Further, there are aspects of Fink's post-ontotheological approach demonstrated in his deliberations upon especially religious fervor, morality, and cult play that might be applied to a Pentecostal Theology. This chapter reads Fink's understanding of the religion-play constellation in light of the "microtheologies" and non-systematic pneumatology developed by the Pentecostal, Nigerian, Systematic Theologian Nimi Wariboko. Fink's understanding of religion prioritizes play over work. And Wariboko's theology embraces an ontological incompleteness, celebrates some forms of metaphysical and logical inconsistency, and prioritizes natality and "creative emergence." Fink's "cult play" symbolizes a cosmic ontology that is at once poetic and creative, yet also germane to any "serious" conceptual thinking. Wariboko's pneumatology conceives the Holy Spirit as a disruptor of social existence, and with whom we participate to creatively generate change. After first detailing core aspects of Wariboko's work, this chapter interprets a few aspects of Fink's understandings of "cult play" and religion in *Spiel als Weltsymbol* to demonstrate the ways in which Fink's work could be used to constructively develop further a "playful" Pentecostal pneumatology. Thus, instead of furnishing "an orthodoxy" of Fink's work, the chapter borrows, applies, and (at times) overextends his insights toward a Pentecostal Christianity. Naturally, Fink's understanding of cult play between persons/gods is perhaps not as radical as the cosmic "playerless play" he also proposes (in both *Play as Symbol of the World* and "Oasis of Happiness"). Yet perhaps religious cult play is more than merely entitative if it truly helps us see alternatives to a substance ontology. As such, cult play helps us imagine openings onto our relationality with the world.

Pentecostal Pneumatology in Nimi Wariboko: A Pneumatology Founded on Difference

Nimi Wariboko brings the two worlds of Nigerian and American Pentecostal Theology and Contemporary European Critical Theory into productive dialogue. This approach emphasizes the importance of various and necessary "splits" in all unifying relations, and provides a refreshing account of how twenty-first-century Christianity can overcome the shop-worn dichotomies between fundamentalism and liberalism. There are three ways his contributions to Christian pneumatology might be characterized: (1) God has a "split subjectivity" that marks a unique self-relation grounded in the work of the Holy Spirit, (2) we should embrace contradiction because it opens creative pathways between God and humans, and (3) natality should prioritized. This is what Wariboko calls the "Pentecostal Principle." All three are demonstrated in Wariboko's *The Split God: Pentecostalism and Critical Theory*, which displays the positive potentials of Pentecostal pneumatology to challenge some of the most basic presuppositions of any "traditional" metaphysical account that would place "thought" before "practice", or insist upon a Platonic and abstract *Eidos*. Wariboko begins with the event of Pentecost—the day the Holy Spirit is said to have descended upon the Church, bringing gifts, a play of languages, and a mission to use those gifts to help other persons. Where most Classic Christian accounts begin with Christology, Wariboko focuses on this dynamic and wild event as *the* founding gesture of the Christianity.

Onlookers at this Pentecost event are said to have believed the early Christians were "drunk with wine" because of their wildness at this event. By beginning with this diverse and chaotic event of Pentecost, we might assume an enigmatic wildness that is directly reflective of the personhood of God.[3] God is diverse and bears a split subjectivity. Wariboko engages current Pentecostal orthopraxy by doing what he calls "microtheology" (a deconstructive unfolding of particular practices) to conclude that the actions and beliefs of Pentecostals visible in their more *playful* engagement with the sacred/profane, the bodily freedom of worship practices, or the spiritual discernment of miracles, demonstrate Pentecostals' belief that reality itself is *split*.[4] Since God is split, so is reality. This split reality tears down the old ontotheological problem of determination. By removing themselves from this game, Pentecostals can live more freely from the bonds of calculation, and instead live according to the principles of grace—a grace that is defined as a break from mere repetition.

Wariboko celebrates how the explosion of languages at Pentecost should relieve us of clamoring to an all-inclusive "systematics" of the world or God that is harmonious (Wariboko 2018: 33), whole, cohesive, and decoupled from culture.[5] This classic, systematic approach was flawed from the beginning: it presumed that God is whole, one, and (with enough hard work and well-invested effort) can be explained clearly. Instead, the nature of God is "split": not only is this God unpredictable but also often is contradictory. Here we notice the preference for a relational, Heraclitean ontology that helps explain the recent growth of Pentecostalism(s) (Wariboko 2018: 33). This all is pneumatological insofar as it sees the Holy Spirit as the one who creates spaces of relation in the inter-Triune life, a life that is "cracked" (Wariboko 2018: 37). A split God bears an internal otherness that prioritizes relation over individual personhood.[6]

This is not to suggest simply that God is the "highest" form of otherness, or that God is "structured precisely around an openness" to alterity (Wariboko 2018: 515). This pneumatological connection is somewhat analogical to humans, who relate with one another in the world. Otherness is an essential *founding feature* of Triune Godhood, and it relieves us from demanding theological sameness. Instead of seeing otherness as an obstacle to be overcome in order to domesticate or "integrate" the enigma of otherness into *our* (possessed) concept of the whole of reality, we need to flip the paradigm to base universality upon otherness. For "What is familiar is ultimately grounded on strangeness: God moves in mysterious ways, the unfinishedness of reality means that it is also a stranger to itself, and the believer is indeed a stranger to herself" (Wariboko 2018: 515). God even eludes Godself.

Further, Wariboko's split God can inhabit incarnationally the "in-between" of the transcendent/immanent. Wariboko affirms that the Holy Spirit truly performs real, material miracles.[7] Such a theology, from the beginning, is rife with a number of contradictions. Wariboko recognizes that Pentecostalism is easily critiqued for its "inconsistencies, unorthodox practices, and orientations to be explained" (Wariboko 2018: 9). Yet this is precisely the "positive condition" of Pentecostalism. It mirrors the split, contradictory God. These contradictions demonstrate play-room and a purposeful "ontological incompleteness" (Wariboko 2018: 54). Since God is not some "master-signifier guaranteeing the harmonious order of reality" (Wariboko 2018: 58), we are able to live in affirmation of what transcends reality.

This also is mirrored in Wariboko's critique of Western "Liberal Christianity" and traditional "death of God" theologies.[8] These movements succeed in properly drawing attention to the inauthenticity of Christian fundamentalisms. Yet the utter failure of Liberalism was not to provide any attractive or viable alternative. Instead, claims Wariboko, such theologies have turned out to be just another form of fundamentalism!: in Liberal theologians believing they may have a "comprehensive (All) notion of reality or God" (Wariboko 2018: 62), they have also claimed to have understood God. Pentecostal theology still maintains the infinite qualitative difference between God/humans, yet vigorously lives out the importance of experience-based, relational activity. As Wariboko believes, "While still believing in their capacity to penetrate the noumenal realm, conservative Pentecostals did what the liberal Christians could not do; they transformed the epistemological obstacle to positive ontological condition: the gap between us and God has now become a positive feature of God" (Wariboko 2018: 68).

Next, Pentecostalism is theologically "promiscuous" as it bears "the threatening image of a community with uncontrolled boundaries" (Wariboko 2018: 21). Emergence is the product of the natality and creative work of the Holy Spirit. Wariboko calls this the "Pentecostal principle": to always begin again. This human principle is analogous to God's own freedom. God is not bound by anything. The radical openness to newness and the hope for a "breakthrough" or event can cause a break with what has happened in the past. Any xenophobia of newness seems to be a moral fear that strikes out on the willingness to play and to fail.

This natality is structural, social, and ever *disruptive* of all that is presumed to be a "closed reality." Where Tillich's "Protestant principle" insisted that there is no way to make "absolute" claims about "relative" reality, Wariboko begins with everyday Pentecostal practices, which are relentless about making absolute claims (Wariboko 2012: 1) about an open-ended renewal. Reflecting emergence theory, Wariboko sees creation as a "pure means" that prioritizes "possibility" over actuality, yet without denigrating the material world (Wariboko 2012: 212). The material world thus becomes "charged" with the Holy Spirit's continuous initiation of creative freedom:

> The Pentecostal principle is the power of emergent creativity that disrupts social existence, generates infinite restlessness, and results in novelty. The notion of the Pentecostal principle rethinks the idea of the Protestant principle as the spirit of creativity, the creative transforming energy that operates within the structures and throughout the process of creation as its law of motion. (Wariboko 2012: 44)

This insistence upon new creation represents a deconstructive hope for tradition. It is a "paleonomic gesture" that simultaneously "erases and preserves the Christian tradition" by maintaining its "old name in order to launch a new concept" (Wariboko 2018: 82). This penchant focus upon newness has earned Pentecostals the accusation of dancing too close to the "boundary of heresy", as they weave in and *out* of Christian orthodoxy (Wariboko 2018: 82).

In short, instead of trying to capture God as an "idealized image" in "theological tomes," Wariboko pursues the opposite: a creative distortion of "the reality or traditional notions of God in order to accent other features that resonate . . . [in] intensive participation in the divine being" (Wariboko 2018: 92). This is not an "Impressionistic" theology that invests all its energies into capturing and describing reality "accurately," as if it were taking a "photograph of God" in a present moment so as to relieve us of the fear it can change (Wariboko 2018: 92). Instead, Wariboko's Pentecostal approach is Expressionistic, insofar as it begins with existential experience rooted in the ultimate alteration of reality so as to stir-up new moods, affects, and intersocial action.

Fink, Play, and Religion

Readers familiar with Heraclitus' dynamic cosmology likely recognize already similarities (and differences) between some of the intuitions of Wariboko's Pentecostalism and Fink's cosmology. A *world in common*, even if it is between persons and God in the way that Wariboko conceives, is established not through industrial *work* but rather a creative playfulness. This is one central insight we might glean from Fink. But we should not be so quick to depict "play" as opposed to "work" and earning—an opposition that depicts not just a mindset but our way of being in the world. In a rather unplayful time in Germany, in the wake of the Second World War in the 1950s, Fink took on such a project with what would become his magnum opus, *Spiel als Weltsymbol* (Fink, 2016, 1977a). As perhaps also a critique of Nazi industriousness, he interpreted that in the Western social imaginary the important role of play—in all its unpredictability and vitality of strengthening social bonds—was so eclipsed to the point that we operate with a certain machine-like accuracy that traps us, even in our leisure time and "play," to working. That is, even when we are at play, we often are working. This amounts to a machination of the human that should lead us to rethink "how" we otherwise might be in the world. Working and machination do not reveal the world. Rather, they more so serve to conceal our interrelations with other persons.

Fink interpreted that the world is revealed to us through the "symbol" of play. Play is the creative combining and intermingling of signs that allows for a thing's meaning to change from one meaning to another. As such, play is the metasymbol by which we can juxtapose our humanity, and the world in which we "are." We typically see ourselves as cogs in the machinery of Being, quarantined off from things and unaffected by them. The world, we think, is partitioned into particular identities and social roles. This is reflective of a rather flawed understanding of *how* we actually live in this world:

> Beings are not positioned in the world like a worm in an apple or gold in the bank. All well-known and familiar modes of the being-in of things in greater things surrounding them cannot be applied to things' being in the universe or *a fortiori*

to the being-in of the human being, who understands Being in the ontological whole of the world. (Fink, 2016: 47)

We are in the world dynamically, and thus playing, laughing, or even dancing help reveal this reality. Although the typical separation of things may be a clever way to depict even accurately how certain physical things are presented phenomenally, *we humans* are not in the world in the way that those objects are. The *Kosmos*, or "order" of things for the "world of people" at a particular moment in time (*aion*), can be revealed through play.[9] Through play we experience a different means of manifestation (*Offenbarkeit*) that helps us imagine "the course of the world" (Fink 2016: 77).[10] We often think of the world as some neutral non-entity, like theater stage on which our lives are played out. Instead, the world is a phenomenon, and play helps us interpret the "total movements" of the world. Human play reveals one piece of the bigger puzzle of how the world operates. Instead of having an i*ntraworldly* existence like things do, humans are *innerworldly*: "The human being is the innerworldly thing that exists in an ecstatic relation to the totality of the world, is addressed by the universe and is turned toward it with understanding" (Fink 2016: 65).[11] Although human play is not something to be experienced like a typical "phenomenal" object, it does reflect "actuality." And although this actuality does not belong to the order of a mere repetitive reproduction, play is also not antithetical to some forms of habituation and repetition. Indeed, "we must attempt to free ourselves from the traditional condemnation of play as mere reproduction of 'actuality'" (Fink, 2016: 125).

Religion and Cult Play

This theory of play becomes even more interesting once it gets applied to religious experience, which Fink thinks far too often is treated as a "work" of labor. Here again, play is a solution to the problem: play should be operative *within authentic* religious life. A number of Fink's contemporaries successfully raised the alarm about how forms of work had entered religion especially in Western Christianity. Economic gain of capital can assimilate religious and cult-like dimensions that help protect its increase of capital (Benjamin), and the outgrowth of Protestant "working" for salvation can deprive us of freedom and imagination (Weber). Fink similarly points to how a certain "dismantling of the religious interpretation of human life and a progressive decline of mythical substance" in part is due to the lack of play, even when we are working. Our primal "Religious fervor" has been channeled into obsessions with economic calculation, striving, and "the explication and the proper ordering of the productive forces moving the course of history" (Fink 2016: 179). Work has replaced religiosity as our most important human endeavor: work has "drawn to itself the most intimate interests of the human being, which otherwise were worked out in religion" (Fink 2016: 179).

What Fink calls "cult play" is one way to break the association between work/seriousness and holy/religion. This kind of play-with-others is expressive of our truest freedoms to access the world and detach us from working repetition. We typically see play as having nothing to do with godliness. We see it as entertainment, distraction, "unreal," or simply folly. We tend to think that the repetitions of work may make money and put us in closer relation to more *things*. Yet cult play helps us access the deeper senses of relations, and can put us in an original relation with God (or as Fink often will say, the gods).[12] Cult play is an act of enchantment, insofar as it charges the profane world with spiritual possibilities and relations that typically are determined to be "unreal" or merely imaginary.

It also is a problem that more often than not Christian moral sanctification and religious life are assumed to be "a kin or a prototype of work" (Fink 2016: 180–1). Yet for Fink, holiness and unity are not achieved through work and business, but rather play. The kingdom of God is characterized by play. Jesus is not the only leader to claim that the kingdom of God belongs to children (those quintessential archetypes of play, laughter, dance, and wildness). So does Heraclitus, the philosopher of "world." Heraclitus likewise insisted that the good life is achieved through childlike play, and that the world itself is like a game we play. Fink will develop this further in terms of "Cult play." Cult play teaches us that to play is to attempt not simply to *imitate* the gods (because this would fall back into the core problematic that Fink reiterates over and over, that play is mere repetition), but rather to have original relations with God (or the gods) via play. When a shaman wears a mask of a God in a spiritual ceremony, this is clearly not serious mimicry but a playful way to garner attention for her gods and from her gods. It is an act of assimilating people in the ways of the gods. In a monotheistic interpretation, we might suggest that our playfulness in religious community emulates a God who plays. Thus, to imitate God is to play in a way that is not merely imitative. This should change how we understand holiness. Holiness now should be seen as a way of playing with God in order to become God-like:

> Cult-play brings to presence the prevailing of the gods and interrupts this "prevailing" as a super-human rule or as a super-human work; in both interpretations rule and work come into an astounding proximity to play, above all through the features of effortlessness, groundlessness, and the impossibility of resistance. (Fink, 2016: 176)

Fink arrives at this conclusion by alluding to the imitation of God. Even when God is "working," God plays. This is one reason why "the truth of the play of the gods is the play of the world" (Fink 2016: 169) The gods embrace this wisdom, and cult play is the emulation of that wisdom, and how they act in relation to the world. There is no promise, however, that this life of play is easy. Perhaps precisely because it is godly, it is difficult: "play is thus what appears to be raised up above all human measure into the super-human" (Fink 2016: 140). Gods that don't play and dance (recalling here Nietzsche's laughing and dancing Zarathustra) are dead and in chains, and therefore are unworthy of adoration, respect, or praise. Instead of engaging in "cultic derivation" and repetition, we should engage in cultic play to access the world. Similarly, since this God's work looks nothing like human work, and since God is always engaged in play (and still can remain serious in this play), it makes sense to think that God created *reason* as a wild form and expression of play also: "Reason is not the cold, pale light that appears to an anemic, withered humanity cut off from the authentic experiences of existence; it is the most passionate passion and the wildest desire, thoroughly aglow with Eros down to its roots, as Plato's dialogues show" (Fink, 2016: 52). Although Plato properly drew the connection between passion and reason, his depiction of playing before the gods (Plato, Laws II 644d VII 803c) mistakenly emphasized how almighty gods simply toy with humans. Fink demonstrates instead that God genuinely enjoys play *with* humans.

Conclusion

This engagement with Fink's work does not properly do justice to his understanding of cult play or religion. However, among several possible insights that might be gained by reading Wariboko's Pentecostal pneumatology through Fink's cosmology, I here would like to highlight two: (1) we are in need of ways of rethinking the "working economy" of pietism, which is not limited to religion or Christianity but indeed is everywhere to be found in culture. In a pneumatological context, play helps establish a new kind of *tone* for moral life. Although the work of the Holy Spirit typically is seen as "serious" business or holy and sanctifying pietism, it is possible to imagine another posture of the moral life. (2) Engagement in "play" can bring one in closer contact with such a playful Holy Spirit: the *esse coram deo,* or "being before God" of humans should not be engaged as a "work like" struggle with God, or a way to earn God's attention or respect. Rather, in a creative and playful "wrestling with God" in which we freely struggle through enchantment and fascination, we might imagine new paths beyond how we typically have understood "imitation," "following," and repetition.

Regarding the first point, the traditional theological opposition between work/earning and freedom/grace is directly relevant here. We might apply Fink's insight that work/play are not opposed, but relate with one another in a playful way. Play can be ever-active in any and all forms of working. Play is a mindset (*Haltung*) or way in which we can also imagine working. This is not unlike the Pentecostal conception of how grace and free will (a point also highlighted by Wariboko) are sutured to one another in ways other systematic theologians often disregard in their practical aspects. Repetition and the seeking of dogmatic harmony certainly are hard work that distracts us from the free play of interrelations—interrelations that are far more important than the "work" we actually do. By understanding Grace and freewill as inseparable, we are provided at least a little space for what Wariboko calls "theological promiscuity," failure, and creativity. As we gain from Fink's understanding of play, we might acknowledge not only that things are constantly in a dynamic movement of freedom. We also can recognize that without this dynamic-ness, our worlds would remain separated from one another. This separation is precisely what allows no room for laughing and dancing—certainly not in any oh-so-serious religious context. Play helps establish genuine relations between persons that often are quarantined off from one another. Humans are not wooden structures distant from their context or "world."

Fink also might lend insight for Pentecostal pneumatology in the context of developing further Weber and Benjamin's thesis that work has become a placebo religiosity. Fink is keen on seeing this problem reversed, namely, in a way that religiosity no longer is completely commandeered by pietistic work, or by industriousness that is supposed to improve the soul or world. The way we are to *connect* with God in this sense would then be through play, laughter, and the full commitment to not hide oneself or present oneself falsely. God is not interested in the human attempt to be demi-gods, or to imitate God's *power*. That would be quite laughable! In this world we are to engage in "cult play" because such play puts us more truly on "the level" of communication with God. As Wariboko's Pentecostal pneumatology teaches, these relations are not for the purpose of winning, losing, or becoming stronger. Rather, it concerns establishing more points of relationality. The Holy Spirit moves, like an expressionist artist, within the split between things to unite them, no matter how contradictory they may seem. Play takes us beyond our human-all-too-human tendencies to engage in hierarchies based upon separation, which belong to the paradigms of work. In Pentecostal pneumatology, although the Spirit's work is one of "sanctification" through bearing the "gifts of the spirit" for witness, this sanctification brings moral repair through playful engagement.

As for the *second point*, Wariboko's rejection of traditional metaphysics seems to also be open for Fink's analysis of dynamic change in the world, which only play can grasp. The celebration of the lack of clear, orderly harmony, founded upon the "play of multiple" forces, pairs well with Fink's idea of cult play, which is motivated by trying to reveal the world (and simultaneously, the human) together. Cult play does not aim to fit a certain moral paradigm or "accurate" framework into a description of God's certain identity. As "cultic" in the most positive sense, this kind of play is communal and not merely individual. Wariboko's concept of the "split" nature of God already opens up a certain space or *Spielraum* between two identities/persons. There is already play between the three persons of the Triune God. Fink's idea of how play is a way to access God can help us better explain this internal diversity in/between persons. Play is a certain *way* of relating with persons and connecting them. Playless work can be done in silence and anonymously. Play calls for laughter and human relatability. Pentecostal pneumatology does not depict the Holy Spirit in terms that fit neatly into either only a substance ontology or a relational ontology but rather both: the Holy Spirit is not only a numinous and non-material power but a person. The Holy Spirit is not a mediator of relations but also relationality itself.

This of course has direct theological consequences, and here Pentecostals have something to learn especially from Fink's understanding of cult play. God's allusivity is not simply to be chalked-up to either a "serious" hiding that requires hard work for holy persons to access, or a mean-spirited and nonempathetic hide-and-seek when we are suffering. As Fink teaches, the distinction between play and seriousness upon which most of us rely in our interrelations is highly flawed. Without overlooking the negative phenomena of God's absence, Pentecostals affirm an affective, holistic way of being embodied in this world. One thing Pentecostal theologians might glean from Fink scholarship is the determination not only that God's "work" is actually a form of playing but also that this kind of working is something humans might playfully imitate, as if in a game. One of the best parts of games is that we can always reset the board, rethink the parameters and rules, and then start over with new strategies. And one thing Fink scholarship might glean from Pentecostal theologians such as Wariboko is found in a modification of Wariboko's "Pentecostal principle": we have the opportunity not only "to always begin again" but also to continue playing games that we thought already were over, and in which we imagined we were playing all alone. Instead of reacting to our aversions to "becoming more holy," we might find here a risk-taking freedom to fail that makes sanctification and holiness more social and fun. Perhaps we all could benefit from a little holy laughter.[13]

15

Ontology of Play and the Ambivalence of Resilience

Alice Koubová

Introduction

"I know of no other manner of dealing with great task, than as play," claims Friedrich Nietzsche in *Ecce Hommo* (2005: 99) and outlines how coping with difficulties and great problems does not exclude playfulness but, rather, the opposite. When facing serious tasks, human beings should remain playful, says Nietzsche. This claim immediately connects Eugen Fink's philosophy of play with what has recently been called resilience thinking. The aim of this chapter is to analyze the ontological implications of play and resilience, namely to relate the so called "ontology of interactive emergence" developed in the framework of the resilience thinking and the ontology of play presented in the play-based cosmology developed by Eugen Fink.

There is a difference of several decades between the extensive proliferation of the concept of play and the "boom" of resilience approaches in the scientific and philosophical debates. Whereas the development of play theories in philosophy, psychology, anthropology, and other disciplines and the overall turn to the topic of playfulness, game, and play culminated in the mid-twentieth century (Sutton-Smith, 1997: ix), the interest in resilience came into prominence at the turn of the century, and it has been researched extensively up till today in the framework of developmental psychology, chaos theory, system theory, disaster studies, and mainly within the Anthropocene paradigm.

The two concepts have, at the same time, important operational similarities: they both challenge linear and static ontologies based on the idea of the sovereign self-aware subject who is principally supposed to govern and control external reality. The play approach as well as the resilience thinking refuse as well the reversal of this equation—that is, that it is the outside reality that in the end governs human beings. Their ontology is based on an understanding of human beings as potentiality-of-being, operating beyond determinism and arbitrariness, beyond lethargic powerlessness and chronical optimism in control and full of governance. Through the phenomenon of playing, or resilience, play thinkers as well as resilience researchers examine possibilities of the intertwined coexistence of humans and reality that includes surprises (and atrocities), emergence, irregularities, generative transformations, relatedness and dependency, and liminality, but also certain kinds of surpluses of meaning, satisfaction, or happiness. They both mention the "vital element" as a key parameter for their ontology.

Regarding the conceptual definition, both the notion of play and the notion of resilience have ambivalent characteristics. Fink speaks about play as a "remarkable phenomenon of life: iridescent and polysemous, mysterious and simple" (Fink 2016: 259), or "very peculiar, though in no way pathological, 'schizophrenia'" (Fink 2016: 24). This description refers both to fragility, to doubleness, and to the stability of the notion. Play denotes a bearable multiplicity of perspectives and a bearable set of transformative responses to the reality. However, if the schizophrenic aspect takes over, it can lead to disintegration. The same dilemma concerns resilience—it is a concept that denotes the capacity to sustain disruptions either in the form a maximal openness to virtual transformation while attentively caring for basic safety and preventing the system to break down into arbitrariness, or in the form of a sophisticated encrypted accomplice of the status quo.

This semantic insecurity is not something that makes play and resilience weaker concepts—they are instead made more intriguing in their character. As is typical of essentially contested concepts, they belong among those qualitative, appraisive, initially ambiguous, and evaluative "concepts the proper use of which inevitably involves endless disputes about their proper uses on the part of their users" (Gallie 1956: 169). Essentially contested concepts are those that exist when it is performed and when it performs. Other examples of essentially contested concepts are "art" or "democracy" (Gallie 1956: 186). The meaning of essentially contested concepts only arises in their practical use, and the way such terms are applied is a matter of perpetual contention among their users.

Play and Resilience in Social Sciences

In social sciences, play and resilience are studied in correlation, for instance in the framework of design theory, or theory of care (Chang, Yarnal, and Chick 2016; Magnuson and Barnett 2013; Buchanan 1992; Wylant 2010). Here, the two concepts are, first, clearly defined and, second, measured and compared. Resilience is defined as the ability to bounce back from adversity, risk, and loss (Ong, Bergeman, and Boker 2009; Smith et al. 2008; Tugade and Fredrickson 2004). Regarding playfulness, social scientists define playfulness as a disposition to engage in play (Barnett 2007), which consists of five behavioural dimensions: creativity, curiosity, pleasure, sense of humour (Guitard, Ferland, and Dutil 2005), and fun (Glynn and Webster 1992). Using the scales for playfulness and resilience, social scientists measure how the activity of playing and the capacity to take part in games correlates with a higher capacity to withstand crises in life and to bounce back from adversity, risk, and loss. The correlation exists and shows that playfulness enhances resilience in life. As for instance Chang, Yarnal and Chick show: "The major finding . . . showed that higher levels of playfulness produced growth in the . . . members' resilience. . . . That is, their experiences of playfulness predicted their resilience growth" (Chang, Yarnal, and Chick, 2016: 223).

Ontology of Play and Resilience

However, correlations measured within these investigations do not question the ontological dimension of play and resilience. They do not ask if the reality of play and resilience is correctly understood and if the concepts as such are used in the relevant way. To give just an example: if resilience denotes a capacity that enables humans to cope with difficulties and to sustain atrocities, it should also be evaluated if the difficulties and atrocities are an unavoidable part of life or rather results of political injustice, or a consequence of one's own destructive behavior. Playfulness can also represent a tool used to make people feel at ease in an unjust world without protesting, or to temporarily escape from harsh reality, or to feel lighter for a while in order to sustain the heaviness longer without solving any problem.

The importance of an ontologically relevant understanding of play and resilience are actualized in the current state of polycrisis. Polycrisis is a term used by the philosopher and system theoretician Edgar Morin; it is defined as a situation of multiple difficulties or social challenges (climate crisis, health crisis, geopolitical conflicts, migration, economic and political instability, fragmentation of societies, political radicalization, poverty) whose origins are different from each other and whose character is too complex to grasp. The situation of polycrisis also has an affective component actualized in humans: feelings of powerlessness, insufficiency, irrelevant particularity. The feelings are amplified by the impossibility of separating from the situation, as humans are part of their problems they need to solve. They are both their carriers, doers, and receivers.

For these reasons, play and resilience must be approached from the philosophical and ontological point of view, and not only studied as ontic phenomena (phenomena that present things as functional parts of our everyday world, as thing at our hand). Eugen Fink belongs among the thinkers who systematically refuse to understand play as an ontic phenomenon, as a useful "affair" or "thing" of our lived world and instead analyzes it as a grounding experience that opens up the way to understand human beings in the world and the being of the world itself. This approach is not only theoretically exciting but also relevant and transformative. In order to find our way out of crises, one probably does not need to change the operational behavior, but one needs to understand the being of the world differently. As Donella Meadows says, we need to transform the "leverage point" that consists in the "society paradigm, or the deepest set of beliefs about how the world works" (Meadows 1999: 17). It is thus not only about trouble-shooting or self-improvement (Fuchs 2021; Coeckelbergh 2022), it is about changing the ontological interpretation of the human condition which has ethical and epistemological consequences.

Eugen Fink's Play-Based Cosmology

In *Play as a Symbol of the World* (2016) Eugen Fink provides a complex analysis of the phenomenon of play as the grounding experience with important ontological and ethical implications. Play enables the study of both "human being's ontological constitution" (Fink 2016: 15) and the search for "the ultimate purpose, the destiny, the true happiness of the human being" (Fink 2016: 20). For this reason, the investigation of play relates the ontological study of subjectivity together with ethico-political study, that is, the question of how to live the subjectivity as potentiality-of-being, as a holder of certain possibilities and power. The main ontological challenge lies in the distinction between play as a human activity and world-play. The second challenge concerns the relationship between human beings and the world totality.

In his philosophical account, Fink subverts the Aristotelian ontological account based in teleology. He agrees with Aristotle that human beings take life as a "task" and strives for the "telos": "Human life appears to stand under a single final end, to which all particular ends and partial strivings are subordinated" (Fink 2016: 212). The final end humans strive for is happiness: "in everything that is done in each case—fundamentally points ahead toward the "ultimate goal" of the human being: felicity, eudaimonia" (Fink 2016: 19). Aristotle claims that human eudaimonia has a form of a harmonious intellectual state of the mind achieved through hard work. In this architecture of hard work and strivings, play (*paidia*) has only a secondary function. It serves as indispensable relaxation when the serious work is too exhaustive. Fink, on the other hand, deconstructs the tension between serious work and play by introducing another ambivalence. He claims that the ultimate paradox lies in the uncertainty with what eudaimonia is. "We are not only affected by the unrest of the striving that carries us along, but also by the unrest of having an 'interpretation' of true happiness . . . in incessantly chasing after *eudaimonia*, we do not reach it" (Fink 2016: 19). And, "The *fatal* situation of the human being . . . is revealed by the fact that he cannot become absolutely certain of his final purpose by himself" (Fink 2016: 20). In order to avoid the hardness of this ambivalence, Fink claims, humans choose "an extremely manic frenzy for work" that only covers the horizon with "gloomy, unbrightened seriousness and . . . ethical rigorism" (Fink 2016: 17) which lets humans "fall captive to the Danaidean deamon of the modern world" (Fink 2016: 16). This compensating (ontic) strategy is revealed as unhappy and destructive, based in a perpetual feeling of self-insufficiency. Any techniques of self-improvement never change the outcome of this endeavor. The compensation of the existential ambivalence leads to an existential exhaustion.

Fink, however, proposes an alternative ontological project. He deconstructs the naive and "popular antitheses of 'work and play', of 'play and the seriousness of life' and so forth" (Fink 2016: 17) and presents play as ontologically primordial: "Play belongs essentially to the ontological constitution of human existence, it is an existentiell, fundamental phenomenon" (Fink 2016: 18). Play allows us to exist beyond the restless rush in the projects to settle and notice another source of movement that has been always already there—the movement of the "breath of the world." In play, thus, the world totality is specifically present, one experiences "pacified present and self-contained sense" (Fink 2016: 20) clearly distinguished from the "forward-rushing orientation toward the future" (Fink 2016: 20). As such, play enables us to experience meaningfulness as it is its own purpose: "Play is existence that is moved in itself. . . . The activity of play has only internal purposes, not ones that transcend it" (Fink 2016: 19–20). The world-relation of human existence in play has, moreover, another important aspect: "Human play has world-significance, has a cosmic transparency—it is one of the clearest world-figures of our finite existence" (Fink 2016: 46). Thanks to experiencing play we can also ask about the world. It seems that for Fink, world has a special characteristic in relationship to the innerworldly beings: "Everything in the world has its ground. But does the world itself, too, have a "ground"—or is the question devoid of sense here?" (Fink 2016: 212). Although all innerworldly being have their grounds, will, directions, the world as such is in "quite a unique sense" groundless: "Without ground and without aim, without sense and without goal, without value and without plan—but it holds within it all the grounds for thoroughly grounded innerworldly beings. . . . It holds spaces and times open for the grounded, purposive, meaningful, and value-laden Being of thing" (Fink 2016: 212). As such the world can never be understood as a subject, as player, as anybody with a ground or will: "Human playing is one way in which, in the midst of the pervasive groundedness of innerworldly things, a groundless oscillating-within-itself of the carrying out of life appears as a symbol of the prevailing world . . . . Human play is thus a symbol of the world" (Fink 2016: 213). The happiness humans can experience is connected with the emancipation from the striving toward the final aim. At the same time, it symbolizes world, that is aimless and groundless itself. But this aimlessness means also omnipotence—openness to possibilities. However this omnipotence is not given to the human being directly, but always in a refracted way, as duality, binarity, multiplicity: "In human play, aspects of the world light up, but in a refracted manner—refracted by the binary of actuality and non-actuality." The non-actuality is not simply an unreal being, or a copy of the actual being. It is an image. Play proposes an imaginary that is productive and transformative, not re-productive, and in this way emancipates humans from the orbits of the actual tasks. What if I do . . ., As if I was . . . What if he says . . . As if we have . . . As "a sphere that is here and yet not here, now and yet not now" (Fink 2016: 205), play "goes around confidently with a broken, fragmented 'understanding of Being'" (Fink 2016: 229). Playing human *is both player (Mitspieler) and toy (Spilzeug) in this play of the world.* The power of play is by Fink denoted as "vital élan" (Fink 2016: 112). Play is according to him "at work in all its metamorphoses as a vital power of mysterious allure and seductive enticement."(Fink 2016: 217) Play has "vitality, . . . transformative power [and] impulsive immediacy" and as such it "Is far removed from the spirit of sober scientific knowledge and philosophy's speculative flight of thought; play does not reason argumentatively and yet it is not thoughtless" (Fink 2016: 234). Therefore, it cannot be reduced to an instrument of human will and control; it embodies a transcendence that does not "allow itself to be incorporated without further ado into the complex architecture of purposes" (Fink 2016: 20). The weapon used against the elan vital of play is irony, ridiculing of enthusiasm, subordination of imagination to thought, and the interpretation of play as a sheer copy, mimesis. To put it shortly—instrumentalization. Although Fink claims that "Play is imitation in the space of the imaginary" (Fink 2016: 90), he refuses Plato's idea, that the "playworld is *less* than the ordinary sensuous thing . . . it is only a reproduction, only the reproductive mirroring of sensuous things" (Fink 2016: 208–9). The reason why Fink refuses Plato's reduction is "the playworld is, notwistanding its being bound to appearance, *more* than ordinary things" (Fink 2016: 209). Thanks to the fact that it provides a frame for epiphany. Fink concludes, "The playworld is thus neither 'less' nor 'more' in comparison to the rest of things; it is unique in that it is less and also more" (Fink 2016: 209).

However, the elan vital is not considered as anything good that must be reached. Fink is not talking in favor of an explanatory triumphalist idea of play and world. "The world in itself is aimless, and it also has no value in itself and remains outside every moralistic assessment, is 'beyond good and evil'" (Fink 2016: 212). Elan vital "just" frees space in which a certain action becomes possible. "In play we mix Being and appearance together without inhibition; we take enigmatic delight in that which is apparent, which occasionally verifies for us a higher truth than the solidly actual things of our everyday environment" (Fink 2016: 209).

Resilience

There are many parallels between Fink"s play theory and resilience theory. The resemblance is proposed for instance by Jan Halak: "Play is, for Fink, a reminder that the reality is not a sum of relationships between objects which can be defined as pure being. Interestingly, such a position is in accord with some of the most progressive thoughts . . . for which the problem of indetermination is frequently crucial (e.g. . . . chaos theory)" (Halak 2015: 5)

Resilience is discussed in the theory of systems and chaos theory. These theories claim that "the stable, predictable world of European modernity were untenable assumptions" (Chandler, Grove, and Wakefield 2020: 9). Later on, within the context of Anthropocene, the debate on indetermination gets more urgent showing that "humanity got embedded within complex social, environmental and technical systems that threaten Earth's habitability" (Chandler, Grove, and Wakefield 2020: 9).

Wicked Problems and Three Episteme for Governing the Complexity

The resilience approach to this challenge consists in an ontological and epistemological move. Its point of departure lies in the presupposition that human beings can never achieve pure security and cannot fully understand the character of reality and problems they face. The reality consists of many "wicked problems." Wicked problems are by definition problems that cannot be fully determined (Coyne 2005). As Kevin Grove explains in more detail:

> Wicked problems are a specific class of problems. They are not simply ill-defined problems that lack specification in terms appropriate for a particular branch of science or engineering to solve . . . [they] transcend disciplinary boundaries and involve stakeholders with competing and incompatible interests and values. Any proposed solution will thus inevitably generate additional and unforeseen problems, which means the problem lacks a stopping rule for terminating the search for solutions. (Grove 2018: 11)

David Chandler explains further how the fact that we face wicked problems influences new ways of governing the complexity. He shows that the emergence of complexity resulted in acceptance that "the unknowable is not a result of hidden determinism . . . nor can it be the results of blind chance or luck" (Chandler 2014: 50). This approach leads to the distinction of three epistemes where the two first ones are undermined by general complex theory and resilience approaches. The first episteme that can be called modernist and liberal, "understands the 'knows knowns' as central to governmental reason, based on linear and universal assumptions of the progressive accumulation of knowledge of laws and regularities of human affairs" (Chandler 2014: 50). The second, neoliberal, episteme regards these "'know knows' to be less important, resulting in merely artificial and potentially counterproductive assumptions that ignore the interactive complexity of life" and rather orients itself toward "known unknowns, the hidden, underlying, processes of determination, which we know we do not fully know" (Chandler 2014: 50). However,

> for resilience approaches, working on the basis of emergent causality or general complexity, there is no deterministic understanding of known unknowns operating underneath or at the deeper level of causation. In the more open interactive ontology of resilience, it is the "unknown uknowns" that have the central role in emergent causation meaning that contingent outcomes only reveal concrete causality after the event and are impossible to know beforehand. (Chandler 2014: 50)

The reality cannot be but governed through a posteriori explanations without any idea of a existing "ground" or "aim" or "exactness." Resilience approaches work instead, as follows: "Nothing is exactly how it appears and entities are not reduced to fixed essences. Instead, relations are key rather than actual entities. . . . It is because resilience approaches focus on the potential powers of life, already real but not actualised, that the key to policy interventions is system or relational understandings" (Chandler, Grove, Wakefield, 8).

Resilience in Psychology

Besides the theory of systems, resilience becomes very important in psychology after the Second World War. The debate focused mainly on the definition of health and what psychology should actually heal. The previous modernistic paradigm forced psychology, according to its critics, to work with the ontology of pathologies—healthy and happy human beings are defined by the absence of sickness, absence of disruptions, and suffering. The healing consists in annihilating suffering and solving problems in their deepest sources. The alternative approach (Donald Winnicott, Martin Seligman, Boris Cyrulnik) argues that health is more about the capacity to flourish in the non-ideal reality, that is, about developing resilience. In other words, one can be healthy although one is somewhat sick. Nobel Prize-winning economist Amartya Sen provides a concrete example of a resilience ontology. Sen claims that absolute levels of education, health, wealth or poverty say very little about the quality of life of an individual. In other words, people consider their lives healthy or having a good quality, not in the case when they have no problems, no issues in economy or education, but in case when they live in satisfactory relations. The relations are satisfactory if the agents have influence on their relational reality, if they can take initiative, if they are visible by the others in their capacities and if their capabilities can become actualized (Sen 1999; Chandler 2013; Reghezza-Zitt and Rufat 2019; Chandler, Grove, and Wakefield 2020: 9). Resilience in this interpretation is presented as the opposite of powerlessness. What it preserves is the capacity to play an active role in one's life and the reality one lives (Peterson, Maier, and Seligman 1993), to be a player regardless of how much one is also played. In cases of long-standing experiences of the absence of the correlation between one's choices and efforts to act and the outcome of such an effort, one can develop so-called learned helplessness. Learned helplessness transforms the self-relationship into a specific pathology characterized by the absence of play. As Seligman puts it: "Learned helplessness is the giving-up reaction, the quitting response that follows from the belief that whatever you do doesn't matter" (Peterson, Maier, and Seligman 1993). People suffering from learned helplessness do not play; they have no distance from their fully serious life. They do not try to avoid painful situations even if the situations were easily avoidable. Instead, they survive. Here, again, it is not important what the play-field is but that one can play in the world-play.

Forms of Instrumentalization of Resilience Approach

The concept of resilience can also be instrumentalized and this instrumentalization paradoxically, resembles many thoughts formulated by Fink in relationship to play.

First, the fact that humans cannot govern their reality because they do not grasp the character of the problems they face (their ground and purpose) might not lead to a transformation of their attitude but to another stronger effort to be in control. This leads to the above-mentioned manic frenzy for work, to the amplified will to stand, cope and manage difficulties, to the will to design, that only covers the horizon with "gloomy, unbrightened seriousness" (Fink 2016: 17). This is one form of instrumentalized resilience.

Second, resilience thinkers as well as play theorists including Fink attribute to the world a vital principle, the elan vital. In Fink's interpretation, this power is neither good nor bad: it presents itself as a refraction of actuality and non-actuality and, it guarantees that there will not be immanence without self-distance. In resilience thinking, the neo-vitalism plays another instrumental role. It claims that life is an excess of being and it is productive and transformative; however, this transformative life power is here for us. In other words, although it is not controllable and unknowable, it will preserve us and our being—it is not a known known, but a known unknown, extracted, and instrumentalized elan vital which is there for us. Thus, it is a new attempt to control the world.

Third, in a real application of resilience thinking, the capacity to sustain uncertainty and insecurity might be in the wrong, put only on the shoulders of those who cannot defend themselves, and the ontological presupposition is transformed into political misuse: "the complexity of unseen or unrecognised policy-feedbacks is rarely framed to take into account the structural causes of resource depletion and social and economic marginalisation, which makes communities and societies more vulnerable to shocks and disturbances" (Neyrat 2019; Whyte 2019). Because of this framing, the policy interventions, based upon enabling and capacity building for resilience, might tend to impose the costs of adaptation upon those who are already in a marginal position, attempting to tackle the effects of crises and shocks but not the structural causes (Moore 2019; Chandler and Reid 2019).

These forms of instrumentalization, governing the ungovernable, transform resilience into a tool for preservation of modern forms of production and consumption: "Ironically, then, resilience approaches seem to be the enemy of resilience in the Anthropocene, striving to continue to preserve and reproduce exactly the same modes of being and thinking that caused anthropogenic climate change in the first place" (Chandler, Grove, and Wakefield 2020: 14).

Fink's Ontology in Resilience Thinking

Fink's play-based cosmology that relates the human being, nonhumans, and the world in a specific way provides highly relevant ontological distinctions that can help to navigate in the turmoil of the current polycrisis without giving advice in the form of ontic "strategies," social engineering, and "implementations."

Fink distinguishes play as a human activity and play as an ontological phenomenon. Whereas in the teleological ontology play is a human activity and is understood as secondary instrumental, in Fink's ontology it is the primary, even grounding experience. It is a symbol of the world linking the actual a non-actual, Being and appearance in the experimental imaginary. In play, human beings step out from the architecture of purposes, strivings, and problem-solving and experience the movement of life that has its aim in itself. This detachment from the architecture of purposes through imagination and duplicity (we play as if we were not only actual) is the source of happiness. Paradoxically enough, this play is a *fragment* symbolizing the *totality* of the world, that itself is groundless, aimless, and deprived of values. The world is neither good nor bad, and as such it disposes of the vital energy. It gives space for grounded beings to strive for purpose and to be in happy contact with a purposeless world. In this way play is above and below the real; it cannot establish any relationship of subordination, hierarchy of more/less to the so-called serious reality, for example, the real problems of the world, and so on. This essential impossibility to place the play-world above or below the real world is a crucial gesture. The play-world cannot include the real world and the real world cannot include the play world. Appearance is more than certainty and certainty is more than appearance. They transcend each other and are *mutual conditions of the possibility* of the other. Therefore, there is no happy ending in Fink's cosmology, no unification, no resolution. But there are moments and places of surplus, satisfaction, happiness, and flourishing that are worth living and that give distance to one's own life. To govern one's life means neither to control it or not to control it. The care of oneself implies noticing world-play as a source of duplicity that is neither frustrating nor pathological, but radically transformative, embodied, and meaningful. If resilience shall be the concept referring to a stance toward uncertainty and insecurity, it should not be instrumentally playful, but it should be playful in the ontological sense of the word. This also includes that humans are being played while they are players and that the vital element is not here to preserve their status quo, but to let humans "see the unseen," to let them be double and not indifferent (excessively immanent, communicating, relating, performing), to let them not be thoughtless even if they are not armed with arguments, to let them not fall into multiplicity of copies, but rather richness of images, to let them avoid learned helplessness. This experimented, embodied distance might refer to the ontology of resilience. It is not an ontology reactivating the modernistic phantom of control and security through seeking the salvation in one's own capabilities to adapt, to sustain, to be well at every occasion. The ontology of resilient human consists in the attentive, non-productive, not indifferent (i.e., differentiating, distancing) encounter with the world.

16

From *Animal Rationale* to *Ens Cosmologicum*

Eugen Fink on Animality

Catherine Homan

In his lecture course of 1951/2, titled "Philosophie der Erziehung" and published as *Natur, Freiheit, Welt*, Fink begins by suggesting that one issue in contemporary pedagogy is that although it focuses on human development, it fails to ask what the human *is* (Fink 1992: 12). Philosophy seems well poised to answer this question of what the human is, yet it, too, has not yet provided an adequate account of what it is to be human. While Fink's focus in this lecture is education, the question of the human appears in nearly all of his writings. Dissatisfied with Western metaphysics' conception of the human as rational animal, which renders the human a "centaur" and relies on dualisms between mind and body, Fink attempts to cast the human instead as *ens cosmologicum*, a cosmological being. Rather than bifurcated between rational human and irrational animal, the cosmological human can relate to herself as in-between. That is, she can understand herself as finite, like all living creatures, and yet also hold herself meaningfully in relation to the infinite play of the cosmos. Fink also warns against thinking of the human as surpassing nature by becoming rational, and instead wants to rethink how it is the human relates to nature. Through play, the human can experience most fully the tension between freedom and necessity that characterizes human experience. This, according to Fink, is both essentially and exclusively human. While other animals demonstrate playful behavior, only the human plays in the truest sense. Similarly, while other animals may produce things, only the human can be said to work. While other animals may mate for life, only the human truly loves. While other animals die, only the human truly experiences death. While other animals spar or fight, only the human truly battles.

In drawing out these differences between humans and nonhumans, is Fink insisting on a distinction of degree or of kind? In recasting the human as *ens cosmologicum*, what happens to the animal dimension of *animal rationale*? Although Fink seeks to maintain the human's status as in-between human and divine, as a living being born of the earth like other creatures, it remains unclear whether humans share in the animality of other living creatures or whether humans are entirely distinct. On the one hand, it seems like Fink preserves the human's animality as a living being comported to nature. On the other hand, he maintains strongly that only the human, unlike other animals, can ask about itself. In Fink's recasting of the human as *ens cosmologicum*, does the animality of the human actually drop out? Or does it remain as ambiguous, the inverse of the human's ambiguous freedom?

In the following, I trace Fink's understanding of the human as a cosmological being set apart from all other things in the world. While Fink does argue that the human not only is fully distinct from other animals but also occupies a privileged status due to its superior capacities, we would be wrong to think that nonhuman animals offer little in helping us understand what it means to be human. Indeed, as demonstrated in Fink's own appeal to Nietzsche, it may be that only by returning to ourselves as animal that we can be fully human.

From Centaur to *Ens Cosmologicum*

We exist, says Fink, in the world, among plants, stones, animals, and humans. What distinguishes the human from these other things is that we know that we are in the world. Moreover, we are not bound to the world in the same way. We can choose the sort of lives we want for ourselves. We can move beyond pure immanence. For those reasons, too, we have moral culpability, whereas other living creatures do not. It is not just that we might have more knowledge than nonhumans, for we also do not fully know the extent of their knowledge. Rather, the human has "specific capacities that raise him above every animal" (Fink 2016a: 63). Thus, it is not only that the human is distinct from but is also superior to every animal. Fink argues that the human can produce things that otherwise would not exist, can form concepts and develop abstract thought, has a moral conscience, has a capacity for language, and, because of this capacity, is also able to have an understanding of Being (2016a: 58–9). For Fink, what is essential to being human is not only that we are in the world but that we also understand ourselves as such. We understand that this distinguishes us from other animals and also raises us closer to the divine.

Western metaphysics has misunderstood this human experience, however, by interpreting the human as "torn asunder" by this intermediate status (Fink 2016a: 63), reflected in defining the human as *animal rationale*. On the one hand, this interpretation views the human as "an intellect stained with sensuousness" and, on the other, "an animal perturbed by intellectuality" (Fink 2016a: 63). This division renders the human a centaur, half human and half animal. Fink does not object to the idea that the human is between animal and divine. Rather, the "disastrous legacy" of the image of the human as centaur is that it confines the human to being simply bound between divine and animal (Fink 2016a: 63). As such, what is most essential about the human, namely the relation to the world, is obscured. The centaur figure does not allow the ecstatic world relation that most characterizes human existence.

Fink argues that what distinguishes the human from other things in the world is not simply a collection of properties, like being rational, bipedal, or created in a divine image. Instead, what distinguishes the human is the specific *way* of being in the world. As he explains in *Sein, Wahrheit, Welt*, the human is "not simply 'in' the world like every other thing, the 'world' is, in a sense, 'in' human beings" (Fink 2018a: 253). By that, Fink means that while all things are gathered into the totality of the world, the world is not like a container that merely holds objects within. Rather, as the totality of all that is, it grants all things time and space. All things in the world are penetrated by the world, yet the world also remains fundamentally distinct from each particular thing. The human differs specifically by recognizing the way in which all things are shot through with the world. Like all things, humans are in the world, but, unlike all other things, they can choose how to comport themselves to the world.

To Be Is to Play

As discussed above, Fink identifies a fundamental difference not only between humans and animals but also between humans and the world. At the root of both of these distinctions is the human's status as a world being. We belong to the world and are open to it. We understand ourselves to be world beings, that is, as finite creatures amid an infinite world totality. The tradition of metaphysics has misunderstood the human as rational animal by covering over this ecstatic nature. Moreover, by maintaining a sharp division between the rational and the animal, metaphysics cannot successfully join its metaphysics of morals with its metaphysics of nature. That is, freedom cannot be married to necessity. For Fink, though, if we are world beings, then our morality, our freedom, cannot be fully separate from our finitude and situatedness. Although we know ourselves to be finite, we can choose how to relate to our finitude. In so doing, we actually participate in something of the world totality. We are able to hold ourselves out beyond mere immanent existence. As we will see, Fink identifies this capacity most clearly in the human play that shares in the play of the world totality.

Before turning more specifically to play, I would like first to outline the distinctions Fink draws between humans and animals. Again, the distinction hinges on the human's existence as a world being. Animals live out their allotted time without any awareness of it. They are "in time but they do not comport themselves to time, they do not comport themselves to their own transience" and "know nothing about their demise" (Fink 2016a: 73). Humans are finite like animals, but humans are "more finite" because they can also comport themselves to this finitude (Fink 2016a: 73). That is, they are nearer to death because they know of their death. Humans know about moving from youth to old age and can determine how to comport themselves to that transience. Thus, what distinguishes the human from the animal is this self-relation.[1]

Similarly, humans, like animals, are corporeal and belong to vegetative life. Yet, we do not belong to vegetative life in the same way. Here, Fink draws not merely a difference of degree but one of kind. It is not that humans belong to nature in a more thoroughgoing way but rather that they do so in a fundamentally different way. Animals are bound by nature, but humans can fabricate things given by nature. Animals are governed by instinct, humans by choice. Because of our fundamental freedom, we can create and give shape to what would otherwise bind us. Importantly, Fink is not here relying on the dualism between reason and animality. The human does not stand over against nature and vegetative life because she is rational. Rather, precisely because the human can understand her existence in nature, she already exists in a different mode of being from plants and animals (Fink 1992: 102).

Whereas much of the history of Western philosophy has seen morality as reason overcoming base animal drives and desires, Fink suggests that ethics is not a matter of getting beyond the natural world. Rather, ethics is grounded in *physis*. By that he means that what characterizes human existence is precisely that we belong both to the world totality that grants all appearance and to the sheltering, concealing earth. Fink explains, "What is often dismissively referred to as our animal nature, the allegedly animalistic, is an originary moral power of human, is a mode of trusting and being close to the quiet granting of the sheltering and giving earth" (Fink 1992: 92). The earth, which resists full comprehension, marks the beginning of morality for it provides the basis of being open to what is other.

If, however, humans belong to the earth in a similar way that other living creatures do, then are not nonhumans also capable of morality? For Fink, decidedly not. Whereas other animals belong to the earth through growth, maturation, birth, and death, humans know they belong to these processes. They play "a great game of love and death," recognizing that while life is finite and dangerous, they are also secure in the "nurturing maternal womb of earth" (Fink 1992: 93). Whereas stones, birds, trees, and so on are also gathered in the world and exist alongside one another, only the human can exist *with* others. Again, this reflects an ethical dimension in that the human remains open to others and, as free, bears responsibility in how she comports herself to this reality. Thus, what distinguishes humans, as world beings, is not only an awareness of our existence as such but the freedom to give shape to our existence.

Fink identifies five basic phenomena of human existence that belong to us as world beings. They are work, death, love, ruling, and play. While animals may share in something akin to these phenomena, they do so only like shadows on the cave wall (Fink 2016a: 143). Fink writes, "No animal can or must work; the bee, which gathers, does not work. It can never relate to its futures, let alone to time. It cannot care and provide" (Fink 1992: 84). Birds may construct a nest or beavers a dam, whereas only humans can set goals for themselves and freely create. For this reason, Fink also insists that only the human can truly be said to work. We can fabricate artificial things through our own labor.

In this way, humans can be said to "go beyond" themselves by being able to relate to their future. While dependent on the environing nature of the earth, humans can give their own stamp to it (Fink 2016a: 150). In this sense, too, only humans can be educated, whereas animals are trained. Education is the development of self-awareness and is more a matter of self-education, of giving shape to oneself, whereas training is done by one to another (Fink 1992: 105). That is, humans can give themselves the task of development, whereas animals are trained according to someone else's goal. Humans understand that they are setting themselves tasks (Bertolini 2017). Animals do not have concepts to understand their actions. Similarly, human struggle is characterized by a desire to win out over something, not the simple instinctual impulse for survival.

Even play, which seems to belong to many species from goats frolicking to kittens pouncing on string to monkeys chasing one another, actually belongs only to humans. Indeed, Fink even goes so far as to say young children do not play in the full sense because they do not yet have a sense of their own futurity (Fink 2016b: 24). They do not understand that they are playing or understand what play is. For Fink, play is not merely a behavior or frivolous action. Instead, it is a meaningful way of standing in symbolic relation to the play of the world.

As discussed above, what distinguishes the human from all other things in the world, and also distinguishes Fink's understanding of the human being from that of Western metaphysics, is that the human being alone is a world being. The world, as the totality of all that is and that allows for all coming into being, surpasses all finite human understanding (Fink 2016a: 132). Yet, because the human exists in understanding, she also knows of this finite understanding. Unlike the animal, who knows neither of its finitude nor of anything beyond its finite conditions, the human being is "more worldly than every other thing" precisely because she comports herself to this understanding of the world and all existence. The human "stands in the slipstream of the immense, is torn open by the supremacy of the universe that at once elevates and bears down on him, is attuned by the native and uncanny proximity and distance of the world-totality" (Fink 2016a: 199). Importantly, for Fink, this relation to the world is not merely cognitive. It is not just a thought but a mode of being.

How, then, do we comport ourselves to the world? Through play. Human play is worldly in the openness that allows things to come into being and to fade away. We are able to transcend ourselves in comporting ourselves to the non-actuality and groundlessness of the playworld we have opened, in stepping out into our freedom. To be sure, we do not escape ourselves, but instead can stand in relation to ourselves and the world in ways otherwise not prefigured. Human play stands in symbolic relation to the play of being and nothing of the world totality. As Fink explains, play is a "cosmic metaphor" (Fink 2016a: 209). The world totality plays, but without a player. As the totality, it is also the groundlessness of all groundlessness. Fink concludes *Play as Symbol of the World* by claiming, "The human being—as a player—exists open to the world most of all precisely when he dismisses all measures and holds himself out into that which is limitless" (Fink 2016a: 215). Thus, it is not that the human abandons her status as a natural being but that she can also take it up as an identity and play with it.

Handling Great Tasks as Play

While animals and even children might take up an object or activity in a novel way or engage with it in a way other than its assumed purpose, because they do not (yet) have language and they cannot hold themselves out in this ecstatic way.[2] They do not play in this truest sense. Above, we saw that Fink does not think that the human is a bundle of characteristics or properties that distinguish her from all other things. Rather, the defining feature is *how* the human exists in the world. If what distinguishes the human, though, is language, then does not Fink seem to slip back into the tradition of metaphysics that defines the human based on essential properties?

Fink explains that linguisticality (*das Sprachliche*) is not simply an ingredient that can be added or subtracted. Instead, it is a condition, a mode of being: "Only because we can speak, only because we can *say* I, are able to observe ourselves, can we reflectively carry out 'inner perceptions,' objectify experiences, 'watch' ourselves as we perform our lives" (Fink 1992: 113). This condition is not such that we can escape ourselves to hold ourselves under a microscope. Nor is language a distortion of self-evident reality. Rather, it is only because language can allow for this reflective capacity that we can understand ourselves as finite world beings and comport ourselves in this mode of existence. Language is a distinguished form of world-disclosure; it is a fundamental mode of human being in the world as dwelling in the open of meaningfully structured coincidence (*Fügung*) (Fink 2018b: 153).

This characterization has three important consequences. First, it is only through language that the world, and our own world being, is disclosed. Second, it is only through language that we can be *with* others. The rock and tree may stand near or alongside others, but they cannot be said to be in community with others. Certainly, animals do live with others and develop companionships or relate to their worlds in specific ways, but they do not have community in the sense of together living out this world relation. Third, language affords the generative creativity that allows the possibility of holding oneself out into the future and having one's life as a task. Without the openness to the world made possible by language, the animal exists in that world totality but cannot comport themselves to it.

Fink describes the human as belonging to nature like all other things in the world but differs in both degree and kind. The human is the "prodigal son" of nature, both abandoned in his isolation and entrusted in his freedom (Fink 1992: 174). He cannot be led by nature like a flock of birds migrating across the sea. Instead, he is always at a crossroads to decide for himself where to go. Yet, it is precisely this exposure (*Ausgesetztheit*) that allows the human to relate to nature, to the world totality, and to other humans. Because the human is free, she is abandoned in this freedom, yet also affirmed in the creative art of transfiguring the world (Fink 2016a: 199). Thus, the human belongs to nature, but stands in a different relation to it from all other natural things.

For Fink, it seems to be the case that the human becomes most human when she remembers that she is not like an animal. She feels encompassed by nature, just as the stone, tree, or fish is, but she also knows that she is estranged from it by being able to act on her freedom. Whereas Western metaphysics, according to Fink, saw this as an impossible divide between the metaphysics of morals and metaphysics of nature, Fink maintains that the human as *ens cosmologicum* is conditioned by nature, but can freely determine how to comport herself to this conditionedness. Moreover, she does this most fully in play.

Fink routinely turns to Nietzsche to make this point. In Nietzsche, Fink identifies the playful tension between measure-giving Apollo and chaotic Dionysus as the play of the universe. For example, in *Natur, Freiheit, Welt*, Fink references Aphorism 150 of *Beyond Good and Evil* as the clue to the human as world being: "Around the hero everything becomes a tragedy; around the demigod, into a satyr-play; and around God,—what? perhaps into 'world'?" (Fink 1992: 196; Nietzsche 2010: 90). The mortal human cannot become god, but as worldly, can act out these world moments of being and nothing, the night and day of being, in play.

What is interesting is that Fink identifies Nietzsche's account of Apollonian-Dionysian play as the key to understanding the human as playful *ens cosmologicum*, yet Fink draws a much stronger distinction between human and animal than Nietzsche does. Nietzsche's philosophy is full of animal metaphors, from the camel to the lion to the cow. On the one hand, it may seem that the use of animals is only metaphorical while still maintaining a clear distinction between human and nonhuman animals. On the other hand, as Vanessa Lemm argues, Nietzsche describes the human as a rope suspended between animal and overhuman. There is continuity, rather than separation, between these seemingly agonistic moments (Lemm 2009: 3). Nietzsche identifies the animal with forgetting and the human with memory. To become human is to recognize the value of forgetting that allows for the revaluation of values.

Nietzsche's philosophy is one of playful self-creation and life-affirmation. It is animal forgetfulness that reminds us that all values are created and subject to revision. For example, animal forgetfulness allows for the gift-giving virtue that resists utilitarian ledgers of debts (Lemm 2009: 73). We find that animal forgetfulness reveals itself in dreams that provide new possibilities for creativity. Moreover, animal thinking is pictorial thinking. As Lemm argues, returning to animal thinking as creative and artistic challenges the hegemony of pure definitions that fails to account for the multiplicitous play of interpretations (Lemm 2009: 122). She highlights Nietzsche's passage in "Truth and Lies in an Extra-Moral Sense":

> The vast assembly of beams and boards to which the needy human being clings, thereby saving himself on his journey through life, is used by the liberated intellect as a mere climbing frame and play-thing on which to perform its most reckless tricks, and when it smashes this framework, jumbles it up and ironically re-assembles it, pairing the most unlike things and dividing those things which are closest to one another, it reveals the fact that it does not require those makeshift aids of neediness, and that it is now guided not by concepts but by intuitions. (Cited in Lemm 2009: 148)

The intellect liberated from the imperative of logic and world of reason can now affirm itself as creative. Animal forgetfulness grants a return to being human as creative life-affirmation.

If, for Fink, what is most human is our playful world relation, particularly as explicated by Nietzsche, I argue we risk failing to remember the animal forgetfulness that enables us to be human if we hold too strongly to human exceptionalism, which is itself a false memory. Even in his extensive Nietzsche interpretation, Fink emphasizes this exceptionalism. Writing about Zarathustra's conversation with his animal companions, Fink explains, "The eternal return is revealed differently to the animals than to humans. They are embraced by change and do not confront it. They are involved in the play of being, they do not play against it like man" (Fink 2003: 88). On Fink's reading, the animal has no task, whereas the human has the task to become overhuman, to play between freedom and necessity. The human, as finite, can play against and within the eternal Dionysian play of time as creation and destruction, whereas the animal is mere animal.

In this discussion of Zarathustra, Fink mentions, but does not dwell at length, on the fact that Zarathustra imagines himself as a bird, citing, "'If I ever suspended quiet heavens above me and flew with my own wings into my own heaven/ If I swam playfully in deep reaches of light and came to the freedom of my bird's wisdom'" (Fink 2003: 101). Fink's point is that the ability to fly above oneself, the "self-expansion of human existence," allows turning toward the world. Similarly, Fink also concludes PSW with this passage, suggesting that the human being becomes most fully human, a player, precisely when "he dismisses all measures and holds himself out into what is limitless" (2016b: 215). While Fink does not say as much, it seems key that Zarathustra accomplishes this by becoming animal, which then enables becoming human in this wider sense.

Fink suggests that Zarathustra's turn to the world is one of love for the infinite (2003: 103). In *Natur, Freiheit, Welt*, Fink also describes the earth's erotic dimension that resists full comprehension. Again, it is comportment to this alterity that opens the possibility for morality. By remaining open to the earth, to our natural, even beastly, elements, we do not abandon ourselves but harmonize ourselves with that dimension. As Gary Shapiro observes, Zarathustra becomes human by becoming bird, becoming other to himself, and by playing with the infinite (2004: 85). Thus, it may be that we become more fully human by remembering we are also animal. The danger of strict human exceptionalism and anthropocentrism is that it precludes the animal forgetfulness that could allow us to affirm ourselves as creative.

While Fink worries that viewing the human as a step between human and divine covers over the human's world relation, cleaving humans fully from both animal and overhuman cleaves us from ourselves. If, instead, we see the tightrope joining the three that allows movement back and forth, we remain in a position to dance across and play with our identities. Returning to ourselves as animal returns us to the infinite world and sheltering, giving earth for it reminds us of how to handle that great task as play.

17

Politics as Social Gameplay? How We Might Reconsider a Phenomenology of Play in Terms of Freedom and Responsibility

Annette Hilt

In Eugen Fink's writings dedicated to the existential role of "play," it is clear this groundphenomenon is crucial for reflecting our self-relation, our understanding of being, and the openness of the world.[1] Yet, Fink is hesitant to use play as a major guideline in his writings on a political self-understanding of our communal being in the world, even if the political realm might be considered in terms of interest-driven games.[2] For Fink, play as an organ of understanding in this realm seems easily to fall prey to being exercised merely for masking power relations, as a strategic way to benefit some happy few, whenever it is used as an instrument to shape political structures not only to represent but to enlarge power. This aspect of power might not apply to the structure of play as a groundphenomenon regarding play's particular possibility to give and gain freedom.[3] From a point of view, where our social affairs are a kind of competitive game, this giving and gaining freedom is easily misunderstood as freedom of a subject which plays against someone or somebody else and is misunderstood as an antagonistic freedom: a negative freedom. Against such misinterpretations of play, Fink enters a different register to interrogate the modes of understanding the structures and situations we face when bringing forth forms of communal life in the sphere of power, that is, politics (cf. Fink 2018b: 418).

Fink states that such a misunderstood form of freedom from play, with which we produce norms, rules, measures, and institutions of being together, turns out to be a game of sheer will to power, a preoccupation of an elite—as he uses a Nietzsche's vocabulary. "Their production bears the character of an idiosyncratic intercourse with the play of their fellow-beings. Whereas the latter are tangled up in their own play for meaning of their existence, the former play with them as players do with toys [. . .], with imaginary tools" (Fink 2018b: 424). It is not only that an elite (mis-)uses their toys as means for their own ends and misses the moral claim of recognition, but they even misunderstand themselves. Such misunderstanding might turn out to swerve into a Hegelian dialectics of master and servant. There will come a time when the oppressed will comprehend that the rules they obey are only at random, without any authority they ought to obey. Fink argues this is the result of the disenchantment of modernity not only by science (cf. Fink 2018b: 293) but also by the age of political revolutions.

For Fink, these learnings of the nihilistic condition of modernity are also a baseline for dealing with our groundless *conditio humana*. Groundless as there is no final foundation we could establish to justify such a condition, but only a web of relational phenomena that might change as we value these phenomena differently. Only by understanding how such values and ideals guiding the ends and means of our social lifeworld become constituted (or instituted), we might capture freedom as a signature of our humaneness. Neither rooted in reason nor in will, freedom is a challenge we face in the fields of politics. Play does not equate with a model for our current understanding of the social world. Rather, for Fink in the political realm it is power. He deals with it as an existential groundphenomenon for the political realm and its challenge to freedom.

What bothers Fink in his *Tractatus on Human Violence* is how human coexistence—our being with other human and nonhuman beings—finds different forms in groundphenomena of human existence (as he does in *Existence and Coexistence*).[4] It is a treatise on our understanding of freedom when there is the existential need to find or rather to invent and produce regimes justified by ideals which are no longer pre-given by any universal norm. For example, a transcendent God, Nature, or any other absolute vantage point like reason, will, or any form of metaphysical precedence over innerworldly structures. The ambiguity or twilight of order to evolve[5] calls for reconsidering three central stances in their interrelatedness which is also symbolized by the web of groundphenomena: subjectivity of the playing agents, their freedom along the lines both of productivity and its structural violence, and finally responsibility in playing the social game. Responsibility is a term we do not find explicitly in Fink,[6] yet we can reconstruct it. For example, in the confrontation of Fink with E. Levinas' "Ethics as First Philosophy."[7]

Which Subjectivity?

Besides in his major work *Groundphenomena of Human Existence* (*Grundphaenomene des menschlichen Daseins*)[8] and in his political *Tractatus* Fink does not speak of "forms" or "ways" of existence but of "institutions" that instantiate order—institutions embedded in a governmental organization of a community.[9] Such institutions differ from forms of living together in a "free and relieved space of conviviality" (Fink 1978: 249); they have to be sharply distinguished from "institutions as deflated forms of life by sheer conventions" (Fink 1978: 249) and their lack of a responsible freedom. For Fink, freedom can and has to be understood as grounded in relations, as a being-with-each other, as set apart from being-for-each other (cf. Fink 2018a: 83–93). This understanding breaks with the Cartesian model of an *ego cogito* and of subjectivity as conceived as a nucleus of self-consciousness which recognizes other subjects by cognitive operations. Like Pragmatism, for Fink, it is rather embodied practice that interrelates the actors of the human world; these practices form the world which is the field where both subjects and subjectivity only can come into play.

What Fink interrogates in the *Tractatus* as a field for instituting our political life aims at a possibility of a "new understanding of being" in our communal being and doing, and this might be brought about in other ways than experiencing our "cognizance of Being" along the lines of the groundphenomena play as a "speculative metaphor" for the "play of the world" (Fink 2010: 28). Instead, this field is to be displayed as a sphere in its own right, having an innerworldly structure.

A *basso continuo* in Fink's diagnosis of politics in the wake of nihilism is that whatever we might understand of man-made order, in the political realm we are still oriented toward implicit metaphysical frames of "a totality," when talking about a political system as grounded in a social contract or as form of "sovereignty of people" or "representative democracy." Openness and the dynamics of our human existence in the political realm have still to be regained from the backdrop of a long tradition, where a political order was and still is only legitimized from unitedness, coherence, and the ideal of constancy, but not from difference or plurality. Fink calls into question the understanding of our freedom for creating these forms of living together (cf. Fink 1978).

Which Freedom?

To misconceive a situation no longer structured by unity, coherence, and constancy in a still metaphysical framework leads to a civil war between ideologies.[10] The operative background of such ideologies stems from our technological self-understanding. Fink's argument takes technology as a practice of our social relatedness. We produce technology itself, yet, it is not a toolmaking tool but an *organ of ourselves* relating to a meaningful reality.[11] We also produce ourselves, who we are, and who we want to be. However, we do not explicitly understand this, we only operate by models or images of this organ, and we lack consciousness about the model. Nevertheless, we produce with the implicit normative paradigms of these models.[12]

Technology then is for Fink a historical watershed. It began with the Enlightenment. It is when hyphenated *pro-duction* becomes prevalent. Production which "brings forward into being" something totally new, no longer foreshadowed in an ideal or some perfection which is conceived by our mind; that is, it is no longer the mimetic ideal of ancient *techné*. Our actions deal with instability, the absence of security, and the loss of permanent truth.[13] *Pro-duction* here no longer means "to unveil" or "to bring into being" something potentially already there but "to move ahead" with no fixed end.[14] "With a common understanding of the producibility of social order, we have not yet accomplished a "form," but we have only "destroyed" an established form."[15]

In misconceiving our freedom to shape and produce our own fundaments of existence, we underscore the prerequisites of our social being, the roles and power relations at play in any form of coexistence.[16] The lack of a set form or ideal (i.e., a permanent reason for production) leads to producing for its own sake. Fink uses the term "unleashed production" to refer to the vicious circle of endless production.[17] It conceives its own end as production for the sake of production. Thus, consumption is how we manifest our freedom and we produce only to consume. This is due to our lack of understanding of how an order of means and ends needs its own time-space to reveal meaningfulness. Such space cannot simply be produced as another good in a technological way but needs an ideal to be meaningful.

As for Fink's preliminary notion of a post-metaphysical ideal for our societal form, he states in *Basic Questions of Systematic Pedagogy* that an ideal is "an interpretation of human happiness that encompasses an entire humanity, a people, a culture" (Fink 1978: 111). Not as a fixed and established order but in the continuous common questioning of what the ideal itself is. The ideal is precisely an expression of human openness to the world, of our finitude which stems from the groundlessness and aimlessness of the world. "We can only understand our circumstances in a 'meaningful' way because we are open to the whole of being, because we stay in the scope of a universal dimension of meaning from which everything gains its meaning" (Fink 1978: 158). Such an ideal is neither pre-given nor brought into the open by a willful production.

As political structures have their own way of understanding of being, we need our own interpretation of the political we are carrying out our social life. Moreover, we need concepts for producing the relations for production[18]—the societal situation, conditions for labor and consumption. Thus far, we are still oriented along the production model of *poiesis*. There is a pre-given ideal of what we produce, but we no longer consider it because it remains hidden and it diminishes our productive freedom that might go beyond imitation. Transcending the imitation model would also mean to examine critically the ontological model of matter and form (cf. Fink 2018b: 414). Producing society in this way means violence is co-constitutive with freedom.

Producing in this way harkens back to the realm of play. Play as a model is a sphere where actualizations are brought about in an imaginative "as if." In PSW, Fink links the cosmic dimension of the world-symbol "play" with the human dimension of play, which in turn symbolizes man as a relationship—to the world, to oneself, to others, and to the play. In play these relationships have no settled purpose, value, or plan. "The meaninglessness of the world shines back into the inner-worldly sphere of human meaningfulness in such a way that man leaves a free space within his purposeful actions, so to speak, in which action becomes possible without a further driving motive for action that projects it towards an end" (Fink 2010: 221).

The "play of the world" encompasses all human activity, including our play and games. We get a sense of the play of the world or learn of it, in our experience of the the twilight of the metaphysical difference between being and appearance, reality and unreality, actuality and possibility. The ambivalence of these relations cannot be contained in a stable ontological theory of categories. Reality in play is not only gained in the mode of imagination, which conveys the reality of appearances, but via the game's own reflexivity itself. In the *Tractatus* Fink states, "The ordinary play produces; it is a creative and productive accomplishment of humans—it produces the world of play in a peculiar dimension of the imaginary; yet the political production brings forth fabrics in the severe sphere of power" (Fink 2018b: 418).

Fink does not follow his discussions of the imaginary status of play as not equating to mere appearance. Rather, he is in search of another form of freedom than the freedom of play when it comes to the realm of power where there is one decisive category, "foreignness" (cf. Fink 2018b: 427f.)—being exposed to others that are strange even inimical. He is seeking another notion of our freedom, another notion of reasonability—apart from play or game and its backdrop of experiencing constitutive differences harbored in irreality. What bothers Fink is a way to conceive freedom in discursive relations—something Fink lines out in his pedagogical writings with the "community of counseling"[19] and its practice of "active passivity," of an admitted perplexity and helplessness, we share especially in crises—and a call to responsibly enact our freedom.

Responsible Freedom?

Fink argues we no longer correspond to what drives and enables the freedom we express in production. Production solely aims at a fetish-like thing in which the power of production is confirmed in the consumption of what is produced. The things produced wear themselves out, and by consumption, the life-world we trust and rely on withdraws in its dimension of providing and bringing together the field or space we might share. Hannah Arendt states a similar point in *The Human Condition*: work—different from labor—produces a certain durable communal world. It produces an architecture for our lives that outlasts immediate consumption and also the "frailty of human affairs." Thus, a world furnished with things and institutions provides a sense of belonging, even of "home," which is a prerequisite for committing ourselves to care for this place as a ground for our communal actions.[20] Again, in unleashed production we conceive a practice of sovereignty which yet neglects what enables our power. In this neglect, power and freedom turn into violence, destroying a space where we can come together to deliberate on our experience of our non-foundational existence.

For Fink *symbola* are meaningful things we share. For example, a meal, the fact of being mortal with a memorial stone on a grave, or any other meaningful thing which opens a space for starting and deepening a relation, even a conflicted one.[21] World evolves around *symbola* which have power to gather people in such ways that we are related to the openness and vastness of the world as we experience meaning. Fink uses *Symbola* in its ancient sense where the practice of verifying a message depended on the uniting of two pieces of a broken token. *Symbola* are therefore fragments of a whole we do not have, and are only given in the outstanding form of a counterpart. *Symbola* are fragments we must gather.

Symbola gather us by bringing us to speak and act with one another. *Symbola* are as fragmented things that do not refer away from themselves to other things; rather, they are "referring to themselves." What is gathered is the meaning we can find in each situation. Thus, the table becomes the place of the meal. "And the meal is worldly, meaningful activity."[22] It is a worldly practice. Yet, what kind of *symbola* and what kind of practices do we need, if there should be not just a mere consumption of symbols?

Symbola gain meaning when they become questionable, because we have to find answers. This creates the world as this questionable space, which is apart from production, but is a place where we share in actual practices. Yet, the creation of community always remains questionable; it must come into conflict repeatedly, has to be reaffirmed over and over again in an understanding about an origin of our togetherness, the aporia of being together in a plurality that is only constituted in differences.

In his pedagogical writings, Fink does not oppose play to social creativity as in the *Tractatus*, where he asks, "Does a 'social system' equal—as long as we don't judge it according to an objective equation with a standard that exists in itself, but as a temporary standard, gaining structures that have sprung from existence's joy of creating—not a context of play, a game world of play, into which the members of this society share?" (Fink 2018b, 417). The sphere of play needs unspoken consent to share its rules, roles, and reliability. But it is this consent we must specifically consider for a social system and its political institutions.

Fink interprets the initial political practice of sharing as a joint situation of consultation in a situation of perplexity which constitutes the heart of our human condition. There are no adequate ways or models to structure this perplexity. A possible access to this situation, which might be debated in common, must first be sought. Counseling together is a practice of freedom. To share in this way relates us together to what is possible in contrast to the impossibility found in the metaphysically tradition with its grid of ideal structures. Yet, the freedom we might gain by experiencing self-efficacy is preceded by our shared interrogation into knowing the situation as complex and aporetic: it is a responsible freedom because it considers its limitations.

The necessity that brings together a counseling community is consideration of foreignness in its complex and aporetic implications for living together. The playful trait in the counseling community can be most valuable when considering ambivalences, ambiguity, and differences. Counseling is not just advisory, deliberative-planned communication about possibilities that are already available. Rather, it develops possibilities only out of a specific situation, which is due to human finiteness and as a constitutive element of human freedom. To be perplexed is something we share within our human condition with all foreignness.

Advice and consultation are thus not to be taken as "professional assistance" authoritatively handed down from an expert but rather as an existential argument between equally perplexed persons. Taken positively, the advice initiates jointly responsible action, creating opportunities for action.[23] Unlike unleashed production, joint consultation creates a language without focusing on a ready-made solutions to the aporetic situation. Rather, it deals with the impact we gain in this situation for acting, as we are interrogating it from our diverse points of views. We find in the situation a way to get into deliberation and then consult each other.

Commitment to Play and Responsibility

Counseling aims at a joint meaning not yet there, a meaning which creates a basis for human action. Only in a joint action does counseling receives its "objectivity," its common reality that must always be figured out. This meaning is not simply given, nor is it just hidden away to be found in a theoretical *epoché* or a methodological abstraction. It is not applied theoretically to the situation; rather, it is found in the combination of activity and passivity, in questions and answers, in the clarification of forgotten, repressed, and unfulfilled experiences, in suggestions and advice (cf. Fink 1970: 187).

In this social structure of counseling and its shared experience, the world is formed in its intersubjective structure. The world is distinguished from the appearance of a subjective inner world of play and also from the antagonistic relations of freedom and its co-constitutive violence. The world is constituted, in part, by one's commitment to the common counseling situation and above all to one's own role in relation to others. These roles are based neither on convention nor on a playful agreement, but on the existential experience that the stage of the theatrical play only has one floor if we are supported by acting together. In sharing the world with one another, play becomes a continuing path of understanding. Yet, this play is no longer played by an actor who sets the rules on her own, who antagonistically tries to fight a game. It is the play between all those persons in the aporetic situation that unfolds and creates sustainable structures for their relations and rules of living together.

It is not autonomy, reason, or arbitrary freedom that is the source of human creativity. It is finiteness and need. Our prevailing lack and limitedness is the core of Fink's concept for a basis from which political freedom might be reconsidered according to a practice of responsibility. For Fink, the self has always been encompassed and held by the sphere of coexistence in which it is physically and historically situated. And it is here that Levinas might come into play to reconstruct the category of foreign strangeness.

My freedom is most doubtful in my relationship with others as they make unexpected demands on me, alter my projects, and distort my intentions. However, it is also in this pushback that the possibility of meaning is most likely.

> Freedom is put into question by the other, and is revealed to be unjustified, only when it knows itself to be unjust. Its knowing itself to be unjust is not something added on to spontaneous and free consciousness, which would be present to itself and know itself to be, *in addition*, guilty. A new situation is created; consciousness's presence to itself acquires a different modality; its positions collapse [. . .] (it) is no longer the principle." (Levinas 1987: 50f)

Our situation with others creates an ethical basis for a responsive dialogue, yet it is always an asymmetrical one due to the impossibility of being able to answer different claims at the same time. The dialogue is not an irresponsible game but one that is challenged by new questions.

Dialogue is the social relationship. It is the non-indifference of the you for the ego. "Dialogue is thus not merely a way of speaking. [. . .] It is transcendence" (Levinas 1998a: 147). It is a chance for understanding, even if it might lead to hate, to struggle, and can degenerate to a reversal of the transcendence as a free self-giving of the other. Dialogue affirms the relationship between what is different, affirms the in-between, in which an understanding of being foreign is also possible.

Levinas ends his little text on dialogue with an outlook on "a kind of phenomenology of the relation" (Levinas 1998a: 148). From Fink's perspective, "of the relations" in the plural means one goes into the multidimensionality of the world and its cosmic play because of the multiple groundphenomena. Perhaps, dialogue might give way to play and might help to create a time-space of the political where through time and space we are referred to others, and to what is foreign, even ourselves. Yet, such dialogue is not just another strategic instrument to produce the structure of our human affair. First of all, it would be a joint commitment to act in concert, and not a means to achieve some goal. In this respect, it resembles play.

Play as it is linked to dialogue might open a space of an interstitial place between freedom and finitude. In between the freedom of relations that comes before monadic subjectivity play emerges. Springing from the tension between freedom and finitude play engenders responsibility. In the end, this in-between might guide us to reconsider why play is only one instance in a relational web of different groundphenomena, and not a sole ground for the human condition. Play is part of a relational web concerned with overcoming power and maintaining empathy, creativity, play, and responsibility.

Part Four

Translations and Commentaries

World, Individuation, and Play

A Critical Introduction to Fink's Conversations with Heidegger

Giovanni Jan Giubilato and Ian Alexander Moore

In chapter nineteen the reader will find the original German and first English translation of two texts from Fink's literary remains that contain notes on two conversations Fink had with Heidegger.[1] Fink's report about the first dialogue, from May 10, 1949, is contained in a still unpublished folder (E15/286) in Fink's archive; it is scheduled to appear in volume 1 of the *Eugen Fink Gesamtausgabe* (*Eugen Fink's Complete Works*): *Nähe und Distanz: Studien zur Phänomenologie* (*Proximity and Distance: Studies on Phenomenology*), edited by Hans Rainer Sepp. The rest of the materials in the same folder deal with Heidegger and especially Hölderlin; they seem to have been intended for a work Fink was planning—already before the onset of the Second World War—on his interpretations of Hölderlin.[2] These materials are expected to be published in volume 10 of the *Eugen Fink Gesamtausgabe*: *Epiloge zur Dichtung* (*Epilogue on Poetry*). The second dialogue with Heidegger took place on March 11, 1953, and Fink's account of it has been recently published, with some transcription errors, in German in volume 16 of the *Eugen Fink Gesamtausgabe*: *Existenz und Coexistenz* (*Existence and Coexistence*), edited by Annette Hilt.[3] Our edition in this volume corrects these errors and notes the differences between the two versions.

Both conversations help to illuminate Fink's philosophy of play and, albeit briefly and through small hints, the still enigmatic and highly complex relationship, both personal and philosophical, between Fink and Heidegger. In this sense, these two dialogues not only contribute to our understanding of Fink's thought but also serve two important purposes: (1) to complement, and fill a gap in, the history of the reception of his philosophy in general, and (2) to mark its specificity with respect to Heidegger's thought, who was certainly an important touchstone for the development of Fink's thinking, but far from the only one. Fink's confrontation with Heidegger can be felt and reconstructed along his entire path of thought and, apart from great affinities and Heidegger's undoubted influence on specific inquiries, produced in Fink's thinking an unending tension and "counter-opposition" between *ontology* and *cosmology*. After remaining for many years in the shadow of the two main names of Freiburg philosophy, Husserl and Heidegger, and thus limited to a small circle of specialists, Fink's philosophy is finally being rediscovered and put at the center of renewed philosophical attention and interdisciplinary research, thanks to the reverberation achieved by translations of some of his works and by publications of the (still ongoing) edition of his *Complete Works*, which since December 2020 has been under the auspices of the Eugen-Fink-Zentrum Wuppertal (EFZW) at the University of Wuppertal.

Fink's divergent—or "heretical," as Patočka would say—position in relation to Husserl marks a remarkable event in the history of phenomenology, which has already been explored in various ways. This is especially true for the position of the young Fink, who integrated and radicalized Husserl's phenomenological-transcendental project into a *phenomenological meontics* (from the Greek words *mē*, "not/non-," and *on*, "being"), thus bringing a new speculative force into phenomenology.[4] Ronald Bruzina, in his exemplary and detailed study on the collaboration between Husserl and Fink titled *Edmund Husserl and Eugen Fink: Beginnings and Ends in Phenomenology*, has portrayed Fink's early intellectual independence from Heidegger's and Husserl's thinking as follows:

> What Fink was working to achieve was a way in which the basic difference dividing Husserl and Heidegger in their own eyes could be linked in one dramatically convergent way, [. . .] by addressing the very issue that lies at the heart of the differences between Husserl and Heidegger, to find therein the resources for moving beyond the achievements of both. [. . .] Fink finds himself compelled to consider "a new third solution", namely "the conception of the freedom from being on the part of spirit". (Bruzina 2004: 130)

To his own philosophical perspective, this so-called "new third solution", Fink had given the name *meontics*—or *meontic integration*. This term/phrase, however, is nowhere used in the writings that Fink published during this period, but appears largely only in his private notes. The reason for the prolonged silence about meontics or the study of non-being is—as Bruzina has again incisively explained—that "the whole idea of meontics is one that is opposed to the dominant character of Husserlian phenomenology, according to which everything must be grounded and must be justified in vivid evidence" (Bruzina 2006: 196). In a quite central note from the years 1930–5, Fink comments on Husserl's position at that time as follows:

> Husserl alludes to the meontic nature of absolute subjectivity, albeit without getting to the root of the matter and without recognizing the full extent of a meontic philosophy; although he has grasped meontic nature only in its peripheral configurations, his expression "pre-being" [*"vor-seiend"*] nevertheless indicates meontic nature; and yet there is still an ontic conceptual schema in the term "pre-being" [. . .]. This is why we use the term: "me-ontic"!!! (Fink 2008: 277)

The extensive result of Fink's far-reaching scrutiny and radicalization of phenomenology thus came to light under the concept of meontics.

Much less evident and discussed than Fink's meontic radicalization of phenomenology, however, is his critical and many-sided position in relation to Heidegger, of whom he has often been considered only a simple commentator or epigone; at most, he has been seen as a further "urbanizer" of the Heideggerian wilderness, as one who managed to turn it into a habitable and comprehensible province.[5] There is a glaring gap, so to speak, in the literature, above all with regard to the tremendous commitment with which the young Fink, already during the prewar years, took up Heidegger's thinking and approached it in a highly critical way. An important task for future philosophical research is thus announced. In contrast, the relationship of Fink's philosophy to Heidegger's thought after the Second World War has been explored—although not always in a manner free from a heuristic effort unidirectionally oriented by Heidegger's philosophy—several times and from different perspectives, in large part on the basis of the famous *Heraclitus Seminar* that they jointly organized in 1966.[6]

On the basis of the diverse collection of notes, drafts, manuscripts and typescripts, partly elaborated writings, and plans for future projects contained in the long-awaited forthcoming volumes 3.3 and 3.4 of the *Eugen Fink Gesamtausgabe*—which will complete the work initiated in the early 1980s by Ronald Bruzina that led to the publication of the first two volumes of the *Phänomenologische Werkstatt* (*Phenomenological Workshop*)[7]—it is now possible to immerse oneself in the course of Fink's painstaking construction of his thought and in a sense to put on display the gradual growth of his own philosophy. In Fink's case, these materials delineate, with unexpected clarity and force, how to "become who you are" (as Pindar once put it). They give us considerable information about how Fink constantly renewed his own thinking and how he defined his own philosophy step by step, ever more precisely and self-consciously—just like a gifted sculptor who carves a finely defined figure from a block of marble. Thus, these texts allow us to gain deeper and more far-reaching insight into the workshop of his thought and the so-called "first phase" of his work (1927–1946), which is enriched with new elements and conceptual components that contribute decisively to the interpretation of his philosophy as a whole and in its specificity.[8]

At the center of Fink's second dialogue with Heidegger lies the question of *individuation*, which is a central theme of Fink's thought and marks the greatest point of contention between the two philosophers in the dialogues. (Many of Fink's other questions are posed with a sense for Heidegger's later philosophy, from whose perspective Fink is asking for clarification or corroboration on how one should approach Heidegger's earlier philosophy.) Individuation is a problem that provides a key to understanding Fink's entire philosophy, one with which Fink was always confronted again and again, from the early years of the *phänomenologische Werkstatt* with Husserl[9]—indeed, individuation is a central theme of the famous *Sixth Cartesian Meditation*, written during the autumn of 1932—to the mature postwar period (1946–1970). In a note dated 1930, Fink writes: "The deepest philosophical problem is that of ontification, that is, the relation between origin and world" (Fink 2008: 7). Several passages from the *Sixth Cartesian Meditation* are quite revealing in this regard, as they allow us to see not only the centrality of the problem of individuation, around which a whole series of phenomenological problems revolve as their gravitational center, but also how Fink's contribution to the final development of Husserl's phenomenology became a program of thought *beyond* Husserl's approach. While surely stemming from the roots of phenomenological philosophy, this led Fink to an early-flowering independence from Husserl's phenomenology. Indeed, the questioning of phenomenology took on a different force and urgency that opened up new aspects for a philosophy that might otherwise have tended to ossify in its habits. Discussing the worldly status of transcendental *phenomenology as intersubjective science*, through which "within transcendental life [...] a countermovement, [i.e.] the constitutive retro-inquiry of the phenomenologizing onlooker," springs up, and thus transcendental subjectivity "comes to itself, "awakens" [...] out of the age-old "sleep" of being-outside-itself," Fink writes:

> while every worldly "we" is rightly understood as a collectivity of really separate and individualized subjects that stand in a common effort, with respect now to the transcendental community of monads it is an open problem whether they are actually built up out of "individuals." The question thus is whether a common phenomenologizing action is a plural cognitive process, or must ultimately be determined as one transcendental tendency that only articulates itself in monadic plurality, therefore, whether the process by which transcendental subjectivity "becomes for itself" is not played out at a depth that lies prior to all monadic "individuation". (Fink 1995: 125)

To understand and to develop the right conceptual tools to even be able to think this "depth that lies prior to all individuation" precisely by understanding its process of individuation and ontification, the phenomenological system has to be conceived of as "the system of life," and "life as concretely playing intentionality" (Fink 1995: 148). This represents one of the main efforts of Fink's entire philosophy. In fact, "the question whether the individuation of the transcendental ego (as an individual monad in monadic intersubjectivity)" corresponds to some "level of the self-objectivation of a transcendental life, which is "one" and lies before all individuation" (Fink 1995: 148), cannot be avoided from Fink's perspective, all the more so if phenomenology, in its aim of genetically reconstructing the constitution process, has to provide a new "encompassing knowledge of the world [...] from out of its constitution" (Fink 1972: 24). The basic question of phenomenology can thus be formulated—as Fink does in his famous essay "The Phenomenological Philosophy of Edmund Husserl and Contemporary Criticism"—as "the question about the origin of the world" (Fink 1970: 136). He thereby not only radically questions "the unity of being and world-form, [...] the combination of "founded" and "founding sphere,"" but also places at the center of phenomenology the need to grasp the *enworlding* (*Verweltlichung*) and humanization (*Vermenschlichung*) process, i.e., *human- and world-constitution*. He explicitly characterizes this new main path of phenomenology—which contrasts with all mundane forms of knowledge and innerworldly ways of knowing, and which must be methodologically anchored in the practice of phenomenological reduction—as an *ontogonic metaphysics*, that is, a metaphysics of the genesis of being; this was already recognized in Fink's 1935 lecture "The Idea of Transcendental Philosophy in Kant and in Phenomenology" (Fink 1976: 7–44). The "transcendental" manner of its phenomenological questioning, which interprets "the whole of being in its constitution" and understands the human within it as the "*mediating cosmological being*" (*vermittelndes Weltwesen*), consists in a "*questioning beyond being*" (*Überfragung des Seins*) that leads Fink to reconsider what seems to him to be "an unexamined presupposition of all phenomenology," namely, "that being appears" (Fink 1976: 249).[10] The appearing of being must be traced back in its constitutive process, and thus brought back conceptually to its non-being (meontic) constitution. The speculative revelation of the processes of world constitution and of "a transcendental life which is 'one' and lies before all individuation" (Fink 1995: 148) leads to a unique understanding of every worldly-being in its "transparency," that is, in its "constitutedness," and lets "the constitutive cosmogony" (Fink 1995: 14) become evident in its transcendental becoming. Thus, Fink concludes,

> questions arise here concerning the universal living complex of the monad community at first given as "open," concerning the transcendental meaning of the mutual intentional implication of monads, etc.—all questions and problems that can only find their solution in the context of the methodic development of the concept of the Absolute. More precisely put their solution is precisely this development and presentation of the concept of the Absolute. What perhaps is shown, then, is that the community of monads itself represents one more constituted stratum in the constitutive becoming of the world. The question is therefore posed whether the transcendental individuation of plural monads is a final and reductively irremovable determination of constituting life. What may then be proven is whether the Absolute itself is articulated in the plural and subjected to an individuation—or whether all articulations are only self-articulations within it, and it itself can only be thought definitively under the Idea of the "One". (Fink 1995: 144–5)

In other words, phenomenological thinking,

> breaking open out of the pathos of the self-assertion of the spirit in the face of chaos and radicalizing itself into the phenomenological reduction, [should lead] finally to an understanding of being—at first impenetrable by the spirit—out of the spiritual fashioning of the world. The fashioning of the world (constitution), as the power and life of absolute spirit, is not like an "objective" happening that is present somewhere, if not in the world, then in a metaphysical space. (Fink 1972: 24, translation slightly modified)

What individuation is basically about is the endless tension and relation between "what is originated" and the "origin" (Fink 2008: 277), between the "end-constitutedness" of worldly being and the "constitutive becoming" of the world, the radical finitude of factual human life and the infinity of the life of the absolute spirit, fragmentation of intraworldly being (*Binnenweltlichkeit*) and the cosmological totality of the world-whole (*Weltganze*).

From this philosophical point of view, according to Fink, what Heidegger does not see is precisely this processuality, or the constitutive process according to which beings "'expose themselves' from out of themselves, 'emerge' from their hidden depths, and let themselves out into appearance" (Fink, Z-XXIX/200b).[11] For Heidegger appearance would be "only understood as the being-for-us of beings" (*Fürunssein*) and not brought into connection with the ontogonic dynamics of the "going outside of itself" (*Außersichgehen*) of a "being-in-itself" (*Ansichsein*), an essence (*Wesen*). Thus, for Fink, the being that shows itself in phenomenality is "not only unconcealed, but also given 'outside itself', i.e. in the appearance" (Fink, Z-XXIX/200/b),[12] in the *Spielraum* (leeway, or more literally "play space") of unconcealed phenomenality that, constitutively, hints back at the concealed essence. A becoming belongs "essentially" to the essence—a becoming that consists in the process of "coming forth," "appearing," "emanating," and "externalizing" mediated by "force" (*Kraft*). Essence (*Wesen*) is therefore *ver-wesend*, that is, animated by a becoming/constituting process by which it is "expressing itself, going outside of itself" (Fink, Z-XXVIII/21b).[13] Exactly in this sense, according to Fink's meontic-ontogonical basic thesis, *all being is always the result of a becoming and the constitutive result of an ontifying or individuating process* that leads to "being" (*Sein*).[14] To understand and analyze this process, and to bring this becoming in its meontic nature to conceptual explication is precisely the task of Fink's philosophical project of an ontogonic metaphysics of cosmological world-play.

Indeed, still in his main work *Play as Symbol of the World* (PSW), after presenting and summarizing his fundamental thesis of "world oblivion" (*Weltvergessenheit*)—according to which "the provenance of the finitude of finite things from out of the prevailing of the world is concealed and falls into oblivion"—we find him addressing the question of individuation at the heart of his philosophical efforts:

> Finitude itself becomes, so to speak, a "phenomenon," a datum in things. "Being" is interpreted as the Being of finitely existing beings; the problem of Being loses its tension vis-à-vis the in-finite, at best is proclaimed as a particular, highest being, God or the absolute as the possessor of "in-finite Being." And that happens all the more, the more the question recedes (or better: is not posed at all) as to how individual things reside within the world-whole. And so long as this question is not posed, the finitude of things cannot be thought back into the world's process of individuation. (Fink 2016: 76). [. . .] The world prevails as the power of universal individuation. (Fink 2016: 214)

Cosmic play, or the world-play of which human play is a symbol, is the constitutive play of individuation, of enworlding and humanization, that is, of human- and world-constitution: the ontogonic process of world-becoming, "what steers all perishing, all emergence and decline of finite things" (Fink 2016: 73).

This idea of the "world-play of being" comes up near the end of the first dialogue. Here, an attempt is made to (re)think what was first thought in Heidegger's *Being and Time*, touching on the issues of (1) the subjectivism that would still affect the fundamental-ontological project of 1927 as developed in an analytic of Dasein, and (2) the very idea of "overcoming metaphysics"—which is a theme that Fink, however, saw differently from Heidegger. Fink's critical gesture and overarching view on the historical development of philosophy should not be understood simply as a repetition of Heidegger's varied attempts to overcome (*überwinden*) or convalesce from (*verwinden*) metaphysics and metaphysical thought. Fink's critique of traditional metaphysics has its own specificity, and is currently one of the most interesting research topics emerging from the most recent publications of his works. Fink's dialectical-cosmological "Metaphysics of Play" arises from a critique of *any* metaphysical or even ontological thought (including, to some extent, Heidegger's) that remains trapped in the idea of being (*Seinsidee*) or is based on the question of being (*Seinsfrage*),[15] and it tries to show the "cosmological horizon" of every ontology and metaphysics.[16]

The great importance of the references to Hegel and Nietzsche in the dialogues should be starting to become apparent. Hegel certainly played a central role in the development of Fink's thought ever since the late 1920s. With the draft of the *Idea of a Transcendental Methodology*, which was intended at least to serve as a guideline for constitutive phenomenology's increasingly intricate investigations, Fink seized the opportunity to further open "the window onto the Absolute (Hegel)" (Fink 1966: 16), a window through which he had glanced for the first time in 1929 on the occasion of his study of phenomenological "single problems," such as acts of presentifications (*Vergegenwärtingugen*) and image-consciousness (*Bildbewusstsein*). Indeed, when it came to a possible tracing back of phenomenological act-intentional analysis into the deep dimensions of constituting transcendental life, Hegel stood in the background as a guiding figure. In the winter semester of 1930–1 Fink took over the so-called "Japanese Seminar," a series of private lectures for a group of Japanese scholars visiting Husserl and Freiburg at that time; Fink chose Hegel's preface to the *Phenomenology of Spirit* as the subject of his conversations and seminar exercises.[17] In the same semester (winter 1930–1), he also listened to Heidegger's lectures on Hegel's *Phenomenology*, which confirmed for him the inevitable confrontation of Husserl's transcendental phenomenology with the ontological insights gained by Heidegger's "hermeneutics of facticity." There is no doubt that Fink's meontic philosophy of absolute spirit, which was the inner core of his entire time as an assistant, was strongly influenced by the study of Hegel's *Phenomenology*. Therefore, Fink's early reading notes on this work, as well as his early attempts to interpret it between the years 1930–8, are particularly important and revealing. Later Fink would publicly reveal his critical examination of Heidegger's interpretation of Hegel in his (Fink's) lecture course of 1950–1 titled *Being and the Human: On the Essence of Ontological Experience*, published posthumously in 1977.[18] In the same year Fink's *Hegel: Phenomenological Interpretations of the Phenomenology of Spirit* appeared, edited by Hans Joll.[19] The book presented the text of Fink's lectures on Hegel which he held in Freiburg for the first time in the winter semester of 1948–9, and eventually developed further from the winter semester of 1966–7 to the summer semester of 1967.

Nietzsche is undoubtedly the other major guiding figure of Fink's thought. A constant confrontation with the profound *crisis* represented by Nietzschean thought accompanies the time span from Fink's youthful experiences in the school of Husserl, through the beginning of his teaching career at Freiburg—which began precisely with a trial lecture on "Nietzsche's Metaphysics of Play" (Fink 2019)—all the way to the great interpretive work on Nietzsche's philosophy in 1960,[20] not coincidentally contemporaneous with the publication of PSW. In Nietzsche, Fink recognizes the flashing of a new, non-metaphysical originality, namely in the thought—or the "cosmic metaphor"—of *play* that supersedes the ontological difference and of the human as "co-player in the cosmic play." Where Nietzsche understands being and becoming as play, he no longer stands under the sway of metaphysics; there, the "will to power" has the character of an Apollonian shaping and constituting force; on the other hand, the "eternal return of the same" is conceived of as the all-encompassing, all-granting and all-erasing playtime (*Zeit-Spiel*) of the world.

Of great importance, finally, is the allusion made in the second dialogue to the desire to propose a joint interpretation of Heraclitus' fragments (Fink & Heidegger 1993), which can be considered the origin of the famous seminar on Heraclitus carried out in 1966. This seminar would crown a philosophical dialogue that lasted half a century.[21]

Zwei Gespräche mit Heidegger / Two Conversations with Heidegger

Eugen Fink, Edited and translated by Giovanni Jan Giubilato and Ian Alexander Moore

May 10, 1949

Conversation with Martin Heidegger

(1) Talk of "overcoming metaphysics"[1] makes students believe that metaphysics should be dismissed. Is it not rather the case that metaphysics, as the thinking (*Denken*) of the beingness of beings, can and must first be understood *more authentically* on the basis of the remembrance (*Andenken*) of the truth of being? Is not metaphysical thinking always also in the light of being, even if metaphysical thinking turns away from it and toward beings as such? Does not the thinking of the truth of being first prove itself when it "understands," *interprets*, *metaphysics* precisely in a manner in which metaphysics cannot see itself?

Heidegger: Yes, that is so. The "difference"[2] is not about keeping the truth of being away from metaphysical truth; rather, metaphysical truth must be thought anew from the truth of being.

(2) Regarding the subjective approach of *Being and Time*: are not *temporality* and *spatiality* and *truth* and the *world* interpreted there "in terms of existence,"[4] whereas existence only is by *standing out* into the open of being? Is not *world-time* primordial time, *world-time-space*?

Being and Time still thinks of "transcendence" from the human side, whereas transcendence must instead be thought from the side of *being*. Not isolated existence, but *ek-sistent* existence[5] is transcendence.

Heidegger: *That is exactly right*. Yes, I still classify *Being and Time* as subjectivism, which it is precisely a matter of overcoming.[6]

(3) *Play*: Play not as constitutive of the being of existence, not as an "existential,"[7] but rather as the *world-play of being*?

Heidegger: Yes, here alone is where it belongs. You see entirely correctly.

(4) *Hegel*? Doubt about thesis "completion of subjectivity,"[8] possibilities to think of dialectics as a *productive* impasse of metaphysics.

Heidegger: That is an entirely central problem. Interpretations of the great thinkers from the "new perspective" of the truth of being are the most important thing to do.

11 März 1953

Gespräch mit Heidegger

1) Einleitend kurz über Sartre, dann über meine Vorlesung "Grundprobleme der menschl. Gemeinschaft," um von da an das Problem des *Todes* anzugehen. Meine Frage war: Ist die Todesanalyse in "Sein und Zeit" nicht vorläufig in dem Sinne, dass sie nur[9] den Bezug von *Tod u. Selbstsein* betrifft u. nicht den "heimatlichen" Charakter des Todes als "Bergung"?[10]

Heideggers Antwort: In der Tat ist die Todesanalyse vorläufig, um den Zeitcharakter der Zukünftigkeit des Daseins u. den Zusammenhang von Selbstsein u. Verstehen herauszustellen, aber "sie berührt nicht einmal ernstlich das *Problem* des Todes selbst."

2) Meine zweite Frage bezog sich auf das Problem der "Individuation" (ob die Vereinzeltheit des Seienden eben ein "Urphänomen" ist—oder es auch der Philosophie möglich[11] ist, "hinter" die Vereinzelung zurückzudenken. Allerdings habe die Metaphysik dieses Problem bislang immer am Modell von Urgrund, Wesen, αἴτιον,[12] ἀρχή gestellt, also auf eine ontolog. Ebene zurückverlegt. Aber es sei fraglich, ob das Problem nicht erst dann dringlich wird,[13] wenn *Sein = Erscheinen* (im Sinne von Aufgehen im Offenen) gedacht wird).[14]

Heidegger wurde durch diese Frage verlegen u. sagte, er verstünde nicht, worauf ich hinauswolle.

Ob ich das Individuationsproblem sehe im Gegenbezug von Gattung u. Exemplar (essentia u. existentia)? Keineswegs, antwortete ich; diese Differenz: Eidos—Exemplar, sei nicht

March 11, 1953

Conversation with Heidegger

1) By way of introduction a bit about Sartre, then about my lecture course *Basic Problems of Human Community*,[36] so as next to proceed to the problem of *death*. My question was: Is not the analysis of death in *Being and Time* provisional in the sense that it concerns only the relation between *death and being a self* and not the "homely" character of death as "sheltering"?[37]

Heidegger's answer: The analysis of death is indeed provisional, so as to bring out the temporal character of the futurality of Dasein and the connection between being a self and understanding, but "it does not even seriously touch on the *problem* of death itself."

2) My second question was related to the problem of "individuation" [*"Individuation"*] (whether the individuatedness of beings is precisely a "primordial phenomenon"—or whether it is also possible for philosophy to think back "behind" individuation [*Vereinzelung*]. Metaphysics, to be sure, has up to now always posed this problem using the model of primordial ground, essence, *aition* [cause], *archē* [source, principle], i.e., has put it back on an ontological level. But it is questionable whether the problem does not first become urgent *when being* is thought *to be equal to appearing* (in the sense of arising within the open)).

Heidegger became perplexed by this question and said he did not understand what I was getting at.

[He asked:] Whether I see the problem of individuation in the correlation of

gemeint, sondern die Frage, ob das Sein (als das *eine* versammelnde[15] Anwesen in allem Anwesenden) wesenhaft durch die Macht des Negativen, als eine ihm einheimische[16] Macht, bestimmt sei, derart dass Seiendes[17] abgerissen u. abgetrennt, unterschieden u. *bestimmt*[18] sei—*unterschieden u. versammelt*[19] oder ob dies nur für den *Tag des Erscheinens* gelte u. nicht für die Nacht des Seins, in der in der Tat "alle Kühe schwarz sind."

Heideggers Antwort war: es gebe für ihn kein Individuationsproblem; man dürfe das "Erscheinen" nicht "zu mager"[20] denken, die "Welt" sei das einzige "Individuum."

Ich erwiderte, diese Antwort hätte ich erwartet. Für Heidegger gäbe es natürlich kein "Wesen," das der Erscheinung zugrundeläge, aber gäbe es nicht das "*Wesenlose*," das "*Nichts*," das *Abwesen*??[21]

Heidegger hüllte sich ins "Dunkel": darüber sei schwer zu sprechen. Dass das[22] Anwesen nicht *alles* sei, sei ja die Erfahrung, die er mit dem zweiten Teil von "Sein und Zeit" gemacht habe. Er habe viel Material darüber in "Messkirch" liegen.

Das *Anwesen* sei die *griechische* Art, das Sein im Horizont der Zeit zu denken,—aber damit, dass man das Ungedachte des griechischen Denkens, nämlich diese verborgene Zeitlichkeit, die "Gegenwart" u. "Unverborgenheit" zugleich meine, herausstelle, komme man selbst in der Sache nicht weiter;[23] hier könne man auch nicht weiterkommen, wie er, Heidegger,[24] nach "Sein u. Zeit" erfahren habe.

Heidegger war überrascht,[25] dass ich sagte, es sei nicht klar in den "Holzwegen," wie weit er selber[26] auf dem Boden der griechischen Seinsinterpretation als "Anwesen" stünde,—nur eben als Einsicht

species and specimen (*essentia* and *existentia*)? In no way, I replied; I do not mean this difference between *eidos* and specimen, but rather the question of whether being (as the *single* gathering presencing in everything present) is determined essentially by the power of the negative, as a power that is native to it, in such a way that beings are torn away and separated, differentiated and determined—*differentiated and gathered*—or whether this holds only for the *day of appearing* and not for the night of being, in which, indeed, "all cows are black."[38]

Heidegger's answer was that there is no problem of individuation for him; one should not think "too meagerly" of "appearing"; the "world" is the only "individual."

I replied that I had expected this answer. For Heidegger, there would naturally be no "essence" that underlies appearance, but could there not be the "*essenceless*," the "*nothing*," *absencing*[39]??

Heidegger veiled himself in "obscurity": it would be difficult to speak about this. The experience he had with the second part of *Being and Time* was indeed that *presencing* is not *everything*. He has a lot of material on this in "Messkirch."[40]

Presencing is the *Greek* way of thinking being within the horizon of time—but one does not get any further in the matter [*Sache*] by drawing out what is unthought in Greek thinking, namely, this concealed temporality that means both "presence" and "unconcealment"; nor can one get any further here, as he, Heidegger, experienced after *Being and Time*.

Heidegger was surprised that I said that it is not clear in *Off the Beaten Path* to what extent he based himself on the Greek interpretation of being as "presencing"—only precisely as insight into the *temporality* of presencing.[41]

in die²⁷ *Zeitlichkeit* des Anwesens. Zumal er auch vom Anwesen spreche, dass das *Abwesen* umfasse,—seine eigene positive Seinsauffassung wäre nicht mit der These Sein = Anwesen zu bezeichnen; diese wäre gänzlich²⁸ anders—und läge in den Messkirchner Manuskripten.²⁹

3) Daran schloss sich eine³⁰ Diskussion, ob *Heraklit*³¹ in das griechische Seinsverständnis (Sein = Anwesen) hineingenommen werden könnte—oder³² nicht, wie ich meinte.

Meine Gesprächsthese war: Heraklit ist nicht an dem³³ Λόγος-Frg. allein oder vorwiegend zu orientieren, sondern am Problem der ἁρμονίη ἀφανής.³⁴

Heidegger war sehr beeindruckt u. sagte, er würde sich für meine Heraklit-Deutung stark interessieren.

Wir vereinbarten, dass wir zusammen³⁵ gelegentlich Heraklit-Fragmente interpretieren wollten.

4) Heidegger frug nach meiner Nietzsche-Arbeit; ermunterte mich zur Publikation; sagte, dass er, als er offiziell von Tübingen angefragt wurde, auch über mich sich positiv geäussert habe.

Especially since he also says of presencing that absencing is what encompasses,⁴²—his own positive conception of being should not be described with the thesis, being = presencing; the thesis would be entirely different—and can be found in the Messkirch manuscripts.

3) This was followed by a discussion of whether *Heraclitus* could be included in the Greek understanding of being (being = presencing)—or not, as I opined.

My thesis for our conversation was that Heraclitus is not to be oriented only or chiefly on the basis of the *Logos*-fragment, but rather on the basis of the problem of the *harmoniē aphanēs*.⁴³

Heidegger was very impressed and said he would be strongly interested in my interpretation of Heraclitus.

We agreed that we wanted to interpret Heraclitus' fragments together sometime.⁴⁴

4) Heidegger asked about my work on Nietzsche; encouraged me to publish it; said that he spoke positively about me when he was officially asked by Tübingen.⁴⁵

Translator's Introduction to "Mask and Cothurnus"

Christopher Turner

"Mask and Cothurnus" is one of Eugen Fink's most important writings on play, occupying a kind of midway point, thematically, between two longer and more well-known works, *Play as Symbol of the World* (1960) and *Fashion: Seductive Play* (1969), though published after both of them in *Epiloge zur Dichtung* (1971). As in his later work on fashion, here too he is focused not merely on play but also on the human body as a site for expressive and polysemous meaning, our own play-space for fashionable charm and the pomp of ceremony. He further develops his conceptualization of the mask's central role in human play, particularly its archaic roots in ancient religious festival and drama. Moving beyond his understanding of the mask as a kind of magic portal into the realm of the daemonic, something with which we do not play as though with a toy but rather through which we become, ourselves, the site for play, for creative transformation, associating with divine powers and leaving ordinary existence behind, Fink here observes that "The poet's words do not sound from behind a lifeless mask, they erupt out of an animated and passionate human mouth, they flare up like tongues of fire in the mime's eloquence, yet the actor is not the poet himself, but is in a sense the poet's transient fleeting manifestation." Thus, while masks are largely absent from contemporary theater and film, they have been replaced by drawing on expressive possibilities latent within an actor's protean face, a surface upon which every conceivable human emotion can come to appearance.

Dramatic play also "unmasks," Fink notes, leading to profound disillusionment (recall, for instance, Oedipus' discovery of the source of the plague or Hamlet's "play within the play"). To an even greater degree, the cothurnus is no longer commonly worn on the stage, yet here too Fink notes that its function remains indispensable today, persisting as "elevation of the banality of existence" into exemplary forms of the essential. Mask and cothurnus remain powerful even today as symbols of "the enchanting powers of the theater." Theater becomes a site of world-play through the enchanting use of such requisites as the mask and cothurnus, and if the physical props themselves are no longer common and familiar, Fink's formulation of theater as "a play that signifies the world" is followed by more general philosophical reflections on play.

In "Oasis of Happiness," Fink compared play to an oasis in the desert of goal- and future-directed striving, while here it is initially likened to a small island in an ocean of darkness or an illuminated tableau. As with the previous contrast of play as masked and as unmasking, so too play is marked by a similar contrast with respect to what it makes visible: play is both illuminating, a source of light, and dazzling, a source of distorted perceptions that are potentially misleading. Play itself is frequently contrasted with (serious) thinking, yet Fink observes that thought has need of play's generation of illusions and error, has need of a kind of "productive irritant," if only so that it can then later correct such error, demystify such illusions. The contrast of play and philosophy, of lighthearted jests and serious contemplation, is one in which each functions as "antipode" and the former is a productive goad for the latter's activity, while what connects the two is that they both share the same world of appearances, the one itself a kind of art of generating appearances, a masking of beings elevated by cothurnus, and the other an art of unmasking such appearances, of disillusionment.

Each of us starts with an everyday familiarity with play that nevertheless must not be confused with knowledge of play. Fink approvingly cites Hegel's dictum to the effect that what is most familiar can also be most unknown, and in the case of play each of us has already done it and yet no one seems to understand what it is, a kind of inversion of Aristotle's ancient problem concerning happiness, namely that everyone is pursuing it while no one agrees about what it is. One shallow understanding of play to avoid, here as elsewhere in Fink, is the facile and by now clichéd contrast of play with work, where it is reduced to a kind of relaxation that helps us maintain our productivity at work, which Fink has already criticized elsewhere, tracing it back to Aristotle's questionable appropriation of Anacharsis' famous dictum, "Play in order that you may work." Instead, Fink again argues for a conception of play as a kind of oasis in the midst of futural and goal-directed striving, relief from finitude in a sense, where we can become anything and time seems to stand still. Many of the most popular kinds of "play" are in fact not play at all in any genuine sense, to the extent that they are still bound up with such striving: exercising at the gym for the sake of one's strength or health, learning a martial art for self-defense, or even just playing a casual game on one's smartphone in order to pass the time.

Play's most important product, its most significant result, is the playworld. Play is an activity that generates a world; conversely, world's activity is speculatively conceived as play. Fink, however, rejects the idea that nature plays, and this is not what he has in mind when he formulates his conception of world-play, which is drastically different from the reflection of a tree shimmering on the surface of a body of water. Rather, play fundamentally generates a playworld that manifests the "hyperreality of essence" precisely through our self-alienation. We are alienated from our actual selves in a creative way and become every possibility at once in an irreal or hyperreal sense, with each possibility imaginatively realized as a symbol, a mask, a timeless sojourn in play's blissful oasis.

Mask and Cothurnus

Eugen Fink, translated by Christopher Turner

We are familiar with mask and cothurnus as requisites of archaic dramatic art, as an almost coarse means of alienation and elevation, which removes the actor from the everyday world and from everyday awareness and raises him to the great figures of fate. The mask is of ancient provenance; it reaches back to times when humanity feared daemons and in its beginnings was a thing of ritual, an unyielding and mysterious image of the face behind which numinous horror lay in wait, from whose empty eye holes incomprehensible powers glare at human beings. Even the masked hierophant left ordinariness behind and was raised to the daemonic status of the sorcerer and shaman. Unrecognizable when shielded behind the motionless mask, he had become free of fixed meaning (*Eindeutigkeit*) and could participate in the polysemy and immense transformative powers of daemons. His ritualistic incantations were perhaps the most ancient magical theater, the magic circle he demarcates the earliest stage and scene. The play (*Schauspiel*) that signifies the world has dark, subterranean roots in the sacred play (*Sakralspiel*) of primeval cults.

The mask has wandered through the years, increasingly lost its shifty power, lost its religious and artistic relevance, and finally dwindled into a masquerade of the carnivalesque impulse. And, nevertheless, an exciting aura still emanates from the mask, like a late echo of a once great dread. The rigid visage, such a contradiction of the living, moving face, entices, and entrances, has a fascinating effect, simultaneously alluring and repelling, seems mysterious and enclosed within a blank surface. Theater as an artistic practice owes much to the mask, to the evocative petrifying power with which it immobilizes time and brings the moment passing over the living face to a standstill. Masks were prominent in the early days of theater; full of the magical charm of concealment and disguise, an extensive stylization holds the actor captive. The dance-play of Indigenous tribes still displays mask-magic and taboo ritual. The theatrical art found other possibilities for the actor's animated and suggestive facial expressions, for his elocution and his restrained control of gestures. The poet's words do not sound from behind a lifeless mask; they erupt out of an animated and passionate human mouth, they flare up like tongues of fire in the mime's eloquence, yet the actor is not the poet himself, but is in a sense the poet's transient fleeting manifestation. There exists a remarkable and strange relation: the dramatic figures and their theatrical figurants (the poet's masks, metaphorically speaking) are certainly not stone-faced, but forms borrowed from imaginative fancy that creates in the medium of an appearance familiar to all, yet difficult to understand.

In the theatrical transmission of art, however, an opposed sense of the mask-motif can emerge. In particular, this happens when art holds up an incorruptible mirror to the audience, tearing away the veils with which human beings shroud themselves and into which they cocoon themselves with their honors and trifling concerns. Art as unmasking can hold court and prove itself to be a "moral institution," when it shows the hollow and dishonest hustle and bustle that we for the most part accept as valid social reality. That which seems to us to be art can project into an insubstantial semblance (*Schein*). Art becomes a process of the institution of truth—in opposition to a nugatory claim to reality, it operates as disenchantment and as disillusionment. And if it ever, as in later times, is itself led astray by an uncertainty as to what is "essential" and "inessential," it seductively begins to mingle being and appearance (*Schein*), playing them off of each other by twisting them together and blending theatrical elements, allowing an author to contrive six characters or even call life a dream. The dance of masks, in which the classical stage came to an end, is a highly significant process in the history of theater that can guide reflections and observations.

It may seem that the cothurnus—which is footwear elevated on stilts by a layer of cork and worn by actors—is far less remarkable and worthy of consideration than the mask. (Cothurnus was originally a lace-up boot worn by the Dionysian throng, later a requisite of the Roman theater.) This elevation at first operated in a merely quantitative manner. Lifted out of the crowd of small and ordinary people, the great heroic human is exquisitely marked for doom or abandoned to the wrath of the gods. "Thus strideth forth no earthly woman, / They are no mortal progeny! / The giant size of each one's person / Transcends by far what's humanly," as the ballad *The Cranes of Ibykus* portrays the unsettling impression of the elevated (Schiller 1985: 339). We have learned to forgo the cothurnus as requisite, yet we cannot dispense with the function that it once forcefully and solemnly performed. Elevation of the banality of existence belongs to art, progressing beyond the factual into the exemplary, from that which contingently occurs to an example of the essential.

Mask and cothurnus have changed, have become more ambiguous and problematic, have become sublime, and have defined the theater's intellectual landscape as one of alienation and excessive exaggeration (although a frosty, haughty, pathos-avoiding naturalism can also be an artistic device, a kind of "inverted cothurnus"). Mask and cothurnus form a significant and momentous dramaturgical problem, particularly when it comes to the history of their metamorphoses. The gradual end of the crude substantial thing, the "mask," and of the stilted effect of the "cothurnus," has not removed the enchanting powers of the theater, which in early times had materialized in those requisites. They are indispensable so long as the theater is a play that signifies the world. We are thus led to ask ourselves what play is, as a general phenomenon of human existence. Play, human play, becomes a philosophical problem. In a certain sense, this is paradoxical. How can one expect a revelation from philosophy concerning a phenomenon that is so contradictory to it? It is precisely the play's unquestionability, its light-spirited exhilaration, its blissful sojourn into itself, the unproblematic in playful performance, which leaves unanswered questions to conceptual thinking.

How is it possible to live in a temporary pastime, as though we were not surrounded by vast darkness, as though the night of concealment, in which the land of knowledge is only a small island, were not itself a miserable island where we know our way around to some degree but get to the bottom of nothing? How is it possible to live as though the heavily burdensome travail of work, constrained and compelled by need (as though human beings did not dreadfully struggle for dominance over each other), as though the futility of the loving heart and the shadows of death, did not loom over all human things? Officially, play is sheer contrast to everything "serious"; it is an attunement of cheerful exuberance that takes life easy and avoids any care or responsibility, especially the sober conceptual rigor of philosophy. In the gloom of our life's scenery, play appears to be an illuminated tableau, a transfigured and transfiguring intermezzo, an activity that needs no motive cause and has no end in view, an action that is self-sufficient and that satisfies its impulses without inhibition. In contrast, philosophy is the most acute form of the "unhappy consciousness," the persistent distrust of everything that exists—even against oneself, a despondent doubt of the given, of what has been acknowledged and passed down, a dismantling of long-established human existence, and indeed by means of an imageless, antagonistically brooding, ice-cold conceptuality, an incessant abstract reflection.

This is the typical way to set up the relation between "philosophy" and "play" precisely as a relation of opposition between "immediacy" and "reflective mediation." We must find it perplexing that play, supposedly simply immediate, effortlessly goes about its business with a fragmented, split understanding of being—and that problematizing philosophy, on the other hand, aims at unambiguous clarity in knowing being. The player's *existentiell* immediacy sensuously moves around the labyrinth of being and appearance—the thinker's *existentiell* fragmentation attempts to force its way through everything apparent to that which is truly essential. Philosophy wants to disenchant, to uncover, to unveil, to wrest things from their age-old concealment and bring them into the light of reason. Philosophy does not want beauty for beauty's sake; at best it wants beauty as an anticipatory trace of truth. It views the charm of disguise with contempt and does not shy away from unmasking the most revered secrets; it wants only sober clear-sightedness into that which is, that is, into what is true. There is more to this contrast than the psychological-typological differentiation of player and thinker; the opposition of antipodes characterizes the world: being and seeming incessantly intermingle in it, and "essence" and "appearance" become distinct; in it things have surface and depth, nature hides itself and opens itself up in the world, and the upsurge and downfall of all beings take place. Playing and thinking seem to be two opposed comportments of the human being with an understanding of being (*des seinsverstehenden Menschen*). The one involves joining the roundelay of worldly things, enjoyment of the polysemy of beings in colorful twilight, where essence becomes surface and appearance becomes core, where the "*peau de pèche* of things" enchants and the mask excites. The other involves the reduction of multicolored, multifarious phenomena to an outline of the essential, conceptual insight into the structure of things, rejection of the contingent, the elaboration of the architecture of the universe. If philosophy nevertheless passionately strives for essence, if it pierces veils and parts curtains to advance toward genuine and actual beings, then it makes its way there on the pathway of appearances that it negates as inessential trumpery—it is chained to what it denies. The illusory in general, whether it be that of deception, of error, of prejudice, or that which is illusory in things themselves, their exterior, their disguised surface or the flickering sheen of the beautiful; all of this becomes productive irritant for thought that comports itself in a negating manner toward the source of human play's bright joy. Play and philosophy have more in common with each other than customary demarcations reveal: in accordance with their immanent understanding of being, they relate to the same appearance and manifestation of beings in the world, even if in respectively opposed ways; they are antipodes on the same globe. This situation defines any philosophical question concerning play that has been raised for us regarding mask and cothurnus; we are not sure whether they are mere theatrical requisites or magical charm, plaything in a significant sense.

Play is familiar to everyone; it is a well-known and recognizable occurrence of the human world. Yet here, too, Hegel's dictum holds true: the familiar is not yet understood (1977: 18 [§ 31]). Each is familiar with play from his own life, has had experience with it, is used to the playful behavior of his fellow human beings, and is familiar with public games, huge circuses, amusements, sports games, contests, child's play, and the strenuous games of adults. Everyone is also familiar with playful elements in nearly all domains of culture. The *homo ludens* is not shielded from *homo faber* and *homo politicus;* there are half-concealed elements of play in the field of work and politics, alluring and seductive games in the interactions of the sexes. Play is a dimension of existence that is interwoven with all other fields of life, and likewise defines associations with fellow human beings such as religious worship, love, work, and dominion. Activities of play are constantly occurring in profusion; they are everyday occurrences and events in the human world. Play is familiar to everyone; each is acquainted with it from the testimony of his own life.

For the most part, an everyday interpretation of human play corresponds to an everyday awareness. This interpretation aims to sideline play as much as possible from its central role in our life, to conceive of it as a peripheral phenomenon, to deprive it of its true significance. To be sure, play's frequency is noted, as is the ardent interest human beings have in play, the intensity with which they pursue it. It is viewed as though it were a mere pastime, however, a break from serious life, as cheerful idleness. Whenever play is only interpreted as a contrast to work or, in general, to the serious business of life, we are confronted by a very shallow view of play that also governs everyday awareness.

What is play, conceived more essentially? We first note the way in which it is performed. Play is an impulsive, spontaneously flowing activity, buoyant action, existence animated in itself, as it were. Yet play's animation does not happen according to the structure of the other forms of human movement. Every serious action is held in tension by a purposive context (*Sinngefüge*) and points, via intermediary goals, to the human being's "ultimate goal," to happiness, *eudaimonia*. For the most part, life is taken on as a "task," an obligation, a project—we have no tranquil sojourn, we know ourselves to be on the way, and we are perpetually driven from each present moment, thrust forward by the force of an inner conception of happiness. We are held in suspense not only by the unrest of the striving for happiness but also by an uncertainty regarding the interpretation of "true happiness." We attempt to work for, obtain, and enjoy happiness and a fulfilling life and are nevertheless driven from everything we have attained; we sacrifice each present moment for the sake of an uncertain "better future." Although play is impulsive existence animated in itself, it is nonetheless spared (*entrückt*) from being propelled into the future, has no goals that lie outside of it, and is already complete in the act itself. It does not occur for the sake of a happiness still to be accomplished in the future; it is already happiness, and has been spared the otherwise universal futurism. To be sure, it has exciting thrills in itself, moments of competition. And yet play does not thereby transcend itself; it does not degrade itself into an intermediary goal for highly problematic final goals of projective existence. We have already lost play if we only engage in it in order to achieve something different from and foreign to play, thus for example in order to strengthen the body, to promote health, to cultivate a martial disposition—or even only to escape boredom and to pass an empty, meaningless stretch of time.

Occasionally, one also hears the explanation that play has biological significance as preparatory training, safe and risk-free, for future serious activities. There are even theories of play in pedagogy that reduce play to a preliminary rehearsal for later serious cases and a staging ground for attempts at existence that are devalued by the opinion that, in guiding children at play, it is important to anticipate the future life of adults, in a kind of sanctuary, to guide students gently and with the disguise of a playmask into a time when there will no longer be any sphere of freedom for gratuitous time. We are skeptical of the widespread view that play exclusively belongs to childhood. To be sure, children play more openly, in a more unobstructed and less disguised, manner than adults, and yet play is fundamentally a possibility of the human being as such.

A strange attunement is specific to the performance of play: the attunement of buoyant delight, which is more than simple joy in being active, it is a delight in the odd mixture of reality and unreality. Playfulness envelops even grief, horror, dread. The playfulness of ancient tragedy quakes with cruel joy at the downfall of heroes and enjoys the cataract of transience. Play-suffering that is sensuously undergone effects a catharsis of the soul—in Nietzsche's words—". . . with the annihilation of the most beautiful phenomena in the world of appearance, Dionysian happiness reaches its zenith" (1910: xxi). Although play is a spirited impulse, sensuous spontaneity, it does not happen without rules. It binds itself to the rules of the game. The player's scope for arbitrary action is not limited by any foreign power, not by nature's resistance to human interventions, not by the opposition of one's fellow human beings in the field of dominion, the player or players themselves set the limits and boundaries. The players remain bound to the self-established rules of the game, whether it is a match, a card game, or child's play. The rules can be "nullified," and new ones can be agreed to, yet as long as one plays and understands play in a sense-suffused manner, one remains bound to rules. Play can even be engaged in as improvisation, a whirl of imaginative powers and a whirring flight of inner visions, as a game played with imaginary partners by someone who is alone. Nevertheless, for the most part, one sticks to prepared games that are already familiar and to be found in every social class. We do not play, however, because there are common and universally loved games. Such games are only occasions and pretexts for a productive and wide-awake dreamworld that wells up in the ground of the human being's essence.

With what do we play? This question cannot be answered succinctly: we play by ourselves, play with others, play with nonhuman things. We also play, however, with matters of thought and imaginary creations, we jumble that which is real and the gossamer threads of dream, and we link being and appearance in an extraordinarily complex way. To put it in plain terms, the player plays with means of play (*Spielmitteln*), with things that are forcefully propelled in space, and with ideas that are only in his head. Really existing means of play include, for example, the playing field, the boundaries, lines, equipment, and various expedients of a material nature. Not all means of play, however, are playthings in the strict sense. Anywhere play manifests itself in the form of games purely involving movement, of sports, competitive performance, and the like, it requires a number of play-instruments. The more that play takes on the features of portrayal, however, the more the play-instrument becomes true plaything. What is a plaything? Surely any child can provide us with information concerning this question, and yet the plaything's nature and mode of being is a difficult problem. The term is ambiguous. We call "plaything" anything that we view as appropriate for use when engaged in play. When we do so, we simply adopt the perspective of the person standing on the sidelines, the nonplayer. Simple natural objects may perhaps seem suitable for an odd game; for instance, seashells on the beach may seem so to children. Aside from that, we are also familiar with the fabricated manufacture of toys for a well-known play-requisite called the "market." The human beings who manufacture toys do not produce them while playing, but rather while working. Indeed, human labor not only produces food and tools for processing natural materials but it also produces everything necessary for life across all dimensions of existence; that is, it produces the soldier's weapons, women's jewelry, the priest's ritual objects, and even the plaything, insofar as it is an artifact. This artificial object, "plaything," is one item in the comprehensive context of one pervasive world reality, and is, in its being, different and yet no less real than the child at play. The doll is a stitched-together bag of artificial matter, marketed for purchase at a specific price. Yet this doll, for the girl playing with it, is a "child" and she its "mother." In doing so, the little girl does not fall victim to any delusion; the doll-thing is not mistaken for a living child, but rather lives in two dimensions at the same time: in ordinary reality and in an irreal, imaginary sphere. In her play, the little girl decides that the doll-thing will be a "child"; the plaything takes on a magical character. It does not come into being through industrial manufacture, not in a work process; it comes into being in and from playing, insofar as this is a projection of a strange sense-dimension that is not assimilated with, but more like an inconceivable sheen lying over, the real. A field of the possible opens up that is not tied to the course of real events; a stage is set, which to be sure requires and takes up room, occupies space and time, yet is not a part of real space and real time, but an irreal place in an irreal space and an irreal tarrying in an irreal time. The plaything has its place if we do not view it superficially as a manufactured product but instead understand it from the player's perspective, that is, if we understand it from within the playworld's immersive sense-field.

The true productivity of play that portrays is the generation, the imaginatively creative construction of the imaginary playworld. For the most part, this is a collective action, a community of players playing together. In the generation of the playworld. However, the players do not remain on "the other side" of what they have generated, they do not remain "outside," and they themselves enter into their playworld and have their "roles" in it. In the playworld's productive and imaginative projection, players as creators lie concealed; they lose themselves in their own constructions, sink into their character roles and likewise confront each other in character. It is by no means the case that playworldly things cover and disguise the real things of the real world. They merely transform them with an atmosphere of produced sense, without really changing anything connected to their being. The play-creative imagination's power is of course in reality an impotence. Play's power to transform being cannot compete with that of human labor and conflict. Is it thereby insubstantial, a negligible product of our frail imagination, which effortlessly builds airy constructs with the imagination's malleable materials? Or is it a reality joined to the festive, in which we are held in tension a thousand different ways, a liberating and loosening contact with the "origin" from out of which solid, stable, and actually recalcitrant being first emerges? Is an "originality" of play, conceived in this manner, a human-all-too-human delusion, an overestimation of an entirely impotent mode of comportment? Or does human play point the way to that which is origin most of all?

The ontological constitution of human play is puzzling, yet it is more difficult to identify the kind of ontological understanding proper for play. The human being is enmeshed in play, in the tragedy and comedy of his finite existence, from which he cannot escape into the pure autonomy of God or into the bestial pleasures of the animal. Can human play, however, be reliably differentiated from what ethologists call "animal play"? Perhaps from the commotion of young animals? A mutual hunt and flight, playing with prey, testing out growing powers by romping about and engaging in mock-battles, the restless and animated exertion of powers and expression of *joie de vivre* that we are acquainted with in animal and human being. There are striking similarities in their form of appearance. As living beings, as "animal," we are related and similar to the animal, so similar and related that for millennia the human being has repeatedly sought new formulations with which to distinguish himself from the animal—and needs to formulate his own self-understanding, to feel himself to be the "crown of creation," the "image of God," as the site where everything that is finds expression in words, or even as vessel of world spirit. The human mind has already, on numerous occasions, established formulations to specify its "uniqueness" and immense importance, to distance itself from all natural creatures. And it may prove difficult to separate, with these distinctions, what stems from our pride, our arrogance, and what stems from the truth. While many of these formulations may be false, nevertheless *that* we distinguish, that we have an ardent interest in distinction, is certain. The human act of self-understanding includes an opposition to all other beings. The animal does not play by imaginatively managing possibilities; it does not relate to an imaginary "appearance." Ethology is no authority when it comes to ontological questions. It becomes more urgent to protect human play from all zoological subsumption even as the findings of animal-psychological research become richer.

In recent theories of play, there is occasionally an attempt to broaden play even beyond animality and discover it in the playful phenomena of inanimate nature, too. The reflection of moonlight on the rippling water's surface, for example, is said to be a play of light, or the cloud drift is said to cast a shadow-play over field and meadow. A certain "closing off" (*Geschlossenheit*) of the play-site, the movement of picturesque scenery by means of lighting effects and shifting shadows, can reveal a play-phenomenon amid the real world of experience that, to a certain degree, as aesthetic sheen, "wafts" (*schwebe*) over real things. Play reveals itself as a freely wafting epiphenomenon, as beautiful gleam, as the fluttering of shadows. In the entire expanse in which nature appears to us, such "plays" as nature's aesthetic productions could exist, as, for example, one quite rightly speaks of the play of the sea's waves. This is by no means merely a metaphor; on the contrary, nature plays first and only then do natural creatures, animals and humans, play in a derivative sense. This is a captivating interpretation that can take on the colorful image-laden speech of the people who frequently adopt the model of play to express in language a humanly experienced scene of nature whose beauty and enchantment moves us. In this way, play is lifted out of the "narrowness" (*Enge*) of an only human manifestation and understood to be an ontic occurrence that is very widely dispersed. Such "plays" of nature obviously do not need any kind of human player—human play becomes a special case of a more extensive play of nature.

In our view, this is fundamentally wrong. One makes a specific aesthetic or aestheticizing natural relationship into the basis for analysis without clearly acknowledging it. Lighting effects and shifting shadows are just as real as the things they illuminate or darken. The natural things of our environment are continuously situated within environmental circumstances: in the light of early morning, under the shadow of a cloudy sky, in the moonlit twilight of night. Each thing near the edge of a body of water casts a reflection on the water's surface. What are called plays of light and shadow are more or less lyrical circumlocutions for how things manifest themselves in environmental circumstances. Of course, it is no accident that we use such metaphors to speak of the play of rippling water or the light sparkling on waves. Nature does not play, but we who are players see playful features in nature—we use the conception of play figuratively to respond to the eddying, the beauty, and the seeming unboundedness of dancing light upon the waves. In reality, the dance of light upon the myriad surfaces of a moving wave is never "unbounded," never "free," is not movement undertaken by anyone themselves. Lighting effects are as little "play" as the ridges of a wave with its breaking white crests are the white steeds of Poseidon. A dreaming soul, naive and immersed in beautiful appearance, may employ poetic metaphors—but not the human being who thinks, forms conceptions, and engages in scientific endeavors, or the one who is concerned with a philosophical conception of play. Whenever a metaphorical or even symbolic extension of the conception of play is ventured, however, the justification, meaning, and consequences of such a transgression of boundaries must be critically discussed and examined.

Our consideration of play to this point has initially foregrounded moments of performance: the attunement of joy, which is able to encompass even its "contrary," such as grief, sorrow, despair, and "is deeper than the day has ever grasped" (Nietzsche

2006: 133); in addition, the pure present moment, abiding in itself, which is not carried away by the futurism of the rest of our life; next, the rules of the game as self-determination and self-limitation of the players, the fundamentally communicative character of interaction within the community of players—the subtle distinction of means of play and plaything, the difference between the outside perspective on an odd game that one does not play and the player's completely different internal perspective on his performance of play. The player's activity is a quite strange kind of production, namely the production of an "appearance," an imaginary creation and nevertheless not nothing but rather the generation of an irreality that has a fascinating, spellbinding, and captivating power that is not contraposed to the player; on the contrary, it draws him in. The term "player" is just as ambiguous as the term "plaything." As the plaything is also a real thing in the imaginary appearance-world with happenings only valid there, so too the player is just a human being who plays and, at the same time, a human being in the play-role. The players withdraw, as it were, sink into their characters' roles, are submerged therein, and conceal their comportment as players with their comportment that is itself played. The "playworld" is the key fundamental concept for the exegesis of every play of portrayal. It is neither in the player's "interiority" nor is it completely independent of the player's inner life like nonhuman natural things. The playworld is neither outside nor inside; it is both outside, namely as a marked-off imaginary domain that the player is aware of and respects, and at the same time inside in the ideas, thoughts, and imaginations of the players themselves. Determining the location of a "playworld" is exceedingly difficult. Conceptual specification becomes onerous precisely regarding a phenomenon that every child is already familiar with and understands. The playworld is nowhere and at no time, and yet it has a play-space in real space and a playtime in real time. The dimensions of these double-spaces and double-times need not be coextensive—an hour of "play" can span a lifetime. The playworld has its own immanent present moment. The playworld-self and the playing-self must be distinguished, although it is the same person. This identity is the presupposition for the distinction between real persons and their "roles." In the performance of play, we generate the playworld. In real actions, however, that are permeated by the magical production and sensuous power of the imagination, we form the playworld, marked off by the rules of play and the portrayal of meaning, in play-communities with others (or sometimes even in an imaginary coexistence with fantasized partners), yet we do not remain facing it like someone viewing an image—we ourselves enter into the playworld and play a role therein.

This characteristic of role-playing can be experienced with varied intensity. There are performances of play in which the playing human being nearly loses himself, completely identifies with his role, becomes absorbed in it, and slips away from himself. Yet this absorption does not remain too long. All play comes to an end, and we awake from the enchanting dream. The player is soon able to play his role easily and effortlessly and may enjoy his freedom knowing that he can retrieve himself at any time. Play soon becomes an ecstatic self-alienation. A real and fleshed-out play of portrayal does not merely involve fellow players who have cocooned themselves in their roles; it refers to a community of players, to the audience for whom the scene has been set. Drama-play (*Schau-Spiel*) shows this clearly and distinctly. Here the audience are not random witnesses to a strange play-activity: they are not uninvolved, but they are the addressees of the play-message. They do not act; they watch, and as they do so they become enchanted. In a certain sense, plays in their traditional form, with enclosed scenery, are like an image. The audience peer into a playworld that opens up before them, as it were. The space, however, in which the audience is aware of itself does not cross over into the stage area—or it only does so insofar as it is a requisite of the play but not the road to Colonus. The space of the playworld occupies a real place and activity in the playworld takes up real time—and yet it still cannot be located or dated within reality's system of coordinates. The setting of the scene is like a window into an imaginary world. The strange playworld does not merely stand at a distance from ordinary reality; it even has the option of fictively "replicating" its distance and contrast to reality one more time in itself. As there are images within images, so there are plays within plays. Replication can occur on many levels, but in all its iterations remains kept within the same medium of playworldly appearance. These instances of replication are no mere artifices. If the indecisive prince of Denmark stages a play within the playworld, one which portrays the regicide, and through this revelatory portrayal corners the murderous mother and her lover, then the play-community presumably also sees the second play-community in the play, becomes witnesses to the latter's own horrifying captivation—and becomes itself spellbound and captivated. The play-community includes players and those watching their play with interest and concern. Players are "in" the playworld, and spectators are "in front of" the playworld, which is not an unfamiliar process to them but rather enthralls them with its enchanting power. Spectators stand in a different relation to play than actors: they have no roles, are not disguised, and are not covered in imaginary masks. They watch the masked role-play, are not themselves figures in the playworld, but are riveted by the playworld-appearance. This does not indicate any factual error; the spectators do not confuse what occurs in the playworld with real processes in plain reality. Of course, play-activities are always also real processes, though the process of playing is not identical to events that are played or achievements within the scene, in this imaginative lighting that shines forth like an exotic island in ordinary reality. The spectators know that a real human being, an "actor" (*Schauspieler*), stands on the stage; they see him in his role. They know he removes his make-up after the curtain falls, that he puts the props away, takes his mask off, and emerges from the realm of enchantment, and the hero becomes a citizen. The playworld's illusory character is known, and such knowledge does not spoil the charm at all. Deception is not the play's substance. Even the actor can distinguish himself, as artist, from what he "is" in the playworld's medium of appearance, he is not deceived concerning himself, and he also does not wish to deceive the spectators. The greatness of an actor's performance is not to be found in deluding his audience into believing that they are vicariously experiencing extraordinary events in everyday reality. The playworld's imaginative character, fundamentally bound to "appearance" (*Schein*), is not supposed to be lost on the viewers; they are not supposed to be overwhelmed with massive and suggestive dazzling effects and forget that they are attending a play. The play of portrayal's revelatory power reaches its apex when what happens in a play is confused with everyday reality, when "fear and pity" seize hold of the audience as though they happened to be eyewitnesses to a terrible car wreck.

The hyperreality of essence (*Wesen*) is manifest in play's unreality. It is always "the" human being who acts and suffers, stands his ground or succumbs, the essential human being in his impotence before fate, his entanglement in guilt, his delusion and decline. To begin with, the unreality of the appearance-woven playworld is de-realization, negation of the specific individual case and, at the same time, it is the elevated cothurnus upon which the playworld-figure achieves representation. Play reveals in a symbolic manner; it is not permeated by the structure of conceptual propositions that operate by distinguishing particular and universal. It reveals in the symbol, that is, in the coincidence of universality and particularity, reveals in the paradigmatic figure who is "unreal" because he is not supposed to signify any particular actual individual and who is "hyperreal" because he signifies that which is essential and possible in every human being. The sense of the play of portrayal is simultaneously unreal and hyperreal, imaginary and essential in one. The spectator from the play-community becomes witness to a process that does not occur in ordinary reality, which appears transported into a utopia and yet stands open to the person looking on. What he sees in the medium of appearance is not some arbitrary fable that concerns others but has nothing to do with him. The witness to the play of portrayal, if he, spellbound, is included in the play-community, is no longer able to draw the otherwise familiar distinction between himself and whoever else happens to be near him. The spectator recognizes, beholds the human being's essential lot, and is unsettled by the insight that, in a mysterious regard, he is identical to the strange figures, and that the woeful son of Laius, cursed Orestes, and the madness-darkened Ajax are in him as uncanny possibilities that are both terrifying and terrible. A play meant to be viewed (*Schau-Spiel*) requires the view (*Schau*) of the play-community, and not merely players and their roles. The spectator is not merely characterized by distraught concern, there is also another comportment, for instance, in comedy, in the laughter-loosening satyr play. Here too it holds true that we really laugh at ourselves, not at the particular individuals for their empirical mistakes, weaknesses, and follies, but at the weakness and folly essential to the human being. Comedy is no less symbolic than tragedy. It sets us free into the human being's ironic distance from the human. Jokes, humor, and irony, the elements of playful exhilaration, cleave a path to the human being's temporary liberation in surmounting himself with laughter.

If we summarize the main features of play—the magical production of the playworldly appearance, the enchanting captivation of the play-community, the identification of the spectator with the players, human existence's vision of the self in play as mirror of life, play's pre-rational depths of meaning, its symbolic power, its paradigmatic function, and its liberation from time in the revocability of all decisions, the playful easing of human existence and its ability to encompass all other basic phenomena of human existence and ultimately itself, and thus not only work, struggle, love, and death but also to play play—then the overall composition that reveals itself is that of play's festive character. The human being plays wherever he celebrates being. The festival interrupts the series of days burdened by hardship, is removed from gray monotony, set apart and elevated as the extraordinary, the unusual. The festival not only stands in contrast to the everyday but it is also of significance for everyday life—it is supposed to uplift life once more and invigorate it. The festival is lifted out of dull workaday business in order to shine over it like a lighthouse. In archaic societies, the festival, in its stimulating essence, was more readily apparent than in our standard chronological order. Where clocks, chronometers, and timepieces of technical precision proliferate, humanity has less and less time for real festivals. Where, however, days and years are counted by the course of sun and stars, solstices are celebrated, the seasons, cosmic processes on which terrestrial life depends, the harvest of cultivated fields, victory over enemies of the homeland, wedding feasts and births are celebrated. Even the return home of the dead is elevated into the festive and solemnly celebrates the memory of ancestors. Music and dance intertwine in the festive round dance and its associated mimed gestures, and all of this culminates in the festival parade (*Festspiel*), where the community of festivalgoers becomes the community of spectators who watch the image of human existence sensuously reflected and are transformed, precisely by this insight. The festival parade in the ancient polis, for instance, makes the essence of all things visibly present, opens up the chthonic depths of the earth with their subterranean gods who watch over oaths, the power of nemesis, the pettiness of human affairs in the face of fate, the curse on powerful families such as that on the Atreides. Play is one of the human roots of religion; it brings the divine and the human—and the world itself—to a shimmering innerworldly epiphany. And from the ground of play the smiling grace of the muses ascends, the dream-flowering of high art with its festive world-theater.

22

Notes on a Translation

Eugen Fink's *Nietzsche's Philosophy*

Goetz Richter

Exposition

I have read philosophy for as long as I can remember. Early pocket money was spent on Leisegang's *Denkformen*. In my early high school years I started reading English philosophers (or those I thought were such). On a visit to Cambridge I discovered Heffers Bookshop and spent my travel allowance on Popper's *Open Society* and *Logic of Scientific Discovery*. After high school I decided to study musical performance. I had enough talent, a strong drive, a lot of passion, and a good teacher. Two reasons seemed to determine my decision: my desire to tackle the impossible and Carl Jasper's advice that philosophers should have other professions. Philosophy requires grounding. Socrates was after all a cobbler and Spinoza had rejected academic business.

I was lucky. My teacher in Munich, the violinist and leader of the Vienna Philharmonic Orchestra Gerhart Hetzel, loved philosophy. He was a remarkable man—curious, intense, infinitely compassionate, persistent and tough. We talked a lot of philosophy, learning and music. He died early. While walking in the mountains he fell. Protecting his valuable hands he fatally injured his head.

After completing my *Staatsdiplom* I accepted a leading performance position in Australia. When I became the associate leader of the Sydney Symphony in my mid-twenties, I decided to study philosophy at Sydney University.

Sydney University still had interesting thinkers at the time. There were two philosophy departments: the analytic philosophers, led by David Armstrong and the "continentals," also known as general philosophy. György Markus, my honours supervisor on Novalis, was a continental but he knew Marx *and* Wittgenstein well. He lectured with intense wonderment and passionate curiosity on Spinoza, Descartes, and Hegel well past semester end until the janitor closed the building for Christmas and the Australian summer break.

I studied at the university for twenty years, finishing with a PhD on the congruence of music and philosophy. In addition to Markus, there were two marvelous thinkers: the Nietzsche and Heidegger interpreter and translator Ted Sadler and my teacher, the brilliant philosopher, and Classics scholar Rick Benitez. Sadler translated some of Heidegger's writings for Bloomsbury. He also directed my attention to Eugen Fink.

Development

Sadler, Markus, and Benitez were real philosophers. They did not just chatter and they were no attention seekers. They were curious, radical, witty, insightful, and competent. They listened, read, and thought. Sadler particularly was not afraid of tackling nonsense that started to invade the university with babbling postmodernists. This did not win him friends, as under the pretense of "interdisciplinary" knowledge, the babblers gradually also seduced analytic philosophy. Today, Sydney has no philosophy department. Anyone working in philosophy is part of a school of social science or such.

Sadler introduced me to Fink in his Nietzsche course, and we frequently discussed the need to make Fink's lectures on Nietzsche available to English readers. Busy battling the pedantic control of Hermann Heidegger while completing his translations, he suggested I take over an assignment from Athlone to translate Fink. I translated a chapter or two and the publisher accepted. Seven years later, when I finally submitted the translation (largely completed on concert tours), I received not even the originally agreed upon paltry fee initially.

A little while after its publication in 2003 my Fink translation received a stunning condemnation by Professor Babich in the *International Studies in Philosophy*. While using the original German version of Fink for her own rambling paper, Babich thought it necessary to mock the translation in a supercilious manner as "disappointingly bad." The translation was "not quite English" and showed a lack of familiarity with philosophical language of all kinds (her list here is a neat example of her confusion). It would be better, Babich suggested, the translation did not exist as its existence would now prevent others from doing it properly (Babich 2005: 177). Supported by theatrical posture ("one might sigh"), Babich's comments were clearly set out in search of attention and authority for herself. Why was that needed? Professor Babich is a flamboyant sophist, someone who writes a lot, tries to impress, and ultimately says little. Her discussion of Fink or Nietzsche lacks depth, order, and direction. She is a postmodern master of an academic business that creates the impression of philosophy. Answering her critique is not really possible. Whether my translation should have been made is no longer relevant. If it is as bad as Babich says, it will disappear. Her comparison of my translation to translations of Fink's essays by others is problematic. Fink's Nietzsche Lectures wrestle with language. He is at times convoluted and repetitive and his thinking turns upon itself. The lectures show blemishes of live speech and failures of expression and systematicity (Moran 2007: 7). While they would have been immensely inspiring for an audience as the thinker reached for the unsayable, the "frozen word" does not always read well. A translation of lectures reflects naturally the original struggle. This has nothing to do with the fact that the translator did not learn English as his first language.

A seemingly more specific criticism of the translation was made by Professor Crowell in his paper in the same journal. Crowell thinks the translation "extremely unreliable" (Crowell 2008: 29), and while citing it, he also changes it. That is perfectly fine. However, why this effortful posture? Why not cite from the German in his own translation? It seems clear that Crowell is not really interested in Fink or Nietzsche. He wants to use them as material to appear as a philosopher. My translation is useful here—an easy strawman.

When we look at Crowell's own altered translations, a substantial task as his essay bamboozles the reader with serpentines of quotes, it becomes clear that Crowell's regret about the translation is entirely insincere and staged. He is seeking an opportunity to manicure his own academic authority. The alterations, where they are made, are insubstantial and ultimately irrelevant. They add nothing to an understanding of Fink's text as such. In three cases, he identifies "serious problems." Two are obvious printing mistakes, that is, a missing "not" and the other a "not" too many. Of course, these mistakes are not good. However, a thoughtful reader who does not just pick sentences out and string them together will see that immediately—just like someone speaking German will detect Crowell's mistakes in his German quotations. In one case where the translation "totally fails" (Crowell 2008: 30) there is room for improvement, I agree. Here, I accept Professor Crowell's criticism, but I do not accept his clumsy alternative. Cycling the text through the Deep-L translation program gives us both a better version.

Recapitulation

My translation of Fink was a training exercise. It was a way to become familiar with the thinking of a real philosopher as philosophy mattered to me. Having the incentive to share my practice gave me a great opportunity to focus. After completing it, my hope was that the practice was sufficiently good to inspire English readers to follow up on Fink. I do not mind what happens next. The text can serve many purposes, including the business of sophists. The thinking that manifests itself in it is awaiting to be discovered always anew. Sophistry on the other hand discovers nothing because it only wants to show its cleverness and secure its authority. Eugen Fink was mindful that we cannot use philosophy to show our cleverness and seek attention. For Fink philosophy is not a business, a worldview, or even a known and available sophistical possibility. Philosophy

> is not known at all, even if we have a learned historical knowledge of the doctrines of the great thinkers since Thales. Philosophy is the questioning of our natural view of the world, is the inverted world. As the suspended foreboding of a more authentic being, as the melancholy of privation, it unsettles man's natural attitude to the world, which is otherwise complacently closed in on itself. (Fink 1985: 21)

Review of Eugen Fink, *Fashion*

Seductive Play[1]

Chester Mlcek

In his 1969 book *Fashion: Seductive Play*, Eugen Fink presents a thorough phenomenological investigation of fashion in its cultural, social, economic, and individual relations to the human. *Fashion*'s English translation offers this comprehensive and influential text to a new audience.

Chapter One, "The Magical Powers of Fashion," elucidates aspects of embodiment, clothing, and the human relation of fashion necessarily overlooked by common and historical attitudes, highlighting fashion as a worthy philosophical problem. Fink initially identifies fashion as that phenomenon which governs human appearance through varying the essentially protective, socially distinguishing, and morally conforming aspects of clothing. While, in many philosophy departments today, the "fashionable" idea often connotates inauthenticity for its deceiving and fleeting qualities, Fink deems such qualities worthy of philosophical investigation, not through the cold calculation of an idle observer but through the playful light in which such phenomena appear in everyday life, as "unnecessary" or embellishing. To think "what remains completely missed" in the reproaches against fashion, Fink draws on Immanuel Kant's 1786 text, *Conjectural Beginning of Human History*, which recounts the biblical "Fall" in the Book of Genesis as an "elevation" of the human to their essential freedom with the development of reason. Fink notices a fundamental "eminent erotic power of covering" (12) in Kant's explanation of heightened desires at variance with nature, which arise from the withdrawal of the object of desire from the wearer. While Kant identifies the anticipation of the future as the opening to *free* choice between instinct and unnatural desires, Fink sees the same anticipation as the comportment toward time as time, or the opening of care. Together, the ecstatic nature of covering (in creating heightened desires), the freedom of choice, and the care of the human toward its destined world constitute the human's central structures. As the body becomes both the site of the human's freeing everyday choice and the connection to the determined natural world, Fink sees the human as an essentially embodied, but displaced being.

Chapter 2, "The Social Phenomenon of Fashion," refutes reductions of fashion's fleeting appearance in human sociality which hold that "what is valid and reliable . . .

must last" (22). As differentiated by its care, the human being comports itself toward the understanding and perception of others, opening the social—a shared, malleable field of meaning whose restructuring drives human history through "an antagonism of conservative forces and proponents of change" (21). The result is that the *presentation* of human actions and events are determined by the *Zeitgeist,* the style of the times, while *in substance*, authoritative laws and traditions determine human actions and events. As the style of appearance, fashion is diverting, fleeting, and constantly in change, yet remains reoccurring "in always new variations on an eternal theme" (22), most drastically so in the realm of clothing. One cannot attack fashion's fleeting nature on the grounds of existence because the emphases of fashion's variation make up a real language of embodied communication. Similarly, fashion cannot be reduced to a mere extravagance, evasion of responsibility, or an industrial ploy to entrap consumers, as the "extravagant" fashion of various designer lines do not constitute the whole of fashion but serve as suggestions of unthought opportunities. Fashion's diverting character is *innovating* in the social, yet never quite divorced or alienated from the essential, reliable, and unchanging forms of human clothing which take the human body as their measure.

Chapter 3, "The Wish to Be Always Different," works to circumvent the *fashionable* opinion of fashion as not serious or frivolous that arises from the conservative and progressive forces of human social relations to better understand fashion's place in human communication. Fashion manifests in public life, contrasting with neither the familial nor private spheres, but instead in oscillation with the individual. At the intersection of the public and individual realms, Fink identifies a "collective fantasy" of unvoiced ideal images, a collective unconscious whose deciphering drives the human "desire" for beauty. With this framework, fashionable clothing may be analyzed from the perspective of consumption, where the consumer selects from an already determined style or line while contributing their own individual "sense" of beauty, or from the perspective of production, where the fashion industry may lead by pondering said incalculable, ideal images, always re-analyzing the emergence of ideals from the mass of consumers. Both perspectives highlight the "language of clothing"—clothing's alteration of and relation to these ideals—as of primary concern. The form of the covered body orients the form of the cover, and the choice of covering constitutes an expression of the adorner. Despite the body's expressions (and therefore its shape) being complex, subtle, and in constant flux, clothing abstracts those expressions, "breaks the impulse's immediate directness and reverses it, driving it back into itself. Clothing mediates our sensual desires, it makes them last longer and spiritualizes our sensuousness" (39). Fink concludes with an examination of the ideals of male and female in fashion's expression: a look at "The Birth of Venus" illustrates the amplifying, abstracting power of material, and an interpretation of Ortega y Gasset's art affirms the body's allure in clothing is more than crude sex appeal.

Chapter 4, "Appeal and Performance in Fashion," discusses appeal, or the occurrences of those "desires at variance with nature" proper to human care, and the *performance* quality of fashion's unique appeal. The human experiences impressions of surrounding sensible things as sense-stimuli which ordinarily do not "stand out" in everyday experience and are left mostly unilluminated by human consciousness. Any slight stimuli, whether conscious, experience-provoking, semi-conscious, or unconscious, may appeal to the human's natural desires, but ultimately, "the human being is, for those like him or her, the strongest stimulus" (46). As the strength of the human's appeal for those of its kind accounts for the creation of culture and society, the human being stands amid a field of reciprocal appeals. The appeal of fashion enters among the others by summoning the natural appeal of the human body. Fashion simultaneously accentuates yet also withdraws this appeal from its corresponding object of desire in a concealment to create a heightened, artificial, and *enchanted* appeal. As the origin of the human's displaced, artificial appeal, fashion acts as the medium of human cultural history. Fink determines that the role of the fashion designer is to balance the interplay of natural and artificial appeals of clothing which perpetuate and update a field of fashion within the field of reciprocal human appeals.

In Chapter 5, "Fashion Has Many Faces," Fink's historical exploration of the network of appeals that constitutes the "language of fashion" reveals fashion's essential play-like character. Moralizing accounts which condemn fashion for its constant change misconstrue its essence, as fashion's essence is "rather ceaseless change . . . a dance through time, the rolling, overflowing frothy foaming head precipitously gushing over itself and pouring onto the difficult, dark waves of our life's flow" (56). With such an axiom in mind, Fink moves to decode the language of fashion's appeals in reference to "cultivated sociability." Sociability, or joyful, embodied being-with, arises out of the serious demands of culture which, in their striving, secured a "free-time" of leisure for an elite few. The Enlightenment and the French Revolution have since democratized free-time as a human right and the newly refined medium of sociability for all. Sociability's juxtaposition against life's "serious" elements of work, love, and power bestows sociability its "tempo" or "gait" of transformation. The elements of serious life are not lost in the sociable realm but instead are transformed and "presented" in a lighthearted manner. The presentation of the serious in the sociable establishes a "parlor game" in which nothing is compelled, but options for community and expression remain available. For Fink, sociability thus belongs to the realm of play, which "does not occur alongside and outside of the carrying out of serious existence, but rather . . . replicates and mirrors all serious undertakings in the mode of as-if . . . conjures a semblance-world [*Scheinwelt*] and yet does not succumb to it" (59). For Fink play essentially creates an enchanted "presentation" of the serious world. Moreover, he understands that fashion (a domain which concerns itself not with necessity but with embellishment) takes up the languages of "culture" and "taste" as the structure of fashion's playworld, that is, the pathways by which the individual journeys toward self-expression.

Because the individual's expressive impulses still might find no fitting pathway in a specific social situation, Chapter 6 examines the methods in which the culture industry of fashion might lead or direct fashion to avoid this tension and ensure its own flourishing. The traditional frameworks of leadership—the authoritative and the pedagogical—have solid structures respective to their domains, but neither can compel in a manner which brings about the normatively binding representation of a fashion. The fashion industry can not only present a suite of pathways or a "collection," it must observe the emergence of ideals from the field of reciprocal appeals and respond to them in a "suggestion." Although some may object that leadership from an industry might reduce fashion to some sort of equipment for an end, Fink argues that, in leading by suggestion, the respective culture industry does not essentialize or reduce fashion, but instead offers it direction, acting more in the way of *seduction* (*Verführung*) than *leadership* (*Führung*). Because the fashion industry engages with objects of propagation, persuasion, and seduction, its manner of suggesting "may only promote within a milieu that has already been promoting" (73) and thus must take the form of advertisement. Fashion, then, must lead through the advertisement of intentionally developed seductive ideals which subtly bridge the familiar with the potentially new, and thereby suggest to the public an option for their free movement into a new fashion.

The final chapter, "Is Fashion Existentially Justified?," argues for fashion's exemption from the measure of contexts external to itself. In the economic context, one assesses fashion on its usefulness for amassing wealth, which itself only has "use" for characterization within a political hierarchy and is too narrow a standard. Similarly, moral contexts assess fashion as either "good" or "bad," but as morals historically arise, shift their formation, and pass away, no one moral code can claim to be an authoritative measure of fashion. Fashion's luxury is not traditionally useful or valuable because fashion's ontological status may not be wholly evaluated "according to standards that are foreign and external to it" (79). When viewed in its own playful light, however, fashion marks the human cultural record of ambiguity in the intersection of natural and artificial appeals. In the enchanting aspect of fashion which blends being and appearance, fashion is "akin to excess and the superfluous and for precisely this reason [is] 'necessary' in a higher sense" (82). Due to the ambiguity of fashion, Fink proposes that one might only recognize fashion's existential justification from within an understanding of fashion as such a seductive play.

Discussing existential justification of Fashion, Fink asks, "Does not everything that exists also already have, through its simple being, the legitimation of its existence, must such legitimation still be brought in addition and from outside?" (81). Subsequently, he engages with critics of fashion who consider it useless or unserious. Here a question arises, if the pathways of free-time may be externally determined "through public programs" (60), might fashion, at least in its current expression through free-time, stand in danger of elimination and therefore in need of external defense or legitimation? Though the realization of free-time as a battleground of capital's structures were not equally revealed in Fink's conditions of 1969, such a defense might still prove valuable considering recent struggles against "fast fashion" and the corporatization of the fashion industry.

Fashion: Seductive Play offers readers an invaluable collection of practical advice and fresh, relevant perspectives for designers, historians, and philosophers of aesthetics, all grounded in a consistent philosophical methodology.

Annotated Bibliography of All Fink English Translations

Anna Luiza Coli and Chester Mlcek

1. Forthcoming. **Presentatification and Image.** Translated and edited by Daniel O'Shiel. Bloomsbury Academic.

Written under Husserl's supervision and Heidegger's evaluation, Fink's PhD thesis (1929) outlines a sort of third way between transcendental phenomenology and the analytic of *Dasein*. The phenomenology of irreality appears in the final considerations on image consciousness.

2. Cairns, Dorian. **Conversations with Husserl and Fink.** The Hague: Nijhoff, 1976.

The meticulous record of the conversations Cairns had with both Husserl and Fink throughout the second period of his Freiburger studies (1931–2)—excluding the initial conversation, dating back to first period (1926)—discloses the restlessness of a dialogical philosophy in constant state of movement and construction, what Husserl called "*syn-philosophizing.*"

3. **"The Phenomenological Philosophy of Edmund Husserl and Contemporary Criticism."** With a preface by Edmund Husserl. In *The Phenomenology of Husserl: Selected Critical Readings*, edited by R. O. Elveton, pp. 73–147. Chicago: Quadrangle, 1970.

The famous article that became known as "Kant-Studien" was published in the homonymous periodical in 1933, and at the request of the editor, it was preceded by the famous note in which Husserl wrote that "there is no sentence by Dr. Fink that I do not recognize as my own." Fink outlines here the program of the Cartesian Meditations (including the sixth) in response to a Neokantian critique of phenomenology.

4. **"What Does the Phenomenology of Edmund Husserl Want to Accomplish? (The Phenomenological Idea of Laying-a-Ground)."** Translated by Arthur Grugan. *Research in Phenomenology* 7, pp. 5–27, 1972.

Published in 1934, this article synthesizes Fink's formulations of a "system of phenomenological philosophy" from the early 1930s. Fink announces how a systematic understanding of the constitutive interpretation of the world is made possible by the phenomenological reduction understood as self-meditation (*Selbstbesinnung*).

5. **"The Problem of the Phenomenology of Edmund Husserl."** Translated by Robert M. Harlan. In *Apriori and World*, edited by William McKenna, Robert M. Harlan, and Laurence E. Winters, pp. 21–55. The Hague: Nijhoff, 1981.

Published in 1939, this article anticipates the idea (which marks Fink's postwar philosophy) that the phenomenological appeal "back to the things themselves" has the specific sense of an appeal not to the immediate experience of things in their familiarity, but precisely in their unfamiliarity. Reduction is reformulated as "astonishment," as the rendering of the familiarity of experience into a philosophical problem—the "inverted world."

6. **"Nietzsche's Metaphysics of Play."** Translated with an Introduction by Catherine Homan and Zachary Hamm. In *Philosophy Today* 63, no. 1, pp. 21–33, 2019.

In this conference, presented in 1946 on the occasion of the defense of his Habilitation thesis (the *Sixth Cartesian Meditation*), Fink traces the general lines of the ontology of becoming which, alongside the interpretation of Nietzsche's philosophy as a metaphysics of play, provide the basis for his ontological project.

7. **"Two Conversations with Heidegger."** Edited and translated by Giovanni Jan Giubilato and Ian Alexander Moore. Included in this edited volume.

A record of two conversations between Fink and Heidegger on the limitations of the subjective perspective in *Being and Time* and the overall limitations on understanding the truth of Being, one in 1949 and one in 1953.

8. **"Ontological Problems of Community."** Translated by Michael R. Heim. In *Contemporary German Philosophy*, vol. 2, pp. 1–19. University Park: Pennsylvania State University Press, 1983.

Originally a lecture held in 1952/3 and 1968/9, this text serves as basis to the published volume *Existence and Coexistence* and articulates the fundamental phenomena of human existence in the context of the problem of community and language. The problem of community becomes an analysis of the experience of others.

9. **"The Teaching of Philosophy in Germany."** In *The Teaching of Philosophy: An International Inquiry of UNESCO.* Paris: United Nations Educational, Scientific and Cultural Organization, 1953.

Representing Germany on the UNESCO Committee of Experts for an inquiry into the teaching of philosophy, Fink examines the state, methods, materials, and shortcomings of philosophical education in Germany's universities in 1951 by responding to a list of standardized questions.

10. **"Operative Concepts in Husserl's Phenomenology."** Translated by William McKenna. In *The Human Being in Action: The Irreducible Element in Man*, Part II: Investigations at the Intersection of Philosophy and Psychiatry, edited by Anna-Teresa Tymieniecka, pp. 56–70. Dordrecht: Reidel, 1978. Republished in Apriori and World, edited by William McKenna, Robert M. Harlan, and Laurence E. Winters, pp. 56–70. The Hague: Nijhoff, 1981.

In this 1957 article Fink systematizes the difference between operative and thematic concepts and argues that operative concepts are those with which thought operates (and thinks thematically) but which are not themselves the object of reflection and problematization. They are thus the "unthought" substrate of all thought. Fink analyzes the operative concepts that remained unthought in Husserlian phenomenology.

11. Schutz, Alfred. **"The Problem of Transcendental Intersubjectivity in Husserl (with Comments of Dorian Cairns and Eugen Fink)."** Translated by Fred Kersten. Schutzian Research 2, pp. 9–51, 2010.

From Schutz's lecture at Husserl-Colloquium in Royaumont in 1957, in which the latter thematizes the experience of the Other in Husserl's Fourth and Fifth Cartesian Meditation, Cairns and Fink wrote a series of commentaries, largely agreeing with Schutz's criticisms regarding the difficulty in the Husserlian exposing of the construction of the Other in the self-experience.

12. **"Oasis of Happiness: Thoughts toward an Ontology of Play."** Translated by Ian Alexander Moore and Christopher Turner. *Purlieu: A Philosophical Journal* 1, no. 4, pp. 20–42, 2012.

Fink attempts to provide conceptual models for the essential structures of play, moving from an examination of play in its everyday and cultural significances to an understanding of play as a reflection of Being in which human beings find their essence.

13. *Play as Symbol of the World and Other Writings*. Translated by Ian Alexander Moore and Christopher Turner. Bloomington: Indiana University Press, 2016.

As Fink's magnum opus, *Play as Symbol of the World* is a full phenomenological exploration of play. Fink traces play's familiarity and "non-seriousness" through its relations to theater, education, labor, sport, art, culture, theology, history, and ontology. The volume also includes various edited manuscripts: the texts "Play and Celebration," "Play and Cult," and (including Fink's respective notes), "The World-Significance of Play" reflect on the historical cultic-festival aspect of play and its modern celebration of embodiment; the texts "Play and Philosophy" (with respective notes) and "Child's Play" provide short elaborations on their titular subjects; and the collected notes of "Sport Seminar," "Play and Sport," and "The Philosophical-Pedagogical Problem of Play" offer valuable fragmented insight on Fink's philosophy of education as communal play.

14. ***Nietzsche's Philosophy***. Translated by Goetz Richter. London: Continuum, 2003.

Published in 1960, this work presents an account of Nietzsche as one of the two central figures for understanding the history of Western metaphysics—the first being Hegel. Unlike Hegel, however, Nietzsche would be the one who advocates nihilism as a way of creating a possible new future for philosophy.

15. With Martin Heidegger. ***Heraclitus Seminar***. Translated by Charles H. Seibert. Evanston, IL: Northwestern University Press, 1993. Earlier published in University: University of Alabama Press, 1979.

Notes of a seminar held by Martin Heidegger and Eugen Fink in the Winter Semester of 1966/7. Fink and Heidegger attempt to elucidate what is unthought in the movements of the one and the many in Heraclitus' fragments, with an emphasis on the often-neglected anthropological fragments.

16. Forthcoming. ***Fashion: Seductive Play***. Edited by Stefano Marino and Giovanni Matteucci, translated by Ian Alexander Moore and Christopher Turner. London: Bloomsbury Publishing, 2023.

Working from a tension between freedom and natural necessity in Kant, Fink investigates fashion's playful and free nature through various intersecting fields of fashion, including its place in industry, advertising, art, and personal expression.

17. **"Mask and Cothurnus."** Translated by Christopher Turner. Included in this edited volume.

Fink takes the dramatic props of the mask and cothurnus as a starting point to reveal the imaginary and elevating powers of play's symbolic representation in theater, games, and festivals.

18. **"Nietzsche's New Experience of the World."** Translated by Michael Allen Gillespie. In *Nietzsche's New Seas: Exploration in Philosophy, Aesthetics, and Politics*, edited by Michael Allen Gillespie and Tracy B. Strong. Chicago: Chicago University Press, 1988.

In this conference delivered at the *Nietzsche Aujourd'hui?* colloquium in Cerisy-la-Salle in 1972, Fink returns to Nietzsche to propose a new experience of the world as the experience of things in their most radical becoming. Fink's ontology of becoming and cosmology clearly overlap here.

19. "**Eugen Fink's Editorial Remarks.**" In Edmund Husserl, *Introduction to the Logical Investigations: A Draft of a Preface to the Logical Investigations* (1913), edited by Eugen Fink, translated by Philip J. Bossert and Curtis H. Peters, pp. 13–15. The Hague: Nijhoff, 1975.

In providing context for the multiple layers of revision and rewriting that comprise Husserl's last "draft of a preface" to his *Logical Investigations*, Fink revisits Husserl's later (1939) perspective on his own work written nearly four decades earlier. Fink reads this late self-interpretation through the reshaping of his own conception of phenomenology.

20. **Sixth Cartesian Meditation**: *The Idea of a Transcendental Theory of Method, with Textual Notations* by Edmund Husserl. Translated with an introduction by Ronald Bruzina. Bloomington: Indiana University Press, 1995.

Conceived as an exposé of a transcendental theory of method—the phenomenology of phenomenology—the "Sixth" should succeed Fink's revision of all Husserl's Cartesian Meditation in its German publication, which ended up not happening. It was, however, an influential text among Husserl's closest circle, although it remained virtually lost until 1988 (when it was published in the Husserliana collection by Guy van Kerckhoven).

Notes

Chapter 1

1 Franz observes that "Indeed, for Fink, all fundamental phenomena are symbols of the world; as modes of human being and understanding, they are also modes of world-understanding" (1999: 124; see also 129). For more on how the world's prevalence is reflected into the human experience of death and mortality, see Dastur, "Worldliness and Mortality" (2017: 167–76).
2 As Franz notes in his reading of this passage, play's engagement with the imaginary occurs on two levels at once, ". . . in a simple sense, as the performance of play, but doubled as a real performance and an activity in the imagination of the playworld" (1999: 123).
3 For Fink's own discussion, see 2016a: 198–204.
4 I discuss Fink's more positive assessment of Plato's philosophy of play in the *Laws* (see for instance Fink, 2016: 100) as well as his interpretation of Heraclitus on play in Turner 2024. More analysis of Fink's interpretations of Plato is needed.
5 See Stenger's superb analysis of world-openness (2011).
6 Using the fundamental phenomenon of work (*Arbeit*) as an example, Stenger observes that "Each fundamental phenomenon opens, while at the same time helping the world and the self in it to their blossoming (φύειν). The fundamental phenomenon of work indicates the emergence of the work-self, just as the 'world of work' is continually enmeshed in its oppositional dialectic. This holds no differently with 'love' and 'play,' as well as the other basic phenomena" (2011: 337).
7 Thanks to Ian A. Moore for bringing this example to my attention.
8 We might even think of today's smartphones, though having everything at one's fingertips without enough time to register it all is not the same as perceiving everything simultaneously. Rather than Borges' "The Aleph," for this we'd have to look to Rilke's account of Nikolai Kuzmich for a potent symbol.
9 As in Edwin Abbott Abbott's *Flatland*, so in Borges' tale perhaps a being from higher dimensions is lifting the narrator into a new dimension, from which everything in the old world is simultaneously visible from all angles, including the insides of living beings. A Square's trip to three-dimensional space is a nice analogue for what the narrator of Borges' tale experiences in Carlos Argentino's basement.

Chapter 2

1 *In memory of Professor. Ronald Bruzina.*
2 When quoting from texts in the original German the English, translations presented in this chapter were prepared by the author with the inestimable help and supervision of Steve Stakland, to whom heartfelt thanks are due. Any errors or inaccuracies are

solely attributable to me. Special thanks to Ian Alexander Moore for his comments and insights on previous versions of this chapter.
3 Cf. Cairns 1976: 57, 67.
4 Cf. Heidegger 1995; see also the extensive discussion of Dasein as "being-in-the-World" and of world as "play of life" in Heidegger 1996b (GA 27).
5 On this fundamental topic see Kerckhoven 2001.
6 See Fink 2008: 103. Also, "Meontic-constitutive phenomenology does not bypass finitude but jumps off from finitude into the infinity of the origin that is enfinitizing itself in the world plunge (Fink 2008: 91)." Cf. Bruzina 2004: 436.
7 During summer 1932 Fink devoted himself to the extensive revisions of Husserl's "Meditations" (cf. Fink 1988b) and then, between August and October, to the writing of the *VI Cartesian Meditation* (cf. Fink 1988a; cf. also Bruzina's explications in Fink 1995: xv, xvii–xxi, and xxxv–lix).
8 In winter semester 1930/1 Fink took over the so-called "*Japanese Seminar*" for Husserl, choosing Hegel's "Preface" to the "*Phenomenology of Spirit*" as the subject of his conversations and seminar exercises in which Tomoo Otaka, Jisho Ushui, Mayumi Haga, and Goîchi Miyake participated (cf. Fink 2008). At the same time, he attended Heidegger's lectures on Hegel's *Phenomenology*. Moreover, around this time, Fink also thought to shape in a planned writing the inevitable confrontation of Husserl's transcendental phenomenology with the ontological insights, to which urged Heidegger's "hermeneutics of facticity" pushed, according to the model of Hegel's "*Differenz-Schrift*" (cf. Fink 2008). See also Fink 2023a; Fink 2023b and Kerckhoven and Giubilato 2023.
9 On philosophy as "catastrophic thinking" cf. Fink 1995: 32, 136; see also Giubilato 2022a.
10 "Being is transcendental surface" (Fink 2008: 108). "The intra-mundane human-object correlation is one that remains in the 'transcendental surface'" (Ibid: 91).
11 On this topic cf. also Nielsen 2010.
12 Cf. Heidegger 1996a: 125: "When we talk in an ontically figurative way about the *lumen naturale* in human being, we mean nothing other than the existential-ontological structure of this being, the fact that it is in the mode of being its there."
13 On this topic see Kerckhoven and Giubilato 2023. Regarding the long dialogue/confrontation with Heidegger, even though an extensive and specific study of Fink's many transcriptions of Heidegger's university courses, lectures, and seminars he attended from 1928/9 until the 1960s is still lacking, see Bruzina 2004 and, here in Chapter 18, the crucial study by Ian Alexander Moore *Fink and Heidegger on Cosmological and Ontological Play: A Confrontation*.
14 Nachlass Eugen Fink, Universitätsarchiv Freiburg, E 15/962. I would like to thank Ian Alexander Moore for drawing my attention to these still unpublished documents.
15 "Martin Heidegger: Der Mann, Das Werk, Die Frage, Der Zuspruch, Die Endlichkeit," radio speech given by Fink on the *Südwestrundfunk* transmitted on 27th September 1964. Cf. Nachlass Eugen Fink, Universitätsarchiv Freiburg, E 15/214.
16 Heidegger is referring to Fink's decision not to accept the appointment as his successor to the Freiburg chair of philosophy. On May 11, 1957, Fink had received a letter from the dean of the Freiburg Faculty of Philosophy: the committee for the reoccupation of the Chair of Philosophy had unanimously decided to make the necessary preparations to propose his appointment to this chair to the faculty. Consequently, the prospect opened up that the chair previously held by Heinrich Rickert, Edmund Husserl, and Martin Heidegger could be filled by Eugen Fink after

a long period of vacancy since, due to a decree of the French military government of December 1946, after the war it had become impossible for Martin Heidegger to return to his chair. Nevertheless, after a long period of careful thought and consideration, on January 17, 1958, Fink informed the dean of the Freiburg Faculty of Philosophy that he could not accept the call.
17 Heidegger probably sent a text or manuscript to Fink with his 1964 letter.

Chapter 3

1 The first translation into English was produced by Garrett Bardon and John Cumming for *Continuum* in 1975. In this chapter I quote the second revised edition published in 2004, revised by Joel Weinsheimer and Donald G. Marshall. I take the fact that the English translator also quotes the German compound word "*Wirkungsgeschichte*" in parentheses as proof of a certain inescapable *Sprachnot* ("linguistic penury") in which we live. The topic of the limits of language (*Sprachkritik*) has been addressed extensively in Gadamer's philosophical hermeneutics.
2 The main figures of the Konstanzer Schule were Hans Robert Jauss and Wolfang Iser (Ferraris 2002: 282–7).
3 Gadamer uses the word "Platonism" (Gadamer 1999b: 13).
4 Gadamer here adopts the metaphor of horizon from Nietzsche and Husserl to stress the openness and mobility of any hermeneutic situation (Gadamer 1999b: 249ff).
5 Other conditions of possibility of the act of understanding developed in this chapter of *Truth and Method* are the hermeneutical circle, the rehabilitation of prejudices, the anticipation of completeness, and the productivity of temporal distance.
6 I have argued elsewhere that there are indeed many concepts of play in Eugen Fink's writings or that his concept of play is multidimensional. See Miras Boronat (2016a, 2016b).
7 In reference to Brian Sutton Smith's (2001) "rhetorical solution," which is introduced in the next section.
8 According to Schiller's popular dictum: "[. . .] man only plays when he is in the fullest sense of the word a human being, and he is only fully a human being when he plays" (Schiller 1967: 107).
9 Gadamer does not specifically use this expression here. Rather, it appears in a short text called "Das Spiel der Kunst" (1977, "The play of the Arts"; Gadamer 1999e: 93), but I do think that the sense fits perfectly on this occasion as well. It is noteworthy that Fink's opening chapter of PSW starts with the heading "Play as a Possible and Worthy Topic for Philosophy" (Fink 2016: 35).
10 This was Fink's doctoral dissertation. It was reprinted in 1930 under the title "Contributions to a Phenomenological Analysis of the Psychological Phenomena Conceived under the Following Denominations: 'Think as if', 'Imagine Something', or 'Fantasy'."
11 "Die Aktualität des Schönen. Kunst als Spiel, Symbol und Fest" (1974) in Gadamer (1999e); "Zur Phänomenologie von Ritual und Sprache" (1992) in Gadamer (1999b).
12 Gadamer had privileged access to the German phenomenological tradition and his philosophical hermeneutics may be regarded as a deepening of that tradition. See short texts on the topic in Gadamer (1999b, 1999c, 1999f).

13 He gave a lecture entitled *Die Spiele der Tiere* ("The Play of Animals") in 1896.
14 Karl Groos is an important reference in Buytendijk's book.
15 I have argued elsewhere that all play concepts in Fink's works refer to each other so that they constitute a kind of closed circle. See Miras Boronat (2016a).

Chapter 4

1 Also in "The Relevance of the Beautiful" Gadamer defines play as an "elementary function of human life" that is based on "a constantly repeated movement," on "a constant coming and going, back and forth, a movement that is not tied down to any goal." More precisely, play appears as "a self-movement that does not pursue any particular end or purpose so much as movement *as* movement, exhibiting so to speak a phenomenon of excess, of living self-representation" (Gadamer 1986: 23–4).
2 With regard to this, Günter Figal has arrived to claim that Gadamer, in his later works on language, quite in contrast to the ontological conception that had been presented in the third part of *Truth and Method*, rather opted for an anthropological "description of life-world comportment" as "a complex of behavior patterns to which one must become accustomed to be able to say and do 'the right thing,' that is, to say that which has meaning in the context of customary behavior" (Figal 2002: 123).

Chapter 5

1 Abbreviations: Heidegger 1975– (= GA); Fink 2010 (= EFGA7); Fink 2016 (= P). All translations for which I do not specify an English edition in the notes are mine. When translating unpublished archival material, I include the original German in a note. Special thanks to Giovanni Giubilato, Tobias Keiling, Chris Merwin, Steve Stakland, and Hakhamanesh Zangeneh for comments on earlier drafts of this chapter.
2 "*In Ihrer Spur geht jeder seinen Weg, der heute denkt. Doch sind Sie nie ein Torgewölb, wo alle Wegen münden, kein 'Haus der Wahrheit' hinter fest verpflöcktem Riegel, die Denkspur die SIE ziehen, weist ins Freie, ins Ungeheuere, in die Heimat WELT.*" In Heidegger 1969: 32. Fink alludes to the preamble of Parmenides's poem.
3 P: 49, 64, 191/EFGA7: 45, 63, 198. Heidegger 1982, 165/GA 24: 234; Heidegger 1962: 93, 131; Heidegger 1967: 65, 98.
4 Heidegger 1962: 185; Heidegger1986: 145.
5 "*Wir spielen nicht weil es Spiele gibt, sondern es gibt Spiele, weil wir spielen. Welt ist der Titel für das Spiel, das die Transcendenz [sic] des Daseins als solche spielt. Dieses metaphysische Spiel hat seine Freiheit, Bindung, Notwendigkeit. Das In der Welt sein ist das ursprüngliche Spielen des Spiels, auf das jedes faktische Dasein sich einspielen muss, um sich abspielen zu können, in der Weise, daß dem faktischen Dasein in der Dauer seiner Existenz so o. so mitgespielt wird. (Dies wohl ein Spiel mit Worten, aber die Sprache spielt mit uns!)*" Nachlass Eugen Fink, Universitätsarchiv Freiburg, call number E 15/433, pages 113–14. (Most of Fink's Nachlass has been digitized and is available here: https://archiv.uni-freiburg.de:8443/actaproweb/archive.xhtml.) Cf. GA 27: 312. Although the final parenthetical sentence of the quotation is missing from

the GA volume, Heidegger made a similar remark about the play of language the following year in 1995, 286/GA 29/30: 414.
6 "*Das Spiel der Transcendenz* [sic] *ist ekstatisch, wir haben immer schon das Seiende umspielt. Der eigentliche Ernst der Existenz ist gegründet auf dem metaphysischen Spiel der Existenz, im Spielraum der Freiheit.*" Ibid., 115. This passage differs significantly from what can be found in GA 27: 313–16.
7 "Die Transcendenz [sic] bezeichnen wir als Spiel. Dies aber kein zufälliges. Die Existenz des Menschen ist auf das Spiel des Seinsverständnisses gesetzt. [. . .] Es wird sich zeigen, daß das Seinsproblem in Einheit mit dem Weltproblem das Thema der Metaphysik ist." Ibid., 119. Cf. GA 27: 323–4.
8 See chapter nineteen in this volume, Eugen Fink, "Zwei Gespräche mit Heidegger/ Two Conversations with Heidegger."
9 For example, although Fink deserves credit for being the first to take play in an *explicitly* ontological or metaphysical, as opposed to existential/transcendentalist, direction, many of the features of play identified by Fink in "Oasis of Happiness" and in PSW can be found already in Heidegger's 1928–29 lecture course (GA 27), especially §§34–6. It would be worth examining, in a future study, how Heidegger's lecture course (along with that of the winter semester of 1929–30 on *The Fundamental Concepts of Metaphysics: World, Finitude, Solitude* [GA 29/30], which Fink also attended and transcribed) influenced Fink's later writings on play. Even though this is not the aim of Ronald Bruzina's monumental study, he does translate and briefly discuss selections from Fink's transcription of GA 27. See Bruzina 2004: 12–14, 131–136, 148, 160–163, 168. For more on the early Fink's relation to Heidegger, see chapter eighteen in this volume, and Giubilato 2022b: 65–91.
10 Heidegger and Fink 1979/ GA 15. See especially the seventh session. The *logos* fragment is numbered first in Diels/Kranz.
11 P: 71/EFGA7: 69; see also 42/38, 53–4/50–1, 204/12. Fink is unequivocal about the limitations of phenomenology for speculative cosmology in his 1950–1 lecture course Fink 1977a: 241: "What is given as a task to the present thinking of philosophy does not entail a further development of thing-ontology beyond German idealism, nor a further transubstantiation of substance. In this regard, the attempt of the 'phenomenological movement' to gain a new and immediate relation to things and simply to describe them unreservedly and impartially, instead of considering them speculatively, is on the wrong track." Quoted with discussion in Schlitte 2020: 185 (my translation).
12 I provide citations and develop these ideas with respect to Heidegger in Moore 2024.
13 On "middle-voiced letting" in Heidegger, including in GA 27 and GA 29/30, see Moore 2019, chapters 5 and 7.
14 I cannot address this here, but Fink's interest in the ontological status of the appearance of play within the realm of the actual dates all the way back to his 1929 dissertation on image-consciousness, for which both Husserl and Heidegger served as referees. Fink 1966: 71. See the material on Fink in O'Shiel 2022, as well as chapters two and nine in this volume.
15 See chapter one in this volume.
16 Nachlass Eugen Fink, Universitätsarchiv Freiburg, E 15/297.
17 Trans. Goetz Richter (New York: Continuum, 2003), 171, 163 (trans. mod.)/*Nietzsches Philosophie*, sixth edition (Stuttgart: Kohlhammer, 1992), 187, 179. For Heidegger's critique, see "Nietzsche's Word: 'God is Dead,'" which was first published in 1950 and

is available in Heidegger 2002: 157–99/GA 5: 209–67. For more on Fink's Nietzsche, see chapter six in this volume.
18 Fink 1976: 128.
19 See Heraclitus, Fragment 52 (in the Diels/Kranz numbering), as well as P: 51/EFGA7: 48, et passim.
20 Heidegger 1951: 127–48 (now in GA 7: 167–87); Heidegger 2001: 163–80. The earlier version can be found in Heidegger 2012: 3–20/GA 79: 3–21.
21 The offprint is available in the Nachlass Eugen Fink, Universitätsarchiv Freiburg, E 15/768.
22 Heidegger 2001: 177; Heidegger1951: 145 (GA 7: 181).
23 Heidegger 2001: 177; Heidegger 1951: 144–5 (GA 7: 180–81).
24 Heidegger 2001: 177, 180; Heidegger 1951: 145, 147 (GA 7: 181, 183).
25 "The rose is without why / it blooms because it blooms // It does not heed itself / asks not if one does see it." "Die Ros' ist ohn warumb / sie blühet, weil sie blühet // Sie achtt nicht jhrer selbst / fragt nicht ob man sie sihet." Silesius 1984: I, 289.
26 Heidegger 1991: 62/GA 10: 91.
27 Ibid., 68 (trans. mod.)/GA 10: 100.
28 Ibid., 38 / GA 10: 58.
29 As Heidegger explains in a letter to Fink from December 14, 1955: "I thank you for your remarks and will put them in the manuscript of my lecture course. [. . .] You say that the 'because' in the verse [by Silesius] 'cuts off, as it were, the justification.' I say that the 'because' in a certain way *disappears*. Notice how I place the emphasis in the proper reading of the saying: 'the rose is without *why*; it *blooms* because it *blooms*' (not: *because* it blooms)." "Ich danke Ihnen für Ihre Bemerkungen u. lege sie in mein Vorlesungsmanuskript. [. . .] Sie sagen, daß das 'weil' im Vers 'die Begründung gleichsam abschneidet.' Ich sage, daß das 'weil' in gewisser Weise *verschwindet*. Achten Sie darauf, wie ich im eigentlichen Lesen des Spruches den Ton lege: 'die Ros ist ohn *warum*; sie *blühet* weil sie *blühet*' (nicht: *weil* sie blühet)." Nachlass Eugen Fink, Universitätsarchiv Freiburg E 15/962. Fink's remarks are available in Heidegger's papers in the Deutsches Literaturarchiv Marbach, Mediennummer HS010785799.
30 Ibid., 113 (trans. mod.)/GA 10: 169. For the translation of *dieweil* as "while" rather than "since," see ibid., 127 (where it is rendered correctly)/GA 10: 186, which also allows us to hear Silesius's phrase as "it blooms *while* it blooms."
31 Quotation by Husserl cited in Bruzina 2004: 69. Heidegger's praise of Fink can be found in a letter that Heidegger sent to his brother Fritz on March 3, 1967, in the Deutsches Literaturarchiv Marbach, Mediennummer HS008539896. In a letter to Fink's wife from July 11, 1975, Heidegger specifies that "Eugen Fink was the outstanding speculative talent of his generation [*Eugen Fink war die überragende spekulative Begabung seiner Generation*]." Nachlass Eugen Fink, Universitätsarchiv Freiburg E 15/962.
32 In addition to passages cited above, see, for example, GA 11: 72 and GA 73: 164–78, as well as Roesner 2003.
33 Quotations found in Bruzina 2004: 67, 314.
34 Cited by Bruzina 2004: 528. Interestingly, Heidegger used the same quotation by Hegel as an epigraph to his Habilitationsschrift. Heidegger 2022: 1/GA 1: 193.
35 See Bruzina's introduction to Fink 1995b.
36 Fink 2019b: 21–33; Fink 2011: 25–37.
37 Heidegger 1995: 359/GA 29/30: 522. Fink transcribed the relevant passages in his notes for the course, preserved in the Nachlass Eugen Fink, Universitätsarchiv Freiburg, E 15/436, pages 134–35. Cf. Fink 1976c: 129.

38 Heidegger 2012: 46/GA 79: 48–49.
39 Heidegger 2012: 69–70/GA 79: 74, et passim.
40 McNeill 2023. On "world" in Heidegger, see Tobias Keiling's recent article "Worlds, Worlding."
41 See, for example, the analysis of several texts by Heidegger in chapters 16–21 of Fink's lecture course from the summer semester of 1949, Fink 1990, especially pages 146 (Heidegger moves from an "'existentiell' concept of world" to a "'cosmic' concept of world'"), 150 ("nowhere is [the problem of world] posed so insistently and with such historical vividness as in Heidegger"), and 175 (Heidegger's invocation of the earth in his artwork-essay = "*world in the cosmic sense*").
42 As Fink summarizes one of the points he made in a letter to Heidegger from December 28, 1951, sent just days after receiving the offprint of "The Thing": "The message of the thing is the onefold-fourfold saying of the mirror-play of the world. For us who have been following your tracks for a long time, this causes great difficulties: 1.) because the "experience" is absent to us; 2.) because I do not grasp how gods and mortals should have the same primordiality as the sky and earth. (Hölderlin's Mother Earth and Father Aether)." "Botschaft vom Ding ist einfache-vierfältige Sage vom Weltspiegelspiel. Uns, die wir seit langem Ihrer Spur folgen, bereitet dies grosse Schwierigkeiten. 1.) weil uns die 'Erfahrung' ausbleibt; 2) weil ich nicht greife, wie Götter u. Sterbliche gleiche Ursprünglichkeit haben sollten wie Himmel u. Erde. (Hölderlins Mutter Erde u. Vater Aether)." The summary (although not the original letter) is available in Fink's correspondence with Heidegger in the Nachlass Eugen Fink, Universitätsarchiv Freiburg, E 15/962.
43 Heidegger 1991: 68/GA 10: 128.
44 Heidegger 1984: 53, 49 (trans. mod.)/GA 5: 367, 363. See also GA 78: 135, and the lecture "Zeit und Sein" with Heidegger's marginalia on *brauchen* in GA 14: 20n6, 21n7, 28nn10–11, 50n3. These marginalia are not available in the published English translation in Heidegger 1972. For more on *Brauch* in Heidegger, see the special topics devoted to Heidegger's recently published text "The Argument against Need (for the Being-in-Itself of Entities)," in the *British Journal for the History of Philosophy* 30, no. 3 (2022) and *Gatherings: The Heidegger Circle Annual Gatherings: The Heidegger Circle Annual* 13 (2023). See also Heidegger's comments on *Brauch* in his personal notes for the seminar he held with Fink on Heraclitus: Heidegger 1997: 9–14.
45 Fink 2008: 22–23, 91, 278. Cf. Fink 1966: 14.
46 "Der Gedanke der Endlichkeit scheint, unseres Erachtens, der am meisten radikale und revolutionäre Grundgedanke der heideggerschen Philosophie zu sein,—der Gedanke, mit dem Heidegger sich gegen die gesamte Tradition stellt. [. . .] Nicht der seinsverstehende Mensch, nicht das *Gefäss* nur ist endlich, welches das Sein 'fasst,' das *Sein selbst*, das ungeheure, weltdurchgreifende Sein, der Ursprung selbst von allem, was ist, schwingt in der Zeit, geschieht als 'Ereignis.' Heideggers Spätphilosophie dreht sich um diesen äussersten Gedanken,—der vielleicht das Verwegenste ist, was in der Menschheit bisher gedacht wurde." Eugen Fink, "Martin Heidegger: Der Mann, Das Werk, Die Frage, Der Zuspruch, Die Endlichkeit," Nachlass Eugen Fink, Universitätsarchiv Freiburg, E 15/214, page 4 of the second, earlier version in the folder. See also Fink 1957: 42.
47 "Nach der Lektüre verweilte ich in einem langen Nachsinnen, das in den Gedanken mündete: 'Er (Fink) wäre doch der einzig mögliche Nachfolger gewesen.'" Letter from November 7, 1964. Nachlass Eugen Fink, Universitätsarchiv Freiburg, E 15/962. See also *Martin Heidegger: 26. September 1969*, 35 = GA 16: 712–13.

48 Letter from Heidegger to Fink, December 8, 1965. Nachlass Eugen Fink, Universitätsarchiv Freiburg, E 15/962.
49 Published as an appendix to Heidegger 1995: 367–9/GA 29/30: 533–36.
50 On being's independence and the question of finitude, see Richard Capobianco's work. In his earlier book Capobianco 2010: 4 et passim, Capobianco argued that, for Heidegger, being was finite, albeit independent of the human, although more recently Capobianco has maintained that "Heidegger's thinking of Being has an 'infinite' character after all; his thinking does indeed arrive at a version of the infinite." Capobianco 2022: 128–9. For an opposing view, which espouses being qua finite meaningfulness and hence correlationism with the human throughout Heidegger's corpus, see Sheehan 2015. Heidegger claims that "beyng is everlasting [*unvergänglich*]" in Heidegger 2018: 256–7/GA 55: 345.
51 Heidegger 2018: 282 (trans. mod.)/GA 55: 379.
52 P: 69–77/EFGA7: 67–76 et passim, and Fink 2019b: 29; Fink 2011: 34.
53 Fink, "Zwei Gespräche mit Heidegger/Two Conversations with Heidegger." See also Giubilato, "Individuation und ontologische Erfahrung," especially 86.
54 I would also consider the problem of the in-itself to be at the center of other apparent differences between Fink and Heidegger such as Heidegger's prioritization of language over other basic phenomena and, relatedly, of unconcealment over concealment. See Fink's 1956 essay "Welt und Geschichte," in *Nähe und Distanz*, 158–79, where he claims that, for Heidegger, "[c]oncealment belongs to being rather like shadow does to light, not like [as is the case for Fink] the lightless, abyssal night" (176). See also Vetter 2011: 184–207. On these counts, however, Heidegger might reply as he did when asked by Fink about the extent to which he prioritizes presence over absence, namely, that the issue is more complicated, especially in view of writings unavailable to Fink at the time. See Fink, "Zwei Gespräche mit Heidegger/Two Conversations with Heidegger," as well as Dastur November 1997: 25–38 (34–36).
55 Heidegger's letter is published in Cristin 2001: 149. Fink's is published in 1972: 94–102.
56 Heidegger 1995: 367/GA 29/30: 534.

Chapter 6

1 (Z III.2.1/KSA 4.197)" refers to *Thus Spoke Zarathustra*, Part Three, chapter two, section 1/(and) *Sämtliche Werke: Kritische Studienausgabe*, volume 4, page 197. Zarathustra, from *Thus Spoke Zarathustra* (Z III.2.1/KSA 4.197). I am translating the important word in Nietzsche's lexicon, *Versuchern* ("researcher", "experimenter", "the one who tries" or "the one who attempts"), here as "tempter." References to translations in English rely predominantly on the Cambridge University Press edition, with various editors and translators. I also reference Walter Kaufman ed. and trans. *Will to Power* (New York: Viking, 1967) and Marianne Cowan trans. *Philosophy in the Tragic Age of the Greeks* (Washington, DC: Regnery, 1962 and 1996). Nietzsche's works in German: KSA *Sämtliche Werke: Kritische Studienausgabe* (vols. 1–15, including *Kommentar* and *Konkordanz*), ed. Giorgio Colli and Mazzino Montinari (Berlin: Walter de Gruyter, 1966–77 and 1998). KSB *Sämtliche Briefe: Kritische Studienausgabe* (vols 1–8), ed. Giorgio Colli and Mazzino Montinari (Berlin: Walter de Gruyter, 1975–84). Citations of Nietzsche's work in English refer to either the

text and aphorism number or the text, part (or ook), chapter, and section. In order to avoid needless repetition, references to the KSA will include the volume and page number.
2 Despite this, Dermot Moran is surely correct to say that Fink is still an obscure figure, even in phenomenological circles (2007), 30. Nevertheless, Fink played an instrumental role in introducing and framing Husserl's work, especially in France, as Leonard Lawlor demonstrates particularly with respect to Derrida (2002: 11–23).
3 As I point out in another essay (Wilkerson 2010: 268–9) we can get a sense of the nature of the Fink-Heidegger relationship by noting with Bruzina that for good and for ill, Heidegger dominated Fink's career path (Bruzina 2004).
4 Fink's objections to Nietzsche's claims, even when he is taking into consideration differences in the "phases" of Nietzsche's thought-path, can easily be challenged by citing contradictory passages from similar phases.
5 I am translating *Ernüchterung* here as "disillusionment" not "sobering." Others have noted the "unreliable" nature of this English translation of Fink's *Nietzsches Philosophie*. See Babich (2005: 177 [fn 3]) and Crowell (2006: 29 [fn 2]). I will make corrections to this translation as I see fit.
6 In a 1971 review of the *Heraclitus Seminar* David Krell notes Heraclitus' significance for Fink's thought, which is best displayed, according to Krell, near the end of Fink's work on Nietzsche, where we find Fink comparing Nietzsche's "Dionysian affirmation of life" favorably to Heraclitus' *Pais Paizon*, the "playing-child" of fragment 52 who holds the "kingly power" of creativity and destruction and who wields it with all the joy and suffering of divine innocence (1971: 138 [fn2]). Following up on this review, in next edition of *Research in Phenomenology*, Krell admits that Fink and Heidegger nowhere mention Heraclitus fragment 52 among the dozens of other sayings considered during the semester. To account for this curious omission, and in an attempt to sustain the prior thesis concerning the importance of *Pais Paison* for Fink and Heidegger, Krell claims that "every issue discussed [in the Heraclitus Seminar] (the relation of the one to all things, the problem of hermeneutics, the problem of death, etc.) requires consideration of the child at play. Fragment 52 is thus the shadow of the philosophers' inquiry, being present yet absent" (1972: 65 [fn4]).
7 Nietzsche's full remarks on this theme state: "[a]mong human beings, Heraclitus as a human being was unbelievable. Even if he were seen observing the game [*Spiel*] of noisy children, what he was thinking surely no other man had thought on such an occasion. He was thinking of the game [*Spiel*] of the great world-child Zeus" (PTG 8/KSA 1.834). Nietzsche ends the chapter with the following: "[w]hat he saw, the teaching of *law in becoming* and of *play* [*Spiel*] *in necessity*, must be seen from now on in all eternity. He raised the curtain in this greatest of all dramas [*Schauspiel*]" (the emphasis is Nietzsche's) (PTG 8/KSA 1.835).
8 See Fink 1993: 108–21.
9 Nietzsche was inclined to calling Zarathustra his "son." See for example a letter addressed to his sister, Elizabeth, dated May 7, 1885 (KSB 7.48).
10 See Babich 2005: 64; Crowell 2006: 15–17 and Krell 1972: 70.
11 See Wilkerson (2012: 130–6).
12 Fink's emphasis. In "*Unterredung mit Professor Heiß*," dated June 24, 1946, from Fink's *Nachlass: Teil II: 1939-1946—Band 4, Abschnitt 2*, edited by Ronald Bruzina (Munich: Karl Alber, 2005). Cited by Bruzina (2004, 532).

Chapter 7

1. PSW, Eugen Fink Gesamtausgabe, Bd. 7, Abteilung II, Ontologie-Kosmologie-Anthropologie, Hrsg. S. Grätzel, C. Nielsen, H. Rainer Sepp, Verlag Karl Alber, Freiburg im Breisgau 2010, followed by English translation, by Ian Alexander Moore and Christopher Turner, Indiana University Press, 2016.
2. Cited from the edition edited and translated by E. M. Wilkinson and L. A. Willoughby, Oxford Clarendon Press, 1982. The letter-form of this work was based on the letters Schiller sent in 1793 to the Duke of Augustenburg to ensure the progress of his philosophical and historical studies, sponsored by the Duke. The letters were originally published in Schiller's journal of literature *Die Horen* in 1795. They were discussed in an interdisciplinary manner, not only in our times but already during Schiller's own lifetime.
3. Schiller 106–7.
4. "Mit Fichte habe ich interessant gesprochen, sehr viel auch über Sie. Er erwartet von Ihnen sehr viel für die Philosophie.[. . .] Das einzige was noch mangle, sei die Einheit. Diese Einheit sei zwar in Ihrem Gefühl, aber noch nicht in Ihrem System. Kämen Sie dahin, und dies hänge allein von Ihnen ab, so wäre von keinem anderem Kopfe so viel und schlechterdings eine neue Epoche zu erwarten." Schiller and von Humboldt1876: 57.
5. See Binkelmann 2019: 140.
6. "A self-producing striving however . . . is called a drive. . . . The drive is thereafter merely in the Subject, and in accordance with its nature does not exceed the region of the latter." In Johann Gottlieb Fichte 1956 [1794]: 204–5.
7. See Schäfer : 2012 129.
8. There is some dispute as to the extent in which the Playdrive is an ontologically independent drive. M. Bondelli argues for the idea in "Schillers Triebkonzept im Ausgang von Reinholds Trieblehre" in *Friedrich Schiller:Über die Ästhetische Erziehung des Menschen in einer Reihe von Briefen,* Klassiker Auslegen, ed. Gideon Stiening. He relies on the 14th Letter to argue that the Playdrive, understood as self-relation in the unity of form and matter, is the beginning of a new systematic conception of drives (133). On the other hand, Sybille Krämer thinks that the Playdrive is nothing more than the coexistence of the two opposed drives and not another, new drive. See Krämer 2007: 169–70.
9. Schiller's doctrine of drives is reminiscent, as was said above, of Fichte's as found also, for example, in *Über den Geist des Buchstaben*. Here, Fichte writes "But the single element in the human being [*das einzige Unabhängige*] that is independent and incapable of being externally determined is what we call Drive [*Trieb*]. This, and only this is the highest and single principle of self-activity [*Princip der Selbstthätigkeit*] in us; only this makes us autonomous, observing and acting beings." *2. Brief,* in Fichte 1965: 277.
10. For example, in Agard 2017: 129–30.
11. Hüni 2008: 14.
12. Hegel 1971: 46.
13. Hegel 1999: 128.
14. Krämer 2007: 168.

Chapter 8

1. Also of significance is an essay by Deleuze referring to Axelos in 1964: "En créant la pataphysique Jarry a ouvert la voie à la phénoménologie," and another from 1970 :

"Faille et feux locaux." Both are now collected in Deleuze (2002). These are translated into English as "How Jarry's Pataphysics Opened the Way to Phenomenology," and "The Fissure of Anaxagoras and Local Fires of Heraclitus," in Deleuze (2004).

2. On the importance of Axelos, see the biographical details in Janicaud (2015). The original French (Janicaud 2001) contains an interview with Axelos not translated in the English edition. In relation to Fink, see the precious article by Francoise Dastur (1997). The entirety of that journal issue is dedicated to "Kostas Axelos et la question du monde."

3. Some of these works have been recently republished. The first, in order of composition, is a version of his 1959 doctoral thesis, *Marx penseur de la technique: de l'aliénation de l'homme à la conquête du monde* ([1969] 2015), followed by *Héraclite et la philosophie: la première saisie de l'être en devenir de la totalité* (1962), then, completing the tryptic: *Vers la pensée planétaire: le devenir-pensée du monde et le devenir-monde de la pensée* ([1964] 2019). He also published in German in this period: *Einführung in ein künftiges Denken, über Marx und Heidegger* (1966). While outside of my scope here, but worth mentioning viz. Fink, is his *Le Jeu du Monde* ([1969] 2018).

4. The journal *Aletheia*, published in Paris, had a short run, just six issues, from 1964 to 1967. In issue five, August 1966, Jean-Michel Rey reviewed Fink's Nietzsche and Denis Hollier reviewed Fink's book on play. Rey also contributed an essay partially on play.

5. Although Len Lawlor presented a groundbreaking work on Fink's approach to Husserl and the importance thereof for Derrida (and Merleau-Ponty), his sources are strictly Fink's works on *Husserlian* phenomenology. See Lawlor (2002). Astonishingly, this crucial book on Derrida says nothing whatsoever about Fink's PSW or Fink's conception of play.

6. Deleuze's book is composed of thirty-four chapters or parts referred to as "series." Thus, the full title is "10th series of the ideal game/play."

7. Compare the entire section "1.C" of Gilson's work on "Common Being."

8. See Deleuze's easily overlooked statement on overcoming metaphysics at the outset of the Jarry essay (Deleuze 2002: 105). On the next page of the same essay, he extends this project backward to Marx and Nietzsche.

9. Statements to this effect, covering such notions, abound in Axelos ([1964] 2019). For brevity's sake, I am not entering Axelos' text in detail here, but propose to do so elsewhere.

10. Deleuze cites E. Brehier ([1908] 1989), V. Goldschmidt (1969).

11. A useful essay is, again, by F. Dastur (2013).

12. Or at least, that is what my heuristically proposed operative assumption from the outset regarding the unity of the phenomenon allows me to suggest.

Chapter 10

1. For Fink, world represents the culmination of the human being's relation to beings—be it time, space, mood, and so on. As the translators of the volume note, Fink uses several German words for world: "*Universum* (universe), *Kosmos* (cosmos), *Weltganze* (world-whole, whole of the world), and *Weltall* and *Weltallheit* (world-totality, totality of the world)" (Fink 2016: 11). Fink's conception of world is largely inspired by Heidegger's, especially in his *Being and Time*; see (Heidegger 1996: 59–70).

2 Fink makes a reference to Hegel's "self-alienation," explaining that it was only natural for his successors such as Marx and Feuerbach to invert Hegel, resulting in philosophy becoming a "resolute anthropology" (Fink 2016: 182).
3 For Heidegger, Plato and Aristotle represent the collapse of truth (ἀλήθεια) in their founding of the roots of metaphysics. Prior to the collapse, Heraclitus, Parmenides, and Anaximander demonstrated a more originary truth that Heidegger characterized as the "first beginning" (*Der erste Anfang*). The goal for Heidegger was to inaugurate the "other beginning" (*Der anderen Anfang*) where thinking was freed from an exclusively propositional and calculative predisposition customary of metaphysics (Heidegger 1989: 359–61).
4 The word choice here "spell" is reminiscent of Popper's "Spell of Plato," which he used to describe Plato's "spell of an alluring philosophy, unequalled in depth and richness." For Popper, Plato used the spell to "close the door" and "arrest society" (Popper 2013: 188).
5 Fink and Heidegger discussed this under the title of the "hermeneutical circle" in their *Heraclitus Seminar*. Fink here asserted that one must enter the circle rather than expect to understand Heraclitus' aphorisms as a whole. As such, every interpretation of Heraclitus cannot yield the "whole" of Heraclitus' thought (Heidegger and Fink 1979: 16–17). Heidegger similarly asserted in his *Contributions to Philosophy* that despite Heraclitus' Πόλεμος holding one of the greatest insights into Western philosophy, it has not been sufficiently developed for understanding truth (Heidegger 1989: 265).
6 The fragment in question is as follows: "The wise is one alone, unwilling and willing to be spoken of by the name of Zeus [ἓν τὸ σοφὸν μοῦνον λέγεσθαι οὐκ ἐθέλει καὶ ἐθέλει Ζηνὸς ὄνομα]" (Kahn 1979: 82–3).
7 The term "pre-Socratics" originates from eighteenth–nineteenth-century German scholarship beginning with Johan Augustus Eberhard. During the early twentieth century, the term was developed by Hermann Alexander Diels and Walther Kranz, who together formed the "Diels-Kranz numbering" system. Both Fink and Heidegger worked with the Diels-Kranz system and translations (Laks 2006: 19–34). For scholarly coverage of Plato in the German tradition, see (Kim 2019).
8 Having studied Kant extensively, Fink ultimately regarded Kant's "world" as something subjective, and a "regulative idea" (Fink 2016: 48).
9 Huizinga's *Homo Ludens* preceded Fink's work on play, having been published in the original Dutch in 1938. Huizinga was more positively disposed toward Plato than Fink and saw that the former had in fact advanced play as the most important of goals: "Play consecrated to the Deity, the highest goal of man's endeavour—such was Plato's conception of religion" (Huizinga 1980: 27). Fink cites *Homo Ludens* in the appendix although it does not appear in the main text; see (Fink 2016: 298).
10 The subject matter of play in Plato's thought has incurred extensive scholarship, for examples, see (Kidd 2019: 49–96; Sermamoglou-Soulmaidi 2014, 2019; Ardley 1967; D'Angour 2013; Thesleff 2023, 167–9).
11 John M. Cooper claimed that for the Neoplatonists "Plato was speaking to us in his writings in the same way that Parmenides or Heraclitus had done, as possessor of his own 'truth'—the real truth—handing that down to other mortals in his own somewhat cryptic way, in dialogues" (Plato 1997: xxiv).
12 Plotinus suffused understanding νόησις from the pinnacle of Plato's "Divided Line" (Republic, 509D–511E) concurrently with Aristotle's "thinking is a thinking on thinking [νόησις νοήσεως νόησις]" (Metaphysics, [9].1074b34, 3650).

13 Neoplatonists understood Parmenides' overarching ontology and epistemological distinctions to be an important influence on Plato. As Proclus noted, the Eleatic dialectical method was evident in Plato's dialogues (Parmenides Commentary: [1000–001]).
14 The *On the Aesthetic Education of Man* (*Über die ästhetische Erziehung des Menschen in einer Reihe von Briefen*) was based on plans for *Kallias, oder über die Schönheit*, which was never composed. It is in these series of letters that Schiller's criterion of beauty conflicted with Kant's view (Beiser 2005: 47–76). For Kant, the lectures *Anthropology from a Pragmatic Point of View* beginning 1772 represents his principal work that deals with idea of play. In these lectures, Kant maintained that play is ultimately confined to the power of imagination despite being nonconceptual (Kant 2006: 22–3). Kant also saw that beauty is a product of nonconceptual "free play" of cognition with representation that is without restriction (Kant 2008: 102–4). That Kant confined the play of beauty to the inner world of imagination was problematic for Schiller, who saw that beauty transports man from form to thought for unification (Schiller 1954: 81).
15 In his *Truth and Method*, Gadamer sought to free play from the subjectivism of Kant and Schiller (Gadamer 1990: 107–39). In Gadamer's understanding of play, Plato did not differentiate between the tragedy of life on the one hand, and the stage on the other. This difference is superseded if one learns to see the meaning of the play as it unfolds (Gadamer 1990: 117–18). Gadamer is consistent here with Derrida's famous essay "*Plato's Pharmacy*". Derrida explained that despite it being thought that Plato condemned play, Derrida argued that Plato saved and praised play (Derrida 1981: 156–71).

Chapter 11

1 Fink's book on fashion (E. Fink (1969). *Mode . . . ein verführerisches Spiel*. Basel: Birkhäuser) and his *Epiloges on poetry* (E. Fink (1971). *Epiloge zur Dichtung*, Frankfurt: Klostermann) might be exceptions, yet they also reconfigure the disciplinary boundaries of aesthetics in a way that cannot be explored here further. Fink's focus on play as an ontological pathway toward art opens obvious interpretative possibilities to thinkers such as Gadamer or Picht.
2 I have made this point in relation to Heidegger in Richter 2022: 198.
3 Translation is my own.
4 See the excellent, differentiated discussion about the importance of speculation in Fink by Coli 2022: 243.
5 "Die Natur des Subjekts also wird neu gedacht, wird gedacht als der lichtende Überstieg über all Gegenstände."
6 Naturally, Husserl's death in 1938 made his personal completion of the path commenced in *The Crisis* impossible. Fink seems to see it as his responsibility to continue his teacher's work in critical dialogue with both Husserl's work and Husserl's challenging student, Martin Heidegger.
7 For Fink *Being and Time* still is committed to Husserlian phenomenology.
8 Gadamer's discussion of art as play ("the art work is play, that is, it does not have a being independent of its presence"; Gadamer 1990: 127) and in particular his insistence that play is the entire of presencing (*Darstellung*) is relevant here ("play itself is the entirety of players and audience . . . the audience is brought into the place of the player"; Gadamer 1990: 115).
9 Gadamer speaks of *Horizontverschmelzung*—or blending of horizons.

Chapter 12

1. When it is scientific, Homan says, "Fink see contemporary pedagogy as fundamentally nihilistic" (293).
2. See Richard Rorty's essay "Education as Socialization and Individualization," in *Philosophy and Social Hope* Penguin, 1999.

Chapter 13

1. Cf., for exempla, the English translation of *Spiel als Weltsymbol* (hrsg. von Cathrin Nielsen und Hans Rainer Sepp [= EFGA II, 7], Freiburg/München): PSW 2016.
2. Friedrich Nietzsche, 248/Friedrich Nietzsche, *Also sprach Zarathustra*, in: ders., *Kritische-Studienausgabe* 4, hrsg. von Giorgio Colli und Mazzino Montinari, München 1999, 380; 385.
3. Friedrich Nietzsche, 249/Friedrich Nietzsche, *Also sprach Zarathustra*, 381.
4. Friedrich Nietzsche, 80/Friedrich Nietzsche, *Also sprach Zarathustra*, 133.
5. Ibid.
6. Ibid.
7. Friedrich Nietzsche, *Nachgelassene Fragmente 1885–1887*, in: Kritische Gesamtausgabe 12, München 1999, 200.
8. Martin Heidegger, *Was heißt Denken?*, hrsg. von Paola-Ludovika Coriando (GA 8), Frankfurt am Main 2002, 54 (Erstauflage: Tübingen 1954).
9. Maybe, in Eugen Fink's idea, "that we want to understand why we are here on this earth" (20/16) the Catholic catechism question "Why are we on earth" finds a resonance (cf. *Katholischer Katechismus der Bistümer Deutschlands*, Freiburg i. Br. 1955, XX).
10. Cf. Hans Urs von Balthasar's *Theodramatik* (Einsiedeln 1973–83) and also Romano Guardini, *Vom Geist der Liturgie*, 23. Auflage, Ostfildern/Paderborn 2013, 57-67 ("Liturgie als Spiel"/ "Liturgy as Play").
11. Eugen Fink, *Spiel als Weltsymbol* (= EFGA II, 7), 184.
12. Friedrich Nietzsche, *Die fröhliche Wissenschaft*, in: *Kritische Gesamtausgabe* 3, hrsg. von Giorgio Colli und Mazzino Montinari, München 1999, § 54.

Chapter 14

1. Given Pentecostalism's frequent association with conservative fundamentalism, this may come as a surprise. However, just as frequent in Pentecostal theology one finds the rejection of such fundamentalisms. In the case of holy laughter, for instance, Pentecostals likely would describe this as an invitation from the Holy Spirit, as opposed to a prescription or requirement for Christians to be "true Christians."
2. *Thus Spake Zarathustra*, 2022 §8, "Reading and Writing."
3. For Wariboko, "The point is that the enigma of the Other that Pentecostals think is an obstacle to integration with the Other is also an enigma within/of Pentecostalism. What eludes the Pentecostals' grasp about the Other eludes not only their own grasp about themselves, but also the Other's grasp about itself" (Wariboko 2018: 516). For a more detailed analysis of Wariboko's pneumatology, see Jason Alvis 2022.
4. Wariboko holds that "Microtheology is an interpretative analysis of everyday embodied theological interactions and agency at the individual, face-to-face level. It is

a study of everyday social interactions of individuals or small groups that demonstrate the link "ages between spirituality (practices and affections) and embodied theological ideas (beliefs)" (Wariboko 2018: 102–3).

5   For Wariboko, multiple languages create disharmony. This principle of embracing disharmony is a part of any acceptance of miracles too: "Because Pentecostals believe that there are cracks in reality, tears in the phenomenal curtain over the noumenal that allow 'miracles' to eventuate or spirit-filled believers to access things-in-themselves, their actions cannot reflect a harmoniously ordered God" (Wariboko 2018: 58).

6   For Wariboko, "The God, qua a notion of Christian God, who inhabits this "between" with them is imagined by Pentecostals to be cracked, a real deity and its fantasmatic supplement; in him multiple, incompatible possibilities exist. From an infinite distance, the notion of pentecostal God is crafted to inspire awe" (Wariboko 2018: 37).

7   For Wariboko, "Pentecostalism's limitation to a split God, that is, the very practices, beliefs, rituals, and interactions that prevent Pentecostals from relating to or conceptualizing a harmonious, consistent God, is, at the same time, the positive condition to its access to a living, active, miracle-working God, and this partly explains its robust growth" (Wariboko 2018: 33).

8   For Wariboko, "the God that 'died' in the 1960s and the God who was 'resurrected' in the 1980s are not the same. God is now a radically split God. Pentecostals have crafted from the materials of their everyday lives a notion of God that is not in (or cannot come into) full identity with Godself, and God is forever interacting with a reality that is ontologically incomplete. Time and again, we see Pentecostalism professing a traditional doctrine of God, yet its very practices continually set the stage for the unraveling, liquidation, or reconstitution of that doctrine" (Wariboko 2018: 24).

9   Fink makes it clear that his work "is not a 'phenomenology' of play but rather the world-significance of play, the recognition of play as a key phenomenon of a truly universal status" (Fink 2016: 71). For a much more thorough description of Fink's work on religion vis Christianity, see Jason Alvis 2019.

10 Fink insists that "world-play is no phenomenon. One cannot point it out or make it the object of a scientific method of research." Fink 2016: 42.

11 For Fink "1. All things in general are intraworldly—or the Being of all existing things must be conceived as "being-in-the-world"; 2. the human being is the innerworldly thing that exists in an ecstatic relation to the totality of the world, is addressed by the universe and is turned toward it with understanding". Fink 2016: 65.

12 It should be mentioned here that much of the time in this text, Fink will refer to "the gods," especially since he is often describing Greek myth and cultic religious play. In some cases, I have taken the liberty of applying these comments also to monotheistic religiosity, and thus I have mostly used the singular "God" here.

13 Acknowledgment: This chapter was written through the generous support of a project grant from the FWF (Austrian Science Fund) for the project "Revenge of the Sacred: Phenomenology and the Ends of Christianity in Europe" (P-3191921).

Chapter 16

1   Distinguishing humans from nonhumans on the capacity for self-relation seems to echo Heidegger's idea of the animal as "world-poor." For a lengthier discussion of Heidegger's attitudes in relation to Fink, see (Bertolini 2017).

2. In his discussions of play, Fink frequently turns to Nietzsche's passage in *Ecce Homo*: "I do not know any other way of handling great tasks than as *play*" (Fink 2016b: 24).

Chapter 17

1. Cf. Fink 2010: 16. All translations of Fink into English are my own (A.H.).
2. Therefore the coupling of the two English terms "play" and "game" in the title of my contribution, since in German "*Wettkampf*," which is an equivalent to some aspects of "game," rather alludes to "strife" and "fight" and not to "play" as Fink captures it: as having its end in itself, without being used strategically as means to an end outside itself.
3. "Freedom" as a heading which brings together a couple of Fink's writings, I will draw on: *Tractatus on Human Violence* (*Traktat ueber die menschliche Gewalt*; originally written in 1969/70 for a journal and published in 1974; Fink 2018b) and to his pedagogical writings *Basic Questions of systematic Pedagogy* (*Grundfragen der systematischen Paedagogik* (Fink 1978) and *Pedagogy and Life lessons* (*Erziehungswissenschaft und Lebenslehre*) (Fink 1970), which originated from lecture courses Fink held in his academic career.
4. Fink 2018a.
5. Referring to B. Waldenfels' phenomenology of the social world as "Order in Twilight": Waldenfels 1996.
6. In fact, Fink states, play would "return to us an irresponsibility which we experience joyfully" (Fink 2010: 215), an aspect Levinas criticized with recourse to Fink as an irresponsible freedom of a freedom of play (cf. Levinas 1998b: 116).
7. Cf. Levinas 1989: 75–87.
8. Here, Fink deals with five groundphenomena (Death, Eros, Labor, Power, and Play) to capture an anthropology which does not start from abstract principles of the human condition (e.g., language or reason), but analyzes institutions differently in different cultures. Cf. Fink 1979.
9. Which, for Fink, does not necessarily end at the borders of a national state, since Fink underlines the global or planetary character of the need for institutions, cf. the last chapter of Fink 2018b.
10. Which Fink discusses not only in the face of a high-time of cold war politics but also in the face of decolonialization, cf. Fink 2018: 419).
11. Cf. Fink 2018b: 291.
12. Cf. Fink 2018b: 432; a similar argument is made by Hannah Arendt in *The Human Condition*, where she differentiates two notions of *archein* as forms of bringing into act: "to begin" and "to rule": Cf. Arendt 1958: 177.
13. Cf. Fink 2018b: 477.
14. Fink 2018b: 480.
15. Fink 2018b: 433.
16. "The tendency towards the complete creation of man by man, towards a total feasibility of all human relationships and institutions, towards the conscious and consistent creation of social institutions characterizes our present in a very essential sense" (Fink 2018b: 297).
17. Cf. Fink 2018b, chapter 15.

18 "Man 'makes' his socialsystems unlike a craftsman 'makes' a tool and also unlike an engineer 'makes' kilowatt-hours. [. . .] Man produces a social role of a blacksmith, and only through this 'role' the technical tools" (Fink 2018b: 413).
19 Fink 1970: chapters 16 and 17.
20 Cf. Arendt 1958, especially chapters 18 and 23.
21 "Any being can become meaningful, not only table and cradle and plow [...] land and sea, clouds and stars, any animal or plant" (Fink 2018a: 127).
22 Ibid., p. 141.
23 Cf. Fink 1970: 185.

Chapter 18

1 Eugen Fink, "Zwei Gespräche mit Heidegger/Two Conversations with Heidegger," ed. and trans. Giovanni Jan Giubilato and Ian Alexander Moore.
2 On Fink's interpretation of Hölderlin see: Boelderl 2022, who also refers to the unpublished folder (E15/286).
3 Cf. Fink 2018: 965–8.
4 See Sepp 1998; Luft 2002; Kerckhoven 2003; Bruzina 2004; Giubilato 2017.
5 As is well-known, Gadamer is said to have "urbanized the Heideggerian province," according to the famous expression of Jürgen Habermas (1981: 393). See also Becker (1958), where the author emphasizes that "Fink's pedagogical intention [is] to present what is customary in Heidegger's circle" (p. 27).
6 Cf. Fink & Heidegger 1993; see also Sallis and Maly 1980. For a masterful exposition of the fundamental guidelines of the confrontation between the two philosophers, developed along the guiding thread of their conceptions of *physis*, cf. Nielsen 2010.
7 Cf. Fink 2006; 2008. The edition of Eugen Fink's "phenomenological workshop" was the life work of Ronald Bruzina. After his premature death in the spring of 2019, it was only natural that Guy van Kerckhoven, himself the editor of several volumes of the *Eugen Fink Gesamtausgabe* as well as close friend of Bruzina, was entrusted, in agreement with the main editors of the Eugen Fink Gesamtausgabe—Cathrin Nielsen (Frankfurt), Alexander Schnell (Wuppertal), and Hans Reiner Sepp (Prague)—with the completion of this gigantic enterprise. Thus, based on what Bruzina had already set and established, volumes 3.3 and 3.4 were prepared during the last few years with the collaboration of Giovanni Jan Giubilato and Francesco Alfieri: see Fink 2023a; 2023b. See also Bruzina's translation of Fink's *Sixth Cartesian Meditation* (Fink 1995), and his detailed introduction to the text.
8 These materials would effectively allow scholars to do with Fink what Theodore Kisiel and Thomas Sheehan have done with Heidegger (cf. Kisiel and Sheehan 2009). A step in this direction has been taken with the editors' detailed introduction to the third and fourth volume of Fink's *Werkstatt* and with the forthcoming study *Weltaufgang: Die Geburt des kosmologischen Denkens* (Kerckhoven and Giubilato 2023).
9 In 1928, the first task with which Husserl entrusted his new assistant Eugen Fink, who at the time was still working on his doctoral thesis, was the preparation of the *Bernauer Manuskripte über das Zeitbewusstsein* for publication. In these manuscripts, Husserl deals extensively not only with the question of temporality and the constitution of consciousness but also with individuation. Fink's familiarity with this material is significantly documented by the remarks and even criticisms outlined

during the preparation of a summary index, dated December 1928 (Fink 2008: 251) and also by an attempt to organize the manuscripts, compiled together with the draft of a preface (Fink 2008: 378). See also footnote 13, below.

10. According to Fink's *philosophical* criticism of Husserl's *phenomenological* approach, with the programmatically established requirement of a presuppositionless science of immediately given phenomena (i.e., phenomeno-logy as *logos* of the *phainomena*) Husserl simply presupposed "phenomenality," the all-encompassing happening of φαίνεσθαι, i.e., of the world-appearance of being, without any further inquiry or questioning. The appearing of being functions as a tremendous, unexamined general presupposition for the infinitesimal intentional analysis to which Husserl subjected human world-experience, purified in its transcendental structures.

11. "das Seiende von sich aus "sich aussetzt," "hervorkommt" aus seiner verborgenen Tiefe und in die Erscheinung ausläßt."

12. "'Erscheinung' also bei Heidegger nur als das *Fürunssein des Seienden* begriffen, nicht als *Außersichgehen des Seienden selber*. Das Seiende ist, wenn 'Wahrheit' geschieht, nicht nur *unverborgen*, sondern auch '*außer sich*,' d. h. in der auf das Wesen hin zielenden Erscheinung gegeben."

13. "Hegel verkennt nicht die Endlichkeit, aber er kämpft gegen ihre Fixation. Endlichkeit und Unendlichkeit = als ein Verhältnis der Kraft begriffen: das Endliche als Verendlichung des Unendlichen, als Selbstbegrenzung im Außersichgehen, im Sichanderswerden. Das Wesen ist ver-wesend, d.i. sich äußernd, außersichgehend."

14. See, e.g., the following passages from Fink, 2008: "Thesis: 'being' [*Sein*'"] (in the broadest sense) [is the] 'result' (of a 'becoming'). (Cf. Hegel!)" (303); "being as the having become [*Gewordenes*] of the constitutive becoming" (168); "'Being' is an abstract moment of the speculative becoming of the constitution of the world: captivation in the world [*Weltbefangenheit*]" (282); "All being is a constitutive-meontic result" (92); "The task of philosophy is to cast out the concept of being from the concept of the absolute. Being is a result. Being is a transcendental surface. Phenomenology is far from being a mere theory of being (ontology). And yet this is a characterization that concerns the whole. *Ti to on* [What is being]? A constitutive result" (108); "The un-nihiliation of the nothing that leads to being is what Hegel calls 'becoming.' Becoming is for him a speculative concept and does not mean an existing being [*ein seiendes Wesen*] or an occurrence in the ordinary sense" (284).

15. See Giubilato 2022.
16. See Fink 1957.
17. Cf. Fink 2008: Z-VIII; Z-VII; Z-VII/Reihe XVI.
18. Cf. Fink 1977a.
19. Cf. Fink 1977b.
20. Cf. Fink 2003; see also Fink 1991.
21. For more on this dialogue, see chapters two and five.

Chapter 19

1. [A common phrase in Heidegger. See, for example, the text bearing this title in Heidegger 2003, chapter 4 / "Überwindung der Metaphysik," in Heidegger (1975–), GA 7: 67–98.]

2 [I.e., the difference between being itself or the truth of being, on the one hand, and beings and *their* beingness, on the other. "Metaphysics," according to the later Heidegger, remains focused on beingness, whereas Heidegger tries to think being itself or the truth of being.]
3 [*Weltalter des Seins*: literally, 'world-age of being.']
4 [In *Being and Time*, Heidegger uses the term "existence" to describe the way of being of the human (the entity whose being is an issue for it), in contrast to ways of being such as 'presence-at-hand' or 'readiness-to-hand,' which are applicable to other entities.]
5 [I.e., of the human who essentially stands (*-sistit*) out (*ek-*) into the truth of being itself. See Heidegger's 1946 text "Letter on 'Humanism,'" trans. Frank A. Capuzzi, in Heidegger 1998: 247–57/GA 9: 323–37. See also Heidegger 2021, Part I, Chapter 1/ GA 49.]
6 [Heidegger develops this self-critique above all in the first part of the recently published volume *Zu eigenen Veröffentlichungen* (GA 82).]
7 [I.e., as a structural trait of the way of being of the human.]
8 [See, for example, Heidegger's essay (2002a), especially p. 99/"Hegels Begriff der Erfahrung," in GA 5, especially p. 132. For Heidegger's use of this exact phrase, see GA 67: 186 and GA 90: 99–102.]
9 [Our transcription differs here from the one published in Fink 2018c: 965–68, which gives "nie" instead of "nur." Further discrepancies will be marked in notes below.]
10 [EFGA 16: "Bezug" instead of "Bergung."]
11 [EFGA 16: "unmöglich" instead of "möglich."]
12 [EFGA 16: the original Greek is transliterated.]
13 [EFGA 16: "wird" is missing.]
14 [EFGA 16: the close parenthesis is missing.]
15 [EFGA 16: "*nur* verschwindende" instead of "*eine* versammelnde."]
16 [EFGA 16: "entschwindende" instead of "einheimische."]
17 [EFGA 16: "demnach das Seiende" instead of "derart dass Seiendes."]
18 [EFGA 16: emphasis missing.]
19 [EFGA 16: emphasis missing.]
20 [EFGA 16: "negativ" instead of "mager."]
21 [Fink underlines "Abwesen" three times in the manuscript. EFGA 16 erroneously gives double underlining for "Wesenlose," "Nichts," and "Abwesen."]
22 [EFGA 16: "Denn dass" instead of "Dass das."]
23 [EFGA 16: "könne man selbst an der Sache nicht arbeiten" instead of "komme man selbst in der Sache nicht weiter."]
24 [EFGA 16: "wie es Heidegger" instead of "wie er, Heidegger."]
25 [EFGA 16: "verwundert" instead of "überrascht."]
26 [EFGA 16: "es selbst" instead of "er selber."]
27 [EFGA 16: "Einrichten in der" instead of "Einsicht in die."]
28 [EFGA 16: "grundsätzlich" instead of "gänzlich."]
29 [Rather than treating this as a single long sentence beginning with "Zumal," EFGA 16 punctuates it as follows, thereby obscuring that this is Heidegger's reply and explanation of his surprise: "[. . .] in der *Zeitlichkeit* des Anwesens, zumal er auch vom Anwesen spreche, dass das *Abwesen* umfasse, – / Seine eigene positive Seinsauffassung [. . .]."]
30 [EFGA 16: "Dann verlor sich die" instead of "Daran schloss sich eine."]
31 [EFGA 16: "*Zeitlichkeit*" instead of "*Heraklit*."]

32 [EFGA 16: "aber" instead of "oder."]
33 [EFGA 16: "den" instead of "dem."]
34 [EFGA 16: "ἁρμονιὴ αφανης" instead of "ἁρμονίη ἀφανής."]
35 [EFGA 16: "zusammen" is missing.]
36 [I.e., Fink's lecture course from the winter semester of 1952–1953, published under the title *Existenz und Coexistenz: Grundprobleme der menschlichen Gemeinschaft*. This lecture course, together with one from the summer semester of 1955 titled *Grundphänomene des menschlichen Daseins* (*Basic Phenomena of Human Existence*), is an indisputable highlight of Fink's philosophical teaching activity. The booklet *Oase des Glücks* (*Oasis of Happiness*, 1957), published two years later, can be regarded as a distillation of the ideas developed above all in the second lecture course. The booklet appeared only three years before Fink's most famous major work, *Spiel als Weltsymbol*, both of which are available in English in Fink 2016b. *Play as Symbol of the World* is based on a lecture course Fink gave during the summer semester of 1957 under the title *Das menschliche und das weltliche Problem des Spiels* (*The Human and the Worldly Problem of Play*).]
37 [Likely a reference to Heidegger's lecture "The Thing," in *Poetry, Language, Thought*, trans. Albert Hofstadter (New York: HarperCollins, 2001), 176/GA 7: 180, a signed offprint of which Heidegger had sent to Fink in 1951 and which they discuss in their correspondence. See also the reference to "death as sheltering and as homecoming to the homely [*Tod als Bergung und Heimkehr ins Heimatliche*]" in Fink's lecture course *Basic Problems of Human Community*, where he discusses the problem of community as a cosmological question and the dialectic that characterizes human existence as a dialectic between love and death, "exposure [*Aussetzung*]" and "sheltering [*Bergung*]." Fink, *Existenz und Coexistenz* (EFGA 16), 276.]
38 Hegel 2018: 12.
39 [Fink underlines "absencing" three times in the manuscript.]
40 [I.e., Heidegger's hometown, where many of his unpublished manuscripts were stored at the time. See, among other private manuscripts composed in the late 1930s–early 1940s, Heidegger 2012/GA 65.]
41 [This was also Fink's question for Heidegger after reading the latter's text "The Thing." As Fink summarizes a letter he wrote to Heidegger on December 28, 1951: "Isn't a basic conception guiding the way? Being = presencing? Presence of the world in things? [*Ist nicht eine Grundauffassung leitend? Sein = Anwesung? Anwesen der Welt in den Dingen?*]" Nachlass Eugen Fink, Universitätsarchiv Freiburg, E 15/962.]
42 [See, for example, *Off the Beaten Path*, 263–4/GA 5: 350.]
43 [In the Diels-Kranz enumeration, the *Logos*-fragment is numbered first; the phrase *harmoniē aphanēs* can be found in Fragment B. 54: ἁρμονίη ἀφανὴς φανερῆς κρείττων, "An unapparent framework [*harmoniē aphanēs*] is more powerful than an apparent one."]
44 [These plans would eventually be realized in a 1966–7 seminar, published as Fink and Heidegger 1979/GA 15.]
45 [Presumably the university there, perhaps for recommendations for an open professorship. In an unpublished letter to his brother Fritz Heidegger dated March 3, 1967, Heidegger speaks of Fink as the most talented philosopher of his age group. Located in the Deutsches Literaturarchiv Marbach, Mediennummer HS008539896. Elsewhere, Heidegger writes that "He (Fink) would have surely been my only possible successor [*Er (Fink) wäre doch der einzig mögliche Nachfolger gewesen*]" (i.e., to his

chair in the Freiburg philosophy department, which Fink had turned down) and that "Eugen Fink was the outstanding speculative talent of his generation [*Eugen Fink war die überragende spekulative Begabung seiner Generation*]." Letters to Eugen Fink and to Fink's wife dated November 7, 1964, and July 11, 1975, respectively, in Nachlass Eugen Fink, Universitätsarchiv Freiburg E 15/962.]

Chapter 23

1 Translated by Ian Alexander Moore and Christopher Turner. Bloomsbury Publishing, 2023. 138 pp.

Bibliography

Agard, Olivier (2017), "L'anthropologie philosophique de Schiller dans les *Lettres sur L'éducation esthétique de l'homme. (1795)*," in F. Fabbianelli and J.-F. Goubet (eds.), *L'Homme entier. Conceptions anthropologiques classiques et contemporains*, 123–42, Paris: Garnier.
Alvis, Jason W. (2019), "God's Playthings: Eugen Fink's Phenomenology of Religion in *Play as Symbol of the World*," *Research in Phenomenology* 49: 88–117.
Alvis, Jason W. (2022), "Charismatic Pneumatology as Ecumenical Opportunity: Orthopraxy, Subjectivity, and Relational Ontologies of the Holy Spirit," in Frances-Vincent Anthony (ed.), *Intercultural Theology vis-à-vis Ecumenical and Interreligious Dialogue*, Special Issue of The Journal, *Religions*, 13.
André, Laks (2006), *The Concept of Presocratic Philosophy: Its Origin, Development, and Significance*. Translated by G. W. Most, Princeton, NJ: Princeton University Press.
Ardley, Gavin (1967), "The Role of Play in the Philosophy of Plato," *Philisophy* 42: 226–44.
Arendt, Hannah (1958), *The Human Condition*, Chicago, IL: Chicago University Press.
Aristotle (1984), *The Complete Works of Aristotle: The Revised Oxford Translation*. Edited by J. Barnes, Princeton, NJ: Princeton University Press.
Axelos, Kostas (1962), *Héraclite et la philosophie: La première saisie de l'être en devenir de la totalité*, Paris: Minuit.
Axelos, Kostas (1966), *Einführung in ein künftiges Denken, über Marx und Heidegger*, Tubingen: Niemeyer.
Axelos, Kostas (2015 [1969]), *Marx penseur de la technique: De l'aliénation de l'homme à la conquête du monde*, La Versanne: Encre Marine.
Axelos, Kostas (2018 [1969]), *Le Jeu du Monde*, Paris: Minuit.
Axelos, Kostas (2019 [1964]), *Vers la pensée planétaire: Le devenir-pensée du monde et le devenir-monde de la pensée*, La Versanne: Encre Marine.
Babich, Babette E. (2005), "Nietzsche's 'Artists' Metaphysics' and Fink's Ontological World-Play." *International Studies in Phenomenology* 37(3): 163–80.
Barnett, Lynn A. (2007), "The Nature of Playfulness in Young Adults," *Personality and Individual Differences* 43: 949–58. https://doi.org/10.1016/j.paid.2007.02.018.
Becker, Oskar (1958), "Eugen Fink, Nachdenkliches zur ontologischen Frühgeschichte von Raum, Zeit und Bewegung," *Philosophische Rundschau* 6(1–2): 26–34.
Beiser, F. C. (2005), *Schiller as Philosopher: A Re-Examination*, Oxford: Oxford University Press.
Bertolini, Simona (2012), *Eugen Fink e il problema del mondo. Tra ontologia, idealismo e fenomenologia*, Milano-Udine: Mimesis.
Bertolini, Simona (2017), "Ist Der Mensch Auch Ein Tier?: Zwei Antworten Der Phänomenologischen Tradition," *Studia Phaenomenologica* 17: 119–49.
Bhavnani, K., J. Foran, P. A. Kurian, and D. Munshi (eds.) *Climate Futures: Reimagining Global Climate Justice*, London: Zed Books.
Binkelmann, Christoph (2019), "Wechselwirkung im Spieltrieb. Schillers konfliktuöser Bezug zu Fichte," in Gideon Stiening (ed.), *Friedrich Schiller: Über die Ästhetische*

Erziehung des Menschen in einer Reihe von Briefen, Klassiker Auslegen, Band 69, 141–56, Berlin and Boston: De Gruyter.
Boelderl, A. (2022), "Der Mensch als Fragment—In der Spur eines anderen Idealismus? Eugen Fink und der arme Hölderlin," *Phänomenologische Forschungen* 2022-2: 225–40.
Bondelli, Martin (2019), "Schillers Triebkonzept im Ausgang von Reinholds Trieblehre," in Gideon Stiening (ed.), *Friedrich Schiller: Über die Ästhetische Erziehung des Menschen in einer Reihe von Briefen, Klassiker Auslegen, Band 69*, Berlin and Boston: De Gruyter.
Borges, Jorge Luis (1999), *Collected Fictions*. Translated by Andrew Hurley. London: Penguin.
Boronat, Miras and Núria Sara (2016a), "Oasis of Happiness: The Play of the World and Human Existence: Eugen Fink's Multidimensional Concept of Play," in M. MacLean, W. Russell, and E. Ryall (eds.), *Philosophical Perspectives on Play*, 95–106, London: Routledge.
Boronat, Miras and Núria Sara (2016b), "La existencia como juego: La antropología filosófica de Eugen Fink," in S. París and I. Comins (eds.), *La interculturalidad en diálogo: estudios filosóficos*, 77–87, Seville: Thémata.
Brehier, Emile (1989 [1908]), *La Théorie des incorporels dans l'ancien stoïcisme*, Paris: Vrin.
Bruzina, Ronald (2004), *Edmund Husserl & Eugen Fink: Beginnings and Ends in Phenomenology 1928-1938*, New Haven, CT: Yale University Press.
Bruzina, Ronald (2006), "Hinter der ausgeschriebenen Finkschen Meditation: Meontik – Pädagogik," in A. Böhmer (ed.), *Eugen Fink: Sozialphilosophie - Anthropologie - Kosmologie - Pädagogik - Methodik*, 193–219, Würzburg: Königshausen & Neumann.
Buchanan, Richard (1992). "Wicked Problems in Design Thinking," *Design Issues* 8: 5–21.
Buytendijk, Frederik Jacobus Johannes (1933), *Wesen und Sinn des Spiels. Das Spielen des Menschen und der Tiere als Erscheinungsform der Lebenstriebe*, Berlin: Kurt Wollf Verlag / Der Neue Geist Verlag.
Cacioppo, J. T. and L. Hawkley (2009), "Perceived Social Isolation and Cognition," *Trends in Cognitive Sciences* 13(10): 447–54. https://doi.org/10.1016/j.tics.2009.06.005.
Cairns, Dorion (1976), *Conversations with Husserl and Fink*, The Hague: Nijhoff.
Capobianco, Richard (2010), *Engaging Heidegger*, Toronto: University of Toronto Press.
Capobianco, Richard (2022), *Heidegger's Being: The Shimmering Unfolding*, Toronto: University of Toronto Press.
Carswell, John (2000), "The Deconstruction of the Dome of the Rock," in S. Auld, R. Hillenbrand, and Y. S. Natshah (eds.), *Ottoman Jerusalem: The Living City*, 1517-917, London: Altajir World of Islam Trust.
Chandler, David (2013), "International Statebuilding and the Ideology of Resilience," *Politics* 33: 276–86.
Chandler, David (2014), "Beyond Neoliberalism: Resilience, the New Art of Governing Complexity," *Resilience* 2(1): 47–63, https://doi.org/10.1080/21693293.2013.878544.
Chandler, David and J. Reid (2019), *Becoming Indigenous: Governing Imaginaries in the Anthro Pocene*, London: Rowman & Littlefield.
Chandler, David, K. Grove, and S. Wakefield (eds.) (2020), *Resilience in the Anthropocene: Governance and Politics at the End of the World*, 1st ed., Routledge. https://doi.org/10.4324/9781003033370.
Chang, Po-Ju, Careen Yarnal, and Garry Chick (2016), "The Longitudinal Association Between Playfulness and Resilience in Older Women Engaged in The Red Hat Society," *Journal of Leisure Research* 48. https://doi.org/10.18666/JLR-2016-V48-I3-6256.
Coeckelbergh, M. (2022), *Self-Improvement: Technologies of the Soul in the Age of Artificial Intelligence*, New York, NY: Columbia University Press.

Coli, A. L. (2022), "'Überlegungen zur Ontologie und zur 'Ontologischen Erfahrung' bei Eugen Fink," *Phainomena* 31(122/123): 237–64. https://doi.org/10.32022/PHI31.2022.122-123.11.
Coyne, R. (2005), "Wicked Problems Revisited," *Design Studies* 26: 5–17.
Cristin, Renato (2001), "L'abissalità del mondo: Grund e Weltproblem in Eugen Fink nel confronto con Heidegger (con una lettera inedita di Heidegger di riposta per l'invio di *Weltbezug und Seins-verständnis*)," *Magazzino di filosofia* 5: 130–67.
Crowell, Steven Galt (2008), "Fink's Untimely Nietzsche: Between Heidegger and Derrida," *International Studies in Philosophy* 308: 15–31.
D'Angour, Armand (2013), "Plato and Play: Taking Education Seriously in Ancient Greece," *American Journal of Play* 5: 293–307.
Dastur, Françoise (1997), "Monde et jeu: Axelos et Fink," *Rue Descartes* 18: 25–38.
Dastur, Francoise (2013), "Fink Reading Nietzsche: *On Overcoming Metaphysics*," in É. Boublil and C. Daigle (eds.), *Nietzsche and Phenomenology: Power, Life, Subjectivity*, 101–14, Bloomington: Indiana University Press.
Dastur, Françoise (2017), *Questions of Phenomenology: Language, Alterity, Temporality, Finitude*. Translated by Robert Vallier, New York: Fordham University Press.
Deleuze, Gilles (1967a), *L'Île Déserte et autres textes*. Edited by D. Lapoujade, Paris: Minuit.
Deleuze, Gilles (1967b), *Logique du Sens*, Paris: Minuit.
Deleuze, Gilles (2004), *Desert Islands and Other Texts 1953–1974*. Translated by M. Taormina, Los Angeles: Semiotext(e).
Derrida, J. (1967), *De la Grammatologie*, Paris: Minuit.
Derrida, J. (1981), *Dissemination*. Translated by B. Johnson, London: The Athlone Press.
Dewey, J. (2012), *Democracy and Education*, Hollywood, FL: Simon & Brown.
Ferraris, Maurizio (2002), *Historia de la hermenéutica*, Madrid: Siglo XXI.
Fichte, J. G. (1956 [1794]), *Grundlage der gesamten Wissenschaftslehre*, Hamburg: Meiner.
Fichte, J. G. (1965), "Über den Geist des Buchstaben," in J. H. Fichte (ed.), *Fichtes Sämtliche Werke*, vol. 8, 333–61, Berlin: de Gruyter.
Figal, Günter (2002), "'The Doing of the Thing Itself': Gadamer's Hermeneutic Ontology of Language," in R. J. Dostal (ed.), *The Cambridge Companion to Gadamer*, 102–25, Cambridge: Cambridge University Press.
Figal, Günter (2007), "Gadamer als Phänomenologe," *Phänomenologische Forschungen* 7: 95–107.
Fink, Eugen (1947), *Vom Wesen des Enthusiasmus*, Essen: Chamier.
Fink, Eugen (1957), *Zur ontologischen Frühgeschichte von Raum—Zeit—Bewegung*, The Hague: Martinus Nijhoff.
Fink, Eugen (1966 [1930]), "Vergegenwärtigung und Bild: Beiträge zur Phänomenologie der Unwirklichkeit," in Fink, *Studien zur Phänomenologie 1930-1939*, 1–78, Den Haag: Martinus Nijhoff.
Fink, Eugen (1966), *Studien zur Phänomenologie 1930–1939*, The Hague: Martinus Nijhoff.
Fink, Eugen (1968), "The Oasis of Happiness: Toward an Ontology of Play," Translated by U. Saine and T. Saine, *Yale French Studies* 41: 19–30. https://doi.org/10.2307/2929663.
Fink, Eugen (1970a), *Erziehungswissenschaft und Lebenslehre*, Freiburg: Rombach.
Fink, Eugen (1970b), "The Phenomenological Philosophy of Edmund Husserl and Contemporary Criticism. With a Preface by Edmund Husserl," in R. O. Elveton (ed.), *The Phenomenology of Husserl: Selected Critical Readings*, 73–147, Chicago: Quadrangle.

Fink, Eugen (1972a), "Weltbezug und Seinsverständnis," in Walter Biemel (ed.), *Phänomenologie Heute: Festschrift für Ludwig Landgrebe*, 94–102, The Hague: Nijhoff.
Fink, Eugen (1972b), "What Does the Phenomenology of Edmund Husserl Want to Accomplish? (The Phenomenological Idea of Laying-a-Ground)," Translated by A. Grugan, *Research in Phenomenology* 7 (1): 5–27.
Fink, Eugen (1976a), *Nähe und Distanz: Phänomenologische Vorträge und Aufsätze*, Freiburg: Karl Alber.
Fink, Eugen (1976b), "Welt und Geschichte," in Franz-Anton Schwarz (ed.), *Nähe und Distanz: Phänomenologische Vorträge und Aufsätze*, 158–79, Freiburg: Alber.
Fink, Eugen (1976c), "Zum Problem der ontologischen Erfahrung," in Franz-Anton Schwarz (ed.), *Nähe und Distanz: Phänomenologische Vorträge und Aufsätze*, Freiburg: Alber.
Fink, Eugen (1977a), *Sein und Mensch. Vom Wesen der ontologischen Erfahrung*. Edited by E. Schütz and F. A. Schwarz, Freiburg: Alber.
Fink, Eugen (1977b), *Hegel: Phänomenologische Interpretationen der "Phänomenologie des Geistes"*, Frankfurt a.M.: Klostermann.
Fink, Eugen (1978), *Grundfragen der systematischen Pädagogik*. Edited by E. Schutz and F. A. Schwarz, Freiburg: Rombach.
Fink, Eugen (1979), *Grundphänomene des menschlichen Daseins*, Freiburg and München: Karl Alber.
Fink, Eugen (1985), *Einleitung in die Philosophie*. Edited by F.-A. Schwarz, Wurzburg: Konigshausen & Neumann.
Fink, Eugen (1988a), *VI. Cartesianische Meditation. Teil 1: Die Idee einer transzendentalen Methodenlehre*. Edited by H. Ebeling, J. Holl, and G. van Kerckhoven, Dordrecht, Boston and London: Kluwer Academic Publishers.
Fink, Eugen (1988b), "Nietzsche's New Experience of World," Translated by Michael Allen Gillespie, in Michael Allen Gillespie and Tracy B. Strong (eds.), *Nietzsche's New Seas*, 203–19, Chicago, IL: Chicago University Press [originally 1973].
Fink, Eugen (1988c), *Teil 2: Ergänzungsband*. Edited by G. van Kerckhoven, Dordrecht, Boston and London: Kluwer Academic Publishers.
Fink, Eugen (1990), *Welt und Endlichkeit*. Edited by Franz-A. Schwarz, Würzburg: Königshausen & Neumann.
Fink, Eugen (1991), "Nietzsches neue Welterfahrung," in A. Guzzoni (ed.), *100 Jahre philosophische Nietzsche-Rezeption*, 126–39, Frankfurt am Main: Athenäum.
Fink, Eugen (1992), *Natur, Freiheit, Welt: Philosophie der Erziehung*. Edited by F.-A. Schwarz, Würzburg: Königshausen & Neumann.
Fink, Eugen (1995a), *Grundphänomene des menschlichen Daseins*, Freiburg am Breisgau and Munich: Karl Alber.
Fink, Eugen (1995b), *Sixth Cartesian Meditation. The Idea of a Transcendental Theory of Method*. Translated by R. Bruzina, Bloomington: Indiana University Press.
Fink, Eugen (2003), *Nietzsche's Philosophy*, 1st ed. Translated by G. Richter, London and New York: Bloomsbury Academic.
Fink, Eugen (2006), *Phänomenologische Werkstatt. Teilband 3.1: Die Doktorarbeit und erste Assistenzjahre bei Husserl (EFGA 3.1)*. Edited by R. Bruzina, Freiburg and München: Alber.
Fink, Eugen (2008), *Phänomenologische Werkstatt. Teilband 3.2: Die Bernauer Zeitmanuskripte, Cartesianische Meditationen und System der phänomenologischen Philosophie (EFGA 3.2)*. Edited by R. Bruzina, Freiburg and München: Karl Alber.
Fink, Eugen (2010), *Spiel als Weltsymbol*. Edited by Cathrin Nielsen and Hans Rainer Sepp, Freiburg: Alber.

Fink, Eugen (2011), "Nietzsches Metaphysik des Spiels," in Cathrin Nielsen and Hans Rainer Sepp (eds.), *Welt denken: Annäherungen an die Kosmologie Eugen Finks*, 25–37, Freiburg: Alber.
Fink, Eugen (2016 [2010]), *Play as Symbol of the World and Other Writings*, Translated by I. A. Moore and C. Turner, Bloomington and Indianapolis: Indiana University Press.
Fink, Eugen (2016a), "Fink's Notes on Play: The Philosophical-Pedagogical Problem of Play," in Moore and Turner ed. and trans., 253–72, Bloomington: Indiana University Press. [originally 1954].
Fink, Eugen (2016b), *Play as Symbol of the World and Other Writings*. Edited by I. A. Moore and C. Turner, Bloomington: Indiana University Press.
Fink, Eugen (2016c), "Oasis of Happiness," in I. A. Moore and C. Turner (trans.), *Play as Symbol of the World and Other Writings*, 14–31, Bloomington: Indiana University Press.
Fink, Eugen (2016d), *Welt und Endlichkeit*, in Sein und Endlichkeit, Gesamtausgabe, sv. 5/2, Freiburg and Munchen: Karl Alber.
Fink, Eugen (2018a), *Sein, Wahrheit, Welt (EFGA 6)*. Edited by V. Cesarone, Freiburg and München: Karl Alber.
Fink, Eugen (2018b), "Traktat ueber die Gewalt des Menschen," in A. Hilt (ed.), *Existenz und Coexistenz*, 287–491, Freiburg and Munich: Alber.
Fink, Eugen (2018c), *Existenz und Coexistenz (EFGA 16)*. Edited by A. Hilt, Freiburg: Karl Alber.
Fink, Eugen (2019a), *Textentwürfe zur Phänomenologie 1930–1932 (EFGA 2)*. Edited by G. van Kerckhoven, Freiburg and München: Karl Alber.
Fink, Eugen (2019b), "Nietzsche's Metaphysics of Play," Translated by Catherine Homan and Zachary Hamm, *Philosophy Today* 63(1): 21–33.
Fink, Eugen (2023a), *Phänomenologische Werkstatt. Teilband 3: Letzte phänomenologische Darstellung: Die "Krisis"-Problematik (EFGA 3.3)*. Edited by R. Bruzina, F. Alfieri, and G. van Kerckhoven, Freiburg: Karl Alber.
Fink, Eugen (2023b), *Fashion: Seductive Play* [1969]. Translated by I. A. Moore and C. Turner, edited by S. Marino and G. Matteucci, London-New York: Bloomsbury.
Fink, Eugen (1928–1929), "Heft Nachschriften V: Heidegger: Einleitung in die Philosophie und Heidegger: Davoser Vorträge," Nachlass Eugen Fink, Universitätsarchiv Freiburg, call number E 15/433.
Fink, Eugen (1928–1931), "Martin Heidegger: Der Mann, Das Werk, Die Frage, Der Zuspruch, Die Endlichkeit," Nachlass Eugen Fink, Universitätsarchiv Freiburg, call number E 15/214.
Fink, Eugen (1953–1964), "Pädagogisches. Gespräch mit Heidegger," Nachlass Eugen Fink, Universitätsarchiv Freiburg, call number E 15/297.
Fink, Eugen "Zwei Gespräche mit Heidegger / Two Conversations with Heidegger." Edited and translated by Giovanni Jan Giubilato and Ian Alexander Moore, in Steven K. Stakland (ed.), *Phenomenology of Play: Encountering Eugen Fink*, London: Bloomsbury.
Fink, Eugen and M. Heidegger (1993), *Heraclitus Seminar*. Translated by C. H. Seibert, Evanston, IL: Northwestern University Press.
Franz, T. (1999), *Der Mensch und seine Grundphänomene*, Freiburg: Rombach.
Franz, T. (2011), "Weltspiel und Spielwelt. Eugen Finks symbolische Kosmologie," in C. Nielsen and H. R. Sepp (eds.), *Welt denken: Annäherung an die Kosmologie Eugen Finks*, 250–66, Freiburg: Alber.
Freud, S. (2003 [1920]), *Beyond the Pleasure Principle*. Translated by J. Reddick, London: Penguin Modern Classics.

Fuchs, T. (2021), *In Defense of the Human Being. Foundational Questions of an Embodied Anthropology*. https://doi.org/10.1093/oso/9780192898197.001.0001.
Gadamer, H. G. (1976), *Philosophical Hermeneutics*. Translated and edited by David E. Linge, Berkeley and Los Angeles: University of California Press.
Gadamer, H. G. (1986), *The Relevance of the Beautiful and Other Essays*. Translated by N. Walker, edited by R. Bernasconi, Cambridge: Cambridge University Press.
Gadamer, H. G. (1990a), *Hermeneutik I: Wahrheit und Methode*, Tübingen, DE: J.C.B. Mohr (Paul Siebeck).
Gadamer, H. G. (1990b), *Wahrheit und Methode – Grundzüge einer philosophischen Hermeneutik. Gesammelte Werke Band I*, Tübingen: Mohr (Siebeck).
Gadamer, H. G. (1999a), *Gesammelte Werke 1. Wahrheit und Methode*, Tübingen: Mohr Siebeck.
Gadamer, H. G. (1999b), *Gesammelte Werke 2. Hermeneutik II*, Tübingen: Mohr Siebeck.
Gadamer, H. G. (1999c), *Gesammelte Werke 3. Neuere Philosophie I*, Tübingen: Mohr Siebeck.
Gadamer, H. G. (1999d), *Gesammelte Werke 4. Neuere Philosophie II*, Tübingen: Mohr Siebeck.
Gadamer, H. G. (1999e), *Gesammelte Werke 8. Ästhetik und Poetik I. Kunst als Aussage*, Tübingen: Mohr Siebeck.
Gadamer, H. G. (1999f), *Gesammelte Werke 10. Hermeneutik im Rückblick*, Tübingen: Mohr Siebeck.
Gadamer, H. G. (2000), "Towards a Phenomenology of Ritual and Language," in L. K. Schmidt (ed.), *Language and Linguisticality in Gadamer's Hermeneutics*, 19–50. Lanham and Oxford: Lexington Books.
Gadamer, H. G. (2004), *Truth and Method* [1960], revised ed. Translated by J. Weinsheimer and D. G. Marshall, London and New York: Continuum.
Gallie, W. B. (1956), "Essentially Contested Concepts," *Proceedings of the Aristotelian Society* 56(1): 167–98.
Gillespie, Michael Allen and Tracy B. Strong (ed.) (1988), *Nietzsche's New Seas*, Chicago, IL: Chicago University Press.
Gilson, Étienne (2019), *John Duns Scotus: Introduction to His Fundamental Positions*. Translated by J. Colbert, London: T&T Clark.
Giubilato, Giovanni Jan (2017), *Freiheit und Reduktion. Grundzüge einer phänomenologischen Meontik bei Eugen Fink (1927–1946)*, Nordhausen: Bautz.
Giubilato, Giovanni Jan (2018), "Beyond the Genesis, Toward the Absolute. Eugen Fink's Architectonic Foundation of a Constructive Phenomenology Between a Meta-Critic of Transcendental Experience and his own Project of a Dialectical Meontic," *Horizon* 7(1): 203–22.
Giubilato, Giovanni Jan (2022a), "Breaking the Hermeneutic Circle. Phenomenology as 'Catastrophe of Man' in Fink's Early Thought," *Phänomenologische Forschungen* 2022-2: 37–56.
Giubilato, Giovanni Jan (2022b), "Individuation und ontologische Erfahrung: Die philosophische Entwicklung des frühen Fink im Lichte seiner Auseinandersetzung mit Heidegger," *Phainomena* 31(122–123): 65–91.
Giubilato, Giovanni Jan and Ian Alexander Moore. "World, Individuation, and Play: A Critical Introduction to Fink's Conversations with Heidegger," in *Phenomenology of Play: Encountering Eugen Fink*, edited by Steven K. Stakland. London: Bloomsbury.
Glynn, M. A. and J. Webster (1992), "The Adult Playfulness Scale: An Initial Assessment," *Psychological Reports* 71: 83–103. https://doi.org/10.2466/PR0.71.5.83-103.

Goldshmidt, Victor (1969), *Le système stoïcien et l'idée de temps*, Paris: Vrin.
Gordillo, Gastón R. (2021), *Rubble*. Durham, NC: Duke University Press.
Gregorio, Giuliana (2008), *Hans-Georg Gadamer e la declinazione ermeneutica della fenomenologia*, Soveria Mannelli: Rubbettino.
Groos, Karl (1922), *Das Spiel. Zwei Vorträge*, Jena: Verlag von Gustav Fischer.
Grove, K. (2018), *Resilience*, 1st ed. Routledge. https://doi.org/10.4324/9781315661407.
Guitard, P., F. Ferland, and E. Dutil (2005), "Towards a Better Understanding of Play in Adults," *Occupational Therapy Journal of Research/Occupation, Participation and Health* 25(1): 9–22.
Habermas, J. (1981), *Philosophisch-politische Profile*, Frankfurt am Main: Klostermann.
Halák, J. (2015), "Beyond Things: The Ontological Importance of Play According to Eugen Fink," *Journal of the Philosophy of Sport*. http://dx.doi.org/10.1080/00948705.2015.1079133.
Hanson, Karen (1993), "Dressing Down Dressing Up: The Philosophical Fear of Fashion," in H. Hein and C. Korsmeyer (eds.), *Aesthetics in Feminist Perspective*, 229–41, Bloomington and Indianapolis: Indiana University Press.
Hegel, Georg Wilhelm Friedrich (1970), *Phänomenologie des Geistes. Werke Band 3*, Frankfurt: Suhrkamp.
Hegel, Georg Wilhelm Friedrich (1971), *Phänomenologie des Geistes*, Hegel Werke 3, Suhrkamp: Frankfurt a. Ms.
Hegel, Georg Wilhelm Friedrich (1977), *Phenomenology of Spirit*. Translated by A. V. Miller, Oxford: Oxford University Press.
Hegel, Georg Wilhelm Friedrich (1999), *Wissenschaft der Logik. Die Lehre vom Wesen (1813)*, Frankfurt: Meiner.
Hegel, Georg Wilhelm Friedrich (2018), *The Phenomenology of Spirit*. Translated by Terry Pinkard, Cambridge: Cambridge University Press, 12.
Heidegger, Martin (1951), "Das Ding," in Bayerische Akademie der schönen Künste (ed.), *Gestalt und Gedanke: Ein Jahrbuch*, 128–49, Munich: Oldenbourg.
Heidegger, Martin (1962), *Being and Time*. Translated by John Macquarrie and Edward Robinson, Oxford: Blackwell.
Heidegger, Martin (1967), *Sein und Zeit*. 11th ed., Tübingen: Niemeyer.
Heidegger, Martin (1969), *Ansprachen zum 80. Geburtstag*. Meßkirch.
Heidegger, Martin (1972), *On Time and Being*. Translated by John Stambaugh, New York: Harper and Row.
Heidegger, Martin (1975–), *Gesamtausgabe*, 102 vols, Frankfurt: Klostermann.
Heidegger, Martin (1980), "Der Ursprung des Kunstwerkes (1935/6)," in M. Heidegger, *Holzwege*, 1–72, Frankfurt: Klostermann.
Heidegger, Martin (1982), *Basic Problems of Phenomenology*. Translated by Alfred Hofstader, Revised ed., Bloomington: Indiana University Press.
Heidegger, Martin (1986), *Sein und Zeit*, Tübingen: Niemeyer.
Heidegger, Martin (1989), *Gesamtausgabe 65: Beiträge Zur Philosophie. Vom Ereignis (1936–1938)*, Frankfurt Am Main: Vittorio Klostermann.
Heidegger, Martin (1991), *The Principle of Reason*. Translated by Reginald Lilly, Bloomington: Indiana University Press.
Heidegger, Martin (1995), *The Fundamental Concepts of Metaphysics: World, Finitude, Solitude*. Translated by William McNeill and Nicholas Walker, Bloomington: Indiana University Press.
Heidegger, Martin (1996a), *Being and Time: A Translation of 'Sein und Zeit'*. Translated by J. Stambaugh, Albany: SUNY.

Heidegger, Martin (1996b), *Einleitung in die Philosophie* (GA 27). Edited by O. Saame and I. Saame-Speidel, Frankfurt a. M.: Klostermann.

Heidegger, Martin (1997), "Aus den Aufzeichnungen zu dem mit Eugen Fink veranstalteten Heraklit-Seminar," Edited by F.-W. v. Herrmann, *Heidegger Studies* 13: 9–14.

Heidegger, Martin (1998), *Pathmarks*. Edited by William McNeill, Cambridge: Cambridge University Press.

Heidegger, Martin (2001), "The Thing," in Albert Hofstadter (trans.), *Poetry, Language, Thought*, 161–84, New York: Perennial.

Heidegger, Martin (2002a), "Hegel's Concept of Experience," in Julian Young and Kenneth Haynes (trans. and ed.), *Off the Beaten Track*, Cambridge: Cambridge University Press.

Heidegger, Martin (2002b), "Nietzsche's Word: 'God Is Dead,'" in Julian Young and Kenneth Haynes (eds. and trans.), *Off the Beaten Path*, Cambridge: Cambridge University Press.

Heidegger, Martin (2010) *Being and Time* [1927]. Translated by J. Stambaugh revised by D. J. Schmidt, Albany, NY: SUNY Press.

Heidegger, Martin (2012a), *Bremen and Freiburg Lectures*. Translated by Andrew J. Mitchell, Bloomington: Indiana University Press.

Heidegger, Martin (2012b), *Contributions to Philosophy: Of the Event*. Translated by Richard Rojcewicz and Daniela Vallega-Neu, Bloomington: Indiana University Press.

Heidegger, Martin (2018), *Heraclitus: The Inception of Occidental Thinking and Logic: Heraclitus's Doctrine of the Logos*. Translated by Julia Goesser Assaiante and S. Montgomery Ewegen, London: Bloomsbury.

Heidegger, Martin (2021), *The Metaphysics of German Idealism*. Translated by Ian Alexander Moore and Rodrigo Therezo, Cambridge: Polity.

Heidegger, Martin (2022a), *Duns Scotus's Doctrine of Categories and Meaning*. Translated by Joydeep Bagchee and Jeffrey D. Gower, Bloomington: Indiana University Press.

Heidegger, Martin (2022b), "Symposium on Martin Heidegger's 'The Argument Against Need,'" *British Journal for the History of Philosophy* 30(3): 508–59.

Heidegger, Martin (2023), "Special Section on a Recent Text from Heidegger's Nachlass: 'The Argument against Need,'" Edited by Christopher D. Merwin and Ian Alexander Moore. *Gatherings: The Heidegger Circle Annual* 13.

Heidegger, Martin and Eugen Fink (1979), *Heraclitus Seminar 1966/67*. Translated by Charles H. Seibert. University, AL: University of Alabama Press.

Heidegger, Martin and Elfride Heidegger (1950–1977), "Briefe und Karten." Nachlass Eugen Fink, Universitätsarchiv Freiburg, call number E 15/962.

Hein, H. (1968), "Play as an Aesthetic Concept," *The Journal of Aesthetics and Art Criticism* 27(1): 67–71. https://doi.org/10.2307/428530.

Heraclitus (1952), *The Cosmic Fragments*, Cambridge: Cambridge University Press.

Homan, C. (2013), "The Play of Ethics in Eugen Fink," *The Journal of Speculative Philosophy* 27: 287–96.

Huizinga, Johan (1955), *Homo Ludens: A Study of the Play Element in Culture*, Boston: The Beacon Press.

Huizinga, Johan (1980), *Homo Ludens: A Study of the Play-Element in Culture*, London: Routledge and Kegan Paul.

Hume, D. (2000 [1739]), *A Treatise of Human Nature: Being an Attempt to Introduce the Experimental Method of Reasoning into Moral Subjects*, Oxford: Oxford University Press.

Hüni, H. (2008), "Die Ursprünglich Geteilte Wachheit bei Heraklit im phänomenologischen Rückblick," in E. Escoubas and L. Tengelyi (eds.), *Affect*

et affectivité dans la philosophie moderne et la phénoménologie, 13–23, Paris: L'Harmattan.
Husserl, E. [HUA IX] (1968 [1925]), *Phänomenologische Psychologie. Vorlesungen Sommersemester*, The Hague: Martinus Nijhof.
Husserl, E. (1992), "Die Krisis der Europäischen Wissenschaften und die Transcendentale Phänomenologie," in E. Husserl and E. Stoiker (eds.), *Gesammelte Schriften 8*, 165–276, Hamburg: Meiner.
Husserl, E. [HUA XXIII] (2005 [1898-1925]), *Phantasy, Image Consciousness, and Memory (1898-1925)*. Translated by J. B. Brough, New York, NY: Springer.
Janicaud, Dominique (2001), *Heidegger en France*, 2 vols, Paris: Albin Michel.
Janicaud, Dominique (2015), *Heidegger in France*, Bloomington: Indiana University Press.
Kaden, C. (1993), *Des Lebens Wilder Kreis- Musik im Zivilisationsprozess*, Kassel: Bärenreiter.
Kahn, C. H. (1979), *The Art and Thought of Heraclitus: An Edition of the Fragments with Translation and Commentary*, Cambridge: Cambridge University Press.
Kant, Immanuel (2006), *Anthropology from a Pragmatic Point of View*. Translated by R. B. Louden with an Introduction by M. Kuehn, Cambridge: Cambridge University Press.
Kant, Immanuel (2000), *Critique of the Power of Judgement*. Translated by P. Guyer and E. Matthews, Cambridge: Cambridge University Press.
Kennan-Kedar, Nurith (2003), *The Armenian Ceramics of Jerusalem: Three Generations, 1919-2003*, Jerusalem and Tel Aviv: Yad Izhak Ben-Zvi and Eretz Israel Museum.
Kerckhoven, Guy van (2001), "Fenomenologia e riduzione tematica dell'idea dell'essere," *Magazzino di Filosofia* 5: 23–46.
Kerckhoven, Guy van (2003), *Mundanisierung und Individuation. Die VI. Cartesianische Meditation und ihr Einsatz*, Würzburg: Königshausen & Neumann.
Kerckhoven, Guy van and G. J. Giubilato (2023, forthcoming), *Weltaufgang: Die Geburt des kosmologischen Denkens. Eine Einführung in den dritten und den vierten Teilband der 'Phänomenologischen Werkstatt' Eugen Finks*, Freiburg: Karl Alber.
Kidd, S. E. (2019), *Play and Aesthetics in Ancient Greece*, Cambridge: Cambridge University Press.
Kierkegaard, S. (1941), *The Sickness unto Death*. Translated by Walter Lowrie, Princeton, NJ: Princeton University Press.
Kim, A. (2019), *Brill's Companion to German Platonism*, Leiden, NL: Brill.
Kisiel, T. and T. Sheehan (2009), *Becoming Heidegger: On the Trail of His Early Occasional Writings, 1910-1927*, Evanston, IL: Northwestern University Press.
Krämer, S. (2007), "Ist Schillers Spielkonzept unzeitgemäß?" in J. Bürger (ed.), *Friedrich Schiller. Dichter, Denker Vor- und Gegenbild*, 158–71, Göttingen: Wallstein.
Krell, David Farrell (1971), Review of "The *Heraclitus Seminar*," *Research in Phenomenology* 1: 137–46.
Krell, David Farrell (1972), "Towards an Ontology of Play: Eugen Fink's Notion of *Spiel*," *Research in Phenomenology* 2: 62–93.
Kripke, Saul A. (1982), *Wittgenstein on Rules and Private Language: An Elementary Exposition*, Cambridge, MA: Harvard University Press.
Lawlor, Leonard (2002), *Derrida and Husserl: The Basic Problem of Phenomenology*. Bloomington, Indiana University Press.
Lemm, V. (2009), *Nietzsche's Animal Philosophy: Culture, Politics, and the Animality of the Human Being*, New York: Fordham University Press.
Levinas, E. (1987), "Philosophy and the Idea of Infinity," in E. Levinas (ed.), *Collected Papers*, Translated by A. Lingis, 47–60, Dordrecht and Boston: Nijhoff.

Levinas, E. (1989), *The Levinas Reader*. Edited by S. Hand, Cambridge, MA: Basil Blackwell.
Levinas, E. (1998a), "Dialogue: Self-Consciousness and Proximity of the Neighbor," in E. Levinas (ed.), *Of God Who Comes to Mind*, Translated by B. Bergo, 137–51, Stanford, CA: Stanford University Press.
Levinas, E. (1998b), *Otherwise than Being, or Beyond Essence*. Translated by A. Lingis, Pittsburgh, PA: Duquesne University Press.
Lucian (1925), *Volume IV*, Cambridge, MA: Harvard University Press.
Luft, S. (2002), *Phänomenologie der Phänomenologie: Systematik und Methodologie der Phänomenologie in der Auseinandersetzung zwischen Husserl und Fink*, Dordrecht: Springer.
Magnuson, C. and L. Barnett (2013), "The Playful Advantage: How Playfulness Enhances Coping with Stress," *Leisure Sciences* 35: 129–44. http://dx.doi.org/10.1080/01490400.2013.761905.
Marino, Stefano (2017), "Philosophical Accounts of Fashion in the Nineteenth and Twentieth Century: A Historical Reconstruction," in G. Matteucci and S. Marino (eds.), *Philosophical Perspectives on Fashion*, 11–45, London and New York: Bloomsbury.
Mason, A. J. (2016), *Flow and Flux in Plato's Philosophy*, Oxon, OX: Routledge, Taylor & Francis Group.
Masten, A. S. (2014), *Ordinary Magic: Resilience in Development*, New York: Guilford Press. ISBN 978-1462517169.
McNeill, William (2023), "Saying the Unsayable: Heidegger on the Being-in-Itself of Beings," *Gatherings: The Heidegger Circle Annual* 13.
Meadows, D. (1999), *Leverage Points: Places to Intervene in a Systém*, Charleston, SC: The Sustainability Institute.
Mpendukana, Sibonile (2022), "Semiotics of Spatial Citizenship: Place, Race and Identity in Post-Apartheid South Africa," PhD thesis, University of the Western Cape, Cape Town, South Africa.
Moore, Ian Alexander (2019), *Eckhart, Heidegger, and the Imperative of Releasement*, Albany: State University of New York Press.
Moore, Ian Alexander (2024), "The (Anarchic) Gift of *Gelassenheit*: On an Undeveloped Motif in Derrida's *Donner le temps II*," *Derrida Today* 17(1).
Moore, Ian Alexander and Christopher Turner (2016), "Translators' Introduction," in Eugen Fink (ed.), *Play as Symbol of the World and Other Writings*, edited by I. A. Moore and C. Turner, Bloomington and Indianapolis: Indiana University Press.
Moore, J. (2019), "Capitalocene and Planetary Justice," *Maize* 6: 49–54. https://www.academia.edu/39776872/The_Capitalocene_and_Planetary_Justice?auto=download.
Moran, Dermot (2007), "Fink's Speculative Phenomenology: Between Constitution and Transcendence," *Research in Phenomenology* 37(1): 3–31. https://doi.org/10.1163/156916407X169799.
Most, G. W. (2002), "Heidegger's Greeks," *Arion: A Journal of Humanities and the Classics* 10(1): 83–98. http://www.jstor.org/stable/20163874.
Navaro-Yashin, Yael (2009), "Affective Spaces, Melancholic Objects: Ruination and the Production of Anthropological Knowledge," *Journal of the Royal Anthropological Institute* 15(1): 1–18.
Neyrat, F. (2019), *The Unconstructable Earth: An Ecology of Separation*, New York: Fordham University Press.
Nielsen, C. (2010), "Kategorien der Physis: Heidegger und Fink," in C. Nielsen and H. R. Sepp (eds.), *Welt denken: Annäherungen an die Kosmologie Eugen Finks*, 154–8, Freiburg: Karl Alber.

Nietzsche, Friedrich (1910), *The Complete Works of Friedrich Nietzsche, Vol. 1 [The Birth of Tragedy]*. Translated by W. M. A. Hausmann, Edinburgh: T.N. Foulis.

Nietzsche, Friedrich (2005), "Ecce Homo," in Aaron Ridley and Judith Norman (eds.), *The Anti-Christ, Ecce Homo, Twilight of the Idols: And Other Writings*, translated by Judith Norman, Cambridge: Cambridge University Press.

Nietzsche, Friedrich (2006), *Thus Spoke Zarathustra: A Book for All and None*. Translated by Adrian Del Caro, Cambridge: Cambridge University Press.

Nietzsche, Friedrich (2010), *Beyond Good & Evil: Prelude to a Philosophy of the Future*, New York, NY: Knopf Doubleday Publishing Group.

Nietzsche, Friedrich, T. Butler-Bowdon, and D. R. Johnson (2022), *Thus Spoke Zarathustra the Philosophy Classic*, Hoboken, NJ: John Wiley & Sons, Incorporated.

Ong, A. D., C. S. Bergeman, and S. M. Boker (2009), "Resilience Comes of Age: Defining Features in Later Adulthood," *Journal of Personality* 77: 1777–804. https://doi.org/10.1111/j.1467-6494.2009.00600.

O'Shiel, D. (2013), "Drives as Original Facticity," *Sartre Studies International* 19(1): 1–15.

O'Shiel, D. (2022), *The Phenomenology of Virtual Technology. Perception and Imagination in a Digital Age*, London and New York: Bloomsbury Academic.

Ossenkop, A., G. van Kerckhoven, and R. Fink (2015), *Eugen Fink (1905–1975). Lebensbild des Freiburger Phänomenologen*, Freiburg and München: Karl Alber.

Ottenberg, Simon (1990), "Thirty Years of Fieldnotes: Changing Relationships to the Text," in Roger Sanjek (ed.), *Fieldnotes*, 139–60, New York: Cornell University Press.

Palmer, J. A. (2002), *Plato's Reception of Parmenides*, Oxford: Clarendon Press.

Peterson, Christopher, Maier, Steven F., and Seligman, Martin E. P. (1993), *Learned Helplessness: A Theory for the Age of Personal Control*, New York: Oxford University Press.

Petropoulos, G. (2021), "Fink's Notion of Play in the Context of Philosophical Inquiry with Children," *Childhood & Philosophy* 17: e56494.

Plato (1997), *Complete Works*. Edited by J. M. Cooper and D. S. Hutchinson, Indianapolis, IN: Hackett Publishing Company.

Plotinus (2018), *Plotinus: The Enneads*. Translated by L. P. Gerson, M. John Dillon, R. A. H. King, A. Smith, and J. Wilberding, Cambridge: Cambridge University Press.

Popper, Karl (2013), *The Open Society and Its Enemies: New One-Volume Edition*, Princeton, NJ: Princeton University Press.

Proclus (1992), *Proclus' Commentary on Plato's Parmenides*. Translated by G. R. Morrow and J. M. Dillon, Princeton, NJ: Princeton University Press.

Proclus (2020), *Proclus: Commentary on Plato's Republic Volume I Essays 1–6*. Edited and translated by D. Baltzly, John F. Finamore, and G. Miles, Cambridge: Cambridge University Press.

Reghezza-Zitt, Magali and Samuel Rufat (2019), "Disentangling the Range of Responses to Threats, Hazards and Disasters. Vulnerability, Resilience and Adaptation in question," *European Journal of Geography* 916.

Richir, M. (2011), "Imagination et Phantasia Chez Husserl," *eikasia*: 13–32.

Richter, G. (2022), "Musical Performance as Poetic Thinking," in C. Rentmeester and J. R. Warren (eds.), *Heidegger and Music*, 195–212, Lanham: Rowman & Littlefield.

Roesner, Martina (2003), *Metaphysica ludens: Das Spiel als phänomenologische Grundfigur im Denken Martin Heideggers*, Dordrecht: Kluwer.

Rogerson, K. F. (2008), *The Problem of Free Harmony in Kant's Aesthetics*, Albany, NY: State University of New York Press.

Rorty, R. (1999), *Philosophy and Social Hope*, New York: Penguin.

Salen, Katie and Eric Zimmerman (2004), *Rules of Play: Game Design Fundamentals*, Cambridge: MIT Press.
Sallis, J. and K. Maly (1980), *Heraclitean Fragments: A Companion Volume to the Heidegger/Fink Seminar on Heraclitus*, Tuscaloosa, AL: University of Alabama Press.
Sartre, J.-P. (2004 [1940]), *The Imaginary. A Phenomenological Psychology of the Imagination*. Translated by J. Webber, London and New York: Routledge.
Sartre, J.-P. (2005 [1943]), *Being and Nothingness. An Essay on Phenomenological Ontology*. Translated by H. E. Barnes, London: Routledge.
Schäfer, R. (2012), *Ich-Welten. Erkenntnis, Urteil und Identität aus der egologischen Differenz von Leibniz bis Davidson*, Münster: Mentis Verlag.
Schiller, Friedrich (1954), *On the Aesthetic Education of Man*. Translated by Reginald Snell, New Haven, CT: Yale University Press.
Schiller, Friedrich (1967), *On the Aesthetic Education of Man in a Series of Letters*, Oxford: Clarendon Press.
Schiller, Friedrich (1982 [1795]), *On the Aesthetic Education of Man in a Series of Letters*. Edited and translated by E. M. Wilkinson and L. A. Willoughby, Oxford: Clarendon Press.
Schiller, Friedrich (1985), *Poet of Freedom*, Vol. 1. Translated by William F. Wertz, Daniel Platt, Muriel Mirak, and John Sigerson, Washington, DC: Schiller Institute.
Schiller, Friedrich and W. von Humboldt (1876), *Briefwechsel zwischen Schiller und W. Von Humboldt*. Edited by A. Leitzmann, Stuttgart: Cotta.
Schiller, Friedrich W. (1993), "Letters on the Aesthetic Education of Man" [1795]. Translated by E. M. Wilkinson and L. A. Willoughby, in W. Hinderer and D. O. Dahlstrom (eds.), *Essays: Friedrich Schiller*, London and New York: Continuum.
Schlitte, Annika (2020), "Eugen Fink—Mitspielen im Spiel der Welt: Zum Verhältnis von Phänomenologie und Kosmologie," in Tobias Keiling (ed.), *Phänomenologische Metaphysik*, 185–210, Tübingen: Mohr Siebeck.
Seligman, M. E. P. (1998), *Learned Optimism*, New York: Pocket Books.
Sen, Amartya (1999), *Development as Freedom*, New York: Anchor.
Sepp, H. R. (1998), "Medialität und Meontik: Eugen Finks spekulativer Entwurf," *Internationale Zeitschrift für Philosophie* 1: 85–93.
Sermamoglou-Soulmaidi, G. (2014), *Playful Philosophy and Serious Sophistry: A Reading of Plato's "Euthydemus"*, Berlin, DE: De Gruyter.
Sermamoglou-Soulmaidi, G. (2019), "Laughter and Play in Plato's Gorgias," *Hermes* 147(4): 406–22. https://doi.org/10.25162/hermes-2019-0036.
Shapiro, G. (2004), "The Halcyon Tone as Birdsong," in C. D. Acampora and R. R. Acampora (eds.), *A Nietzschean Bestiary: Becoming Animal Beyond Docile and Brutal*, 83–8, Lanham: Rowman & Littlefield.
Sheehan, Thomas (2015), *Making Sense of Heidegger: A Paradigm Shift*, London: Roman & Littlefield.
Silesius, Angelus (1984), *Cherubinischer Wandersmann: Kritische Ausgabe*. Edited by Louise Gnädinger, Stuttgart: Reclam.
Smith, B. W., J. Dalen, K. Wiggins, E. Tooley, P. Christopher, and J. Bernard (2008), "The Brief Resilience Scale: Assessing the Ability to Bounce Back," *International Journal of Behavioral Medicine* 15: 194–200. https://doi.org/10.1080/10705500802222972.
Spariosu, M. (1989), *Dionysus Reborn*, Ithaca, NY: Cornell University Press.
Spiegelberg, Herbert (1960), *The Phenomenological Movement: A Historical Introduction*. 2 vols, The Hague: Nijhoff.

Spolsky, Bernard (2009), *Language Management*, Cambridge: Cambridge University Press.
Stenger, G. (2011), "Finks Weltkosmoi," in C. Nielsen and H. R. Sepp (eds.), *Welt denken: Annäherung an die Kosmologie Eugen Finks*, 321–46, Freiburg: Alber.
Stroud, Christopher and Sibonile Mpendukana (2012), "9 Material Ethnographies of Multilingualism," in Sheena Gardner and Marilyn Martin-Jones (eds.), *Multilingualism, Discourse, and Ethnography*, 149–62, London: Routledge.
Sutton-Smith, Brian (1997), *The Ambiguity of Play*, Boston: Harvard University Press.
Sutton-Smith, Brian (2001), *The Ambiguity of Play*, Cambridge, MA: Harvard University Press.
Svendsen, Lars F. (2006), *Fashion: A Philosophy*, London: Reaktion Books.
Thesleff, H. (2023), "Play," in G. A. Press and M. Duque (eds.), *The Bloomsbury Handbook of Plato*. 2nd edn, 167–9, London: Bloomsbury Academic.
Tomlinson, G. (2015), *A Million Years of Music – The Emergence of Human Modernity*, New York: Zone Books.
Tugade, M. M. and B. L. Fredrickson (2004), "Resilient Individuals Use Positive Emotions to Bounce Back from Negative Emotional Experiences," *Journal of Personality and Social Psychology* 86: 320–33. https://doi.org/10.1037/0022-3514.86.2.320.
Turner, Christopher (2024), "Fink's Play as Symbol of the World and Its Relevance for Interpreting Ancient Greek Conceptions of Play," in Iulian Apostolescu (ed.), *Phenomenology, Metaphysics, Ontology: Essays on Eugen Fink*, Berlin: De Gruyter University Press.
Vassilopoulou, P. (2021), "Plotinus: Philosophical Thinking as Self-creation," in P. Vassilopoulou and D. Whistler (eds.), *Thought: A Philosophical History*, 117–34, Abingdon, OX: Routledge, Taylor & Francis Group.
Vetter, Helmut (2011), "Die nächtliche Seite der Welt: Anmerkungen zu Martin Heidegger und Eugen Fink," in Cathrin Nielsen and Hans Rainer Sepp (eds.), *Welt denken: Annäherungen an die Kosmologie Eugen Finks*, 184–207, Freiburg: Alber.
Voegelin, Charles F. (1933), "Linguistics: Language and Languages: An Introduction to Linguistics," *American Anthropologist* 35(2): 356–8.
Volvach, Natalia (2022), "Shouting Absences: Disentangling the Ghosts of Ukraine in Occupied Crimea," *Language in Society*, 1–26.
Wacquant, Loïc (2003), "Ethnografeast: A Progress Report on the Practice and Promise of Ethnography," *Ethnography* 4(1): 5–14.
Waldenfels, B. (1996), *Order in the Twilight*. Translated by D. J. Parent, Athens, OH: Ohio University Press.
Wariboko, Nimi (2011), "'Fire from Heaven' Pentecostals in the Secular City," *PNEUMA: The Journal of the Society for Pentecostal Studies* 33: 391–408.
Wariboko, Nimi (2012), *The Pentecostal Principle: Ethical Methodology in New Spirit*, Pentecostal Manifestos, Grand Rapids: Wm B. Eerdmans.
Wariboko, Nimi (2018), *The Split God: Pentecostalism and Critical Theory*, New York: SUNY Press.
Whyte, K. (2019), "Way Beyond the Lifeboat: An Indigenous Allegory of Climate Justice," in K. Wilkerson Dale (ed.), (2010), "A 'Dictatorship of Relativism' and the Specter of Nietzsche: Between Heidegger and Fink," *American Catholic Quarterly* 84(2): 257–81.
Wilkerson, Dale (2012), "Preservation-Enhancement as Value-Positing Metaphysics in Heidegger's Essay, 'The Word of Nietzsche: God is Dead,'" in Babette Babich, Alfred Denker, and Holger Zaborowski (eds.), *Heidegger & Nietzsche in Elementa: Schriften zur Philosophie und ihrer Problemgeschichte 82*, 121–43, Amsterdam: Rodopoi.

Winnicott, D. (2009), *Playing and Reality*, London: Routledge.
Wittgenstein, Ludwig (1999), *Philosophical Investigations*, Oxford: Blackwell.
Wittgenstein, Ludwig (2003), *Philosophical Investigations* [1953]. Translated by G. E. M. Anscombe. 50th Anniversary edn, Oxford: Blackwell.
Wylant, Barry (2010), "Design Thinking and the Question of Modernity," *The Design Journal* 13: 217–31.

Contributors

Emile Alexandrov is Assistant Professor at the School of Advanced Studies, University of Tyumen, Russia. His research areas focus on ancient Greek philosophy, especially late Antiquity to Early Middle Ages, and German philosophy from Kant to Heidegger. Emile has published on Plato, neoplatonism, and Heidegger. Emile's most recent research publication focuses on the reception of Aristotle's interpretation of Plato in Neoplatonism and early Islamic philosophy, for example, "Poetisation of Nature and Thinking in Heidegger and Emerson" and "Saving Plato from Reductivism."

Jason W. Alvis is Senior Research Fellow at the University of Vienna in the Institute for Philosophy, and teaches in the Department of Theology at the University of Oldenburg. His fields of research are systematic theology, philosophy of religion, and phenomenology, and he most recently has been researching how to use phenomenology to explore Charismatic pneumatology more closely.

Núria Sara Miras Boronat is Associate Professor in Moral and Political Philosophy at the University of Barcelona. Her research interests focus on feminism, pragmatism, and contemporary theories of injustice and oppression. She has published on play, games, phenomenology, and hermeneutics. Her most recent book is *Filòsofes de la contemporaneïtat* (Women Philosophers for Our Times, 2023).

Anna Luiza Coli completed her PhD on Eugen Fink at the Universities of Wuppertal (Bergische Uni Wuppertal) and Prague (Uni Karlova v Praze). She has a postdoctoral degree from the State University of Londrina (UEL) and is currently attending a second postdoctoral internship as a CAPES-PrInt fellow and professor of the Federal University of Minas Gerais (UFMG). She works mainly in the areas of German and French phenomenology, philosophy of mind and cognition, aesthetics and philosophy of art, psychoanalysis.

Giovanni Jan Giubilato is independent writer and researcher with an international academic trajectory. Member of the *Eugen-Fink-Zentrum Wuppertal (EFZW)*. His research interests focus on philosophy, anthropology, and aesthetics. He is author of several scientific papers, translations, and books. His most recent publication is *Weltaufgang: die Geburt des kosmologischen Denkens Eugen Finks* (2023).

Annette Hilt is Professor for Philosophy at Hochschule fuer Gesellschaftsgestaltung in Koblenz, Germany. Her research interests focus on phenomenology and hermeneutics on systematic and ethical fields, philosophical anthropology, philosophy of culture and society, and philosophy of education and of medicine. Her most recent book is *Erzaehlend philosophieren—ein Lehr—und Lesebuch* (2020).

Catherine Homan is Associate Professor of Philosophy and Chair, Department of Theology and Philosophy at Mount Mary University. Her research interests focus on the philosophy of play, especially in relation to education and interspecies play. She has published multiple articles and chapters on Hans-Georg Gadamer and Eugen Fink in addition to her book, *A Hermeneutics of Poetic Education: The Play of the In-Between* (2020).

Alice Koubová is Senior Researcher at the Institute of Philosophy, Czech Academy of Sciences, and Associate Professor and Vice-Dean for Research at the Academy of Performing Arts in Prague, Czech Republic. Her main research interests range from resilience and ludic thinking, performance and performativity to relational ethics and citizen science. Her most recent books are *Play and Democracy* (2021), *Resilient Society—between Powerlessness and Tyranny* (in Czech, 2023), and the 2021 article "Ethical Dimensions of Play and Care: reflections Based on Donald Winnicott's Theory of Play and the Ethics of Care."

Stefano Marino is Professor of Aesthetics at the University of Bologna. His main research interests and research fields are hermeneutics, critical theory, somaesthetics, philosophy of music, and aesthetics of fashion. He is the author of the books *Verità e non-verità del popular* (2021), *La filosofia dei Radiohead* (2021), *Le verità del non-vero* (2019), *Aesthetics, Metaphysics, Language* (2015), *La filosofia di Frank Zappa* (2014), and *Gadamer and the Limits of the Modern Techno-Scientific Civilization* (2011). He has co-edited several volumes and special issues of philosophical journals: *Varieties of the Lifeworld* (2022), *Popular Culture and Feminism* (2022), *Pearl Jam and Philosophy (2021), The "Aging" of Adorno's Aesthetic Theory* (2021), *Kant's "Critique of Aesthetic Judgment" in the 20th Century* (2020), *Adorno and Popular Music* (2019), *Philosophical Perspectives on Fashion* (2017), and *Theodor W. Adorno: Truth and Dialectical Experience* (2016). He has translated books of Th. W. Adorno and H.-G. Gadamer from German into Italian, and books of C. Korsmeyer and R. Shusterman from English into Italian.

Chester Mlcek is an undergraduate at Loyola Marymount University studying English and philosophy. His research interests focus on phenomenology, ontology, post-structuralist political philosophy, and twentieth-century poetry.

Ian Alexander Moore is Assistant Professor of Philosophy at Loyola Marymount University. He specializes in continental philosophy, especially Heidegger and post-Heideggerian thought. He is the author of *Dialogue on the Threshold: Heidegger and Trakl* (2022) and *Eckhart, Heidegger, and the Imperative of Releasement* (2019). With Christopher Turner, he translated Eugen Fink's *Fashion: Seductive Play* (2023) and *Play as Symbol of the World* (2016).

Daniel O'Shiel is an independent researcher and teacher working in the environmental sector. In philosophy his expertise is in phenomenology, and he has additional interests in philosophical anthropology, philosophy of technology, and environmental philosophy and ethics. His publications include two monographs, *Sartre and Magic* (2019) and *The Phenomenology of Virtual Technology* (2022).

Goetz Richter is Associate Professor at the University of Sydney's Conservatorium of Music. A performing musician and philosopher, his research covers major intersections between music and philosophy. He is the translator of Fink's book on *Nietzsche's Philosophy* (2003). His most recent publication is a paper on Musical Performance as Poetic Thinking in *Heidegger and Music* edited by C. Rentmeester & J. R. Warren (2022).

Susanne Schilz is Lecturer in the Department of Philosophy & Modern Languages, at California State University, Stanislaus. Her main interests are in aesthetics, phenomenology, German idealism, and twentieth-century French philosophy. She has published translations in her areas of interests between French and German.

Steve Stakland is Professor of Philosophy at Northern Virginia Community College. He thinks about the philosophy of education especially as it relates to phenomenology and Heidegger. He is the author of *Exploring What Is Lost in the Online Undergraduate Experience: A Philosophical Inquiry into the Meaning of Remote Learning* (2023). He also contributed the chapter "Fink's *Oasis of Happiness* and John Dewey: Play, Education and Ontology" to the German anthology on Eugen Fink's "Oase des Glücks: Gedanken zu einer Ontologie des Spiels" (2023).

Christopher Turner is Associate Professor in the Department of Philosophy & Modern Languages at California State University, Stanislaus. His research interests include ancient philosophy, existentialism, and phenomenology, as well as Western Marxism. He has published articles on Plato, Aristotle, the Cynics, Sartre, Adorno, and is currently focused on Fink. He has also co-translated two recent publications by Eugen Fink in English, *Play as Symbol of the World* (2016) and *Fashion: Seductive Play* (2023).

Dale Wilkerson is Lecturer of Philosophy at the University of Texas Rio Grande Valley. His current research focuses on the intersection of Nietzsche's interest in the history of Western culture and cosmopolitanism. He has published on Nietzsche and Heidegger's and Fink's readings of Nietzsche. He is the author of the *Internet Encyclopedia of Philosophy's* entry on Nietzsche (2010) and *Nietzsche and the Greeks* (2006).

Holger Zaborowski is Professor of Philosophy at the University of Erfurt. His work focuses on phenomenology, theology, and German philosophers. He has published many articles and books and is one of the editors of the *Heidegger Jahrbuch* as well as one of the principle organizers of regular academic conferences in Heidegger's home town of Messkirch.

Hakhamanesh Zangeneh is Associate Professor of Philosophy at California State University, Stanislaus. He primarily works on the intersection of German and French Philosophy in the twentieth century. His articles have appeared in *Journal of the British Society for Phenomenology*, *International Journal of Philosophical studies*, and *MLN Comp Lit*. He is working on a book about Heidegger's conception of time.

Index

agency 79, 80, 84, 105, 107
Aletheia 111
alienation 63, 180–1
alterity 129, 154
ambiguity 76, 156, 160, 198
American ix, 114, 119, 128
Amor fati 34–5
Anaximander 6, 65
apeiron 6
Apollo 67, 152, 179
aporetic 109, 160
a priori 19, 21
Arendt, Hannah x, 159
Aristotle 4, 92–6, 99, 140, 179
attunement 25, 107, 111, 112, 182, 184, 187
authenticity 24–6, 112
autonomy 106, 161, 186
autotelic 44–5
awe 94

babies 103
bad faith 90
being-in-the-world 6, 14, 16, 50, 111
being-with 197
biblical 47, 124–5, 195
biological 61, 184
boredom 25, 184
Bruzina, Ronald 13, 166–7, 203

calculation 97, 129, 132, 195
capitalism 29
categories 36, 66, 68, 107, 158
causality 44, 50, 54, 66, 78, 143
centaur 90, 147, 148
chaos 137, 142, 169
childlike 99, 133
children 32, 47, 91, 115, 117–19, 124, 133, 150–1, 184–5
Christianity 124, 127–30, 132, 134
clearing 20, 24, 52, 111

collective unconscious 196
common sense 30
comportment 95–7, 154, 182, 186, 188, 190, 195
creativity 4, 60, 66, 88, 95, 120–1, 126, 130, 134, 138, 152–3, 160–2

das Man 25
demise 149
despair 5, 9, 47, 187
Dewey, John 114, 115, 119
dialogue(s) 43, 51, 96, 99, 109, 128, 134, 161–2, 165, 167, 170–2
dignity 29
Dionysus 63, 67, 69 152
discursive 159
dread 180, 184
dream 5, 122–3, 126, 153, 181, 185, 187–8, 191

economics 36
emotion 26, 33, 178
emulate 116, 133
enigmatic 45, 68, 129, 142, 165
Enlightenment 64, 99, 157, 197
entities 43, 46, 54, 79, 120, 143
environment 119, 122, 142, 187
epistemology 15, 39, 62, 71, 98, 106
Eros 34, 134
ethics x, 4, 12, 24–5, 37, 150, 156
etymology 17
everydayness 25, 122

faith 60, 125, 127
fascism 33
feeling 33, 111, 112, 139, 140
Fichte, Johann Gottlieb 70–1, 75
film 178
food 185
forgetting 60, 65, 153
Foucault, Michel 123

fourfold   43, 49, 51
French Revolution   197
futurity   151

Germany   9, 114, 131, 201
gift   19–20, 44, 129, 135, 153
givenness   14, 15, 18, 107
Greeks   64, 86

Habermas, Jürgen   28
heterotopias   123
Hölderlin, Friedrich   68, 111, 165
home   20, 107, 159, 191
Homer   9–10
horror   180, 184
Huizinga, Johan   32–3, 37, 97–9
Hume, David   86
humor   7, 190

idealism   15, 18, 70, 117
identities   131, 135, 154
impulse   13, 98, 107, 150, 180, 182, 184, 196
inauthenticity   130, 195
infinity   8, 74, 80, 169
information   13, 28, 103, 167, 185
intentionality   13, 103, 110, 168
intuition   22, 24, 62, 104–5, 108, 113
irony   32, 105, 141, 190
irrational   147

Jesus   124, 133
Judaism   124

Kantian   70–2
Kierkegaard, Søren   5, 23

language game   37
Leibniz, Gottfried Wilhelm   50
leisure   131, 197
leveling   18, 22
Levinas, Emmanuel   156, 161
listen   103–4
logos   43, 47, 54, 177
love   xi, 3, 34, 46, 48, 123, 147, 150, 154, 183, 190, 192, 197

machination   131
magic   8, 178, 180

magical   9, 34, 125–6, 180, 183, 185, 188, 190, 195
market   185
Marx, Karl   63, 77, 192
mathematics   118
mental   85, 87–8, 90
Meontic   13–15, 17, 22–3, 116, 166–7, 169–71
Mimesis   46, 73, 115–16, 120, 141
Mirror-like   6
modernity   68, 123, 142, 156
moods   22, 25, 131
mystery   8, 94

Nazi   ix, 51, 87, 131
necessity   x, 42, 49–51, 96, 147, 149, 153, 160, 197, 202
negation   73, 81, 190
Neoplatonists   96
nihilism   65, 77, 123, 126, 157, 202
non-human   145, 156
non-seriousness   7, 88, 201

objectivity   44, 160
ontotheological   129
optimism   137
ousia   53

Parmenides   94
pedagogy   x, 12, 114–15, 147, 184
perception   10, 85, 87, 89–91, 152, 179, 196
plastic   4, 86
play-space   42, 50, 52, 188
plaything   6–8, 45–6, 96, 116, 120, 183, 185, 188
poetic thinking   67
poetry   93, 165
Poiesis   112, 115–16, 120, 158
politics   xi, 36, 155–7, 183
powerlessness   137, 139, 144
pragmatism   28, 156
presencing   19, 55, 72, 176–7
pre-Socratics   7, 92
principle of sufficient reason   50
production   7, 97, 116, 145, 155, 157–60, 187, 188, 190, 196
projection   21, 24, 41–2, 185–6
propositional   6, 24, 110

proximity 27, 133, 151, 165
psychological 26, 61, 64, 111–12, 182, 186

recognition 39, 85, 113, 155
release 4, 13
representation 3, 9–10, 18, 23, 30, 61–3, 190, 197, 202
reproduction 6–8, 73, 132, 141
resemblance 28, 142
reverence 93
Rilke, Rainer Maria 35
Romanticism 29, 68, 119

semblance 28, 45, 142, 181, 197
sensuous 9, 45, 73, 141, 148, 182, 184, 188, 191, 196
shadows 64, 73, 93–4, 103, 150, 182, 187
skepticism 60
Socrates ix, 64–6, 96, 99, 109, 192
song 103–4
Spielraum 19, 42, 52, 135, 170
Spinoza, Baruch 192
spiritual 64, 106, 129, 133, 169
stage 4, 11, 24, 64, 96, 118, 125, 132, 161, 178, 180–1, 185, 189

Stoicism 80
sublime 25, 181
substance 66, 128, 132, 135, 189, 196
survival 34, 91, 150
symbola 159

technology 157
temporality 29, 45, 80, 103, 110, 174, 176
theological 63, 93–6, 99, 125, 128, 129, 131, 134–5
thrownness 21, 25
toy 45, 118, 134, 141, 155, 178, 185

uncanny 11, 151, 190
unconcealment 19, 24, 49, 53, 176
unicorns 87

violence 156, 158–9, 161
vocation 84
voice 44, 79, 105–7, 109

Wittgenstein, Ludwig 30, 33, 37, 192

youth 32, 149

Zeus 62, 116

www.ingramcontent.com/pod-product-compliance
Lightning Source LLC
Chambersburg PA
CBHW071822300426
44116CB00009B/1399